THE STORY
OF THE
139th INFANTRY

BY

CLAIR KENAMORE

1920

GUARD PUBLISHING CO.

ST. LOUIS, MO.

FOREWORD

When the History Committee of the 139th Infantry put the production of this book into the hands of the Guard Publishing Company early in September, 1919, that company arranged with me to write it. Many difficulties have arisen in the collection of data, principally through my inability to obtain the regimental records.

Officers and men of the regiment have resumed their civilian pursuits and some of them have wandered far afield since they were discharged from the army, so far indeed that letters and telegrams are unanswered. The Regimental History, which would have been of great assistance, has not been found. Such officers and men as I have been able to get in touch with have been most kind and helpful, and whatever value the book has is due to them.

I am fully aware that the narrative given here does not do justice to the fine regiment with which it deals, but no book could do that. The great bravery of these men, the grim persistence, the fortitude in the face of great odds, have made for them a fame which should live forever.

My poor words cannot add to their glory. All I can hope to do is briefly to tell their story and offer a book which will preserve the pictures of these gallant men in the uniforms they wore with so much honor on the fields of France.

Clair Kenamore

CONTENTS

Illustrations are on all pages from the beginning to Page 141, and from that page on, they occur occasionally. The company pictures are not on the pages with the same company's roster.

VAUQUOIS HILL AND CHAUDRON FARM

The crosses in the snow-covered field of Chaudron Farm are at the heads of graves of 35th Division men.

The picture of the top of Vauquois Hill was made from an airplane at a height of about 400 feet. The craters were made by mines exploded by the French and Germans before we entered the war. Trenches can be seen on either side.

A COMPANY

ONE of the firm convictions of natives of Missouri and Kansas used to be that the citizens of the other state were a bad lot. This impression came down from the days when we Missourians, out of the goodness of our hearts, used to go over into Kansas and help them hold their elections. Even before Kansas was a state, Missourians were trying to lead them onward and upward to better things. We took them by the hand, led them to the ballot box, showed them how to vote, told them which way to vote, voted ourselves to give them the benefit of our example. Often we voted for them when they were backward or timorous. Did they appreciate it? They did not. They called us many things that were not pleasant to listen to. We called them things which sounded even worse. Twenty years ago the boys in any respectable Missouri school had a bitter contempt for Kansas and its people. In my own family there was an uncle who moved to Kansas and bought a farm. We spoke in low tones of him in the family circle afterward.

Now all that feeling has passed away. The prejudice and intolerance of Civil War days are forgotten. The only rivalry is in the tilt yards of trade, and the only bitterness is upon the foot-ball field. The last vestige of this old rancor was swept away by regiments such as the 139th Infantry of the United States Army. This regiment was made up of the 4th Missouri Infantry and the 3rd Kansas Infantry, two National Guard outfits of enduring fame. They were united soon after they were called to the colors, they were trained as one unit. By the time they were sent to France, all state lines had been lost. In France they worked and learned and trained

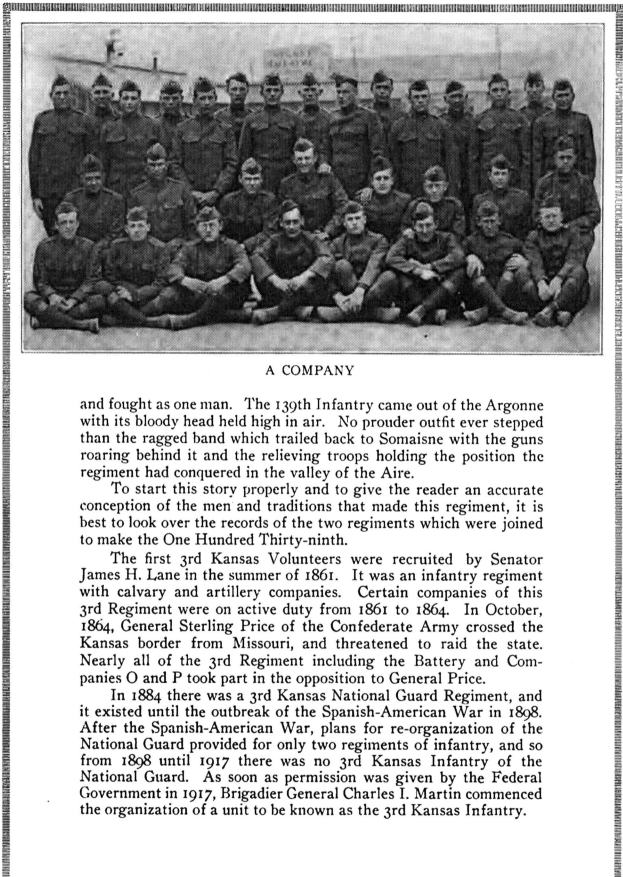

A COMPANY

and fought as one man. The 139th Infantry came out of the Argonne
with its bloody head held high in air. No prouder outfit ever stepped
than the ragged band which trailed back to Somaisne with the guns
roaring behind it and the relieving troops holding the position the
regiment had conquered in the valley of the Aire.

To start this story properly and to give the reader an accurate
conception of the men and traditions that made this regiment, it is
best to look over the records of the two regiments which were joined
to make the One Hundred Thirty-ninth.

The first 3rd Kansas Volunteers were recruited by Senator
James H. Lane in the summer of 1861. It was an infantry regiment
with calvary and artillery companies. Certain companies of this
3rd Regiment were on active duty from 1861 to 1864. In October,
1864, General Sterling Price of the Confederate Army crossed the
Kansas border from Missouri, and threatened to raid the state.
Nearly all of the 3rd Regiment including the Battery and Companies O and P took part in the opposition to General Price.

In 1884 there was a 3rd Kansas National Guard Regiment, and
it existed until the outbreak of the Spanish-American War in 1898.
After the Spanish-American War, plans for re-organization of the
National Guard provided for only two regiments of infantry, and so
from 1898 until 1917 there was no 3rd Kansas Infantry of the
National Guard. As soon as permission was given by the Federal
Government in 1917, Brigadier General Charles I. Martin commenced
the organization of a unit to be known as the 3rd Kansas Infantry.

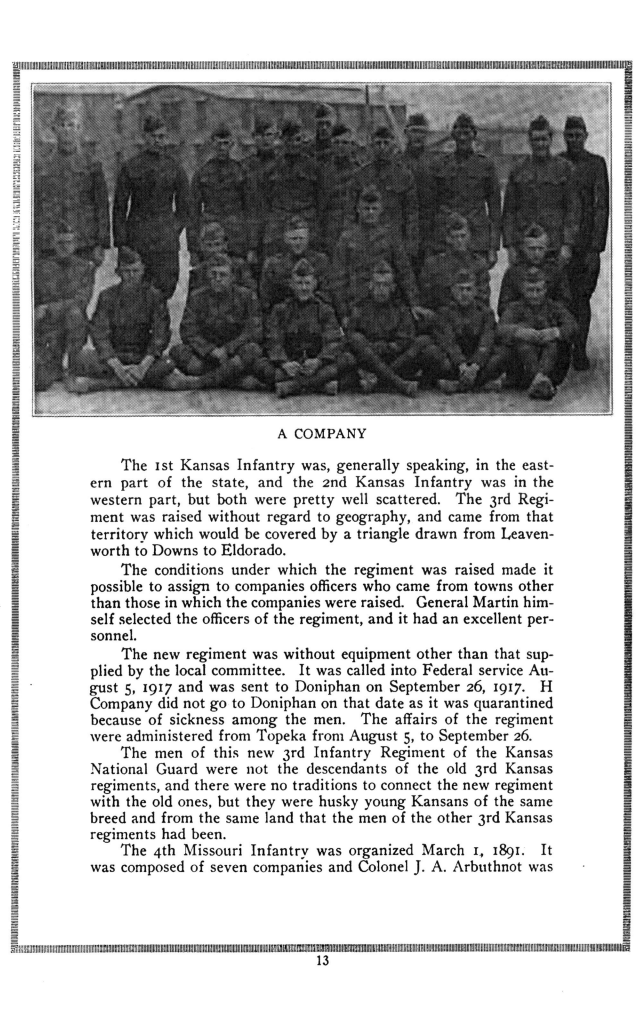

A COMPANY

The 1st Kansas Infantry was, generally speaking, in the eastern part of the state, and the 2nd Kansas Infantry was in the western part, but both were pretty well scattered. The 3rd Regiment was raised without regard to geography, and came from that territory which would be covered by a triangle drawn from Leavenworth to Downs to Eldorado.

The conditions under which the regiment was raised made it possible to assign to companies officers who came from towns other than those in which the companies were raised. General Martin himself selected the officers of the regiment, and it had an excellent personnel.

The new regiment was without equipment other than that supplied by the local committee. It was called into Federal service August 5, 1917 and was sent to Doniphan on September 26, 1917. H Company did not go to Doniphan on that date as it was quarantined because of sickness among the men. The affairs of the regiment were administered from Topeka from August 5, to September 26.

The men of this new 3rd Infantry Regiment of the Kansas National Guard were not the descendants of the old 3rd Kansas regiments, and there were no traditions to connect the new regiment with the old ones, but they were husky young Kansans of the same breed and from the same land that the men of the other 3rd Kansas regiments had been.

The 4th Missouri Infantry was organized March 1, 1891. It was composed of seven companies and Colonel J. A. Arbuthnot was

A COMPANY

its first commander. It was located generally in the northern part of the state, and many towns have been represented in its organization. The forming and mustering-out of companies have gone on steadily since that time.

Concerning the early life of the regiment Col. William E. Stringfellow says:

"In those days, there was no state appropriation for the maintenance of the companies. Equipment was issued. The companies had to be maintained by the officers and men. Some small amount in dues was paid by each member and the officers had to dig up to supply the deficiencies. We held our annual encampments much in the manner that a street carnival is held. We approached the various towns in north and northwest Missouri of suitable size to be interested, and saw what they would allow us in the way of camping grounds, wood and water, and anything else we might get, including a percentage of the receipts of a sham battle, which usually was given as the principal means of obtaining any ready cash. The officers made up the deficiency.

"From the date of my acquaintance with the regiment, which was practically at the beginning of its organization, there has been a high degree of military spirit and willingness to serve on the part of a nucleus, which spirit has been maintained until now, and it is my sincere belief that a part of the splendid spirit shown by the One Hundred Thirty-ninth in France was due to the esprit de corps created in the early days and maintained until now."

The regiment volunteered for service in the Spanish-American

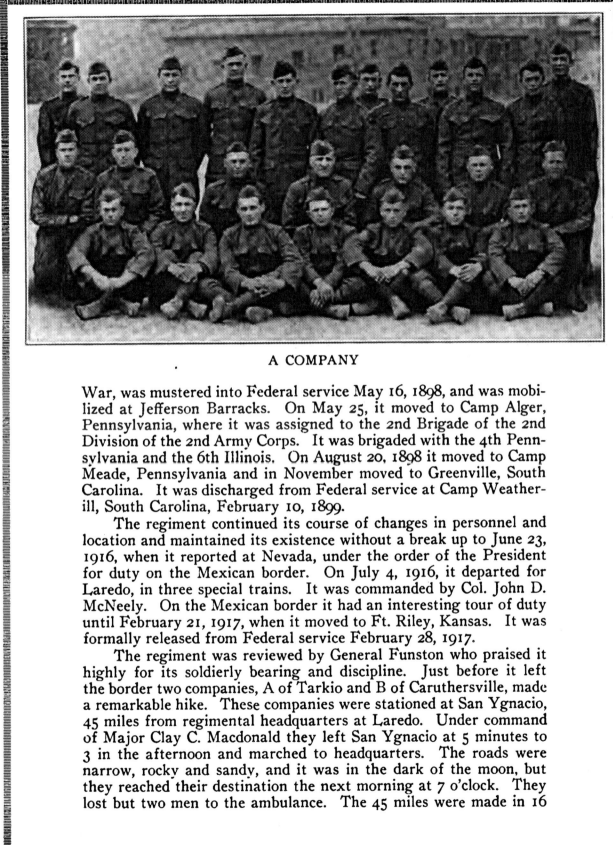

A COMPANY

War, was mustered into Federal service May 16, 1898, and was mobilized at Jefferson Barracks. On May 25, it moved to Camp Alger, Pennsylvania, where it was assigned to the 2nd Brigade of the 2nd Division of the 2nd Army Corps. It was brigaded with the 4th Pennsylvania and the 6th Illinois. On August 20, 1898 it moved to Camp Meade, Pennsylvania and in November moved to Greenville, South Carolina. It was discharged from Federal service at Camp Weatherill, South Carolina, February 10, 1899.

The regiment continued its course of changes in personnel and location and maintained its existence without a break up to June 23, 1916, when it reported at Nevada, under the order of the President for duty on the Mexican border. On July 4, 1916, it departed for Laredo, in three special trains. It was commanded by Col. John D. McNeely. On the Mexican border it had an interesting tour of duty until February 21, 1917, when it moved to Ft. Riley, Kansas. It was formally released from Federal service February 28, 1917.

The regiment was reviewed by General Funston who praised it highly for its soldierly bearing and discipline. Just before it left the border two companies, A of Tarkio and B of Caruthersville, made a remarkable hike. These companies were stationed at San Ygnacio, 45 miles from regimental headquarters at Laredo. Under command of Major Clay C. Macdonald they left San Ygnacio at 5 minutes to 3 in the afternoon and marched to headquarters. The roads were narrow, rocky and sandy, and it was in the dark of the moon, but they reached their destination the next morning at 7 o'clock. They lost but two men to the ambulance. The 45 miles were made in 16

A COMPANY

hours, or leaving out the rest for supper and the 5 and 10 minute rest periods on the march, a marching time of 13 hours. The last 12 miles of the march was covered in 3 hours and 5 minutes. Major Macdonald was the first officer inducted into Federal service in May, 1917, and the only officer who served with the regiment in the Spanish War, on the Mexican border and in France.

Among its officers on the border were Major Macdonald, commanding the 1st Battalion; Captain Williamson, commanding D Company; Major James E. Rieger, commanding the 2nd Battalion; Captain Wilson, commanding G Company; Captain McQueen, commanding H Company and Major Stepp, commanding the 3rd Battalion. We shall hear of these men again in France.

Major Ralph Ramer who served with the South Carolina troops in the world war, Major Donald Bonfoey who served on the Border and in France, and Captain Donald Duncan of the Marines, who fell in battle near Chateau Thierry, all had their training with the old Fourth Missouri.

When the 139th Regiment, U. S. Infantry was formed, A Company was made by joining A Company of the 3rd Kansas and A Company of the 4th Missouri. The ranking Captain took command of the company. Since the Kansas regiment had been newly organized, most of the regimental and company commands went to Missouri officers for the time being. Displaced officers were attached, or were sent to the Depot Brigade. Colonel McNeely commanded the regiment and to assist, advise and instruct him there was a procession of regular army officers, none of whom stayed long with the regiment.

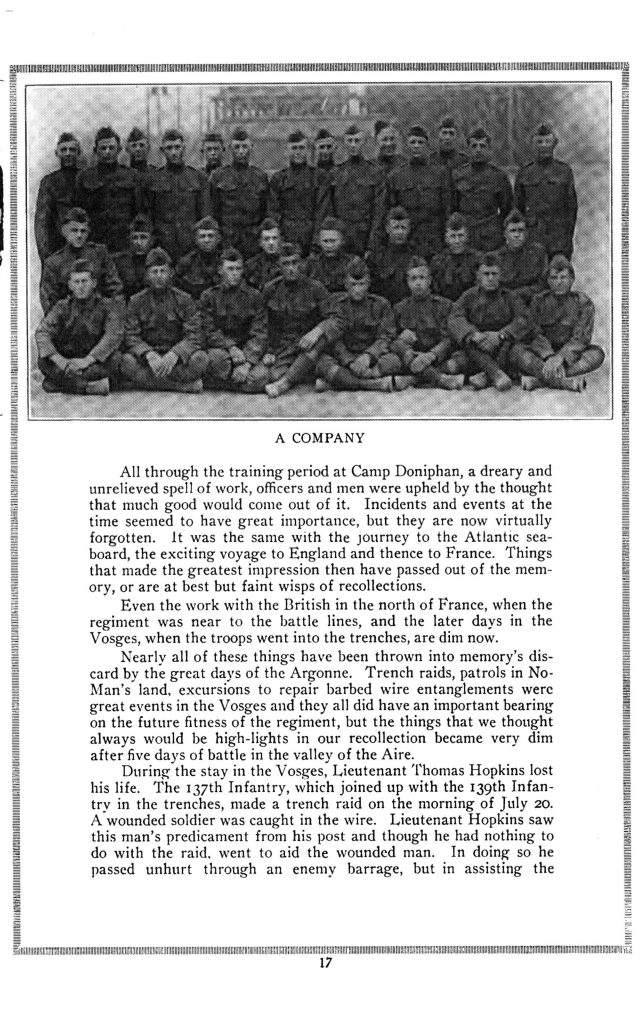

A COMPANY

All through the training period at Camp Doniphan, a dreary and unrelieved spell of work, officers and men were upheld by the thought that much good would come out of it. Incidents and events at the time seemed to have great importance, but they are now virtually forgotten. It was the same with the journey to the Atlantic seaboard, the exciting voyage to England and thence to France. Things that made the greatest impression then have passed out of the memory, or are at best but faint wisps of recollections.

Even the work with the British in the north of France, when the regiment was near to the battle lines, and the later days in the Vosges, when the troops went into the trenches, are dim now.

Nearly all of these things have been thrown into memory's discard by the great days of the Argonne. Trench raids, patrols in No-Man's land, excursions to repair barbed wire entanglements were great events in the Vosges and they all did have an important bearing on the future fitness of the regiment, but the things that we thought always would be high-lights in our recollection became very dim after five days of battle in the valley of the Aire.

During the stay in the Vosges, Lieutenant Thomas Hopkins lost his life. The 137th Infantry, which joined up with the 139th Infantry in the trenches, made a trench raid on the morning of July 20. A wounded soldier was caught in the wire. Lieutenant Hopkins saw this man's predicament from his post and though he had nothing to do with the raid, went to aid the wounded man. In doing so he passed unhurt through an enemy barrage, but in assisting the

COL. CARL L. RISTINE

A National Guard Officer, who, at the age of 32, led a combat regiment in the Argonne-Meuse offensive with such skill and daring that his troops made the farthest advance accomplished by the 35th Division. He was promoted to Colonel for his work in battle. He was a hard taskmaster on the drill ground, but won the love of his regiment by his valor on the field, and his untiring devotion to his men.

B COMPANY

wounded man to cover, Lieutenant Hopkins was himself fatally wounded.

The Distinguished Service Cross and the Croix de Guerre were both awarded to Lieutenant Hopkins and an American Legion Post in his home in Wichita, Kansas has been named for him.

The regiment also lost Captain Alexander M. Ellett in the Vosges. He was commanding I Company and had done, excellent work in rounding the company into shape. Near Amiens in the spring, his company won first place in the competitive drill within the battalion and one of his platoons won first place in the competition among platoons. His company in the Vosges occupied the town of Metzerall. The explosion of a hand-grenade while he was inspecting an intermediate line of defense caused wounds from which Captain Ellett died before reaching the hospital.

Captain Charles H. Browne, who had commanded H Company of the 3rd Kansas and later E Company of the One Hundred Thirty-ninth and who had done such good work in Alsace was sent back home as an instructor August 11. He became a Major and while he never saw the Argonne, the work he had done in training the men lived after him on that field.

Colonel McNeeley, who had commanded the regiment at Doniphan was relieved after several weeks in France. He was promoted to a corps job and did not see any further service with the One Hundred Thirty-ninth. But I am sure he would have forgone the promotion for the privilege of staying with his outfit.

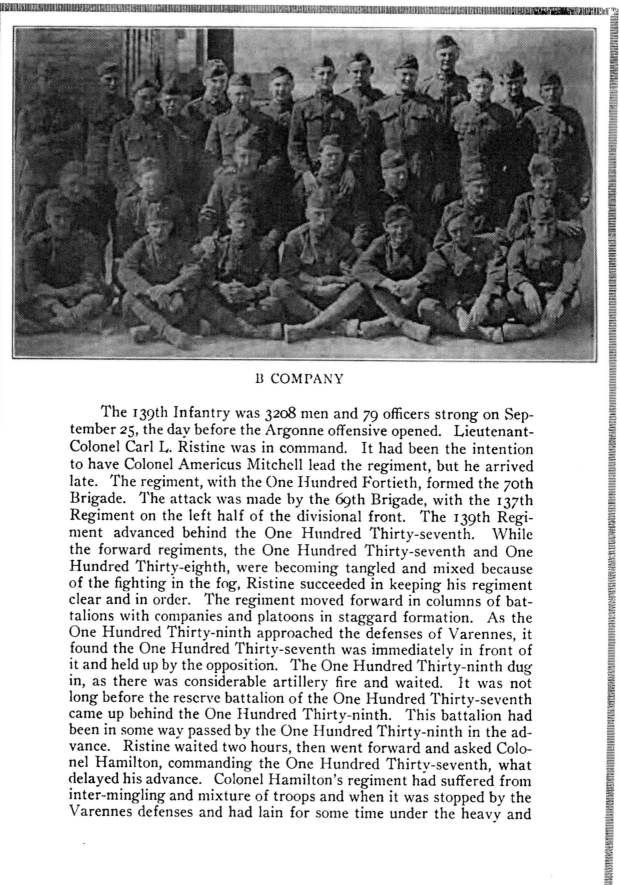

B COMPANY

The 139th Infantry was 3208 men and 79 officers strong on September 25, the day before the Argonne offensive opened. Lieutenant-Colonel Carl L. Ristine was in command. It had been the intention to have Colonel Americus Mitchell lead the regiment, but he arrived late. The regiment, with the One Hundred Fortieth, formed the 70th Brigade. The attack was made by the 69th Brigade, with the 137th Regiment on the left half of the divisional front. The 139th Regiment advanced behind the One Hundred Thirty-seventh. While the forward regiments, the One Hundred Thirty-seventh and One Hundred Thirty-eighth, were becoming tangled and mixed because of the fighting in the fog, Ristine succeeded in keeping his regiment clear and in order. The regiment moved forward in columns of battalions with companies and platoons in staggard formation. As the One Hundred Thirty-ninth approached the defenses of Varennes, it found the One Hundred Thirty-seventh was immediately in front of it and held up by the opposition. The One Hundred Thirty-ninth dug in, as there was considerable artillery fire and waited. It was not long before the reserve battalion of the One Hundred Thirty-seventh came up behind the One Hundred Thirty-ninth. This battalion had been in some way passed by the One Hundred Thirty-ninth in the advance. Ristine waited two hours, then went forward and asked Colonel Hamilton, commanding the One Hundred Thirty-seventh, what delayed his advance. Colonel Hamilton's regiment had suffered from inter-mingling and mixture of troops and when it was stopped by the Varennes defenses and had lain for some time under the heavy and

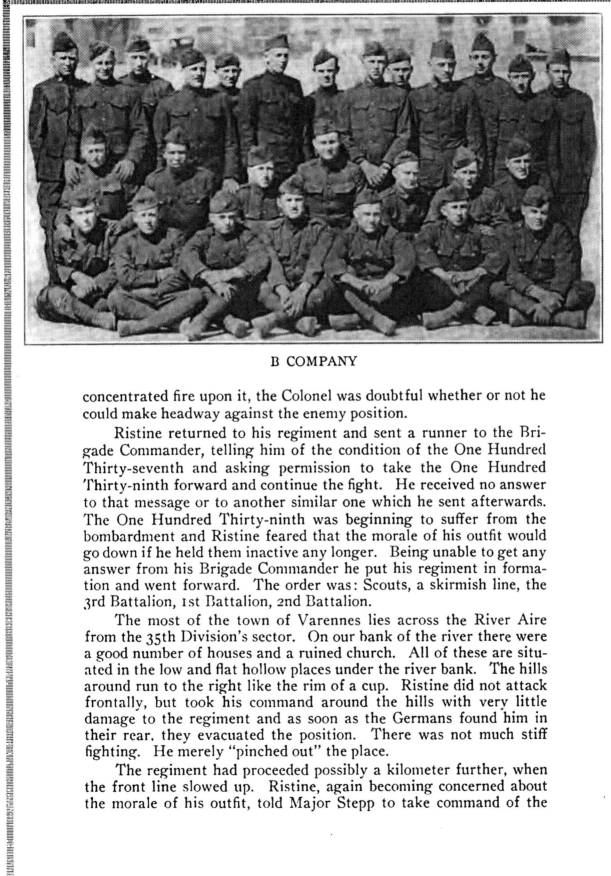

B COMPANY

concentrated fire upon it, the Colonel was doubtful whether or not he could make headway against the enemy position.

Ristine returned to his regiment and sent a runner to the Brigade Commander, telling him of the condition of the One Hundred Thirty-seventh and asking permission to take the One Hundred Thirty-ninth forward and continue the fight. He received no answer to that message or to another similar one which he sent afterwards. The One Hundred Thirty-ninth was beginning to suffer from the bombardment and Ristine feared that the morale of his outfit would go down if he held them inactive any longer. Being unable to get any answer from his Brigade Commander he put his regiment in formation and went forward. The order was: Scouts, a skirmish line, the 3rd Battalion, 1st Battalion, 2nd Battalion.

The most of the town of Varennes lies across the River Aire from the 35th Division's sector. On our bank of the river there were a good number of houses and a ruined church. All of these are situated in the low and flat hollow places under the river bank. The hills around run to the right like the rim of a cup. Ristine did not attack frontally, but took his command around the hills with very little damage to the regiment and as soon as the Germans found him in their rear, they evacuated the position. There was not much stiff fighting. He merely "pinched out" the place.

The regiment had proceeded possibly a kilometer further, when the front line slowed up. Ristine, again becoming concerned about the morale of his outfit, told Major Stepp to take command of the

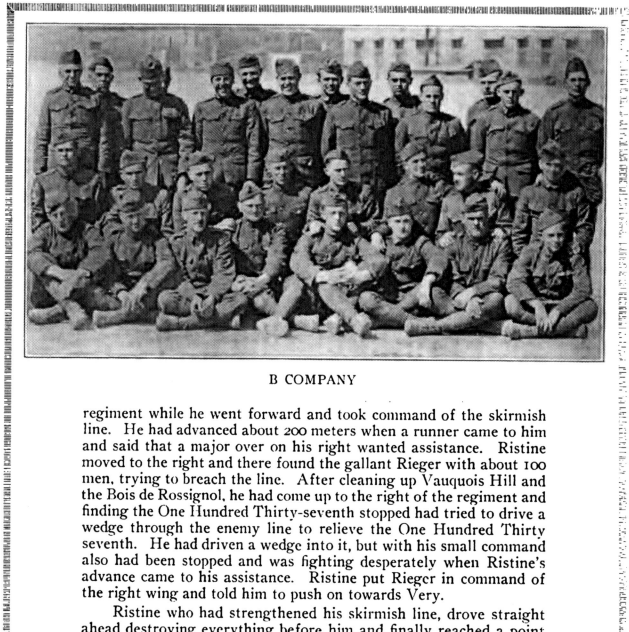

B COMPANY

regiment while he went forward and took command of the skirmish line. He had advanced about 200 meters when a runner came to him and said that a major over on his right wanted assistance. Ristine moved to the right and there found the gallant Rieger with about 100 men, trying to breach the line. After cleaning up Vauquois Hill and the Bois de Rossignol, he had come up to the right of the regiment and finding the One Hundred Thirty-seventh stopped had tried to drive a wedge through the enemy line to relieve the One Hundred Thirty seventh. He had driven a wedge into it, but with his small command also had been stopped and was fighting desperately when Ristine's advance came to his assistance. Ristine put Rieger in command of the right wing and told him to push on towards Very.

Ristine who had strengthened his skirmish line, drove straight ahead destroying everything before him and finally reached a point about a kilometer and a half south of Charpentry, where he ran into a very heavy enfilading fire. He told his detachment to dig in and wait for the regiment to come up. When the regiment failed to appear, Ristine left his skirmish line, holding the front, and went back to the regiment. There he learned Major Stepp had been killed and the regiment had not moved. He reformed his command in a column of battalions and took the regiment forward and the men dug in just back of the skirmish line at nightfall.

Rieger had volunteered for the mopping up of Vauquois Hill and the Bois de Rossignol. Captains Wilson and McQueen had matched coins for the privilege. Wilson with two companies had attended

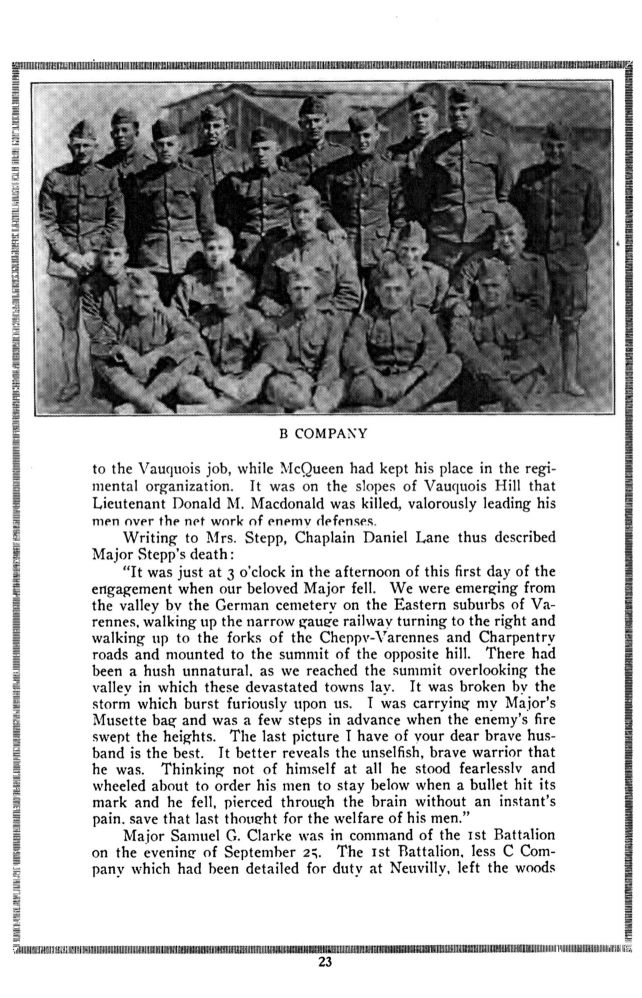

B COMPANY

to the Vauquois job, while McQueen had kept his place in the regimental organization. It was on the slopes of Vauquois Hill that Lieutenant Donald M. Macdonald was killed, valorously leading his men over the net work of enemy defenses.

Writing to Mrs. Stepp, Chaplain Daniel Lane thus described Major Stepp's death:

"It was just at 3 o'clock in the afternoon of this first day of the engagement when our beloved Major fell. We were emerging from the valley by the German cemetery on the Eastern suburbs of Varennes, walking up the narrow gauge railway turning to the right and walking up to the forks of the Cheppy-Varennes and Charpentry roads and mounted to the summit of the opposite hill. There had been a hush unnatural, as we reached the summit overlooking the valley in which these devastated towns lay. It was broken by the storm which burst furiously upon us. I was carrying my Major's Musette bag and was a few steps in advance when the enemy's fire swept the heights. The last picture I have of your dear brave husband is the best. It better reveals the unselfish, brave warrior that he was. Thinking not of himself at all he stood fearlessly and wheeled about to order his men to stay below when a bullet hit its mark and he fell, pierced through the brain without an instant's pain, save that last thought for the welfare of his men."

Major Samuel G. Clarke was in command of the 1st Battalion on the evening of September 25. The 1st Battalion, less C Company which had been detailed for duty at Neuvilly, left the woods

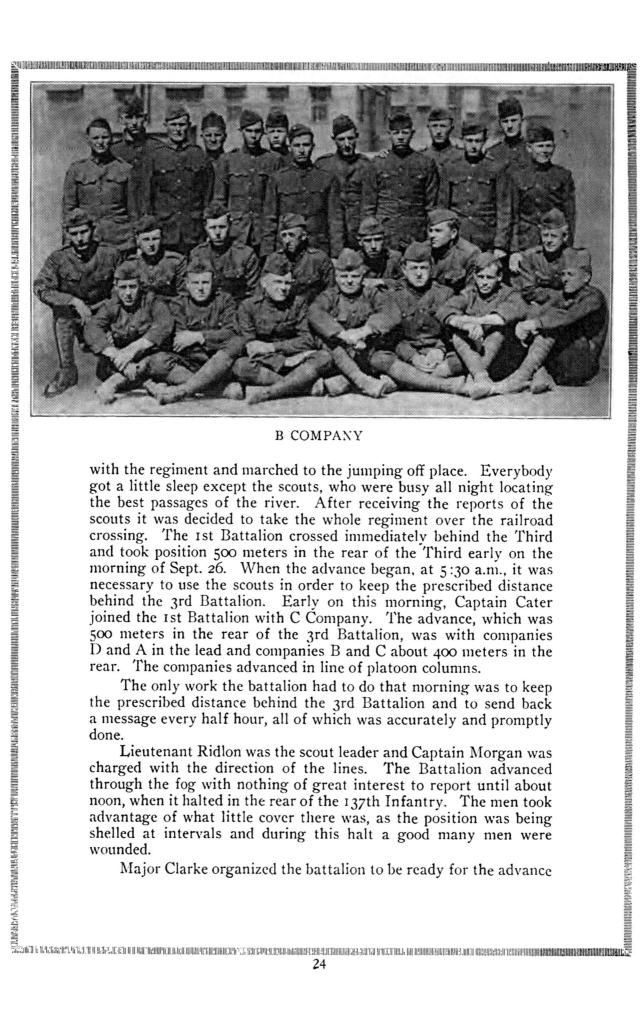

B COMPANY

with the regiment and marched to the jumping off place. Everybody got a little sleep except the scouts, who were busy all night locating the best passages of the river. After receiving the reports of the scouts it was decided to take the whole regiment over the railroad crossing. The 1st Battalion crossed immediately behind the Third and took position 500 meters in the rear of the Third early on the morning of Sept. 26. When the advance began, at 5:30 a.m., it was necessary to use the scouts in order to keep the prescribed distance behind the 3rd Battalion. Early on this morning, Captain Cater joined the 1st Battalion with C Company. The advance, which was 500 meters in the rear of the 3rd Battalion, was with companies D and A in the lead and companies B and C about 400 meters in the rear. The companies advanced in line of platoon columns.

The only work the battalion had to do that morning was to keep the prescribed distance behind the 3rd Battalion and to send back a message every half hour, all of which was accurately and promptly done.

Lieutenant Ridlon was the scout leader and Captain Morgan was charged with the direction of the lines. The Battalion advanced through the fog with nothing of great interest to report until about noon, when it halted in the rear of the 137th Infantry. The men took advantage of what little cover there was, as the position was being shelled at intervals and during this halt a good many men were wounded.

Major Clarke organized the battalion to be ready for the advance

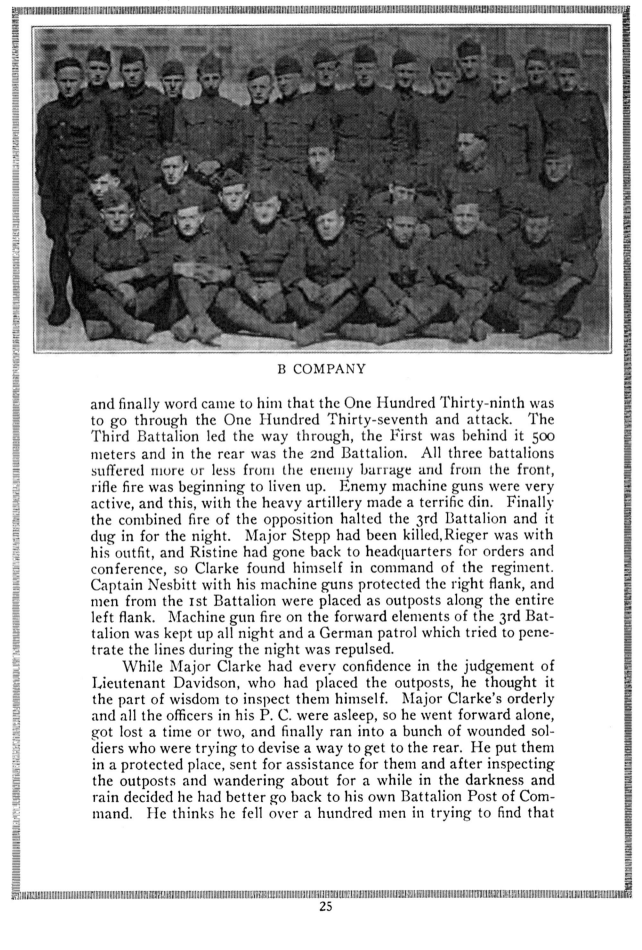

B COMPANY

and finally word came to him that the One Hundred Thirty-ninth was to go through the One Hundred Thirty-seventh and attack. The Third Battalion led the way through, the First was behind it 500 meters and in the rear was the 2nd Battalion. All three battalions suffered more or less from the enemy barrage and from the front, rifle fire was beginning to liven up. Enemy machine guns were very active, and this, with the heavy artillery made a terrific din. Finally the combined fire of the opposition halted the 3rd Battalion and it dug in for the night. Major Stepp had been killed, Rieger was with his outfit, and Ristine had gone back to headquarters for orders and conference, so Clarke found himself in command of the regiment. Captain Nesbitt with his machine guns protected the right flank, and men from the 1st Battalion were placed as outposts along the entire left flank. Machine gun fire on the forward elements of the 3rd Battalion was kept up all night and a German patrol which tried to penetrate the lines during the night was repulsed.

While Major Clarke had every confidence in the judgement of Lieutenant Davidson, who had placed the outposts, he thought it the part of wisdom to inspect them himself. Major Clarke's orderly and all the officers in his P. C. were asleep, so he went forward alone, got lost a time or two, and finally ran into a bunch of wounded soldiers who were trying to devise a way to get to the rear. He put them in a protected place, sent for assistance for them and after inspecting the outposts and wandering about for a while in the darkness and rain decided he had better go back to his own Battalion Post of Command. He thinks he fell over a hundred men in trying to find that

B COMPANY

P. C. He finally reached it and soon was asleep but was almost immediately awakened by a runner who said the Regimental Adjutant wanted to know if he would not come at once to the regimental P. C., as he was expecting the Germans to attack on our left. No attack came and about dawn Ristine returned. He gave out information concerning the advance and placed the 1st Battalion in the line with the Third. Major Clarke went back to his battalion to give the necessary orders for the advance. In getting into position the air seemed alive with machine gun bullets. Everybody walked close to the ground. A sudden machine gun burst pinned Major Williamson and Major Clarke to the ground. Williamson was hit on the left side, but not badly hurt. Clarke was hit four times with machine gun bullets, once in the left wrist, once in the left leg and two minor wounds in the right leg below the knee. His left leg was useless, but he remained where he was for some time, thinking it might be possible for him to go forward again when the time came.

He crawled a little to the rear to get into the path of the litter bearers and he thought he would be able to stay throughout the day, but Colonel Ristine saw him and ordered that he be taken to the rear. So ended his part in the Meuse-Argonne Battle. He was in the hospital until November 25, then returned to duty, but had to go back to the hospital again as he was not yet fit. He finally rejoined the regiment December 21, 1918.

On September 27, the second day of the battle, the attack was to be resumed at 5:30 a.m. by the 70th Brigade which had been in support on the first day. It was not necessary for the One Hundred

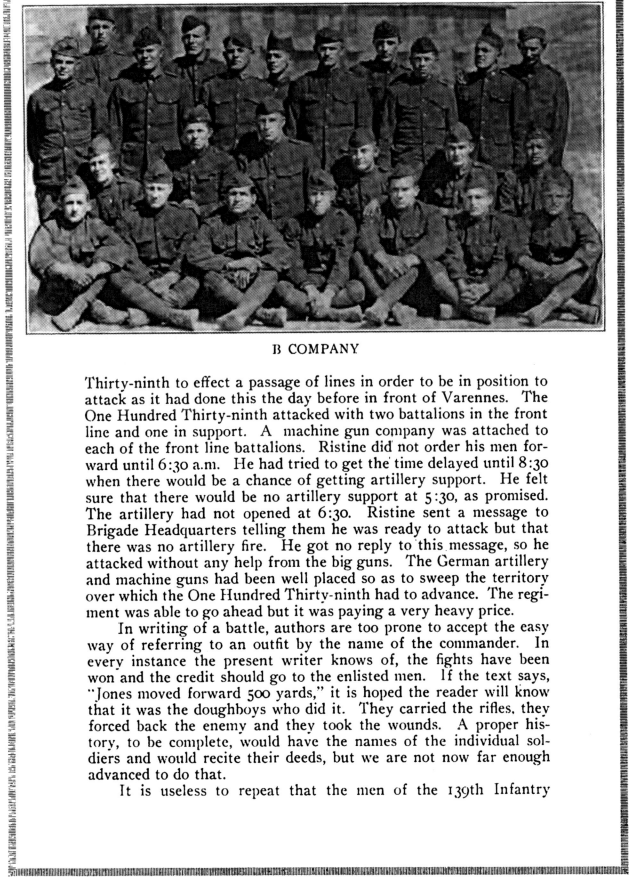

B COMPANY

Thirty-ninth to effect a passage of lines in order to be in position to attack as it had done this the day before in front of Varennes. The One Hundred Thirty-ninth attacked with two battalions in the front line and one in support. A machine gun company was attached to each of the front line battalions. Ristine did not order his men forward until 6:30 a.m. He had tried to get the time delayed until 8:30 when there would be a chance of getting artillery support. He felt sure that there would be no artillery support at 5:30, as promised. The artillery had not opened at 6:30. Ristine sent a message to Brigade Headquarters telling them he was ready to attack but that there was no artillery fire. He got no reply to this message, so he attacked without any help from the big guns. The German artillery and machine guns had been well placed so as to sweep the territory over which the One Hundred Thirty-ninth had to advance. The regiment was able to go ahead but it was paying a very heavy price.

In writing of a battle, authors are too prone to accept the easy way of referring to an outfit by the name of the commander. In every instance the present writer knows of, the fights have been won and the credit should go to the enlisted men. If the text says, "Jones moved forward 500 yards," it is hoped the reader will know that it was the doughboys who did it. They carried the rifles, they forced back the enemy and they took the wounds. A proper history, to be complete, would have the names of the individual soldiers and would recite their deeds, but we are not now far enough advanced to do that.

It is useless to repeat that the men of the 139th Infantry

"On the morning of September 26, Major James E. Rieger with his battalion made the frontal attack on the heights of Vauquois, capturing this almost impregnable position in forty minutes. Reorganizing his battalion he pushed forward and on the evening of September 27, without regard for his own safety, personally led the charge into Charpentry with such speed and dash that a large body of the enemy were cut off and captured. He, with his battalion, captured the foremost point reached by the Division."—From his citation.

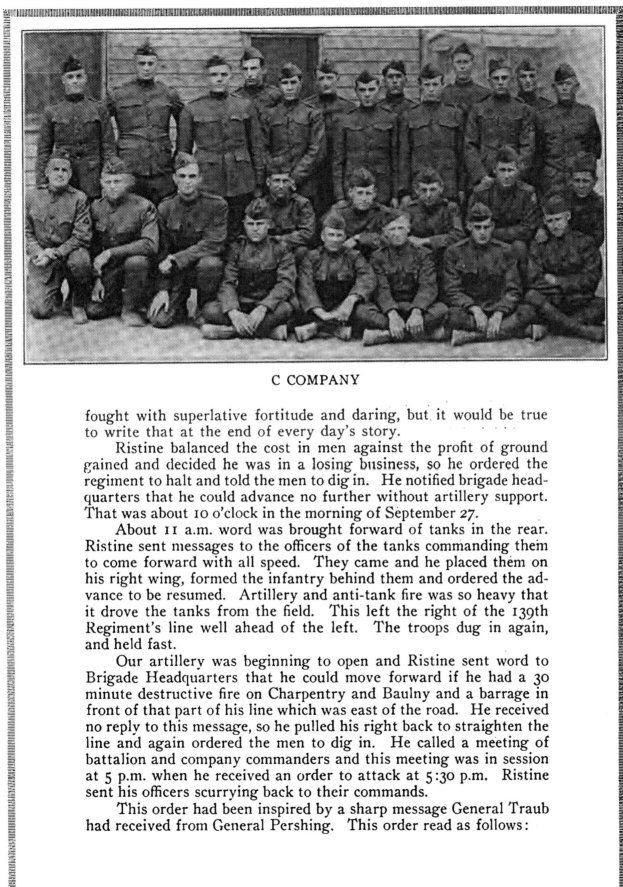

C COMPANY

fought with superlative fortitude and daring, but it would be true
to write that at the end of every day's story.

Ristine balanced the cost in men against the profit of ground
gained and decided he was in a losing business, so he ordered the
regiment to halt and told the men to dig in. He notified brigade headquarters that he could advance no further without artillery support.
That was about 10 o'clock in the morning of September 27.

About 11 a.m. word was brought forward of tanks in the rear.
Ristine sent messages to the officers of the tanks commanding them
to come forward with all speed. They came and he placed them on
his right wing, formed the infantry behind them and ordered the advance to be resumed. Artillery and anti-tank fire was so heavy that
it drove the tanks from the field. This left the right of the 139th
Regiment's line well ahead of the left. The troops dug in again,
and held fast.

Our artillery was beginning to open and Ristine sent word to
Brigade Headquarters that he could move forward if he had a 30
minute destructive fire on Charpentry and Baulny and a barrage in
front of that part of his line which was east of the road. He received
no reply to this message, so he pulled his right back to straighten the
line and again ordered the men to dig in. He called a meeting of
battalion and company commanders and this meeting was in session
at 5 p.m. when he received an order to attack at 5:30 p.m. Ristine
sent his officers scurrying back to their commands.

This order had been inspired by a sharp message General Traub
had received from General Pershing. This order read as follows:

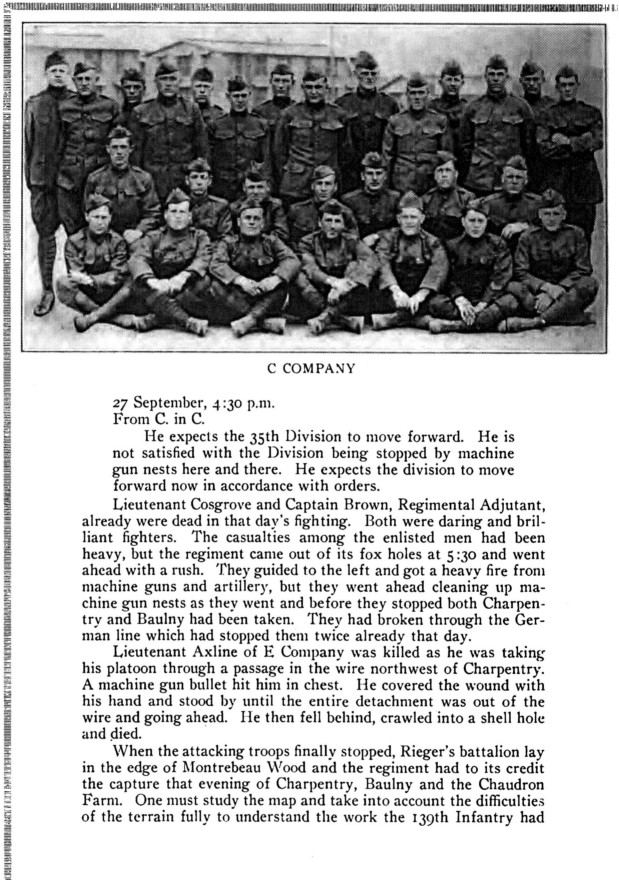

C COMPANY

27 September, 4:30 p.m.
From C. in C.

He expects the 35th Division to move forward. He is not satisfied with the Division being stopped by machine gun nests here and there. He expects the division to move forward now in accordance with orders.

Lieutenant Cosgrove and Captain Brown, Regimental Adjutant, already were dead in that day's fighting. Both were daring and brilliant fighters. The casualties among the enlisted men had been heavy, but the regiment came out of its fox holes at 5:30 and went ahead with a rush. They guided to the left and got a heavy fire from machine guns and artillery, but they went ahead cleaning up machine gun nests as they went and before they stopped both Charpentry and Baulny had been taken. They had broken through the German line which had stopped them twice already that day.

Lieutenant Axline of E Company was killed as he was taking his platoon through a passage in the wire northwest of Charpentry. A machine gun bullet hit him in chest. He covered the wound with his hand and stood by until the entire detachment was out of the wire and going ahead. He then fell behind, crawled into a shell hole and died.

When the attacking troops finally stopped, Rieger's battalion lay in the edge of Montrebeau Wood and the regiment had to its credit the capture that evening of Charpentry, Baulny and the Chaudron Farm. One must study the map and take into account the difficulties of the terrain fully to understand the work the 139th Infantry had

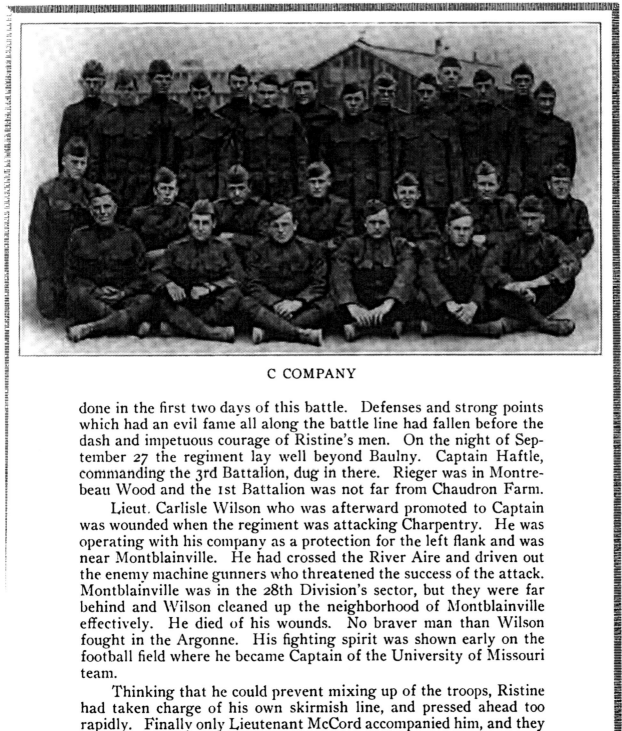

C COMPANY

done in the first two days of this battle. Defenses and strong points which had an evil fame all along the battle line had fallen before the dash and impetuous courage of Ristine's men. On the night of September 27 the regiment lay well beyond Baulny. Captain Haftle, commanding the 3rd Battalion, dug in there. Rieger was in Montrebeau Wood and the 1st Battalion was not far from Chaudron Farm.

Lieut. Carlisle Wilson who was afterward promoted to Captain was wounded when the regiment was attacking Charpentry. He was operating with his company as a protection for the left flank and was near Montblainville. He had crossed the River Aire and driven out the enemy machine gunners who threatened the success of the attack. Montblainville was in the 28th Division's sector, but they were far behind and Wilson cleaned up the neighborhood of Montblainville effectively. He died of his wounds. No braver man than Wilson fought in the Argonne. His fighting spirit was shown early on the football field where he became Captain of the University of Missouri team.

Thinking that he could prevent mixing up of the troops, Ristine had taken charge of his own skirmish line, and pressed ahead too rapidly. Finally only Lieutenant McCord accompanied him, and they became separated in crossing a small stream. McCord guided to the left and, unable to find his colonel, joined a party which penetrated far into the enemy territory near the bank of the river.

Ristine went ahead. He believed the American front line was still in front of him and seeing some soldiers through the dusk climb-

C COMPANY

ing a hill across the valley made this belief stronger. They were the retreating Germans, but he was not close enough to them to distinguish their uniforms. Indeed our troops had stopped and there was nothing ahead of Ristine but the Germans. He reached a hill just south of the valley which leads to Exermont and found himself quite near one of these lines of troops. "What outfit is this?" he yelled through the gathering darkness, but got no answer. He drew nearer and found it was a German outfit in retreat.

The Colonel was up against it. What he knew of the terrain he had learned from the map and it had now grown so dark that he could not put this knowledge to any use. He had lost his flash light, and probably would not have dared to examine his map even if he had had the light. He was in a quandary. He surely did not want to be surrounded by the enemy and he had a natural reluctance to retire from a retreating foe. With him at this time were a lieutenant and five privates of the 137th Infantry, whom he had run across on the field after leaving McCord. The seven men went to the crest of the hill and crawled into a big new shell hole. They organized it by digging the soft earth out of the bottom and putting it around the rim for a barricade. They had made four automatic rifle positions in the sides of the hole, when a German machine gun began to shoot across their position. Soon it appeared that two guns were crossing their fire over the shell hole.

After a period of waiting, Ristine decided the detachment could do better as individuals and gave each man permission to look out for himself. Ristine explained to them his idea, which was to crawl

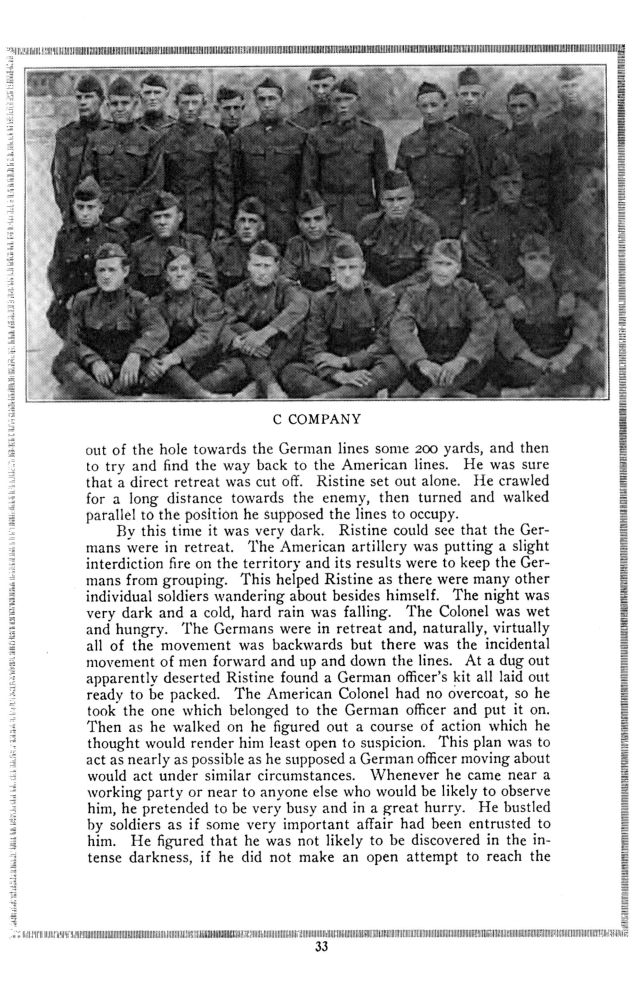

C COMPANY

out of the hole towards the German lines some 200 yards, and then to try and find the way back to the American lines. He was sure that a direct retreat was cut off. Ristine set out alone. He crawled for a long distance towards the enemy, then turned and walked parallel to the position he supposed the lines to occupy.

By this time it was very dark. Ristine could see that the Germans were in retreat. The American artillery was putting a slight interdiction fire on the territory and its results were to keep the Germans from grouping. This helped Ristine as there were many other individual soldiers wandering about besides himself. The night was very dark and a cold, hard rain was falling. The Colonel was wet and hungry. The Germans were in retreat and, naturally, virtually all of the movement was backwards but there was the incidental movement of men forward and up and down the lines. At a dug out apparently deserted Ristine found a German officer's kit all laid out ready to be packed. The American Colonel had no overcoat, so he took the one which belonged to the German officer and put it on. Then as he walked on he figured out a course of action which he thought would render him least open to suspicion. This plan was to act as nearly as possible as he supposed a German officer moving about would act under similar circumstances. Whenever he came near a working party or near to anyone else who would be likely to observe him, he pretended to be very busy and in a great hurry. He bustled by soldiers as if some very important affair had been entrusted to him. He figured that he was not likely to be discovered in the intense darkness, if he did not make an open attempt to reach the

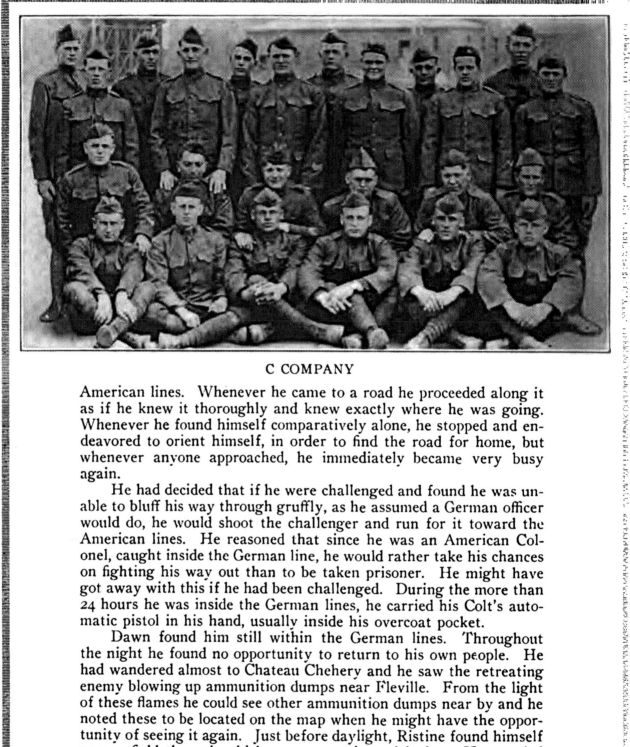

C COMPANY

American lines. Whenever he came to a road he proceeded along it as if he knew it thoroughly and knew exactly where he was going. Whenever he found himself comparatively alone, he stopped and endeavored to orient himself, in order to find the road for home, but whenever anyone approached, he immediately became very busy again.

He had decided that if he were challenged and found he was unable to bluff his way through gruffly, as he assumed a German officer would do, he would shoot the challenger and run for it toward the American lines. He reasoned that since he was an American Colonel, caught inside the German line, he would rather take his chances on fighting his way out than to be taken prisoner. He might have got away with this if he had been challenged. During the more than 24 hours he was inside the German lines, he carried his Colt's automatic pistol in his hand, usually inside his overcoat pocket.

Dawn found him still within the German lines. Throughout the night he found no opportunity to return to his own people. He had wandered almost to Chateau Chehery and he saw the retreating enemy blowing up ammunition dumps near Fleville. From the light of these flames he could see other ammunition dumps near by and he noted these to be located on the map when he might have the opportunity of seeing it again. Just before daylight, Ristine found himself near a field through which ran an untrimmed hedge. He crawled under the rows of the hedge and crept stealthily forward until he found a place from which he could watch both sides. Then he made himself as comfortable as he could to spend the day.

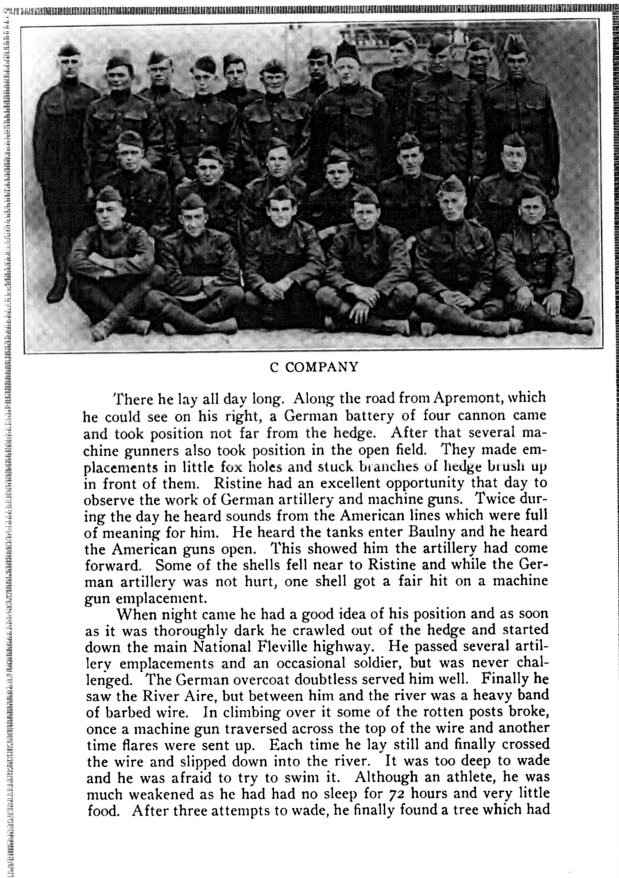

C COMPANY

There he lay all day long. Along the road from Apremont, which he could see on his right, a German battery of four cannon came and took position not far from the hedge. After that several machine gunners also took position in the open field. They made emplacements in little fox holes and stuck branches of hedge brush up in front of them. Ristine had an excellent opportunity that day to observe the work of German artillery and machine guns. Twice during the day he heard sounds from the American lines which were full of meaning for him. He heard the tanks enter Baulny and he heard the American guns open. This showed him the artillery had come forward. Some of the shells fell near to Ristine and while the German artillery was not hurt, one shell got a fair hit on a machine gun emplacement.

When night came he had a good idea of his position and as soon as it was thoroughly dark he crawled out of the hedge and started down the main National Fleville highway. He passed several artillery emplacements and an occasional soldier, but was never challenged. The German overcoat doubtless served him well. Finally he saw the River Aire, but between him and the river was a heavy band of barbed wire. In climbing over it some of the rotten posts broke, once a machine gun traversed across the top of the wire and another time flares were sent up. Each time he lay still and finally crossed the wire and slipped down into the river. It was too deep to wade and he was afraid to try to swim it. Although an athlete, he was much weakened as he had had no sleep for 72 hours and very little food. After three attempts to wade, he finally found a tree which had

KILLED IN ACTION

1. Capt. Sanford Brown, Jr.
2. Lieut. Arthur A. Axline
3. Capt. Carlisle R. Wilson
4. Capt. Edgar H. Dale
5. Lieut. John D. Cosgrove

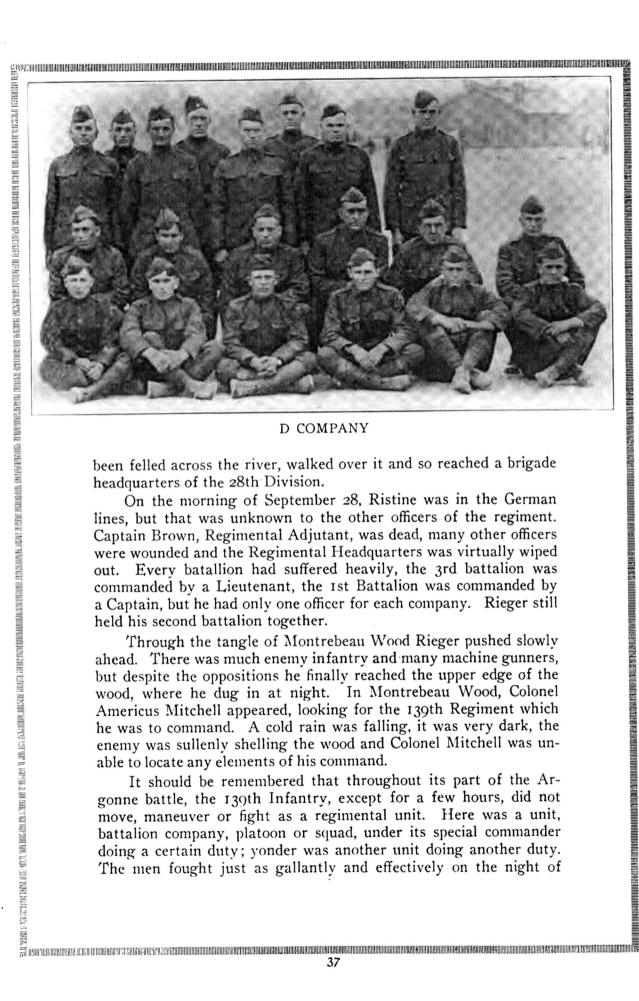

D COMPANY

been felled across the river, walked over it and so reached a brigade headquarters of the 28th Division.

On the morning of September 28, Ristine was in the German lines, but that was unknown to the other officers of the regiment. Captain Brown, Regimental Adjutant, was dead, many other officers were wounded and the Regimental Headquarters was virtually wiped out. Every batallion had suffered heavily, the 3rd battalion was commanded by a Lieutenant, the 1st Battalion was commanded by a Captain, but he had only one officer for each company. Rieger still held his second battalion together.

Through the tangle of Montrebeau Wood Rieger pushed slowly ahead. There was much enemy infantry and many machine gunners, but despite the oppositions he finally reached the upper edge of the wood, where he dug in at night. In Montrebeau Wood, Colonel Americus Mitchell appeared, looking for the 139th Regiment which he was to command. A cold rain was falling, it was very dark, the enemy was sullenly shelling the wood and Colonel Mitchell was unable to locate any elements of his command.

It should be remembered that throughout its part of the Argonne battle, the 139th Infantry, except for a few hours, did not move, maneuver or fight as a regimental unit. Here was a unit, battalion company, platoon or squad, under its special commander doing a certain duty; yonder was another unit doing another duty. The men fought just as gallantly and effectively on the night of

D COMPANY

the 27th and all through the day of the 28th as they did at any other time, and the losses were very heavy.

It was on September 28 that Lieutenant Everett B. Mosier met his death. This officer was new to the regiment, but had made a very good impression. He had been an athlete and sportsman in Philadelphia when the United States entered the war. He was one of the organizers of the Philadelphia District Lawn Tennis Association and was considered probably the best racket player in Philadelphia. He had applied for admission to the first officers' training camp, passed the physical examination, but was not called. He then applied for admission to the Fort Oglethorpe training camp but was not called there. Soon afterward he was drafted. In January, 1918, he was selected for the third officers' training camp at Camp Gordon, passed satisfactorily and was sent to France in May. July 18 he was commissioned Second Lieutenant and transferred from the 82nd Division to the 35th Division.

On this day he was leading parts of two companies of the 2nd Battalion near the edge of Montrebeau Wood. The Germans, filtering forward threatened to surround him. He ordered his men to fall back for safety, but before this was possible for many of them, the detachment was surrounded. The last seen of Mosier he was fighting desperately with a few of his men. He was entirely surrounded by the Germans. He and this little band did not surrender, but died fighting. He was at first listed as missing, but his grave was found afterwards about 700 yards north of Chaudron Farm.

Captain Dale was killed on September 28. He was in command

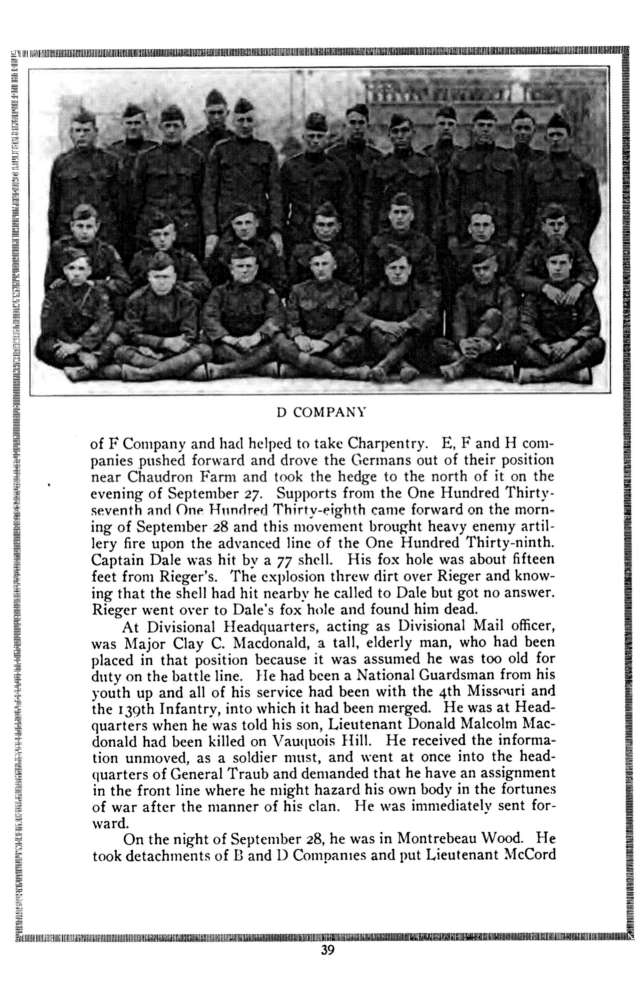

D COMPANY

of F Company and had helped to take Charpentry. E, F and H companies pushed forward and drove the Germans out of their position near Chaudron Farm and took the hedge to the north of it on the evening of September 27. Supports from the One Hundred Thirty-seventh and One Hundred Thirty-eighth came forward on the morning of September 28 and this movement brought heavy enemy artillery fire upon the advanced line of the One Hundred Thirty-ninth. Captain Dale was hit by a 77 shell. His fox hole was about fifteen feet from Rieger's. The explosion threw dirt over Rieger and knowing that the shell had hit nearby he called to Dale but got no answer. Rieger went over to Dale's fox hole and found him dead.

At Divisional Headquarters, acting as Divisional Mail officer, was Major Clay C. Macdonald, a tall, elderly man, who had been placed in that position because it was assumed he was too old for duty on the battle line. He had been a National Guardsman from his youth up and all of his service had been with the 4th Missouri and the 139th Infantry, into which it had been merged. He was at Headquarters when he was told his son, Lieutenant Donald Malcolm Macdonald had been killed on Vauquois Hill. He received the information unmoved, as a soldier must, and went at once into the headquarters of General Traub and demanded that he have an assignment in the front line where he might hazard his own body in the fortunes of war after the manner of his clan. He was immediately sent forward.

On the night of September 28, he was in Montrebeau Wood. He took detachments of B and D Companies and put Lieutenant McCord

D COMPANY

in immediate command and with them formed a line facing the enemy. Major Macdonald on September 29 took command of A and B Companies by direction of Colonel Ristine. Lieutenant McCord on September 29 was wounded and sent to the rear. On the morning of September 30 Major Macdonald, still capable and efficient, turned over A and B Companies to Captain Williamson, commanding the 1st Battalion of the One Hundred Thirty-ninth, and under orders of Colonel Mitchell took command of the 2nd Battalion of the 137th Infantry and formed a line just in the rear of that line held by Stayton and the Engineers. He stayed with the One Hundred Thirty-seventh until the regiment was withdrawn, when he was returned to the One Hundred Thirty-ninth where he took command of his old battalion. Despite his 61 years, Major Macdonald endured great physical hardships and the pounding and wear of battle better than some of the younger men and when he came home it was as a Lieutenant-Colonel, a promotion won on the field.

On the morning of September 26, the morning which, as one officer grimly said, was "to separate the men from the boys," Captain Heiny was one of many men who wondered how he was going to stand the strain. It was a dubious question with him. Four days later, after he had taken two severe wounds and had kept fighting with the forward elements at all times and had voluntarily gone forward through an enemy barrage to get information, there was not much doubt in any body else's mind as to whether he was a soldier.

The morning of September 29 dawned dark and gray on the

40

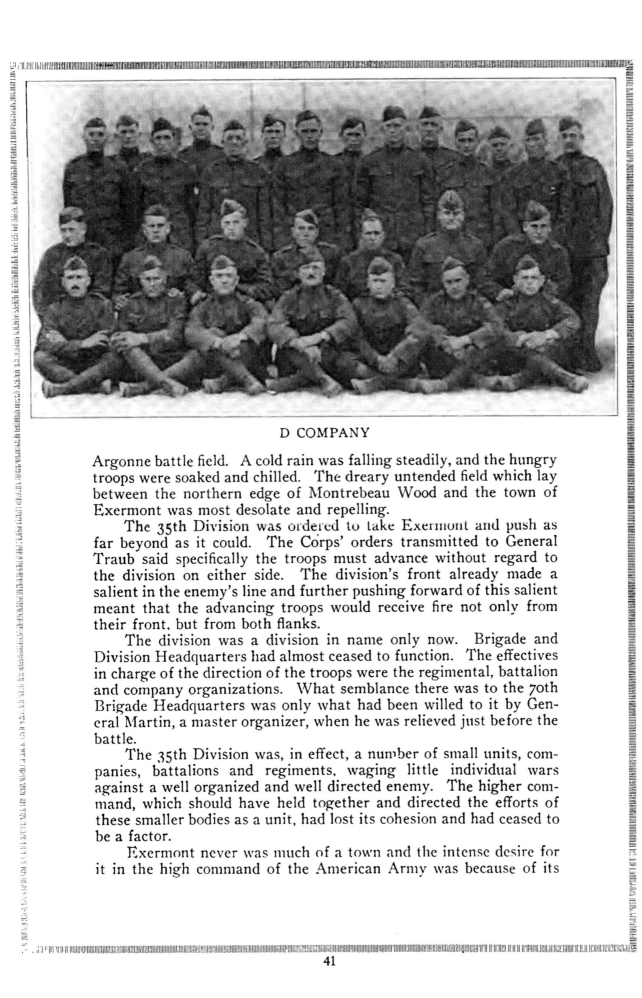

D COMPANY

Argonne battle field. A cold rain was falling steadily, and the hungry troops were soaked and chilled. The dreary untended field which lay between the northern edge of Montrebeau Wood and the town of Exermont was most desolate and repelling.

The 35th Division was ordered to take Exermont and push as far beyond as it could. The Corps' orders transmitted to General Traub said specifically the troops must advance without regard to the division on either side. The division's front already made a salient in the enemy's line and further pushing forward of this salient meant that the advancing troops would receive fire not only from their front, but from both flanks.

The division was a division in name only now. Brigade and Division Headquarters had almost ceased to function. The effectives in charge of the direction of the troops were the regimental, battalion and company organizations. What semblance there was to the 70th Brigade Headquarters was only what had been willed to it by General Martin, a master organizer, when he was relieved just before the battle.

The 35th Division was, in effect, a number of small units, companies, battalions and regiments, waging little individual wars against a well organized and well directed enemy. The higher command, which should have held together and directed the efforts of these smaller bodies as a unit, had lost its cohesion and had ceased to be a factor.

Exermont never was much of a town and the intense desire for it in the high command of the American Army was because of its

D COMPANY

position and the fact that it had been strongly fortified by the Germans. It blocked the way. For its further defense the enemy had brought into it since the beginning of the Argonne Battle, large numbers of veteran machine gunners. These were in the prepared emplacements in the town and scattered over the open field between Montrebeau Wood and the Exermont Ravine.

The first to make the attempt on Exermont was Major Kalloch with about 125 men, mostly of the 137th Infantry. Kalloch was beaten back and his command was virtually destroyed. He left his dead and wounded on the field. After him came Major James Rieger, a devout man, who was not in the custom of spending his Sunday mornings in such a scene. His battalion had suffered heavy losses, for it had been through all the fighting at Vauquois Hill, the Bois de Rossignol, at the taking of Charpentry, Baulny and Chaudron Farm and the Montrebeau Wood. Those unwieldy French names for places were hardly known to us then, but they will live in history as long as Missourians and Kansans read of martial deeds and revere their soldier dead. The little dots on the map of France were that day passing from the obscurity of rural villages, to the blaze of flame in the Midlands of America thousands of miles across the sea.

Rieger formed the remnants of his battalion behind Montrebeau Wood, intending to pass through it for the sake of the shelter it would give against enemy fire, and to advance directly from its upper edge towards Exermont. Colonel Nuttman, commanding the brigade met him just as he was entering the wood and insisted that Exermont lay "that way," pointing due east. Rieger assured his superior of-

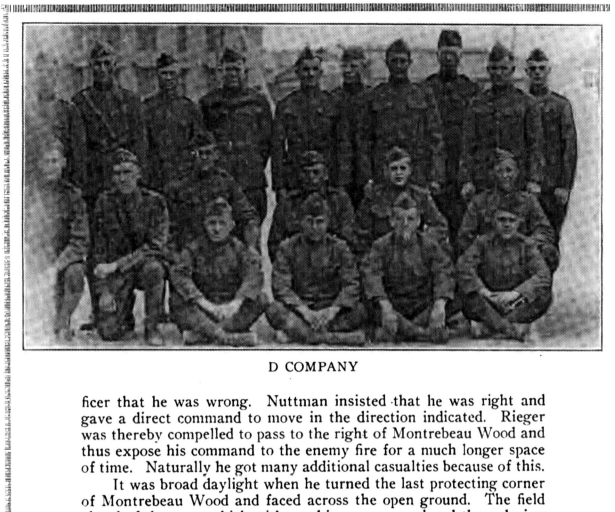

D COMPANY

ficer that he was wrong. Nuttman insisted that he was right and gave a direct command to move in the direction indicated. Rieger was thereby compelled to pass to the right of Montrebeau Wood and thus expose his command to the enemy fire for a much longer space of time. Naturally he got many additional casualties because of this.

It was broad daylight when he turned the last protecting corner of Montrebeau Wood and faced across the open ground. The field ahead of them was thick with machine gunners, placed there during the night, rifle fire from every protection was brought to bear on the attacking troops, artillery from three sides pounded them. Rieger's men had been without warm food for four days. They were chilled with the rain and they were extremely tired because of the constant work of battle.

So heavy was the fire from the front that men were seen to turn their faces from it while still advancing, as one will do in a gale of wind.

The command was "Forward." There was no barrage and if General Berry's artillery was aiding the infantry, the infantry did not know it. That was the General Berry who spent so much time at Camp Doniphan trying to get rid of Major Rieger, and this was the Major Rieger that stayed. Both had reached the day of supreme trial.

Across the open field the worn infantry went, the losses growing heavier every minute. Across the little valley of Exermont and the creek. Fairly against the town they charged and they took it, grimly killing the enemy machine gunners at their guns, and bombing the

D COMPANY

dug outs with awful thoroughness. Through the town they passed and to the heights beyond. There they dug a line and held it, and there the 2nd Battalion, the 139th Infantry and the 35th Division reached the height of their glory.

Captain McQueen was badly wounded in Exermont; Lieutenant McManigal was shot through the chest and with Private Joe Simpich lay three days without care or attention. This story has been told in detail in the first chapter of "From Vauquois Hill to Exermont."

Of all of McManigal's detachment in the desperate move on Exermont, Leroy Moss, who did as much fighting as anyone else, was the only man who was not either killed or wounded.

Not far behind Rieger came Delaplane with part of the One Hundred Fortieth, making firm and sure the American occupation of Exermont.

On the field behind these advanced units, in Montrebeau Wood, about Chaudron Farm and on both sides of it, the troops were suffering as the result of confused orders and loss of capable officers. On our right, Colonel Walker commanding the 69th Brigade had ordered two advances and a retirement. Ristine, again with his own division, reached that part of the field as the troops were coming back. He tried in vain to stop what elements he met, declaring he had later orders from high authority that the whole division was to advance and support the forward troops. He was too late, but if there had been another like him the farthest advance might have been held.

Colonel Walker's message ordering a withdrawal and an officer

FELL IN BATTLE

1. Capt. Alexander M. Ellett   3. Major W. D. Stepp
2. Lieut. Everett B. Mosier   4. Lieut. Thomas Hopkins
5. Lieut. Donald Malcolm Macdonald

E COMPANY

patrol from Colonel Mitchell reached Exermont about the same time. Delaplane evacuated the town and fell back slowly and in order. Behind him came Rieger's outfit fighting constantly over the ground they gave up. On three sides of him the enemy pressed forward with infantry and automatic riflemen. Rieger's splendid rear guard action brought his outfit safely back to the Engineer's line.

An act of merit and justice which followed was the promotion of Rieger for gallantry in action. He was always loved by his men for his unfailing kindness and humanity, and this reward of his bravery and skill in battle thrilled every heart.

The widespread belief that the armistice would end the war for the 139th Infantry was soon disproved. The winter of 1918-19 in the Commercy area was a most dreary one. The army command thought it would try to make soldiers out of the men. The riddled ranks were filled with replacements and beautiful military problems were worked out in the rain and mud.

The men were as a rule in unheated billets, hay lofts and the like, and there was the chronic shortage of clothing. Colds and pneumonia grew alarmingly and Major Smith and Col. Ristine wrestled unceasingly with the Divisional command to have the drill hours reduced and to give the men a chance to keep their health.

Each man was entitled to a razor. The requisition for them had been sent in at Doniphan, and they finally were received, after many urgings, after the armistice. Though the men were cold, wet and for long periods unbathed, they must be clean shaven.

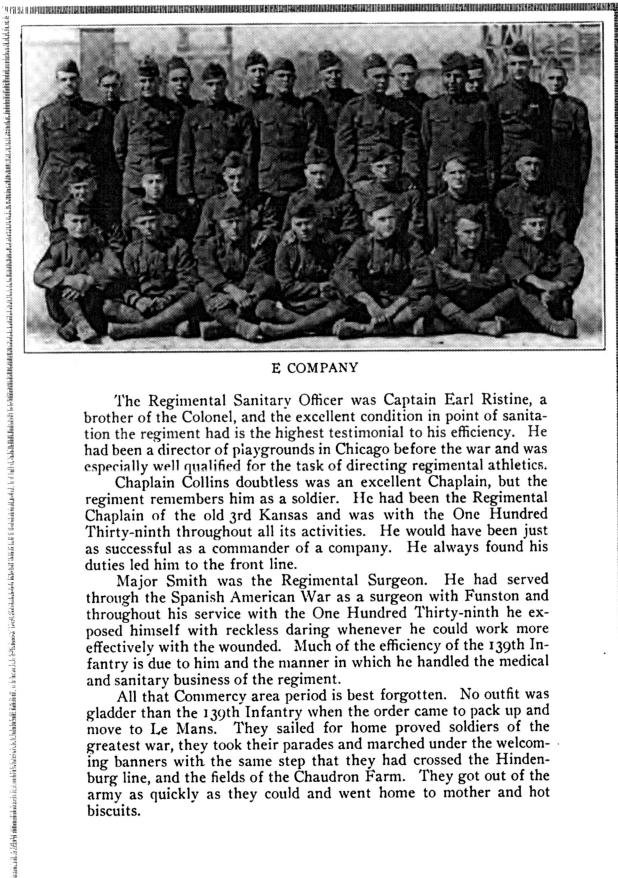

E COMPANY

The Regimental Sanitary Officer was Captain Earl Ristine, a brother of the Colonel, and the excellent condition in point of sanitation the regiment had is the highest testimonial to his efficiency. He had been a director of playgrounds in Chicago before the war and was especially well qualified for the task of directing regimental athletics.

Chaplain Collins doubtless was an excellent Chaplain, but the regiment remembers him as a soldier. He had been the Regimental Chaplain of the old 3rd Kansas and was with the One Hundred Thirty-ninth throughout all its activities. He would have been just as successful as a commander of a company. He always found his duties led him to the front line.

Major Smith was the Regimental Surgeon. He had served through the Spanish American War as a surgeon with Funston and throughout his service with the One Hundred Thirty-ninth he exposed himself with reckless daring whenever he could work more effectively with the wounded. Much of the efficiency of the 139th Infantry is due to him and the manner in which he handled the medical and sanitary business of the regiment.

All that Commercy area period is best forgotten. No outfit was gladder than the 139th Infantry when the order came to pack up and move to Le Mans. They sailed for home proved soldiers of the greatest war, they took their parades and marched under the welcoming banners with the same step that they had crossed the Hindenburg line, and the fields of the Chaudron Farm. They got out of the army as quickly as they could and went home to mother and hot biscuits.

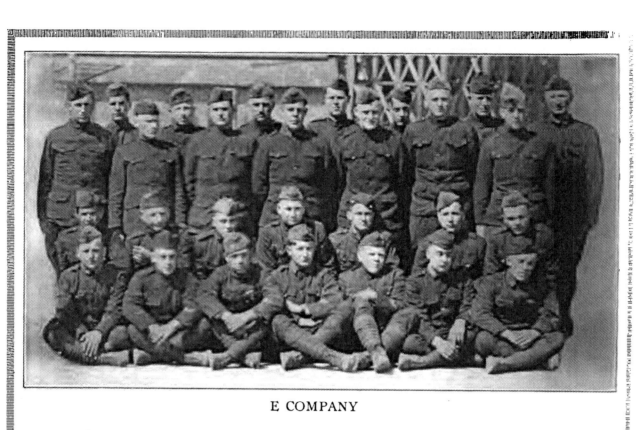

E COMPANY

They do not like to talk about it yet. There really is not much of it that makes good telling at the supper table. Many a mother wonders why Jimmie who used to be such a talker, is so silent on the topic of the Great War. She must wait a while. It is too new. Let the memories begin to mellow and ripen, and she will hear some mighty tall tales of the things her boy did in France.

CASUALTIES OF THE 139th INFANTRY

COMPANY OR DETACH.	KILLED		WOUNDED		GASSED		MISSING		TOTAL		Percentage Casualties "Fourth Battalion"
	Men	Off.	Men	Off.	Men	Off.	Men	Off	Men	Off.	
Hdq.	3		18	1	45	3	8		74	4	Total strength.
M. C. Gun	4		38	3			10		52	3	449 men, 24 officers.
San. Det.			4				3		7		Loss.
Field Amb.		3		1						4	29.62% 45.83%.
A	1		34		15		32		82		First Battalion.
B	10		82	1	11	1	3		106	2	Total strength.
C	12		88			1	9		109	1	934 men, 18 officers.
D	6		62	1	12		6		86	1	Loss, 41.557. 22.48 %.
E	12		41	1	8	1	42		103	2	Second Battalion.
F	11	1	49	2	6	1	36		102	4	Total strength.
G	4	1	61	1	8		54	1	127	3	931 men, 19 officers.
H	11		70	3			29	1	110	4	Loss, 49.12% 68.42%.
I	4		52	2	10	1	42		108	3	Third Battalion.
K	11	1	55	2	2		47		115	3	Total strength.
L	7		49	1	4		30		90	1	894 men, 18 officers.
M	2		42	2	3		24		71	2	Loss, 47.00% 50.60%.
Total	98	6	745	21	124	8	375	2	1342	37	Loss Regiment total.
											Men Officers.
%	3.36	6.33	23.22	26.58	3 87	10.12	11.78	2.50	41.82	46.84	41.82% 46.84%.

Total strength, Sept. 25th, 3208 men, 79 officers.

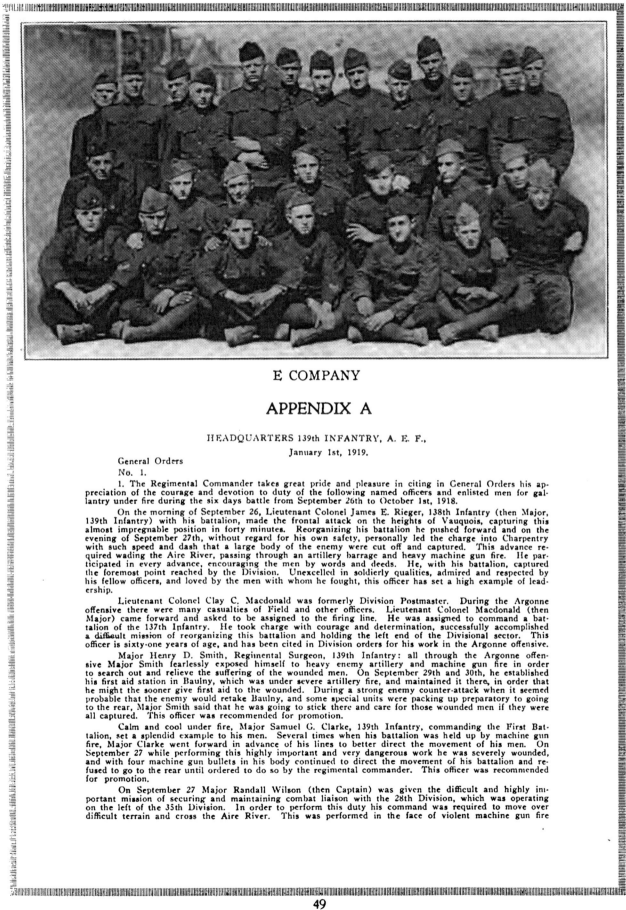

E COMPANY

APPENDIX A

HEADQUARTERS 139th INFANTRY, A. E. F.,

January 1st, 1919.

General Orders

No. 1.

1. The Regimental Commander takes great pride and pleasure in citing in General Orders his appreciation of the courage and devotion to duty of the following named officers and enlisted men for gallantry under fire during the six days battle from September 26th to October 1st, 1918.

On the morning of September 26, Lieutenant Colonel James E. Rieger, 138th Infantry (then Major, 139th Infantry) with his battalion, made the frontal attack on the heights of Vauquois, capturing this almost impregnable position in forty minutes. Reorganizing his battalion he pushed forward and on the evening of September 27th, without regard for his own safety, personally led the charge into Charpentry with such speed and dash that a large body of the enemy were cut off and captured. This advance required wading the Aire River, passing through an artillery barrage and heavy machine gun fire. He participated in every advance, encouraging the men by words and deeds. He, with his battalion, captured the foremost point reached by the Division. Unexcelled in soldierly qualities, admired and respected by his fellow officers, and loved by the men with whom he fought, this officer has set a high example of leadership.

Lieutenant Colonel Clay C. Macdonald was formerly Division Postmaster. During the Argonne offensive there were many casualties of Field and other officers. Lieutenant Colonel Macdonald (then Major) came forward and asked to be assigned to the firing line. He was assigned to command a battalion of the 137th Infantry. He took charge with courage and determination, successfully accomplished a difficult mission of reorganizing this battalion and holding the left end of the Divisional sector. This officer is sixty-one years of age, and has been cited in Division orders for his work in the Argonne offensive.

Major Henry D. Smith, Regimental Surgeon, 139th Infantry: all through the Argonne offensive Major Smith fearlessly exposed himself to heavy enemy artillery and machine gun fire in order to search out and relieve the suffering of the wounded men. On September 29th and 30th, he established his first aid station in Baulny, which was under severe artillery fire, and maintained it there, in order that he might the sooner give first aid to the wounded. During a strong enemy counter-attack when it seemed probable that the enemy would retake Baulny, and some special units were packing up preparatory to going to the rear, Major Smith said that he was going to stick there and care for those wounded men if they were all captured. This officer was recommended for promotion.

Calm and cool under fire, Major Samuel G. Clarke, 139th Infantry, commanding the First Battalion, set a splendid example to his men. Several times when his battalion was held up by machine gun fire, Major Clarke went forward in advance of his lines to better direct the movement of his men. On September 27 while performing this highly important and very dangerous work he was severely wounded, and with four machine gun bullets in his body continued to direct the movement of his battalion and refused to go to the rear until ordered to do so by the regimental commander. This officer was recommended for promotion.

On September 27 Major Randall Wilson (then Captain) was given the difficult and highly important mission of securing and maintaining combat liaison with the 28th Division, which was operating on the left of the 35th Division. In order to perform this duty his command was required to move over difficult terrain and cross the Aire River. This was performed in the face of violent machine gun fire

E COMPANY

from the enemy then located in the village of Montblainville. On September 29th and 30th, Major Wilson, with his command, held an advanced post north of Chaudron Farm and covered the evacuation of 140 wounded men from that place, remaining on duty for twenty-six hours and repelling numerous attacks made by the enemy, and he did not retire to the new lines being held by the Division until the last man had been evacuated.

Major William C. Williamson (then Captain) while commanding the First Battalion, 139th Infantry, on September 29 and 30, took an advanced position north of Baulny near the north edge of Montrebeau Woods, organized and held said position so as to allow an advance force to retire, and defeated two counter-attacks made by the enemy, this was done under continuous artillery and machine gun fire. On September 30, while in command of said battalion he reorganized a defensive line on Chaudron Farm and defeated a determined enemy attack.

In order to get food up to his regiment Captain Charles J. Hall, Supply Officer, turned his supply train off the main highway and drove it across the fields in order to get around a jam which was blocking the traffic on the highway. After getting around the jam he resumed the main highway, which was under direct observation of the enemy and being shelled continuously. As he neared Baulny his difficulties increased, as the shelling became more severe and mixed with gas. He lost 19 horses and had five wagon tongues shot off, but persevered and made it into Baulny with 22 wagon loads of food which contained seven days rations for 4,000 men; and for several days furnished rations to almost the entire Division. This officer was recommended for promotion.

On September 26 Captain J. W. McQueen personally led his company to mop up Vauquois and Bois du Rossignol, and captured many prisoners and war material. On September 27 he led one of the attacking companies against the enemy line of Charpentry and Baulny, the attack resulting in the capture of Charpentry, Baulny and Chaudron Farm buildings, his company reaching the ridge east of Montrebeau Woods and maintained its position there notwithstanding the assaults of the enemy. He personally led his company in the attack on Exermont, which resulted in the capture of that town. He advanced with his company beyond the town, and while driving off an assault by the enemy was seriously wounded. This officer was recommended for promotion.

Captain Henry F. Halverson, 139th Infantry, led his company with spirit and determination. On the evening of September 26, upon the death of Major Stepp, he assumed command of the battalion. He assisted in the capture of Charpentry and Montrebeau Woods on September 27, and by his splendid example of courage and self-sacrifice inspired his troops to make these advances through destructive artillery and machine gun fire. On September 29th, during the attack on Exermont he was gassed and wounded, but refused to go to the rear until ordered to do so by the regimental commander.

On September 27, Captain John D. Heiny organized men separated from the front line and turned them over to company officers and assisted in the organization of disorganized units under enemy fire and though wounded twice (marked severe) remained on duty during the entire action. Went through barrage and gave our artillery location of enemy batteries that were doing great damage to our troops, this notwithstanding great personal danger. On the night of September 29th he remained in the first aid station at Chaudron Farm, and assisted in the care and evacuation of the wounded. During the entire action this officer showed great bravery and gallantry in action. This officer was recommended for promotion.

Captain Matthew Guilfoyle (then First Lieutenant), led his platoon against machine gun nests near Charpentry, with spirit and determination. On September 26 assumed command of Company I, and assisted in the capture of Charpentry, advancing through destructive machine gun and artillery fire with such rapidity that many prisoners were captured. Reorganized and continued the advance, capturing and pushing on beyond Chaudron Farm. On September 29th, when all other officers senior to him had become casualties, assumed command of the battalion until the regiment was relieved.

E COMPANY

During every advance Captain Ralph W. Martin, was always in front and by his calmness and qualities of natural leadership inspired everyone near him. On the morning of September 28, while his battalion and adjoining units were held up by destructive machine gun fire from both front and right flank, he led a patrol around the right flank, reducing machine gun nests and protecting the advance on Montrebeau Woods.

1st Lieutenant Donald M. Macdonald, was the first of the regiment to make the supreme sacrifice. In the early hours of the morning, September 26, Lieutenant Macdonald while gallantly leading his platoon and considerably in advance thereof, started to dash up the heights of Vauquois when he was killed by a machine gun bullet, but his spirit lived on in his splendid example of courage and gallantry, in the determination with which his men avenged his death in the capture of Vauquois.

1st Lieutenant Coburn Hull, on September 27, without regard to personal danger, led his company in the attack behind the tanks against the defenses of Charpentry, passing through a dense artillery and machine gun barrage. His company had suffered severe losses and it required an officer of exceptional ability and courage to handle the situation. He reorganized his company and that evening led it in a gallant attack, assisting in the capture of Charpentry. He was pushing forward beyond Charpentry when he was wounded. This officer was recommended to be a Captain, but failed to receive this merited promotion on account of being dropped from the rolls of the Division by reason of being in a base hospital.

On September 26, 1st Lieutenant John W. McManigal personally led his platoon of Company H to mop up Vauquois and Bois du Rossignol, and captured many prisoners and much war material. On September 27 he led one of the attacking platoons against the enemy line of Charpentry and Baulny, the attack resulting in the capture of Charpentry, Baulny and Chaudron Farm buildings, his platoon reaching the ridge east of Montrebeau Woods, and maintained its position there notwithstanding the assaults of the enemy. He personally led his platoon in the attack on Exermont, which resulted in the capture of that town. He advanced with his platoon beyond the town, and while driving off an assault by the enemy was seriously wounded. This officer was recommended for promotion.

1st Lieutenant William H. Morse while acting adjutant of the Third Battalion, showed courage and resourcefulness under difficult conditions on September 26 and 27. He made personal trips from one end of the line to the other, encouraging the men and assisting in locating enemy machine gun emplacements, then disposing the trench mortars and one pounders so that they could be effectively used against them. While engaged in this highly important work Lieutenant Morse was severely wounded. This occurred about one kilometer south of Charpentry.

1st Lieutenant Homer J. Henney (then 2nd Lieutenant), gathered together a detachment of men who had lost their organizations and repulsed a counter-attack on the right of Montrebeau Woods on the night of September 28-29. The following morning he resolutely pushed forward with the detachment in the attack on Exermont, assisting in the capture of that place.

Chaplain Myron S. Collins, senior Chaplain of the regiment, in addition to his official duties as Chaplain in administering spiritual comfort to the wounded soldiers, ably assisted the regimental surgeon in administering physical comfort to the wounded. He worked without rest and without fear while under most severe artillery, machine gun fire and rifle fire. This officer was recommended for promotion.

1st Lieutenant George T. Worthen was in command of a company in the Argonne fight, and although suffering from mustard gas burns he stayed with his troops during the entire fight. He was always found at the head of his troops when an attack was on, and performed all of his work most excellently. This officer was recommended to be a Captain, but failed to receive this merited promotion on account of being in a hospital and having been dropped from the rolls of the Division.

1st Lieutenant Edward S. Carmack had been in charge of the message center some time prior to the Argonne fight, and was in charge of same during the fight and did excellent work as such. Although

E COMPANY

he was gassed in the early part of the fight he did not permit himself to be evacuated until after the order for the relief of our Division had been received. This officer was recommended for promotion.

1st Lieutenant George H. Stephens was regimental scout officer in the Argonne fight, and did excellent work as such until he was wounded. He was severely wounded with a fragment of high explosive and while waiting to be evacuated was gassed. This officer was recommended for promotion.

In the drive commencing September 26, 1st Sergeant Harry R. Kelsey, Company E (deceased) was at all times at the side of the company commander. In the afternoon of September 27, while under very heavy shell fire, Sergeant Kelsey volunteered to carry a vry important message from the company P. C., which was located about 100 yards to the right of the road leading north into Charpentry and about 1,000 yards south of Charpentry, to the battalion P. C., about 800 yards to the left of the company P. C. With no regard for his own safety, knowing the message was of the utmost importance and time valuable, he took the most direct route by which he must go through a very heavy barrage and cross the road swept by machine gun fire. 1st Sergeant Kelsey was killed while performing this great service.

1st Sergeant John J. Kirkpatrick, Co. M, on September 28, near Apremont, with great courage exposed himself to enemy machine gun and rifle fire from all sides while locating an enemy gun nest, against which he led a bombing attack. On September 28, after his Captain was wounded and the company scattered, he gathered together and organized as much of his company as he could find and attached himself to Co. D, 138th Infantry, and held the front line against a German counter-attack.

On the morning of September 26, at Varennes, Sergeant Frank J. Kilfoyle, Co. M, led an automatic rifle squad into the town under heavy machine gun and artillery fire, capturing a machine gun nest. On September 28 he led his platoon, after his platoon commander had been severely gassed, with great valor and courage thereby setting an example to all his men, against a German machine gun nest and line of skirmishers, forcing them to retire.

Sergeant Wayne C. Newcomb, Co. M, (deceased) was painfully wounded while leading his platoon against a German machine gun nest, but refused to go back to the hospital, remaining in command of his platoon and thereby setting a splendid example of courage to his men.

Corporal Albert E. Suess (wounded and missing) Co. M, on September 27 volunteered to carry ammunition through intense machine gun fire and a heavy bombardment, to the front lines near Charpentry. This ammunition was sorely needed. He later joined the fight, in which he was severely wounded.

Corporal Winfield P. Shahan, Co. M, as regimental liaison N. C. O., did on September 26, 27 and 28, with the greatest of courage and bravery constantly expose himself to heavy enemy machine gun and shell fire in order to help maintain liaison between the different companies and regimental headquarters. Later, on September 29, near Exermont, single-handed, he attacked a German machine gun nest, killing a number of Germans and while taking one prisoner was fired upon by another German machine gun and attacked by his prisoner. He was wounded in the right arm and being unable to use his rifle drew his pistol and killed the German attacking him, thereby making his escape.

On the evening of September 29, near Apremont, when the enemy counter-attacked, preparing their way by throwing smoke grenades thereby shielding our fire and succeeding in planting machine guns to check our advance, Corporal Frank L. Motley, Co. M, advanced single handed, killed the machine gunner and loader, jumped into the enemy nest of fifteen and thereby aided in breaking up the counter-attack.

Mechanic Benjamin E. Foust, Company F, displayed a high standard of bravery in the Argonne fight. On September 29th, after having one eye shot out and administering first aid to himself, showing no regard for his own safety, he refused to leave the field and remained administering first aid to the wounded men of his own organization and men of other organizations who were near. He continued his work through a gas attack, wearing his gas mask over the wounded eye.

CITED IN ORDERS

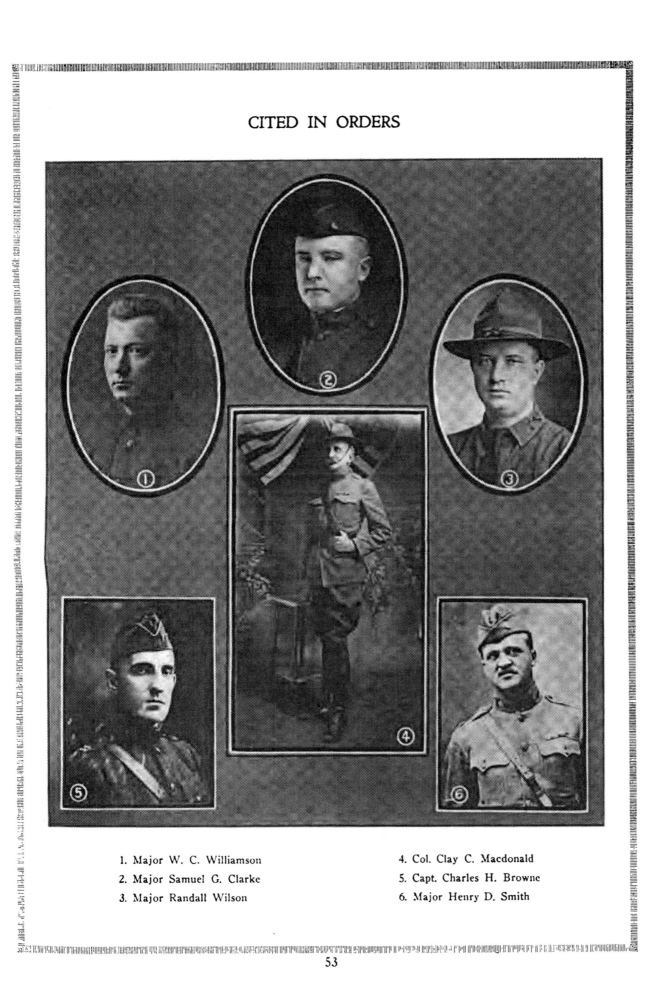

1. Major W. C. Williamson
2. Major Samuel G. Clarke
3. Major Randall Wilson
4. Col. Clay C. Macdonald
5. Capt. Charles H. Browne
6. Major Henry D. Smith

F COMPANY

Private 1st Class Russell M. Dudley, Sanitary Detachment, displayed great gallantry in action. On September 27, near Cheppy, he went through heavy enemy artillery fire, without regard for his own safety, and carried Lieutenant Colonel Dickey, who was severely wounded, to the first aid station.

Private Herbert F. Stoffle, Sanitary Detachment, displayed great gallantry in action near Exermont, September 29th, going through an enemy artillery barrage to dress a wounded comrade who had one leg shot off. While attending to this patient the line was drawn back. He remained with the wounded man and was captured by the enemy. He assisted in getting his patient to a German aid station and thereby saved his life.

Private Cecil L. Smith, Co. M, was a stretcher bearer, and on the morning of September 26, near Varennes, with great courage and bravery advanced through machine gun and artillery fire to the aid of the wounded and assisted in bringing them to the dressing station. On the same day and on September 27, without thought of his own safety, voluntarily carried water through intense shell fire to the wounded who could not be carried back to the first aid station. On September 28 he refused to retire from his stretcher after being badly gassed, until it became necessary to assist him from the field.

Private Anton J. Benson, Co. F, showed exceptional bravery and a disregard for his own safety while working as a stretcher bearer in the Argonne battle. He continued his work through heavy machine gun and artillery barrages and when his comrades who were helping him were shot, he carried the wounded back alone. His work was the means of saving many lives.

Private George W. Wood, Co. F, while performing his duty as an automatic rifleman in the Argonne battle showed great bravery and a disregard for his own safety in advancing against the enemy. He had cleared the way of many machine gun nests and had worked his way to the farthest advance point. It was during an advance against a machine gun nest by himself that he was killed.

CARL L. RISTINE, Colonel, 139th Infantry.

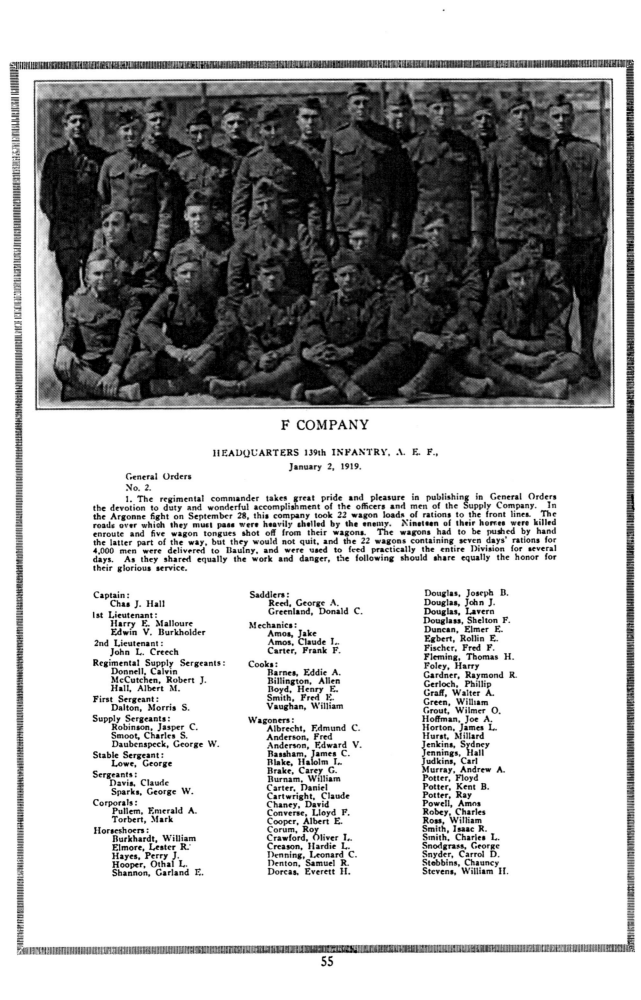

F COMPANY

HEADQUARTERS 139th INFANTRY, A. E. F.,

January 2, 1919.

General Orders
No. 2.

1. The regimental commander takes great pride and pleasure in publishing in General Orders the devotion to duty and wonderful accomplishment of the officers and men of the Supply Company. In the Argonne fight on September 28, this company took 22 wagon loads of rations to the front lines. The roads over which they must pass were heavily shelled by the enemy. Nineteen of their horses were killed enroute and five wagon tongues shot off from their wagons. The wagons had to be pushed by hand the latter part of the way, but they would not quit, and the 22 wagons containing seven days' rations for 4,000 men were delivered to Baulny, and were used to feed practically the entire Division for several days. As they shared equally the work and danger, the following should share equally the honor for their glorious service.

Captain:
Chas J. Hall

1st Lieutenant:
Harry E. Malloure
Edwin V. Burkholder

2nd Lieutenant:
John L. Creech

Regimental Supply Sergeants:
Donnell, Calvin
McCutchen, Robert J.
Hall, Albert M.

First Sergeant:
Dalton, Morris S.

Supply Sergeants:
Robinson, Jasper C.
Smoot, Charles S.
Daubenspeck, George W.

Stable Sergeant:
Lowe, George

Sergeants:
Davis, Claude
Sparks, George W.

Corporals:
Pullem, Emerald A.
Torbert, Mark

Horseshoers:
Burkhardt, William
Elmore, Lester R.
Hayes, Perry J.
Hooper, Othal L.
Shannon, Garland E.

Saddlers:
Reed, George A.
Greenland, Donald C.

Mechanics:
Amos, Jake
Amos, Claude L.
Carter, Frank F.

Cooks:
Barnes, Eddie A.
Billington, Allen
Boyd, Henry E.
Smith, Fred E.
Vaughan, William

Wagoners:
Albrecht, Edmund C.
Anderson, Fred
Anderson, Edward V.
Bassham, James C.
Blake, Halolm L.
Brake, Carey G.
Burnam, William
Carter, Daniel
Cartwright, Claude
Chaney, David
Converse, Lloyd F.
Cooper, Albert E.
Corum, Roy
Crawford, Oliver L.
Creason, Hardie L.
Denning, Leonard C.
Denton, Samuel R.
Dorcas, Everett H.

Douglas, Joseph B.
Douglas, John J.
Douglas, Lavern
Douglass, Shelton F.
Duncan, Elmer E.
Egbert, Rollin E.
Fischer, Fred F.
Fleming, Thomas H.
Foley, Harry
Gardner, Raymond R.
Gerloch, Phillip
Graff, Walter A.
Green, William
Grout, Wilmer O.
Hoffman, Joe A.
Horton, James L.
Hurst, Millard
Jenkins, Sydney
Jennings, Hall
Judkins, Carl
Murray, Andrew A.
Potter, Floyd
Potter, Kent B.
Potter, Ray
Powell, Amos
Robey, Charles
Ross, William
Smith, Isaac R.
Smith, Charles L.
Snodgrass, George
Snyder, Carrol D.
Stebbins, Chauncy
Stevens, William H.

F COMPANY

Stoltz, George W.
Sturm, Clarence E.
Vendel, Claude W.
Walker, Oliver
Welch, Henry C.
Wheeler, William W.
Wiley, Carter W.
Williams, Forrest H.
Williams, Russel H.
Wright, Mike

Privates, First Class:
Allen, Leslie
Dalton, Charles
Frantz, Donald
Gunn, Clarence T.
Hayes, Chester A.
Lamb, Edward
Limle, Harry
Rossie, Charles
Vrana, Joseph
Wilson, Lorn T.

Privates:
Anderson, John L.
Arlt, William H.
Arnold, Hobart
Brewster, Willard O.
Brogdon, John I.
Cooper, Noah
John, Claude I.
Jorgenson, Albert W.
Judkins, Cecil
Kelly, George J.
Kindler, Ernest

Kinder, William F.
King, Joseph
Knox, Fred
Long, William N.
Maxwell, Joseph L.
McHugh, John E.
McClure, Norvie J.
Mountain, Delbert
Oglevie, Lloyd V.
Olsen, Andy L.
Pauls, Rudolph
Kennedy, Leo J.
Kearn, Earl R.
Larson, Leonard
Madden, John L.
McGarry, James
Michels, Anton J.
Murname, William, M.
Myers, Oscar L.
Nolen, Henry
Persson, Linus
Reed, James E.
Reilly, John J.
Reisenauer, Wendel
Sharkey, Walter M.
Simpson, Orin S.
Smith, Albert

Ordnance Detachment:

Ordnance Sergeant:
Barnes, Henry E.
Ordnance Corporal:
Collier, Woodson E.

Private, 1st Class:
Burke, Russel

Privates:
Shea, Daniel D.
McAuliffe, Joseph
Collier, John

Attached:

Privates:
White, Wilfred, Hdq. Co.
Blumhagen, Willie, Co. C.
Scanlon, Leo T., Co. C.
West, Harvey, Co. E.
Walling, Charles F., Co. E.
Hoskins, Willie, Co. E.
Webster, Wesley, Co. E.
Coppock, Charlie
Doramus, Elmer C.
Douglass, John J.
Dowell, George W.
Engler, Louis K.
Jennings, Carl
Johnson, Harold F.
Johnson, Robert L.
Trosper, Roy, Co. I.
McDiffett, Patrick, Co. I.
Hicks, Luther
Wilson, Dessie T., Co. M.
Dawson, Ben., Co. M.

Corporal:
McMurray, Harold, Co. I.
CARL L. RISTINE, Colonel, 139th Infantry.

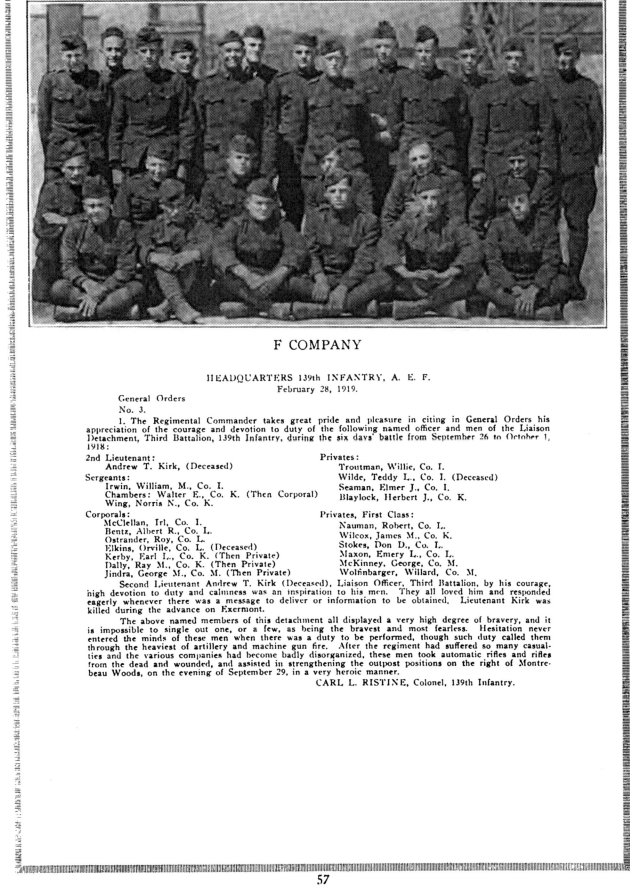

F COMPANY

HEADQUARTERS 139th INFANTRY, A. E. F.
February 28, 1919.

General Orders

No. 3.

1. The Regimental Commander takes great pride and pleasure in citing in General Orders his appreciation of the courage and devotion to duty of the following named officer and men of the Liaison Detachment, Third Battalion, 139th Infantry, during the six days' battle from September 26 to October 1, 1918:

2nd Lieutenant:
Andrew T. Kirk, (Deceased)

Sergeants:
Irwin, William, M., Co. I.
Chambers: Walter E., Co. K. (Then Corporal)
Wing, Norris N., Co. K.

Corporals:
McClellan, Irl, Co. I.
Bentz, Albert R., Co. L.
Ostrander, Roy, Co. L.
Elkins, Orville, Co. L. (Deceased)
Kerby, Earl L., Co. K. (Then Private)
Dally, Ray M., Co. K. (Then Private)
Jindra, George M., Co. M. (Then Private)

Privates:
Troutman, Willie, Co. I.
Wilde, Teddy L., Co. I. (Deceased)
Seaman, Elmer J., Co. I.
Blaylock, Herbert J., Co. K.

Privates, First Class:
Nauman, Robert, Co. L.
Wilcox, James M., Co. K.
Stokes, Don D., Co. L.
Maxon, Emery L., Co. L.
McKinney, George, Co. M.
Wolfinbarger, Willard, Co. M.

Second Lieutenant Andrew T. Kirk (Deceased), Liaison Officer, Third Battalion, by his courage, high devotion to duty and calmness was an inspiration to his men. They all loved him and responded eagerly whenever there was a message to deliver or information to be obtained. Lieutenant Kirk was killed during the advance on Exermont.

The above named members of this detachment all displayed a very high degree of bravery, and it is impossible to single out one, or a few, as being the bravest and most fearless. Hesitation never entered the minds of these men when there was a duty to be performed, though such duty called them through the heaviest of artillery and machine gun fire. After the regiment had suffered so many casualties and the various companies had become badly disorganized, these men took automatic rifles and rifles from the dead and wounded, and assisted in strengthening the outpost positions on the right of Montrebeau Woods, on the evening of September 29, in a very heroic manner.

CARL L. RISTINE, Colonel, 139th Infantry.

F COMPANY.

HEADQUARTERS 139th INFANTRY, A. E. F.,
February 27, 1919.

General Orders
No. 4.

1. The Regimental Commander takes great pleasure in citing in General Orders the officers, non-commissioned officers and men of L Company, 139th Infantry. During the recent Regimental competition to determine the best drilled company of the regiment, L Company came out victorious with A Company a close second.

I realize the great amount of work performed and the wonderful spirit shown by L Company in preparing for the Division competition. You went out on the field with your clothing and equipment spotlessly clean. Your appearance and performance on the field was a credit to yourselves and your regiment. The judges specified the movements you were to execute and I have no quarrel with them for giving the company of the 137th or 138th Infantry one-half point more than you, but I do know that if they had made a rigid inspection of all companies first, and then given each company fifteen minutes to drill in order to show what they really could do, that you would have demonstrated that you were by far the cleanest, best equipped, and best drilled company in the division.

I and the Regiment are very proud of each and every one of you.

Captain:
    Charles Haftle

1st Lieutenants:
    Spencer Otis, Jr.
    George Walters

2nd Lieutenants:
    Lonnie Young
    George Gleason

1st Sergeant:
    Schoonover, Orville

Mess Sergeant:
    Greenway, Raymond

Sergeants:
    Gibson, Hugh
    Cardinell, John
    Roberts, Jack A.
    Netherton, Charles
    McJunkins, John
    Montgomery, William S.
    Bickel, Fred E.
    Weightman, Ray
    Zook, Russel
    Renn, George
    Sunderland, Roscoe
    Lawrence, Earl

Corporals:
    Casselman, Phillip
    Duncan, Thomas

Hopper, Frank C.
Bentz, Albert
Beattie, James I.
Ostrander, Roy M.
Anderson, Archie
Browning, Frost
Bell, Cecil
Ward, Harold
Hill, Roy
Jackson, Orville
Rerick, Charles
Gomel, Louis
Scott, Francis
Windsor, Glen
Wilson, Roscoe
Meredith, Warren
Barner, Lee
Cook, Charles
Overby, Jesse
Allison, Albert
Potucek, Charles
Reynolds, Floyd
Tucker, Robert
Caples, Russel
Spahr, Orville
Anderson, Carl
Wilson, Julian

Buglers:
    Hadden, Harry
    Litts, Dewayne

Privates, First Class:
    Adams, George
    Anno, Trevor
    Ballinger, James
    Banghart, Merle
    Barlow, Harry
    Beattie, Harols
    Bartram, William
    Bohart, Ora
    Bose, Charles
    Braukman, Harry
    Brickley, Henry
    Buckles, Carl
    Crimmons, Leo
    Cross, Lemmie
    Curtin, Joseph
    Denny, Martin
    Donan, Francis
    Fitzmaurice, Michael
    Hamel, Melvin
    Hatch, Alfred
    Holmes, Cecil
    Hopkins, Emmit
    Kinsella, Thomas
    Kraeszig, Adam
    Lane, Edward
    Mannign, Charles
    McLees, Walter
    Miller, Paul
    Moore, Delmar

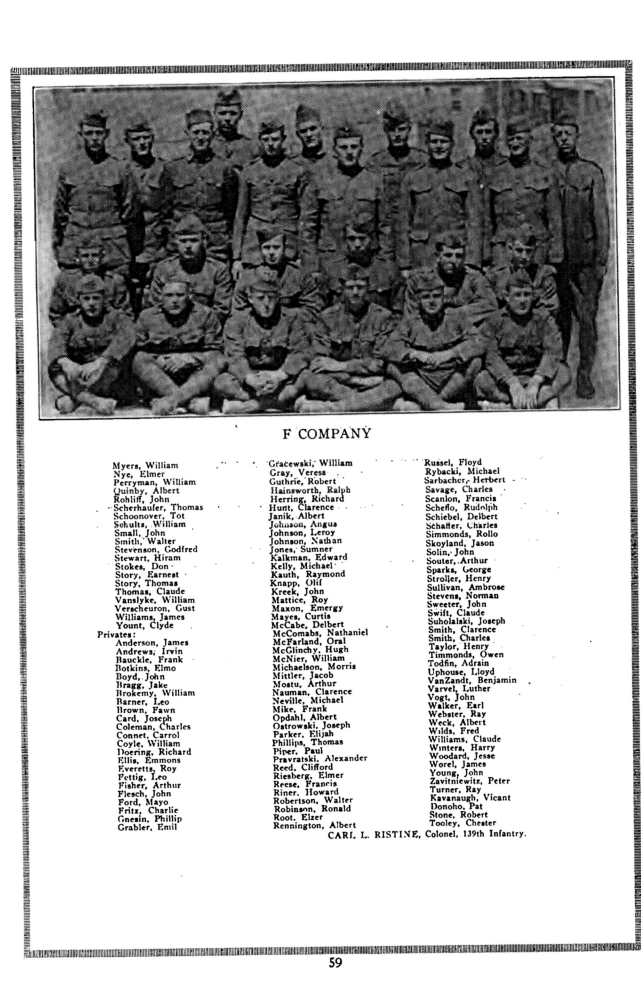

F COMPANY

Myers, William
Nye, Elmer
Perryman, William
Quinby, Albert
Rohliff, John
Scherhaufer, Thomas
Schoonover, Tot
Schultz, William
Small, John
Smith, Walter
Stevenson, Godfred
Stewart, Hiram
Stokes, Don
Story, Earnest
Story, Thomas
Thomas, Claude
Vanslyke, William
Verscheuron, Gust
Williams, James
Yount, Clyde
Privates:
Anderson, James
Andrews, Irvin
Bauckle, Frank
Botkins, Elmo
Boyd, John
Bragg, Jake
Brokemy, William
Barner, Leo
Brown, Fawn
Card, Joseph
Coleman, Charles
Connet, Carrol
Coyle, William
Doering, Richard
Ellis, Emmons
Everetts, Roy
Fettig, Leo
Fisher, Arthur
Flesch, John
Ford, Mayo
Fritz, Charlie
Gnesin, Phillip
Grabler, Emil

Gracewski, William
Gray, Veress
Guthrie, Robert
Hainsworth, Ralph
Herring, Richard
Hunt, Clarence
Janik, Albert
Johnson, Angus
Johnson, Leroy
Johnson, Nathan
Jones, Sumner
Kalkman, Edward
Kelly, Michael
Kauth, Raymond
Knapp, Olif
Kreek, John
Mattice, Roy
Maxon, Emergy
Mayes, Curtis
McCabe, Delbert
McComabs, Nathaniel
McFarland, Oral
McGlinchy, Hugh
McNier, William
Michaelson, Morris
Mittler, Jacob
Mostu, Arthur
Nauman, Clarence
Neville, Michael
Mike, Frank
Opdahl, Albert
Ostrowski, Joseph
Parker, Elijah
Phillips, Thomas
Piper, Paul
Pravratski, Alexander
Reed, Clifford
Riesberg, Elmer
Reese, Francis
Riner, Howard
Robertson, Walter
Robinson, Ronald
Root, Elzer
Rennington, Albert

Russel, Floyd
Rybacki, Michael
Sarbacher, Herbert
Savage, Charles
Scanlon, Francis
Scheflo, Rudolph
Schiebel, Delbert
Schaffer, Charles
Simmonds, Rollo
Skoyland, Jason
Solin, John
Souter, Arthur
Sparks, George
Stroller, Henry
Sullivan, Ambrose
Stevens, Norman
Sweeter, John
Swift, Claude
Suholalski, Joseph
Smith, Clarence
Smith, Charles
Taylor, Henry
Timmonds, Owen
Todfin, Adrain
Uphouse, Lloyd
VanZandt, Benjamin
Varvel, Luther
Vogt, John
Walker, Earl
Webster, Ray
Weck, Albert
Wilds, Fred
Williams, Claude
Winters, Harry
Woodard, Jesse
Worel, James
Young, John
Zavitniewitz, Peter
Turner, Ray
Kavanaugh, Vicant
Donoho, Pat
Stone, Robert
Tooley, Chester

CARL L. RISTINE, Colonel, 139th Infantry.

F COMPANY

HEADQUARTERS 139th INFANTRY, A. E. F.,
March 2, 1919.

General Orders
No. 5.

1. The Regimental Commander desires to publish in General Orders his appreciation of the Battalion Commander, Officers, non-commissioned officers and men of the Third Battalion, 139th Infantry.

It was with profound satisfaction that the Regimental Commander after viewing the divisional contest to determine the best drilled Battalion in the Division saw the winning work performed by the Third Battalion, 139th Infantry and heard this Battalion acclaimed, without dissenting voice,- to be the best drilled in the division.

You did not win because the other contenders did poorly, for their work was of a very high order, but you won because from the beginning your every action, every movement was uniform, harmonious and exact to perfection. It has been my privilege to see many contests of this character, yet I never saw better team work, better movement or better spirit, than in the contest you so deservedly won.

The entire regiment is very proud of you and the regimental commander desires to thank each of you and to commend you for your earned title as the best Battalion of the 35th Division.

FIELD AND STAFF
Major:
    Robert C. Heyward
1st Lieutenants:
    Homer J. Henney
    Walter A. Ruch
2nd Lieutenant:
    Thomas R. D. Donoghue
        I Company
Captain:
    Ralph W. Martin
1st Lieutenant:
    William D. Turnbull
2nd Lieutenant:
    Robert L. Lovern
Sergeants:
    Danielson, Herbert E.
    Love, Wesley O.
    Calkins, Arthur
    Ostrander, Clarence
    Hoskins, George
    Krause, John
    Diegelman, John
    McCourt, John
    Cramner, William S.
    Hoskins, Frank
Corporals:
    Rauber, Floyd

Pottorf, Frank
Kohler, Ervin
Volkman, Arthur
Sheridan, Delmer
Rogers, Thomas
Staunk, Milton
Rader, Proctor E.
Wakefield, Fred
Rayle, Lawrence
Schrader, Herbert C.
Schrolick, Martin
Wright, Earl
Stone, Marion
Sage, Orpha
Bratcher, Homer
Moore, Samuel
Zimmermann, Harvey

Company K:
Captain:
    Marcus J. Morgan
1st Lieutenants:
    Charles M. Flynn
    W. H. Ellenburg
    Burr A. Davidson
    Truman O. Pooler
1st Sergeant:
    Frazer, Eldon M.
Sergeants:
    West, Frank

Arnold, Irvin
Barnett, Carl D.
Helman, Charles H.
Wilson, Coburn
Chambers, Walter
Hampson, Thomas C.
Hill, James W.
Smith, Emmett E.
Shepard, John T.
Corporals:
    Daily, Allen
    Daily, Lee
    Moberly, Harry
    Hankins, James L.
    Branum, Roy
    Mitchell, Thomas W.
    Wright, Marion C.
    Wallace, Delmar L.
    Spinner, Richard
    Wilson, Otis E.
    Simmons, Lester L.
    Daily, Ray M.
    Fuller, Ellis R.
    LaFoe, Lawrence
    Hartman, Joseph
    Krick, Albert
    Pletcher, Paul
    Roberts, Erskine
    Duncan, John S.

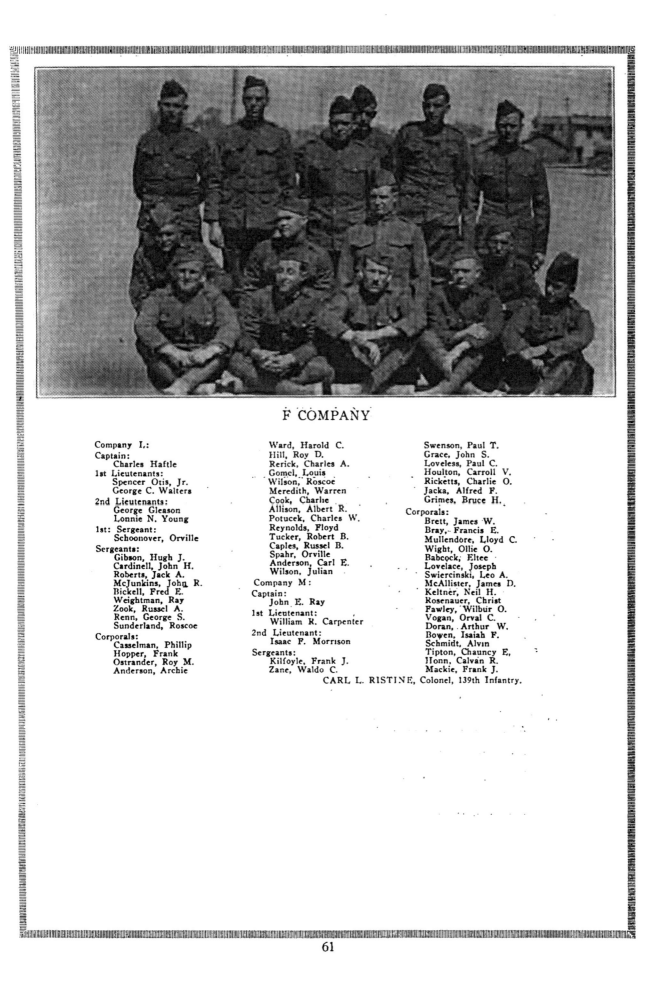

F COMPANY

Company I.:
Captain:
 Charles Haftle
1st Lieutenants:
 Spencer Otis, Jr.
 George C. Walters
2nd Lieutenants:
 George Gleason
 Lonnie N. Young
1st: Sergeant:
 Schoonover, Orville
Sergeants:
 Gibson, Hugh J.
 Cardinell, John H.
 Roberts, Jack A.
 McJunkins, John R.
 Bickell, Fred E.
 Weightman, Ray
 Zook, Russel A.
 Renn, George S.
 Sunderland, Roscoe
Corporals:
 Casselman, Phillip
 Hopper, Frank
 Ostrander, Roy M.
 Anderson, Archie

Ward, Harold C.
Hill, Roy D.
Rerick, Charles A.
Gomel, Louis
Wilson, Roscoe
Meredith, Warren
Cook, Charlie
Allison, Albert R.
Potucek, Charles W.
Reynolds, Floyd
Tucker, Robert B.
Caples, Russel B.
Spahr, Orville
Anderson, Carl E.
Wilson, Julian
Company M:
Captain:
 John E. Ray
1st Lieutenant:
 William R. Carpenter
2nd Lieutenant:
 Isaac P. Morrison
Sergeants:
 Kilfoyle, Frank J.
 Zane, Waldo C.

Swenson, Paul T.
Grace, John S.
Loveless, Paul C.
Houlton, Carroll V.
Ricketts, Charlie O.
Jacka, Alfred F.
Grimes, Bruce H.
Corporals:
 Brett, James W.
 Bray, Francis E.
 Mullendore, Lloyd C.
 Wight, Ollie O.
 Babcock, Eltee
 Lovelace, Joseph
 Swiercinski, Leo A.
 McAllister, James D.
 Keltner, Neil H.
 Rosenauer, Christ
 Fawley, Wilbur O.
 Vogan, Orval C.
 Doran, Arthur W.
 Bowen, Isaiah F.
 Schmidt, Alvin
 Tipton, Chauncy E.
 Honn, Calvan R.
 Mackie, Frank J.

CARL L. RISTINE, Colonel, 139th Infantry.

F COMPANY

INTRODUCTION TO ROSTER

When the idea of publishing a history of the 139th Infantry was first agreed upon, personnel adjutants, company commanders were instructed to make up rosters to be used in this history. These rosters were to contain the name of each man who had been a member of the organization, his rank, home address and his previous service record and his service in the Great War. The editor of this history has obtained such rosters and they are published herewith from the following companies: A, B, C, E, F, H, I, K, L, M and Supply Company. These rosters are believed to be nearly complete and to convey all the information for which they were designed.

The roster of D Company was made up July 19, 1918. The special history roster, if it ever had been made, cannot be found.

The G Company roster is not dated but it appears to have been made up during the tour of duty in Alsace.

The Machine Gun Company roster is dated August 18, 1918, and as in the case of D Company the editor has been unable to obtain a special history roster, if it was made.

The Headquarters Company roster is undated and no special history roster has been found.

The other units such as Brigade Headquarters detachment and Sanitary detachment are the best rosters obtainable.

There are doubtless some names which will appear more than once in these rosters. These will be officers or men who were transferred from one outfit to another and whose names got on both rosters. It has not been thought advisable to eliminate these names.

In the original rosters the serial numbers of the men were given. They are not used in this book as being of little value outside of the army.

Some of the rosters failed to credit the men with participation in the Saint Mihiel offensive, but they should have this credit as the division was reserve for that operation.

A key to the initials used follows:

OS, Overseas.
MA, Meuse-Argonne.
A. Argonne
St. M., Saint Mihiel.
MGF (?), Machine Gun Fire
TRFD, Transferred.
K, Killed.
KIA, Killed in Action.
MP, Military Police.

THEY WON THEIR SPURS IN BATTLE

1. Lieut. George T. Worthen
2. Lieut. J. W. McManigal
3. Capt. James H. McCord, Jr.
4. Lieut. Edward S. Carmack
5. Lieut.-Chaplain Myron S. Collins

G COMPANY

ROSTER OF COMPANY A, 139th INFANTRY

NAME AND RANK	HOME ADDRESS AND REMARKS
Frank D. Mathias, Captain	Humboldt, Kansas, M. G., 3rd Kans. OS-MA. Base Hosp. 91.
Ross Diehl, Captain	Chillicothe, Missouri, Co. L, 4th Mo.. MA.
Blanton U. Bentley, 1st Lt.	Coffeyville, Kansas. Co. A, 3rd Kans. OS. Returned to states for instructor.
Charles W. Barndollar, 1st Lt.	Coffeyville, Kansas. Co. A, 3rd Kans. OS-MA. Trans. Co. C, 139th Inf.
Homer Yale, 1st Lt.	Tarkio, Missouri. Co. A, 4th Mo. Trans. to Co. A, 139th Inf. OS-MA.
Edward Johnson, 1st Lt.	808 Coffey St., Indianapolis, Indiana.
Albert Sheridan, 1st Lt.	Mangum, Okla. Trans. from 6th Division.
Benjamin J. Wells, 1st Lt.	820 Bankville Avenue, Pittsburgh. Pennsylvania. Trans. from 6th Division.
George S. Downing, 2nd Lt.	53 Butternut Street, Detroit, Michigan.
Harry Ross, 2nd Lt.	New York City, New York. Trans. Co. A, 139th Inf.
Paul A. Cannady, 1st Lt.	Yates Center, Kansas, 3rd Kans. OS-MA.
Jensen, Carl O., 1st Sgt.	606 Elm St., Coffeyville, Kans. OS. Officers' Training School.
Cosler, Raymond E., 1st Sgt.	Coffeyville, Kansas. Co. A, 3rd Kansas. OS. Returned to States for instructor.
Brunner, Alfred C., 1st Sgt.	Coffeyville, Kansas. Co. A, 3rd Kans. OS-MA. Officers' Training school.
Nichols, Irwin, 1st Sgt.	Tarkio, Missouri. Co. A, 4th Missouri. OS-MA.
Trickett, Dean Sup. Sgt.	310 W. 12th St., Coffeyville, Kansas. Co. A, 3rd Kans. OS-MA.
Swearngin, Carl E., Mess Sgt.	112 W. Hickory St., Coffeyville, Kansas. Co. A, 3rd Kans. OS-MA.
Vinyard, Jess, Sergeant	Witt's Foundry, Tennessee. Co. A, 4th Mo. OS-MA.
Askren, Bert, Sergeant	Coffeyville, Kansas. Co. A, 3rd Kans. OS-MA.
Morgan, William O., Sergeant	Tarkio, Missouri. Co. A, 4th Missouri. OS-MA.
Dooley, Floyd C., Sergeant	Coffeyville, Kansas. Co. A, 3rd Kans. OS-MA.
Meeks, Clyde Sergeant	Coffeyville, Kansas. Co. A, 3rd Kans. OS-MA.
Huddleston, George R. Sergeant	Delaware, Okla. Co. A, 3rd Kans. Inf. OS-MA.

NAME AND RANK	HOME ADDRESS AND REMARKS
Dana, Merle H. Sergeant	Coffeyville, Kansas, Co. A, 3rd Kans. OS-MA.
Smith, Herman I.. Sergeant	Tarkio, Missouri, Co. A, 4th Mo. OS-MA.
Rogers, Earnest H. Sergeant	Coffeyville, Kansas, Co. A, 3rd Kans. OS-MA.
McElfish, Earl E. Sergeant	Tarkio, Missouri. Co. A, 4th Mo. OS-MA Trans. M. P. Co.
Clark, Hugh W. Sergeant	Coffeyville, Kansas, Co. A, 3rd Kans. OS-MA.
Welch, John Sergeant	Tarkio, Missouri. Co. A, 4th Mo. OS-MA.
Burkhall, Walter H. Sergeant	Coffeyville, Kansas, Co. A, 3rd Kars. OS- Trans. Hosp.
Bradbury, Frank W. Sergeant	Coffeyville, Kansas, Co. A, 3rd Kans. OS- Trans. Hosp.
Henson, Jason Sergeant	Tarkio, Missouri. Co. A, 4th Mo. OS-MA. Officers Training School
Yale, Walter Sergeant	Tarkio, Missouri. Co. A, 4th Mo. OS-MA. Officers Training School
Dillon, Keith Corporal	Coffeyville, Kansas, Co. A, 3rd Kans. OS-MA. Trans. Hdqrs. Co 139th Inf.
Miller, Claude A. Corporal	Nowata, Okla. Co. A, 3rd Kans. OS-Trans. Hdqrs. Co. 139 Inf.
Robert, H. Jones Corporal	Coffeyville, Kansas, Co. A, 3rd Kans. OS-MA.
Piner, George W. Corporal	Coffeyville, Kansas, Co. A, 3rd Kans. OS-MA.
Van Winkle, Earl Corporal	Coffeyville, Kansas, Co. A, 3rd Kans. OS-MA. Captured.
Crosely, Oral E. Corporal	Tarkio, Missouri, Co. A, 4th Mo. OS- Trans. Hospital
Allen, Lee W. Corporal	Tarkio, Missouri. Co. A, 4th Mo. OS-MA.
Tucker, Max A. Corporal	Coffeyville, Kansas, Co. A, 3rd Kans. OS-MA.
Cundiff, Roy E. Corporal	Coffeyville, Kansas, Co. A, 3rd Kans. OS-MA.
White, Guy L. Corporal	Coffeyville, Kansas. Co. A, 3rd Kans. W-HE- Trans. Hosp.
Dragoo, Dale, Corporal	Tarkio, Missouri. Co. A, 4th Mo. OS-MA. Captured.
Long, Roy D. Corporal	Coffeyville, Kansas. Co. A, 3rd Kans. Trans. 110 Am. Train.
Cotton, Harry C. Corporal	Nowata, Oklahoma. Co. A, 3rd Kans. OS-MA- G. Hosp.
Deboard, Frank C. Corporal	Tarkio, Missouri. Co. A, 4th Mo. OS-MA. W-S.
Tabor, Calvin A. Corporal	Hartford, Kansas. Co. A, 3rd Kans. OS-MA.
Love, Blanton D. Corporal	Nowata, Okla. Co. A, 3rd Kans. OS-MA.

64

G COMPANY

Jones, Edgar L. Corporal — Coffeyville, Kansas. Co. A, 3rd Kans. OS-MA.

Shaw, Ronald F. Corporal — Star City, Ind. Camp Dodge. OS-MA. Trans. University.

Kaup, Clarence Corporal — Shakopee, Minn. Camp Dodge. OS-MA.

Brown, Paul Corporal — 55 South Washington Street, Chillicothe, Missouri. Co. A. 4th Mo. OS-MA.

Gunsolley, Bernard W. Corporal — Glen Wood, Iowa. Camp Dodge, Iowa. OS-MA.

Fredlund, John A. Corporal — Scandia, Kansas. Camp Funston, Kans. OS-MA.

Howe, Robert W. Corporal — Delaware, Oklahoma. Co. A, 3rd Kans. OS-MA.

Martin, Samuel J. Corporal — Nowata, Oklahoma, Co. A, 3rd Kans. OS-MA.

Mueller, Fred Corporal — Tarkio, Missouri. Co. A, 4th Mo. OS-MA.

Perry, Robert Corporal — Olmit, Iowa. Camp Dodge, Iowa. OS-MA.

Hayes, Don Corporal — Sigourney, Iowa. R. F. D. 3, Camp Dodge, Iowa. OS-MA.

Garst, Jonathan Corporal — Iowa, Camp Dodge, Iowa. OS-MA. Trans. University.

Higginbotham, James H. Corporal — Depew, Oklahoma. Co. A, 3rd Kans. OS-MA.

Meek, Charley Corporal — Tarkio, Missouri. Co. A, 4th Mo. OS-MA.

Pevehouse, John D. Corporal — Coffeyville, Kansas. Co. A, 3rd Kans. OS-MA.

Sharp, Nuell Corporal — Tarkio, Missouri. Co. A, 4th Mo. OS MA.

Snoderly, Dewel E. Corporal — Coffeyville, Kansas. Co. A, 3rd Kans. OS-MA.

Tangney, Ralph M. Corporal — Decatur, Illinois. Camp Dodge, Iowa OS-MA.

Wrinkle, Ola E. Corporal — Tarkio, Missouri. Co. A, 4th Mo. OS-MA.

Hanes, James B. Corporal — Coffeyville, Kansas. Co. A, 3rd Kans. OS-MA. Trans. M. P.

Kortekaas, Leonard Corporal — Minn. Camp Dodge, Iowa. OS-MA. Trans. MP.

Perry, Henry E. Corporal — Olmitz, Iowa. Camp Dodge. OS-MA. Trans. MP.

Petrus, Antony Corporal — Unknown. Trans. MP.

Yael, William N. Sergeant — Tarkio, Missouri. Co. A, 4th Mo. OS-MA.

Wise, Robert Sergeant — Coffeyville, Kansas. Co. A, 3rd Kans. OS-MA.

Lupton, Clifford L. Sergeant — Missouri. 3rd Mo. Trans. M. P.

Nelson, George E. Corporal — Coffeyville, Kans. OS. Trans. Co. A, 130th Machine Gun Bn.

Gailey, Bert Corporal — Tarkio, Missouri. Co. A, 4th Mo. OS-MA.

Woolhether, Lawrence A. Corporal — Tarkio, Missouri. Co. A, 4th Mo. OS-MA. Trans. Hosp.

Herrick, Ben F. Corporal — Coffeyville, Kansas. Co. A, 3rd Kans. OS-MA.

Kelley, Olin F. Corporal — Tarkio, Missouri. Co. A, 4th Mo. Trans. Hospital.

Hutson, Rufus Corporal — 719 South 19 St. Independence, Kansas. Co. A, 3rd Kans. OS-MA.

Lindley, Robert H. Corporal — Tarkio, Missouri. Co. A, 4th Mo. OS-MA. Captured.

Farley, Grover C. Mechanic — Fairfax, Missouri. Co. A, 4th Mo. OS-MA.

Vernon, Joe Mechanic — Tarkio, Missouri. Co. A, 4th Mo. OS-MA.

Martin, Verne Mechanic — 112 East Cottonwood Street, Independence, Kans. Co. A, 3rd Kans. OS MA.

Hogue, Robert G. Mechanic — Tarkio, Missouri. Co. A, 4th Mo. OS-MA.

Arnold, Clarence Cook — Nowata, Oklahoma. Co. A, 3rd Kans. OS-MA.

Dragoo, Carl Cook — 206 East Valley Street, St. Joseph, Mo. Co. A, 4th Mo. OS-MA.

Walton, Grover C. Cook — Coffeyville, Kansas. Co. A. 3rd Kans. OS-Trans. Hosp.

Bucher, Tilden Cook — 209 East 11th St., Coffeyville, Kans. Co. A, 3rd Kans. OS-MA.

Cobb, Charles R. Cook — Nowata, Oklahoma. Co. A, 3rd Kans. OS-MA.

Duncan, Paul W. Bugler — Tarkio, Missouri. Co. A, 4th Mo. OS-MA.

Searcy, Alvie Bugler — Tarkio, Missouri. Co. A, 4th Mo. OS-MA.

Ahnert, Walter E. Pvt. 1cl. — Kansas. Camp Funston, Kans. OS-MA. Trans. Hosp.

Benedict, Harry W. Pvt. 1cl. — Corning, Missouri. Co. A, 4th Mo. OS-MA.

Boom, Samuel J. Pvt. 1cl. — Nowata, Oklahoma, Co. A, 3rd Kans. OS- Trans. Hosp.

Brown, Leon M. Pvt. 1cl. — Minn. Unknown.

Bacon, Ford F. Pvt. 1cl. — Ithaca, Mich. 8 Co. 2nd Bn. 160 Depot Brig.

Berg, Earl Pvt. 1cl. — Tarkio, Missouri. Co. A, 4th Mo. OS-MA W-S.

Boston, Levi S. Pvt. 1cl. — Delaware, Oklahoma. Co. A, 3rd Kans. OS-MA.

Bucher, Barney Pvt. 1cl. — 209 E. 11th St. Coffeyville, Kans. Co. A, 3rd Kans. OS-MA.

Brunning, George Pvt. 1cl. — 349 Sander St. Indianapolis, Indiana, Camp Zachary Taylor, Ky.

Bunbury, Dennis L. Pvt. 1cl. — 415 South 3rd St. Niles, Mich. Camp Zachary Taylor, Ky.

Carlson, Carl F. Pvt. 1cl. — 711 East Danaher Street, Ludention, Mich. Camp Custer.

Carlson, Carl E. Pvt. 1cl. — 711 East Danaher Street, Ludention, Mich. Camp Custer.

Carlson, Emil Pvt. 1cl. — 1105 Hawthorne Avenue, St. Paul, Minn. Camp Dodge, OS-MA.

Carter, Frank A. Pvt. 1cl. — Tarkio, Missouri. Co. A, 4th Mo. OS-MA.

Cathers, Charles P., Jr. Pvt. 1cl. — Coffeyville, Kansas, Co. A, 3rd Kans. OS-MA.

Clanton, Thomas I. Pve. 1cl. — Tarkio, Missouri. Co. A, 4th Mo. OS-MA.

Curran, Lawrence A. Pvt. 1cl. — Coffeyville, Kansas. Co. A, 3rd Kans. OS. Hosp.

65

G COMPANY

Combs, Joel A.	Pvt. 1cl.	1302 West 11th St. Coffeyville, Kansas. Co. A, 3rd Kans. OS-MA.
Crowford, Claude C.	Pvt. 1cl.	Deward, Michigan. Camp Custer.
Dohm, Vaughn D.	Pvt. 1cl.	East Claire, Michigan. RFD1, Camp Custer.
Farley, Clyde	Pvt. 1cl.	Tarkio, Missouri, Co. A, 4th Mo. OS-MA.
Fuzzell, David W.	Pvt. 1cl.	Nowata, Oklahoma. Co. A, 3rd Kans. OS-MA. Trans. Hosp.
Friend, James O.	Pvt. 1cl.	Tarkio, Missouri, Co. A, 4th Mo. OS-MA.
Grady, George E.	Pvt. 1cl.	Nowata, Oklahoma. Co. A, 3rd Kansas. OS-MA.
Glidwell, Marion D.	Pvt. 1cl.	Liberty, Kansas. Co. A, 3rd Kans. OS-MA.
Guthrie, Belt D.	Pvt. 1cl.	Tarkio, Missouri. Co. A, 4th Mo. OS-MA Trans. Co. A, 139th Infantry.
Gray, Charley A.	Pvt. 1cl.	Goodrich, North Dakota. Camp Dodge, Iowa. OS-MA.
Harmon, Claude	Pvt. 1cl.	Tarkio, Missouri. Co. A, 4th Mo. OS- Trans. Hosp.
Harsh, Cecil P.	Pvt. 1cl.	Tarkio, Missouri. Co. A, 4th Mo. OS-MA Trans. M. P.
Haring, Myron L.	Pvt. 1cl.	516 South Sarah St. Escanaba, Michigan. Camp Custer.
Henson, Caston	Pvt. 1cl.	Tarkio, Missouri. Co. A, 4th Mo. OS-MA.
Hughey, Charle M.	Pvt. 1cl.	Bartlesville, Oklahoma. Co. A, 3rd Kans. OS-MA.
Hull, William P.	Pvt. 1cl.	Tarkio, Missouri. Co. A, 4th Mo. OS-MA.
MacHatton, Joe	Pvt. 1cl.	Coffeyville, Kansas. Co. A, 3rd Kans. OS-MA. Trans. Hosp.
McElfish, John	Pvt. 1cl.	Tarkio, Missouri. Co. A, 4th Mo. OS-MA Trans. Mech. School
Isley, Crayton W.	Pvt. 1cl.	Shelby, Michigan. Camp Custer.
Karns, Jess W.	Pvt. 1cl.	Pleasantville, Iowa. Camp Dodge.
Kaup, Nick H.	Pvt. 1cl.	Shakopee, Minn. Camp Dodge. OS-MA.
Keeppen, Henry A.	Pvt. 1cl.	Kill, Wis. RFD1. Camp Grant.
Latta, John	Pvt. 1cl.	Coffeyville, Kansas. Co. A, 3rd Kans. OS-MA.
Lyons, Roscoe M.	Pvt. 1cl.	Olid, Michigan, Camp Custer.
Marshall, Irvin	Pvt. 1cl.	Tarkio, Missouri. Co. A, 4th Mo. OS-MA.
Meyer, Paul L.	Pvt. 1cl.	1326 Stophlet Street. Fort Wayne, Indiana. Camp Dodge.
Miller, Clarence M.	Pvt. 1cl.	Thornton, Iowa, Camp Dodge, OS-MA.
Moody, Harrison	Pvt. 1cl.	Turon, Kansas. Camp Funston. OS-MA.
Montague, Harold	Pvt. 1cl.	621 Walnut St. Cadillac, Michigan. Camp Custer.
Mussleman, Earl A.	Pvt. 1cl.	212 Kenwood Avenue. Beloit, Michigan. Camp Grant.
Olson, John B.	Pvt. 1cl.	Litchfield, Minnesota. RFD2. Camp Dodge. OS-MA.

Orme, John H.	Pvt. 1cl.	North Fork, Kentucky. Camp Zachary Taylor.
Patterson, Claude A.	Pvt. 1cl.	Nowata, Oklahoma. Co. A, 3rd Kans. OS-MA.
Perry, Alva B.	Pvt. 1cl.	Coffeyville, Kansas. Co. A, 3rd Kans. OS-MA. Trans. Hosp.
Peterson, Charles G.	Pvt. 1cl.	Chicago, Illinois. Camp Wheeler.
Rhino, Alphonse	Pvt. 1cl.	Champion, Michigan. Camp Grant.
Rice, Harold S.	Pvt. 1cl.	Coffeyville, Kansas. Co. A, 3rd Kans. OS-MA.
Roup, Guy O.	Pvt. 1cl.	Dewitt, Iowa. Camp Dodge. OS-MA.
Richards, John	Pvt. 1cl.	Tarkio, Missouri. Co. A, 4th Mo. K-
Renfro, Earl E.	Pvt. 1cl.	Tarkio, Missouri. Co. A, 4th Mo. Trans. Co. K, 139th Inf.
Scholes, Richard C.	Pvt. 1cl.	Coffeyville, Kansas. Co. A, 3rd Kans. OS-MA.
Smith, Herbert	Pvt. 1cl.	Coffeyville, Kansas. Co. A, 3rd Kans. OS-MA.
Schiffern, Roy	Pvt. 1cl.	Tarkio, Missouri. Co. A, 4th Mo. OS-MA. Captured.
Scott, Albert B.	Pvt. 1cl.	Indiana. Camp Dodge. OS-MA. Trans. Co. M, 139th Inf.
Schwartz, Vincent B.	Pvt. 1cl.	Iowa. Camp Dodge. OS-MA Trans. Hospital.
Shirer, Fred	Pvt. 1cl.	Chanton, Iowa. Camp Dodge. OS-MA.
Silsbee, Glendon H.	Pvt. 1cl.	606 East Green Street, Hastings, Michigan. Camp Grant.
Stagner, Claude M.	Pvt. 1cl.	Redding, Iowa. Camp Dodge. OS-MA.
Stone, Roy	Pvt. 1cl.	Tarkio, Missouri. Co. A, 4th Mo. OS-MA.
Trough, Lloyd	Pvt. 1cl.	Coffeyville, Kansas. Co. A, 3rd Kans. OS.
Romish, Mile	Pvt. 1cl.	Trans. MP. Unknown.
Tharp, Roy C.	Pvt. 1cl.	Trans. Hospital Unknown.
Vanderford, Earl E.	Pvt. 1cl.	1402 West Seventh Street. Coffeyville, Kansas. Co. A, 3rd Kans. OS-MA. W-S.
Van Sickle, Selah	Pvt. 1cl.	Iowa. Camp Dodge. OS- Trans. University.
Walton, Ellis P.	Pvt. 1cl.	Coffeyville, Kansas. Co. A, 3rd Kans. OS.
Wade, John A.	Pvt. 1cl.	1802 West Tenth Street, Coffeyville, Kansas. Co. A, 3rd Kans. OS-MA.
Warren, Fred	Pvt. 1cl.	Tarkio, Missouri. Co. A, 4th Mo. OS-MA
Wymer, Clarence B.	Pvt. 1cl.	1212 Elm Street, Dubuque, Iowa. Camp Dodge. OS-MA.
Withrow, Floyd C.	Pvt. 1cl.	Tarkio, Missouri. Co. A, 4th Mo. 110 Am. Train.
World, Herman	Pvt. 1cl.	Tarkio, Missouri. Co. A, 4th Mo. OS Trans. Hosp.
Wilson, William R.	Pvt. 1cl.	Iowa. Camp Dodge. OS-MA. W-HE Trans. MP.
Zeiger, Conrad	Pvt. 1cl.	Medora, North Dakota. Camp Grant.
Allen, Sylvester	Private	Tarkio, Missouri. Co. A, 4th Mo. OS-MA-K.

G COMPANY

Agee, Arthur L.	Private	Tarkio, Missouri. Co. A, 4th Mo. Trans. Co. A, 130th Mch. Gun Bn. OS.
Adleman, William	Private	Minot, North Dakota. Camp Dodge. OS-MA.
Amundson, Norman	Private	Dallas, Wis. Camp Dodge. OS-MA.
Anderson, Walter C.	Private	Olds, Iowa, Camp Dodge. OS-MA.
Bachman, Ross B.	Private	Union, Iowa. Camp Dodge. OS-MA.
Bragg, Harley W.	Private	Tarkio, Missouri, Co. A, 4th Mo. OS-D.
Barnes, William	Private	Page, North Dakota. Camp Dodge. MA.
Barlund, Albin,	Private	Iowa. Camp Dodge. Trans. Hosp.
Barrett, Ranson H.	Private	Allen Mills, Pa. Camp Dodge. MA.
Benefiel, Lelan J.	Private	Coffeyville, Kansas. Co. A, 3rd Kans. OS-MA.
Bennett, Jess	Private	Tarkio, Missouri. Co. A, 4th Mo. OS-MA.
Billgren, John	Private	Williston, North Dak. Camp Dodge MA.
Blackstead, Ola A.	Private	Minot, North Dakota. Camp Dodge. MA.
Blatter, Berthold	Private	Tarkio, Missouri. Co. A, 4th Mo. OS-MA.
Boetcher, Edward	Private	Stanton, North Dakota. Camp Dodge. MA.
Bogg, Earnest	Private	Champion, Ill. Camp Wheeler.
Boxsted, Herman	Private	Lakota, North Dak. MA.
Branderhort, Ralph J.	Private	Crosby, North Dakota. Camp Dodge MA.
Brodie, Dale C.	Private	St. John, Kansas. Camp Funston. OS-MA.
Brown, Leo R.	Private	Kulm, North Dak. Camp Dodge. MA. OS.
Bunch, John R.	Private	Melrose, Iowa. Camp Dodge. OS-MA.
Boumpensiero, Salviator	Private	Milwaukee, Wis. Camp Grant.
Busse, Ben E.	Private	Unknown. Trans. Hospital.
Butcher, Roy L.	Private	Lovila, Iowa. Camp Dodge. OS-MA.
Butcher, Lee	Private	Lovila, Iowa. Camp Dodge. OS-MA.
Carlson, Herbert	Private	St. Paul, Minn. Camp Dodge. OS-MA. Captured.
Cheesman, William M.	Private	Tarkio, Missouri. Co. A, 4th Mo. OS. Trans. Hosp.
Clark, Allen G.	Private	Tarkio, Missouri. Co. A, 4th Mo. OS- Trans. Hosp.
Campbell, James	Private	Abline, Kans. Co. H, 3rd Kans. OS-MA.
Charmichael, Charles V.	Private	Mt. Ayre. Iowa, Camp Dodge. OS-MA.
Christianson, Carl A.	Private	Landa, North Dak. Camp Dodge. OS-MA.
Christlock, Harold J.	Private	Redwing, Minn. Camp Dodge. OS-MA.
Clanton, Thomas,	Private	Tarkio, Missouri. Co. A, 4th Mo. OS-MA.
Coltveit, Thomas E.	Private	Williston, North Dak. Camp Dodge. OS-MA.
Collison, Elba A.	Private	Hastings, Mich. Camp Custer. MA.
Coon, William D.	Private	Chillicothe, Mo. Co. A, 4th Mo. OS-MA. W-S.
Costas, Francis	Private	New York City, New York Trans. MP.
Crotty, Francis W.	Private	Bernard, Iowa. Camp Dodge. OS-MA.
Davenport, Frank C.	Private	Osceola, Iowa. Camp Dodge. OS-MA.
Denzler, William	Private	Carlton, Minn. Camp Dodge. OS-MA.
Donelson, Dean	Private	Tarkio, Mo. Co. A, 4th Mo. OS.
Dodge, Emery	Private	Tarkio, Missouri. Co. A, 4th Mo. OS-MA. Trfd. MP.
Dyson, Melvin	Private	Oskaloosa, Kansas. 3rd Kans. MA.
Engelke, Otto A.	Private	Saginaw, Michigan. RFD1. Camp Custer. MA.
Engen, Hans	Private	Williston, North Dak. Camp Dodge. OS-MA.
Fall, Earl C.	Private	La Moure, North Dakota. Camp Dodge OS-MA.
Farris, John	Private	Tarkio, Missouri. Co. A, 4th Mo. OS-MA.
Fischer, Edward	Private	Deulah, North Dak.
Fisher, Guy K.	Private	Greenville, Mo. Co. A, 3rd Kans. OS-MA.
Foster, Grover R.	Private	Minot, North Dakota. OS-MA. Camp Dodge.
Franklin, George T.	Private	Minot, North Dak. Camp Dodge. MA.
Gleason, Walter	Private	Tarkio, Missouri. Co. A, 4th Mo. OS-MA.
Grasso, Alfreddo	Private	Cella Cerbetta, Italy, Camp Dodge OS-MA.
Gray, Charles A.	Private	Denhoff, North Dak. Camp Dodge. OS-MA.
Gunsallus, John	Private	Osage, Iowa. Camp Dodge. OS-MA.
Halvorson, Andrew	Private	Calvin, North Dak. OS.
Hancock, William L.	Private	119½ W. 9th St., Coffeyville, Kansas. Co. A, 3rd Kans. OS-MA.
Hannon, John F.	Private	Litchfield, Minn. Camp Dodge. OS-MA.
Henson, Loyd	Private	Mansfield, Missouri. Co. A, 4th Mo. OS-MA.
Hollick, Phillip	Private	Kenmare, North Dak. Camp Dodge OS-MA.
Hover, Ray R.	Private	Minot, North Dak. OS.
Howell, Harvey P.	Private	Grinnell, Iowa. Camp Dodge. OS-MA.
Irwin, Willie E.	Private	Osceola, Iowa. Camp Dodge. OS-MA.
Jacobsmeyer, Joseph	Private	RFD1 Luxenburg, Iowa. Camp Dodge. OS-MA.
Janke, William	Private	Janesville. Minn.
Jones, James	Private	Tarkio, Missouri. Co. A, 4th Mo. OS-MA.
Jundy, Dewey	Private	707 East 11th St. Coffeyville, Kansas. Co. A, 3rd Kans. OS-MA.
Keasling, Lloyd F.	Private	Hayesville, Iowa. Camp Dodge. OS-MA.
Kuster, Henry	Private	RFD 4, Buffalo Lake, Minn.

67

G COMPANY

Latta, James — Private — 1209 Elm St. Coffeyville, Kans. Co. A, 3rd Kans. OS-MA. W-G.

McGlothen, Ora R. — Private — RFD2 Larmar, Iowa. Camp Dodge. OS-MA.

Mowery, Merle — Private — Tarkio, Missouri. Co. A, 4th Mo. OS-MA.

Olstad, Olai R. — Private — 1st. St. Willmer, Minn.

Osing, John H. — Private — Memphis, Missouri. Camp Dodge. OS-MA.

Palmer, Magnus — Private — Foxholme, North Dak. Camp Dodge. MA.

Papen, James B. — Private — Linn Creek, Missouri. Co. A. 3rd Kans. OS-MA.

Peterson, Roy V. — Private — Box 30, Appleton, Minn.

Plank, William F. — Private — Webster, Iowa. Camp Dodge OS.

Platt, Clyde A. — Private — Dickens, Iowa. Camp Dodge OS-MA.

Proffitt, Harry L. — Private

Richard, Ben — Private — Tarkio, Missouri. Co. A, 4th Mo. OS-MA.

Schimmelpfennig, John — Private — RFD1, Harper, Iowa. Camp Dodge. OS-MA.

Sevier, Earnest — Private — Coffeyville, Kansas. 120-1 -2 W. 8th St. Co. A, 3rd Kans. OS-MA.

Smeback, Carl O. — Private — Roseau, Minn. OS-MA Camp Dodge.

Stagner, Claude M. — Private — RFD1 Redding, Iowa. Camp Dodge. OS-MA.

Steele, Albert F. — Private — FFD1, New Sharon, Iowa. Camp Dodge. OS.

Stephens, Clyde G. — Private — Mt. Ayr, Iowa. Camp Dodge. OS.

Stephens, Ray — Private — Maloy, Iowa. Camp Dodge OS Trans. Hosp.

Sunday, Clarence — Private — Hastings, Nebr. Co. A, 4th Mo. OS. Trans. Hosp.

Swenson, Harry M. — Private — Svea, Minn. Camp Dodge. OS-MA.

Shelton, Irwin — Private — Kirksville, Missouri. MA.

Thompson, Oscar — Private — RFD5, Red Wing, Minn. Camp Dodge. OS.

Tintes, Hubert — Private — RFD1, Eden Valley, Minn. Camp Dodge, OS-MA.

Turner, Harry — Private — Tarkio, Missouri. Co. A, 4th Mo. OS-MA.

Walker, Frank M. — Private — Grand View, Iowa. Camp Dodge. OS-MA.

Walters, Ruben L. — Private — 1511 Gnaban St. Burlington, Iowa. Camp Dodge. OS-MA.

Wallen, Henry J. — Private — Browningston, Mo. Co. A, 3rd Kans. OS-MA.

Wheeler, Fred — Private — Westboro, Mo. Co. A, 4th Mo. OS-MA.

Walker, Worley M. — Private — Tarkio, Missouri. Co. A, 4th Mo. OS-MA.

Witthoeft, Henry — Private — RFD5, Long Prairie, Minn. OS-MA.

Yochum, Walter L. — Private — Longville, Minn. Camp Dodge. OS-MA.

Yoerg, Sheldon E. — Private — RFD1, Little Falls, Minn. Camp Dodge. OS-W-S.

Zulick, Harry H. — Private — RFD1, Judson, North Dak. Camp Dodge. OS. Trans. Hosp.

Zeiner, Eldwood — Private — 344 East 44th St. New York City, New York. OS-MA.

Boxsted, Herman — Private — Lakota, North Dak. OS-

Brown, Leo R. — Private — Halbright Sask, G. Camp Dodge.

Gehard, Ben J. — Private — Bonner Springs, Kansas. MA.

G COMPANY

ROSTER OF COMPANY B, 139th INFANTRY

NAME AND RANK	HOME ADDRESS AND REMARKS
Blevins, Theodore R. 1st Sgt.	Oskaloosa, Kansas. OS-MA-St.M.
Kimmel, William 1st Sgt.	1400 West 6th St., Topeka, Kansas. OS-MA-St.M.
Culpepper, Henry G. 1st Sgt.	Caruthersville, Mo. Discharged to accept commission, 2nd Lt. OS.
Streiff, John P. Sup. Sgt.	Hayti, Mo. MA-MGF. OS. St.M.
Taylor, James R. Sup. Sgt.	Lawrence, Kans. OS-MA-St.M.
Chance, Benjamin H. Mess Sgt.	Atwood, Kans. OS-MA-St.M.
Cecil, Clarence C. Sergeant	Steele, Mo. OS.
Brey, Marlin Sergeant	Oskaloosa, Kans. OS-MA-MGF-St.M.
Gibson, Perry F. Sergeant	Winchester, Kans. OS. Trfd. to 110th Ammu. Tr. Aug. 18, 1918.
Harr, Lloyd T. Sergeant	Emporia, Kans. OS. Trfd. to U. S. A. Aug. 15, 1918.
Kennedy, John L. Sergeant	Scotts Hill, Tenn. OS.
Larner, Leland S. Sergeant	Oskaloosa, Kans. OS. Discharged to accept 2nd Lt. Commission.
Segraves, Victor L. Sergeant	Oskaloosa, Kans. OS-MA-K-St.M.
Vendel, Joseph J. Sergeant	Oskaloosa, Kans. OS-MA-G-MGF-St.M.
Williamson, Sherman H. Sergeant	Oskaloosa, Kans. OS-MA-MGF-S-St.M.
Young, Karles C. Sergeant	Ft. Worth Tex. OS. Discharged to accept 2nd Lt. Commission.
Kelley, Fred Sergeant	Steele, Mo. OS-MA-St.M.
Edwards, James H. Sergeant	Oskaloosa, Kans. OS-MA-St.M.
Robohn, Walter E. Sergeant	Oskaloosa, Kans. OS-MA-St.M.
Farris, Earl A. Sergeant	Lawrence, Kans. OS-MA-MGF-St.M.
Gutschenritter, Samuel B. Sergeant	Oskaloosa, Kans. OS-MA-MGF- St. M.
Shepard, John W. Sergeant	Blytheville, Ark. OS-MA-MGF-G Trfd. Co. K, 139th Inf. Feb. 15, 1919.
Miller, Virgil W. Sergeant	Howard, Kans. OS-MA-MFG-St.M.
Roberts, Herbert R. Sergeant	Blytheville, Ark. OS-St.M.
Anderson, Alba W. Sergeant	Valley Falls, Kans. OS-St.M.
Langley, Arbie F. Sergeant	Oskaloosa, Kans. OS-MA-St.M.
Baynes, John W. Sergeant	Caruthersville, Mo. OS-MA-St.M.
Davis, Lewie E. Sergeant	Winchester, Kans. OS-MA-St.M.
Adams, Carl Sergeant	Caruthersville, Mo. OS-MA-St.M-HE
Gibson, Lucien P. Corporal	Winchester, Kans. OS-MA-St.M-MGF.
Ham, William Corporal	Caruthersville, Mo. OS-St.M-MA.
McCullum, John L. Corporal	Steele, Mo. OS-St.M-MA-MGF.
McGhee, Robert L. Corporal	Caruthersville, Mo. OS-St.M-MA-G.

NAME AND RANK	HOME ADDRESS AND REMARKS
Neel, Robert N. Corporal	Nortonville, Kans. OS-St.M-MA-MGF
Neel, Lawrence C. Corporal	Kennett, Mo. OS-St.M-MA.
Pratt, William M. Corporal	Emporia, Kans. OS. Killed in Alsace trenches.
Quaney, Lawrence F. Corporal	Ozawakie, Kans. OS-St.M-MA-MGF.
Cole, Fred G. Corporal	Ellsworth, Kans. OS-St.M-MA-S.
Pottorf, Frank H. Corporal	Oskaloosa, Kans. OS-St.M-MA. Trfd. to Co. I, 139th Inf. Feb. 15, 1919.
Conley, Loren Corporal	Emporia, Kans. OS. Trfd. in Sept. OS-St.M-MA-MGF. Trfd to Co. I, Feb. 15, 1919.
Grossman, Edmund A. Corporal	Winchester, Kans. OS-St.M-MA-MGF.
Robertson, Lee W. Corporal	Emporia, Kans. OS-St.M-MA-K.
Sill, Richard I. Corporal	Goldendale, Wash. OS-St.M-MA.
Radcliff, George D. Corporal	Steele, Mo. OS-St.M-MA.
Woolbright, Everett Corporal	Howard, Kans. OS-St.M-MA.
Barckman, Donnel Corporal	Oskaloosa, Kans., OS-St.M-MA.
Bliss, Stanley V. Corporal	Dunavant, Kans. OS-St.M-MA-S.
Ramsey, David W. Corporal	Steele, Mo. OS-St.M-MA-MGF.
Wells, Mervin Corporal	Tyler, Mo. OS-St.M-MA.
Hillard, Clark H. Corporal	Oskaloosa, Kans. OS-St.M-MA.
Davis, Clinton Corporal	Caruthersville, Mo. OS-St.M-MA.
Lawrence, Melvin C. Corporal	
Flynn, James S. Corporal	153 Stephens Ave., St. Paul, Minn. OS-St.M-MA.
Lacoe, Mat J. Corporal	Thief River Falls, Minn. OS-St.M-MA.
Dark, Stanley Corporal	Wardell, Mo. OS-St.M-MA.
Hammond, William F. Corporal	Valley Falls, Kans. OS-St.M.
Shively, Charles W. Corporal	Valley Falls, Kans. OS-St.M-MA.
Gallion, Ruff Corporal	Steele, Mo. OS-St.M-MA-MGF.
Glock, John H. Corporal	Oskaloosa, Kans. OS-St.M-MA-MGF.
Hesser, Fred S. Corporal	Alta Vista, Kans. OS-St.M-MA.
Blair, Charles H. Corporal	Glennwood, Minn. OS-St.M-MA.
Heskett, Alvin J. Corporal	Antelope, Kans. OS-St.M-MA.
Hudson, William B. Corporal	Oskaloosa, Kans. OS-St.M-MA-MGF.
Kalin, Thomas Corporal	826 North Street, Peru, Ill. OS.
Massow, Charles A. Corporal	Eldora, Iowa. OS-St.M-MA.
Severn, Arnold Corporal	Steele, Mo. OS-St.M-MA.
Walters, Austin M. Corporal	Oskaloosa, Kans. OS-St.M-MA.
Hanson, Sophus W. Corporal	128 Van Street, Neenah, Wis. OS-St.M-MA.

G COMPANY

Clark, George R. Corporal
Lost Springs, Kans. OS-St.M-MA-G.

Gilliland, Hiram A. Corporal
Coffeyville, Kans. OS-St.M-MA.

Ellefson, Herbert Corporal
708 2nd Ave., Minot, N. D., OS-St.M-MA.

Ayers, Richard Corporal
Wardell, Mo. OS-St.M-MA.

Golden, Philip Corporal
Louiston, Mich., OS.

Vendel, William F. Corporal
Oskaloosa, Kans. OS-St.M-MA-G.

Larkins, William J. Corporal
Oskaloosa, Kans. OS-St.M-MA.

Warren, Carl D. Corporal
Tyler, Mo. OS-St.M-MA-MGF.

Vigus, Frank M. Corporal
Ozawakie, Kans. OS-St.M-MA-K.

Duke, William R. Corporal
OS-St.M-MA-S 18

Davison, Curtis L. Corporal
OS. Joined Oct. 19.

Paul, Clinton Corporal
Ellsworth, Kansas. OS-MA-G. 18.

Krick, Albert Corporal
OS. Jained Oct. 19.

Giese, Richard E. Corporal
James Town, N. D. OS. Wounded in Alsace trenches.

Citius, Henry L. Cook
Caruthersville, Mo. OS-St.M-MA.

Fletcher, Charles W. Cook
Oskaloosa, Kansas. OS-St.M-MA.

Hagendeffer, Ernest F. Cook
Oskaloosa, Kans. OS-St.M-MA.

Kellogg, Harry Cook
71 Turriel Ave. LaPeer, Mich. OS. Trfd. July 1918 to Hq. Co.

Brandon, Benjamin F. Mechanic
Caruthersville, Mo. OS-St.M-MA-MGF.

Cratty, Ollie B. Mechanic
Dyersburg, Tenn. OS. Trans. to Mg. Bn. May, 1918.

Craiglow, John H. Mechanic
Stanley, N. D. OS-St.M-MA-S-K.

Hebert, Henry W. Mechanic
Spring Valley, Ill. OS. Admitted to Hosp. Sept. 1918.

Haremski, Ignatius L. Mechanic
Kenneth, Mo. OS.

Rodgers, Virgel C. Mechanic
Dow, N.D. OS-St.M-MA.

French, Enos G. Mechanic
Halls, Tenn. OS-St.M-MA.

Jennings, Carl Mechanic
Halls, Tenn. OS-St.M-MA.

Jennings, Hall Mechanic
Caruthersville, Mo. OS-St.M-MA-MGF.

Esters, Lexie C. Bugler
Howard, Kans. OS-St.M-MA.

Young, Clark Bugler
Caruthersville, Mo. OS-St.M-MA-G. OS.

Bennett, Curtiss Pvt. 1cl.
Armstrong, Thomas E. Pvt. 1cl.
Oskaloosa, Kans. OS-St.M-MA-MGF.

Bateman, Lumeul E. Pvt. 1cl.
Oskaloosa, Kans. OS-St.M-MA-MGF.

Blockwitz, Birt Pvt. 1cl.
Caruthersville, Mo. OS-St.M. Trans. to MP.

Brown, Homer Pvt. 1cl.
14 Wisconsin St. Indianapolis, Ind. OS.

Amsler, William Pvt. 1cl.
Osawkie, Kans. OS-St.M-MA.

Abbott, Dean A. Pvt. 1cl.
Oskaloosa, Kans. OS-St.M-MA-MGF.

Austin, Robert A. Pvt. 1cl.
Hayti, Mo. OS-St.M-MA.

Byrd, Lawrence Pvt. 1cl.
Oskaloosa, Kans. OS-St.M.

Brann, Everett W. Pvt. 1cl.
Chaska, Minn. OS-St.M-MA.

Burkhart, William H. Pvt. 1cl.
Oskaloosa, Kans. OS-St.M-MA-K-MGF.

Blevins, William E. Pvt. 1cl.
Albia, Iowa. OS-St.M-MA-K-S.

Bishop, Chester M. Pvt. 1cl.

Boik, Mike Pvt. 1cl.
L'Anse, Mich. OS.

Buckley, Houston H. Pvt. 1cl.
Hayti, Mo. OS-St.M.

Adams, Shelby Pvt. 1cl.
Steele, Mo. OS-St.M-MA.

Cottier, Albert Pvt. 1cl.
Western Union, Iowa. OS-St.M-MA-G.

Coons, Kenneth Pvt. 1cl.
Oskaloosa, Kans. OS-St.M-MA.

Davis, Lester M. Pvt. 1cl.
Winchester, Kans. OS-St.M.

Deitrich, Peter Pvt. 1cl.
Ellis, Kans. OS-St.M-MA.

Dodge, Alfred D. Pvt. 1cl.
Lyndon, Kans. OS-St.M-MA.

Douglass, Shelton F. Pvt. 1cl.
Kennett, Mo. OS-St.M-MA.

Davis, William L. Pvt. 1cl.
Oskaloosa, Kans. OS-K. Alsace Trenches.

Duncan, Elmer E. Pvt. 1cl.
Williamstown, Kans. OS. Trfd. May, 1918. OS.

Dickes, Forrest H. Pvt. 1cl.
Hayti, Mo. OS-St.M-MA.

Edwards, Thomas H. Pvt. 1cl.
Caruthersville, Mo. OS-St.M-MA.

Evans, Nathaniel, Pvt. 1cl.
Dunavant, Kans. OS.

Fletcher, Clair Pvt. 1cl.
Nortonville, Kans. OS-St.M-MA-MGF.

Greeley, Charles E. Pvt. 1cl.
Topeka, Kans. OS-St.M-MA.

Guay, John Pvt. 1cl.
Steele, Mo. OS-St.M-MA-K-HE.

Golf, George Pvt. 1cl.
Tyler, Mo. OS. Trfd. to Hq. Co. May, 1919.

Gilliland, Gilbert Pvt. 1cl.
Herman, Mo. OS-St.M-MA.

Hagen, Tony C. Pvt. 1cl.
322 2nd Ave. Evansville, Ind. OS-St.M-MA.

Hall, James E. Pvt. 1cl.
Windledom, N. Dak. St.M-MA-OS.

Hanson, Almer W. Pvt. 1cl.
Virginia, Minn. OS-St.M-MA.

Hauts, Vaino H. Pvt. 1cl.
Virgil, Kansas. OS-St.M-MA.

Hays, John W. Pvt. 1cl.
Brocket, N. D. OS-St.M-MA.

Holte, Karle Pvt. 1cl.
Caruthersville, Mo. OS-St.M-MA-OS.

Harper, Lynn, Pvt. 1cl.
Tyler, Mo. OS-St.M-MA-K.

Holmes, Clyde Pvt. 1cl.
Oskaloosa, Mo. OS-St.M-MA-K.

Hudson, Leslie A. Pvt. 1cl.
Caruthersville, Mo. OS-St.M-MA-W-MGF.

Herndon, Charles E. Pvt. 1cl.
Steele, Mo. OS-St.M-MA-W-MGF. OS-St.M-MA.

Hudson, George A. Pvt. 1cl.
Lowry, Minnesota. OS-St.M-MA.

Henson, Everett C. Pvt. 1cl.
Paullina, Iowa. OS.

Hanson, Henry M. Pvt. 1cl.
Pike, Arkansas. OS-St.M-MA.

Idso, Oscar Pvt. 1cl.
Faust, Mo. OS-St.M-MA.

Ingram, Joseph Pvt. 1cl.
Caruthersville, Mo. OS-St.M.

Jenkins, Lloyd Pvt. 1cl.
Moorehead, Minnesota. OS-St.M-MA.

Johnson, Fred W. Pvt. 1cl.
Hayti, Mo. OS.

Knutson, Oliver G. Pvt. 1cl.
Madison, Mo. OS-St.M-MA-G.

Knight, Dan R. Pvt. 1cl.
Walcott, N. D. OS-St.M-MA.

Lamboy, Tommie J. Pvt. 1cl.
Oskaloosa, Kans. St.M-MA-OS-S.

Lee, Melvin A. Pvt. 1cl.
Caruthersville, Mo. OS-St.M.

Langley, Ernest L. Pvt. 1cl.
Bloomfield, Iowa. OS-St.M-MA-MGF-W.

Little, George A. Pvt. 1cl.
St. Paul, Minn. OS-St.M-MA.

Lunsford, Dorcie D. Pvt. 1cl.
Bragg City, Mo. OS-St.M-MA.

Laverty, Clarence B. Pvt. 1cl.
Hayti, Mo. OS-St.M-MA-W-G.

Marcus, Elmer Pvt. 1cl.
Rigely, Tenn. OS-St.M-MA.

Maxey, Shirley Pvt. 1cl.

Madox, Bennie Pvt. 1cl.

70

CITED FOR VALOR

1. Capt. J. W. McQueen
2. Lieut. Coburn Hull
3. Capt. John D. Heiny
4. Capt. N. B. Loman
5. Lieut. William Perrigo

H COMPANY

McCalley, Carl R. Pvt. 1cl.
McDaniel, Hillary F.
    Pvt. 1cl.
McLees, Guy, Pvt. 1cl.
Moose, Joseph Pvt. 1cl.
Morrissey, Leo A. Pvt. 1cl.
Morley, Roy C. Pvt. 1cl.
Morton, Jason S. Pvt. 1cl.

Mott, Roy A. Pvt. 1cl.
Meyers, Newton E. Pvt. 1cl.

McGowen, Paul Pvt. 1cl.
Nilson, Ole Pvt. 1cl.

Nemecek, Milo V. Pvt. 1cl.

Nichols, Ralph M. Pvt. 1cl.

Olson, Theodore R. Pvt. 1cl.
Owen, Albert A. Pvt. 1cl.
O'Brion, William M.
    Pvt. 1cl.
Owen, Wade R. Pvt. 1cl.
Olmstead, Hugh Pvt. 1cl.
Popejoy, William R.
    Pvt. 1cl.
Powell, Odis L. Pvt. 1cl.
Pottorf, Fred G. Pvt. 1cl.
Rushing, Herman H.
    Pvt. 1cl.
Ray, Hugh V. Pvt. 1cl.
Shilley, Carl Pvt. 1cl.
Smith, Shirley M. Pvt. 1cl.
Snelson, Ben H. Pvt. 1cl.
Stowe, John M. Pvt. 1cl.
Shultz, Everett J. Pvt. 1cl.
Spencer, Marshall Pvt. 1cl.
Southern, Walter Pvt. 1cl.
Trapp, Merle A. Pvt. 1cl.
Vance, Claborn Pvt. 1cl.
Vandruff, Grover Pvt. 1cl.

Ware, George E. Pvt. 1cl.

Wilbanks, Jack W. Pvt. 1cl.
Wind, Fred J. Pvt. 1cl.

Woessner, Otte E. Pvt. 1cl.

Watts, Chester Pvt. 1cl.

Winrick, Clarence E.
    Pvt. 1cl.
Zidek, Rafeal Pvt. 1cl.
Abernathy, Claborn Private
Akers, Howard Private
Ahl, Gust E. Private

Andrews, John M. Private

Waker, Iowa. St.M.
Caruthersville, Mo. OS-St.M-MA.

Genoa, Wisconsin. OS-St.M-MA.
Daune, Minn. OS-St.M-MA-W-G.
Anamosa, Iowa. OS-St.M-MA.
Goodrich, N. D. OS-St.M-MA.
Atwood, Kans. OS-St.M-MA-W-S-MGF.
Oskaloosa, Kans. OS-St.M-MA.
Oskaloosa, Kans. OS-W-S. Alsace trenches.
Hayti, Mo. OS-St.M-MA-W-MGF.
210 A St., North Moorehead, Minn. OS-St.M-MA.
1019 Ninth Ave., East Cedar Rapids, Iowa. OS.
Oskaloosa, Kans. OS-St.M-MA-MGF.
Florence, Wis. OS-St.M-MA.
Winchester, Kans. OS-St.M-MA.
OS-Trfd. to Hq. Co. 139th Inf. July 16/19.
Oskaloosa, Kansas. OS-St.M-MA-K.
Oskaloosa, Kans. OS-St.M-MA.
Decatur, Tex. OS-St.M-MA.

Hayti, Mo. OS-St.M-MA-S.
Oskaloosa, Kans. OS-St.M-MA-S.
Sikeston, Mo. OS-St.M-MA.

Senath, Mo. OS-St.M-MA-G.
Steele, Mo. OS-St.M-MA.
Steele, Mo. OS-St.M-MA-S.
Lovilia, Iowa. OS-St.M-MA-MGF.
Foley, Minn. OS-St.M-MA.
Oskaloosa, Kans. OS-St.M-MA.
Steele, Mo. OS-St.M.
Steele, Mo. OS-St.M-MA-K.
Oskaloosa, Kans. OS.
Tyler, Mo. OS-St.M-MA.
McClouth, Kans. OS. Trfd. to 130th M.G. Co. May 4/19.
103 S. Franklin St., Junction City, Kans. OS-St.M-MA.
Hayti, Mo. OS-St.M-MA.
113 Market St., Emporia, Kans. OS-St.M-MA-W-G.
Parkers Prairie, Minn. OS-St.M-MA.
Caruthersville, Mo. OS-St.M-MA-W-MGF.
Ozawkie, Kans. OS-St.M-MA-MGF.

Maryville, Kans. OS-St.M-MA-K.
Kennett, Mo. OS-St.M-MA.
Reedsville, Ky. OS.
1219 7th St., South Minneapolis, Minn. OS-St.M-MA-K.
OS.

Anueswitz, Jacob Private

Arsenaue, Howard J.
    Private
Bartels, Otto C. Private
Baron, Michael Private
Bevelhymer, Harry A.
    Private
Biggs, Noah M. Private
Borlaugh, Gerhard E.
    Private
Brown, Lyle J. Private
Braun, Frank H. Private
Brown, Ira Private
Blank, Harry J. Private
Bousfield, George H. Private

Chapman, Homer H. Private
Cottier, Albert Private

Crawford, Willard I. Private
Creason, James H. Private
Collins, Joseph R. Private
Carleton, Guy Private

Creason, Hardie Private

Carmicheal, Dolph Private

Dunavan, Merle L. Private

Doran, Henry P. Private
Darnell, William B. Private

Derry, Samuel Private
Duranto, Antonio Private
Edling, Reuben W. Private

Ekstrom, Oscar Private
Engene, Amund Private
Flannigan, John C. Private

Fletcher, Louis H. Private
Foelker, Walter H. Private

Foster, John W. Private
Fromm, Edwin H. Private
Furcht, Francis F. Private
Frederickson, Frank H.
    Private
Froehlick, Andrew Private
Given, John Private

Glomstead, Elmer Private
Grassmidt, Jacob Private
Gray, John Private
Grondale, Henry Private
Gundberg, John, Private

Goeke, Raymond A. Private

Trfd. to Co. K, 139th Inf., Feb. 15/19. OS.
OS-Trfd. Co. K, 139th Inf., Feb. 15/19.
Gregory, Iowa. OS-St.M-MA.
Mandon, N. D. OS-St.M-MA.
Ceder, Mich. OS. Trfd. to Co. K.

Sparta, Mich. OS-St.M-MA.
Calmer, Iowa. OS-St.M-MA.

Oxford, Mich. OS.
Rothsay, Minn. OS-St.M-MA-K.
Norwood, Mo. OS-St.M-MA-K.
OS. Trfd. May 1918.
Valley Falls, Kansas. OS-St.M-MA-Trfd. to Hq. Co., 139th Inf.
Versailles, Kentucky. OS.
West Union, Iowa. OS-St.M-MA-W-G.
Sawyer, N. D. OS-St.M-MA-W-S.
Conran, Mo. OS-St.M-MA.
Winnelk, Ill. OS.
Caruthersville, Mo. OS. Trfd. to Hq. Co., 139th Inf., May 1919.
Conran, Mo. OS. Trfd. to Supply Co., May 1919.
OS-St.M-MA-Trfd. to Hq. troop Jan. 1919.
1313 Brooklyn Ave., Kansas City, Mo. OS. Trfd. to Hq. 35th Div.
OS. Trfd.
Huntsville, Ala. OS. Trfd. to M Co.
OS.
OS. Trfd. to K Co. 139th Inf.
Robinsville, Minn. OS-St.M-MA-W-S.
Plaza, N. D. OS-St.M-MA.
Casselton, N. D. OS-St.M-MA.
2303 Gerard Ave., Minneapolis, Minn. OS.
Boyle, Kans. OS-St.M-MA.
1036 S. 3rd Ave., Wausau, Wis. OS-St.M-MA.
Dyesberg, Tenn. OS-St.M.
1712 N. Ave., Milwaukee, Wis. OS.
Dallas, Iowa. Joined Jan. 1919 OS.
Portland, N. D. OS. Wounded in Alsace Trenches.
Mandon, N. D. OS-St.M-MA.
7122 Ingleside Ave., Chicago, Ill. OS.
Wheelock, N. D. OS.
856 11th St., Grand St., Mich. OS.
Cosell, Mich. OS.
Roy, N. D. OS-St.M-MA-W-MGF.
Detroit, Mich. OS-St.M-MA-W-MGF.
OS-St.M-MA-K.

H COMPANY

Gifford, Leon D.	Private	Minneapolis, Minn. OS-St.M-MA.
Goetze, Albert L.	Private	Mora, Minn. OS-Trfd. May, 1918.
Gibler, Forrest S.	Private	Joplin, Mo. OS.
Harrington, Clifford	Private	Trenton, N. D. OS-St.M-MA.
Hau, Henry J.	Private	Newberry, St. Appleton, Wis. OS.
Hedland, John	Private	Kindred, N. D. OS-St.M-MA.
Heine, Henry	Private	Krem, N. D. OS-St.M-MA.
Helgeson, Henry L.	Private	Mohawk, N. K. OS-St.M-MA.
Henrickson, Nicolai	Private	Appam, N. D. OS-St.M-MA-W-G. Grenade in Alsace Trenches.
Hanson, Martin C.	Private	Newton, Minn. OS-St.M-MA.
Hill, Alfred	Private	Park Hill, Ontario, Canada.
Hilleren, Henry C.	Private	Troga, N. D. OS-St.M-MA.
Hoffman, Leslie L.	Private	Amherst Junction, Wis. OS.
Hogan, George F.	Private	5616 Green St., Chicago, Ill. OS.
Hopp, Charles A.	Private	230 Fullerton Ave., Detroit, Mich. OS.
Houts, Jehrias	Private	Masion, Iowa. OS-St.M-MA.
Hubbard, Felix	Private	Brock, Ky. OS.
Harlow, Luther T.	Private	Leonard, N. D. OS-St.M-MA.
Hartman, Charles L.	Private	Stanley, N. D. OS-St.M-MA-K.
Harris, Robert	Private	Mohall, N. D. OS-Trfd. to Hospital as sick in Aug., 1919.
Hatling, Walter H.	Private	Crosley, N. D. OS-St.M-MA-S.
Hellerud, Paul	Private	Minton, N. D. OS-St.M-MA.
Hiatt, Elmer	Private	Minton, N. D. OS-St.M-MA.
Hilderbrandt, Edward	Private	Watseka, Ill. OS-St.M-MA-S.
Hiterdal, Clifford	Private	Moorehead, Minn. OS-St.M-MA-MGF.
Hoard, Clement	Private	Jamestown, N. D. OS.
Haugland, Conrad	Private	OS-St.M.
Hargrave, Glen N.	Private	OS-St.M-MA. Trfd. Co. M.
Irwin, Kelley O.	Private	Belle Prairie, Ill. OS.
Johnston, Traynor	Private	Ft. Wayne, Ind. OS.
Johnson, Robert L.	Private	Caruthersville, Mo. OS. Trfd. to Supply Company, May, 1918.
Kilmer, James T.	Private	Ozawkie, Kansas. OS-St.M-MA.
Kosan, Frank J.	Private	4950 South Seely Ave., Chicago, Ill. OS.
Kilroy, James P.	Private	1514 East 9th St., Minneapolis, Minn. OS.
Kreul, Anton J.	Private	Highland, Wis. OS.
Kramer, Reuben L.	Private	Wabash, Minn. OS-St.M-MA.
Koenig, August W.	Private	Moorehead, Minn. St.M-MA-K.
Kruchten, Edward A.	Private	St. Cloud, Minn. OS-St.M-MA.
Lewis, George S.	Private	271 13th St., Milwaukee, Wis. OS.
Large, Oral F.	Private	Numa, Iowa. OS.
Laverty, Clarence	Private	26 West Winfred St., St. Paul, Minn. OS-St.M-MA.
Lewis, Ira E.	Private	416 West 6th Ave., Flint, Mich. OS.
Logsdon, Shirley B.	Private	Caruthersville, Mo. OS-St.M-MA.
Lunsford, Dorcie D.	Private	Bloomfield, Iowa. OS-St.M-MA-W-GMGF.
Lake, Artie C.	Private	Topeka, Kansas. Trfd. to Hq. Co. July/18.
Marlin, Delmar R.	Private	Caruthersville, Mo. OS-St.M-MA.
Mally, George A.	Private	Chicago, Ill. OS.

Malpiede, Clyde	Private	Denver, Colo. OS.
Mannion, Michael	Private	Glenamaddy, Ireland. OS.
Martin, Theodore F.	Private	Stuttgart, Ark. OS.
Mattfolk, Alfred	Private	Muskegon, Mich. OS.
Matson, Herbert	Private	Ludington, Mich. OS.
Meyer, John	Private	Conway, Mo. OS.
Miller, Howard	Private	Manceloa, Mich. OS.
Monroe, Alvin J.	Private	Elleston, Iowa. OS-St.M-MA. Wounded in Alsace trenches.
Moore, David W., Jr.	Private	Peoria, Ill. OS.
Moore, John	Private	Minconning, Mich. OS.
Myhand, Wyatt Y.	Private	Opelika, Ala. OS.
Marley, James J.	Private	Hayti, Mo. OS-St.M-MA-W-G.
McAninch, Howard	Private	OS-St.M-MA-K.
Miles, George H.	Private	Caruthersville, Mo. OS-MA.
Miller, Grover C.	Private	Valley Falls, Kans. OS-St.M-MA-W-S.
Martin, Wilson M.	Private	Dunvant, Kans. OS-St.M-MA-W-G.
Nordberg, John	Private	Minneapolis, Minn. OS-St.M-MA.
Oelkers, Albert J. C.	Private	Redwing, Minn. OS-St.M-MA.
Oman, Ernest	Private	Chicago, Ill. OS.
Ostile, Oscar O.	Private	Northwood, N. D. OS.
Owens, Earl D.	Private	Akron, Mich. OS.
Olson, Herbert	Private	Spirit Lake, Iowa. OS-St.M-MA. OS. Trfd. to K Co. 139 Inf. Feb. 16, '19.
Ozzelo, Emil	Private	
Palmer, Frank	Private	Corydon, Iowa. OS.
Park, John	Private	Galesville, Wisc. OS.
Parson, Clint	Private	Brownell, Kans. OS-St.M-MA-W-S.
Patrick, James W.	Private	Paris, Mo. OS-St.M.
Plester, Charles R.	Private	Harbor Beach, Mich. OS.
Parson, Tolmie A.	Private	Kent Center, Ontario, Canada. OS.
Peterson, Verner G.	Private	Shauer, Mich. OS.
Pollock, Newton D.	Private	Chicago, Ill. OS.
Prall, Ross L.	Private	Carlisle, Iowa. OS-St.M-MA.
Pride, Frank	Private	Caruthersville, Mo. OS-MA.
Pfleuger, Chester H.	Private	Ortonville, Minn. OS.
Pepples, Joseph	Private	Pascola, Mo. OS. Trfd. to M. G. Gun July 1, '19.
Remoga, Nick	Private	Saint Andrea, Sulloneo Province, Contonzaro, Italy. OS.
Renner, Harley	Private	Indianapolis, Ind. OS.
Reynolds, Roy L.	Private	Lansing, Mich. OS.
Rothel, Arthur F.	Private	Cleveland, Wis. OS.
Reed, Daniel W.	Private	Beaukiss, Tex. OS-St.M-MA.
Rockstroh, Ernest R.	Private	Chicago, Ill. OS.
Rice, William M.	Private	St. Johns, Mich. OS.
Russell, Willard P.	Private	Hayti, Mo. OS-St.M.
Ralph, Harry	Private	Hayti, Mo. OS. Trfd. to Hosp. as sick.
Robertson, Lee W.	Private	Winchester, Kans. OS-St.M-MA-W-MGF.
Rogers, Clyde J.	Private	Nortonville, Kans. OS-St.M-MA-K. OS. Trfd. to Hosp. as sick.
Repologe, Karl M.	Private	Caruthersville, Mo. OS-MA.
Roberts, Frank D.	Private	Caruthersville, Mo. OS-MA.
Ray, George W.	Private	OS. Trfd. to Hosp. sick.
Reed, Mansie	Private	OS. Trfd. to Hosp. sick.

H COMPANY

Riveria, Ventura	Private	OS. Trfd. to M Co. 139th Inf.
Sandel, Walter E.	Private	Covington, Ky. OS.
Sapinza, Anthony	Private	Detroit, Mich. OS.
Scarnton, Samuel B.	Private	Grand Rapids, Mich. OS.
Schaffer, George W.	Private	Watertown, Wis. OS.
Selter, William G.	Private	Roniulus, Mich. OS.
Sensor, Harley R.	Private	West Union, Iowa. OS-St.M-MA.
Shultz, Mark L.	Private	Spirit Lake, Iowa, OS-St.M-MA.
Slatten, John D.	Private	Poretville, Cal. OS.
Southern, Robert	Private	Steele, Mo. OS-St.M-MA.
Smith, William W.	Private	Winston, Mo. OS-St.M-MA.
Smith, Jetha L.	Private	Des Moines, Iowa. OS-St.M-MA.
Snyder, Lewis F.	Private	Harbor Springs, Mich. OS.
Sorensen, Henry B.	Private	Chicago, Ill. OS-St.M-MA-MGF.
Stephanon, Neofitos J.	Private	Chicago, Ill. OS.
Storey, William F.	Private	Junction, Kans. OS-St.M-MA.
Snelson, Ben H.	Private	Knoxville, Iowa. OS-St.M-MA.
Stovern, Oscar	Private	Fergus Falls, Minn. OS.
Swanson, Albert C.	Private	Spirit Lake, Iowa. Trans.
Swanson, Gilbert E.	Private	Red Wing, Minn. OS-St.M-MA.
Trudel, Armile	Private	Detroit, Minn. OS-St.M-MA.

Tinsley, George	Private	Caruthersville, Mo. OS-St.M-MA.
Tressen, Morgan	Private	OS-St.M-MA.
Tessin, Edward	Private	OS. died Hosp.
Vaughn, Floyd	Private	Lost Springs, Kans. OS-St.M-MA.
Vanorsdall, Seef	Private	Coffeyville, Kans. OS-St.M-MA.
Wachs, William A.	Private	Kenosha, Wis. OS.
Walters, Frank	Private	Winchester, Kans. OS-St.M-MA-MGF.
Wh'ting, Howard	Private	Ripley, W. V. OS.
Wiegert, Lewis C.	Private	Milwaukee, Wis. OS.
Wiiliams, John W.	Private	Noble, Iowa. OS-St.M-MA.
Wrobbel, Oscar C.	Private	Plymouth, Mich. OS.
Woessner, Otto E.	Privat?	Stanley, N. D. OS. Trans. to Hosp.
Ware, John	Private	Caruthersville, Mo. OS-St.M-MA.
Warnert, Louis E.	Pr'vate	Bimidji, Minn. OS-W in Alsace.
Wertz, Steve	Private	Mandan, N. D. OS-W. in Alsace.
Witchi, Thomas	Private	Linton, N. D. OS-St.M-MA-K. in Arg.
Willis, Charley F.	Private	Adel, Iowa. OS-St.M-MA-K.
Yearout, Thomas H.	Private	Emporia, Kans. OS.
Baldwin, James M.	Private	OS.
Miniti, Antonio	Private	South GRCO Reopieteiaria, Reggealabea, Italy. OS.

H COMPANY

ROSTER OF COMPANY C, 139th INFANTRY

NAME AND RANK		HOME ADDRESS AND REMARKS
Jasper N. Gates	Captain	Spartensburg, S. Carolina. C Co. 4th Mo.
Oscar C. Brownlee	Captain	Lawrence, Kans. OS. 1st Kans. Inf.
Thilip H. Slocum	Captain	Boston, Mass.
Raymond W. Cater	Captain	Kirksville, Mo. C Co. 4th Mo. OS-MA. Gassed.
William Perrigo	Captain	Junction City, Kans. C Co. 3rd Kans.
Samuel Daugherty	1st Lt.	Junction City, Kans. C Co. 3rd Kans.
George H. Stephens	1st Lt.	Topeka, Kans. Officers Reserve. OS-MA-G-S.
Lewis E. Hansen	1st Lt.	Sedalia, Mo. Officers Reserve. OS.
Paul A. Cannady	1st Lt.	Yates Center, Kans. 1st Kans. Inf. OS-MA.
Paul O. Botkin	1st Lt.	Wichita, Kans. Bn. Adj. 3rd. Kans. OS-MA-G.
David C. Mewhiter	1st Lt.	Replacement.
Frank L. Armstead	1st Lt.	Replacement.
George L. Prindel	1st Lt.	Replacement.
John L. Creech	2nd Lt.	Poor Fork, Arkansas. Officers Reserve. OS. Trans. to Sup. Co. 139th Inf.
Harold G. Dean	2nd Lt.	Alderson, Ala. Replacement.
Charles Lynch	2nd Lt.	Columbia, Penn. Replacement.
Richard P. McDonald	2nd Lt.	Kansas City, Mo. Trans. fr 140th Inf. OS-MA.
Peterson, John L.	1st Sgt.	Kirksville, Mo. C Co. 4th Mo. OS. Now 2nd Lt. with 5th Division.
McKeehan, Carl	1st Sgt.	Grand Meadow, S. Dak. OS. Returned to U. S. as instructor. C Co. 4th Mo.
Kent, Claude J.	1st Sgt.	Green City, Mo. C Co. 4th Mo. OS-MA. Commissioned as 2nd Lt. ORC.
Wimber, Van	1st Sgt.	Kirksville, Mo. C Co. 4th Mo. OS-MA-G.
Ferguson, Stephen	Sup. Sgt.	Kirksville, Mo. C Co. 4th Mo.
Howey, Earl W.	Sup. Sgt.	Kirksville, Mo. C Co. 4th Mo. OS-MA.
Bauer, Leon	Mess Sgt.	Junction City, Kans. C Co. 3rd Kans.
Harding, David	Mess Sgt.	Kansas City, Mo. C Co. 3rd Kans. OS-MA.
Anderson, Grover	Mess Sgt.	Junction City, Kans. C Co. 3rd Kans. OS-MA.
Ray, Boyd E.	Sergeant	Junction City, Kans. C Co. 3rd Kans. OS-MA-HE.
Denton, Manvil S.	Sergeant	Kirksville, Mo. C Co. 4th Mo. OS-MA-G.
Bennett, Alva	Sergeant	Kirksville, Mo. C Co. 4th Mo. OS-MA-G.
Loder, John L.	Sergeant	Kirksville, Mo. C Co. 4th Mo. OS-MA.
Rutherford, Joe	Sergeant	Kirksville, Mo. C Co. 4th Mo. OS-MA.
Daul, John F.	Sergeant	Quincy, Ill. C Co. 4th Mo. OS-MA.
Moon, Frank B.	Sergeant	Kirksville, Mo. C Co. 4th Mo. OS-MA.
Hanks, Ackland	Sergeant	Kenneth, Mo. Trans. fr 140th Inf. OS-MA.
Barnes, William	Sergeant	Kirksville, Mo. C Co. 4th Mo. OS-MA.
Singley, Chas.	Sergeant	Green City, Mo. C Co. 4th Mo. OS-MA.
Singley, Riley	Sergeant	Green City, Mo. C Co. 4th Mo. OS-MA. Trans. to G Co. 139th Inf.
MacDougal, Hubert	Sergeant	Kirksville, Mo. C Co. 4th Mo. OS-MA-MG died of wounds.
Jones, Earl L.	Sergeant	Junction City, Kans. OS-MA. Missing in action.
Brassfield, Orrin	Sergeant	Kirksville, Mo. C Co. 139th Inf. Trans. Romsey, England. OS.
Clark, John C.	Sergeant	Junction City, Kans. C Co. 3rd Kans. Trans. Romsey, England.
Deitrich, William	Sergeant	Junction City, Kans. C Co. 3rd Kans. Deserted at Camp Doniphan, Okla.
Foley, Timothy J., Jr.	Sergeant	Junction City, Kans. C Co. 3rd Kans. OS-MA. Gassed.
Fiscus, Ray	Sergeant	Kirksville, Mo. C Co. 4th Mo. Trans. to U. S. as instructor.
Otnes, Fred J.	Sergeant	Junction City, Kans. C Co. 3rd Kans. OS-MA.
Pegues, Henry	Sergeant	Junction City, Kans. C Co. 3rd Kans. OS-MA. Comm. 2nd Lt. 137th Inf.
Turner, Ben E.	Sergeant	Kahoka, Mo. C Co. 4th Mo. OS-MA. Comm. 2nd Lt. 28th Division.
Woods, Oliver S.	Sergeant	Queen City, Mo. C Co. 4th Mo. OS-MA. Trans. to sanitary detachment 139th Inf.
Crawford, Chas.	Sergeant	Kirksville, Mo. C Co. 4th Mo. OS. Trans. to U. S. as instructor.
Eggert, Ralph	Sergeant	Kirksville, Mo. C Co. 4th Mo. OS-MA-HE.
McKinney, Earl H.	Sergeant	Junction City, Kans. C Co. 3rd Kans. OS. Comm. 2nd Lt. 28th Division.
Rubin, LeRoy	Sergeant	Kirksville, Mo. C Co. 4th Mo. OS-MA. Gassed.
Foutch, Chase	Sergeant	Kirksville, Mo. C Co. 4th Mo. OS-MA. Comm. 2nd Lt. ORC.

75

FIGHTING LINE OFFICERS

1. Lieut. Robert Warren Roberts
2. Lieut. Paul A. Cannady
3. Lieut. J. H. Wilson
4. Lieut. Paul O. Botkin
5. Capt. Ralph Lucier
6. Lieut. Will H. Morse
7. Lieut. F. A. Appenfelder
8. Lieut. C. M. Flynn
9. Lieut. Charles W. Barndollar

I COMPANY

Storey, Fred L. Sergeant Junction City, Kans. C Co. 3rd Kans. OS-MA. Trans. B Co. 139th Inf.

Conkin, William Sergeant Green City, Mo. C Co. 4th Mo. OS-MA.

Unfer, Louis Sergeant Kirksville, Mo. C Co. 4th Mo. OS-MA.

Webber, Thomas Sgt. Major Laplata, Mo. C Co. 4th Mo. OS-MA. Trans. to Army Hdq.

Bentley, William Sergeant Junction City, Kans. C Co. 3rd Kans. OS-MA. Gassed.

Bailey, Kenneth Corporal Kirksville, Mo. C Co. 4th Mo. OS-MA-G.

Lawrence, Brown Corporal Kirksville, Mo. C Co. 4th Mo. OS-MA.

Beall, Orrin O. Corporal Kirksville, Mo. C Co. 4th Mo. OS-MA-HE.

Crawford, Henry F. Corporal Kirksville, Mo. C Co. 4th Mo. OS-MA.

Dawdy, Leslie Corporal Laplata, Mo. C Co. 4th Mo. OS-MA-HE.

Estes, John W. Corporal Junction City, Kans. C Co. 3rd Kans. OS-MA.

Guthrie, Belt D. Corporal Tarkio, Mo. A Co. 4th Mo. OS-MA-HE.

Gates, Alfred L. Corporal Kirksville, Mo. C Co. 4th Mo. OS-MA. Gassed.

Mallon, George W. Corporal Junction City, Kans. C Co. 3rd Kans. OS-MA-GSW.

Miles, Lloyd B. Corporal Laplata, Mo. C Co. 4th Mo. OS-MA. Gassed.

Oliver, Fay E. Corporal Kirksville, Mo. C Co. 4th Mo. OS-MAG.

Plemmons, Thomas D. Corporal Laplata, Mo. C Co. 4th Mo. OS-MA.

Robinson, Levy C. Corporal Green City, Mo. C Co. 4th Mo. OS-MA.

Stahl, Earl L. Corporal Kirksville, Mo. C Co. 4th Mo. OS-MA.

Thompson, George H. Corporal Yarrow, Mo. C Co. 4th Mo. OS-MA-HE.

Taylor, LeRoy G. Corporal Junction City, Kans. C Co. 3rd Kans. OS.

Warnock, Charles Corporal Junction City, Kans. C Co. 3rd Kans. OS-MA-HE.

Wellman, Elba Corporal Kirksville, Mo. C Co. 4th Mo. OS-MA-HE.

Wiggins, Richard C. Corporal Trenton, Mo. D Co. 4th Mo. OS-MA-HE.

Hartung, Harry E. Corporal Junction City, Kans. C Co. 3rd Kans. OS-MA.

Brueggeman, Theodore Corporal Fort Washington, Wis. repl. MA.

Martin, Eddie A. Corporal Caro, Michigan. repl. MA.

Mead, William O. Corporal Caro, Michigan. repl. MA.

Shepard, Edwin L. Corporal Hillsdale, Michigan. repl. MA.

Collins, Elmer L. Corporal Connelsville, Mo. C Co. 4th Mo. OS.

Durham, Earl Corporal Kirksville, Mo. C Co. 4th Mo. Comm. 2nd Lt. Aviation.

Davenport, Leslie J. Corporal Junction City, Kans. C Co. 3rd Kans.

Fisher, Earnest Corporal Kirksville, Mo. C Co. 4th Mo. OS. Trans. to Veterinary Corps.

Glynn, Derby Corporal Kirksville, Mo. C Co. 4th Mo. OS-MA.

Hurley, Daniel T. Corporal Junction City, Kans. C Co. 3rd Kans. OS.

Halfpenny, Gordon Corporal Junction City, Kans. C Co. 3rd Kans.

Hood, Martin E. Corporal Junction City, Kans. C Co. 3rd Kans. OS-MA-HE.

Hull, Warren Corporal Junction City, Kans. C Co. 3rd Kans. OS.

Kerr, Paul Corporal Junction City, Kans. C Co. 3rd Kans. OS-MA.

Lowe, Mannie Corporal Kirksville, Mo. C Co. 4th Mo. OS-MA. Killed in action.

McKinney, Earl H. Corporal Junction City, Kans. C Co. 3rd Kans. OS-MA. Comm. 2nd Lt. 28th Div.

Martin, Earl Corporal Kirksville, Mo. C Co. 4th Mo. OS. Trans. to Ambulance Co.

Miller, Ralph Corporal Green City, Mo. C Co. 4th Mo.

O'Meara, Paul A. Corporal Junction City, Kans. C Co. 3rd Kans.

Piersee, Charley Corporal Kirksville, Mo. C Co. 4th Mo. Trans. to 110 Motor transport Bn.

Ross, Clyde J. Corporal Junction City, Kans. C Co. 3rd Kans.

Rivers, Leo E. Corporal Junction City, Kans. C Co. 3rd Kans. OS-MA. Gassed.

Rieber, Carl S. Corporal Junction City, Kans. C Co. 3rd Kans. OS.

Scanlon, Leo T. Corporal Junction City, Kans. C Co. 3rd Kans. OS. Trans. to RR Engineers.

Thompson, Vance E. Corporal Junction City, Kans. C Co. 3rd Kans.

Taylor, Leroy G. Corporal Junction City, Kans. C Co. 3rd Kans. OS.

Winn, William Corporal Kirksville, Mo. C Co. 4th Mo. OS-MA.

Bozarth, Allen Corporal Kirksville, Mo. C Co. 4th Mo. OS-MA.

Cole, John B. Corporal Green City, Mo. C Co. 4th Mo. OS-MA. Gassed.

Dowis, Carl C. Corporal Kirksville, Mo. C Co. 4th Mo. OS-MA.

Foster, Earl Corporal Kirksville, Mo. C Co. 4th Mo. OS-MA-HE.

Leas, Clyde A. Corporal Green City, Mo. C Co. 4th Mo. OS-MA.

Pinkerton, Joseph A. Corporal Kirksville, Mo. C Co. 4th Mo.

Story, William F. Corporal Junction City, Kans. 3rd Kans. OS.

Vetsch, John H. Corporal Junction City, Kans. C Co. 3rd Kans. OS-MA-HE.

I COMPANY

Ceas, Lester	Corporal	Junction City, Kans. C Co. 3rd Kans. OS-MA.
Chancelor, Clarence	Corporal	Kirksville, Mo. C Co. 4th Mo. OS-MA. Killed in action.
Griswold, Levi W.	Corporal	Yarrow, Mo. C Co. 4th Mo. OS-MA. Killed in action. D.S.C.
Hampton, Earl	Corporal	Kirksville, Mo. C Co. 4th Mo. OS-MA-HE.
Jennings, Ray L.	Corporal	Junction City, Kans. C Co. 3rd Kans. OS-MA.
Jones, Otis K.	Corporal	Junction City, Kans. C Co. 3rd Kans. OS-MA.
Kelley, Leo	Corporal	Junction City, Kans. C Co. 3rd Kans. OS-MA.
Moore, Omer	Corporal	Junction City, Kans. C Co. 3rd Kans. OS-MA.
Mallon, George W.	Corporal	Junction City, Kans. C Co. 3rd Kans. OS-MA-GSW.
Osbern, Raymond	Corporal	Green Castle. C Co. 4th Mo. OS-MA-GSW.
Saunders, Clinton J.	Corporal	Laplata, Mo. C Co. 4th Mo. OS-MA
Joss, Phillip E.	Corporal	Beulah, N. D. Repl. MA. Killed in action.
Bentley, William	Corporal	Junction City, Kans. C Co. 3rd Kans. OS-MA-Gass.
Hartnett, Lester	Corporal	Repl. MA.
Huitt, Edward	Corporal	Junction City, Kans. C Co. 3rd Kans. OS-MA. Killed in action. Repl. MA. Trans. to 3rd Army Corps.
Pallberg, Edward	Corporal	Junction City, Kans. C Co. 3rd Kans. OS-MA. Killed in action.
Snell, Clyde R.	Corporal	Junction City, Kans. C Co. 3rd Kans. OS-MA-GSW.
Valmar, John O.	Corporal	Kirksville, Mo. C Co. 4th Mo. OS. Trans. to 110 Motor Supply Train.
Hardister, Orbie	Sergeant	Junction City, Kans. C Co. 3rd Kans. Trans. at Ft. Sill, Okla.
Gouin, Forrest F.	Cook	Junction City, Kans. C Co. 3rd Kans. OS-MA.
Gaunt, Herman M.	Cook	Kirksville, Mo. C Co. 4th Mo. Trans. at Romsey, England.
Standforth, David	Cook	Unionville, Mo. C Co. 4th Mo. OS-MA-GSW. Gassed.
Kaup, Harrison L.	Cook	Junction City, Kans. C Co. 3rd Kans. OS-MA.
Brazil, Chester G.	Cook	Junction City, Kans. C Co. 3rd Kans. OS-MA.
Huey, Archie	Cook	Kirksville, Mo. C Co. 4th Mo. OS-MA.
Paris, Alva R.	Cook	Junction City, Kans. C Co. 3rd Kans. OS. Trans. at Romsey, England.
Asher, Gene	Cook	Junction City, Kans. C Co. 3rd Kans. OS-MA.
Briddell, William S.	Cook	Kirksville, Mo. C Co. 4th Mo. OS-MA.
Summers, Richard	Cook	Kirksville, Mo. C Co. 4th Mo. OS-MA-GSW.
Kent, William H.	Mechanic	

Kirby, Martin E.	Mechanic	Junction City, Kans. C Co. 3rd Kans. OS-MA.
Petit, Harry	Mechanic	Junction City, Kans. C Co. 3rd Kans. Trans. at Ft. Sill, Okla.
Runyon, Erwin	Mechanic	Green Castle, Mo. C Co. 4th Mo. OS-MA.
Fickle, Roy E.	Mechanic	Kirksville, Mo. C Co. 4th Mo. OS-MA-GSW.
Conley, James W.	Mechanic	Kirksville, Mo. C Co. 4th Mo. OS-MA-HE.
Alln, Noble	Bugler	Junction City, Kans. C Co. 3rd Kans. OS-MA.
Thomas, George	Bugler	Green City, Mo. C Co. 4th Mo. OS. Trans. at Romsey, England.
Sperry, Clifford F.	Bugler	Trenton, Mo. D Co. 4th Mo. OS-MA.
Paschal, Luther	Bugler	Kirksville, Mo. C Co. 4th Mo. OS-MA.
Andrea, Walter L.	Pvt. 1cl.	Elsworth, Kans. Replacement OS-MA.
Alverson, Archie	Pvt. 1cl.	Junction City, Kans. C Co. 3rd Kans.
Archbold, George	Pvt. 1cl.	Replacement. MA.
Bullock, Milan A.	Pvt. 1cl.	Stanton, Kans. OS-MA.
Barnett, Edgar	Pvt. 1cl.	Kirksville, Mo. C Co. 4th Mo. OS-MA.
Bedford, Charles E.	Pvt. 1cl.	Junction City, Kans. C Co. 3rd Kans. OS.
Burris, Ross S.	Pvt. 1cl.	Kirksville, Mo. C Co. 4th Mo. Trans. at Ft. Sill, Okla.
Bentz, Edward	Pvt. 1cl.	Junction City, Kans. C Co. 3rd Kans. OS-MA-HE.
Cater, Bert	Pvt. 1cl.	Kingman, Kans. repl. OS-MA.
Chrisman, Willie	Pvt. 1cl.	Kirksville, Mo. C Co. 4th Mo. OS-MA-GSW.
Cooper, Glen	Pvt. 1cl.	Kirksville, Mo. C Co. 4th Mo. OS-MA-HE.
Cox, Curtis	Pvt. 1cl.	Junction City, Kans. C Co. 3rd Kans.
Commack, Ralph	Pvt. 1cl.	Lewistown, Mo. C Co. 4th Mo. Trans. to aviation corps.
Cowgill, Isaic M.	Pvt. 1cl.	Green City, Mo. C Co. 4th Mo. OS
Czlapelski, Vincent	Pvt. 1cl.	Parkview, Ill. Repl. MA.
Cameron, George	Pvt. 1cl.	Sacramento, California. Repl.
Courneya, Ernest J.	Pvt. 1cl.	Standish, Mich. Repl.
Card, Richard	Pvt. 1cl.	Repl. MA.
Detrich, Fred	Pvt. 1cl.	Junction City, Kans. C Co. 3rd Kans. OS-MA. Gassed.
Diegelman, Joseph	Pvt. 1cl.	Junction City, Kans. C Co. 3rd Kans. OS-MA.
Deason, Henry M.	Pvt. 1cl.	Junction City, Kans. C Co. 3rd Kans.
Draper, William H.	Pvt. 1cl.	Caro, Michigan. Repl.
Dean, Charles W.	Pvt. 1cl.	Carrol, Mich. Repl.
Deaton, Walter	Pvt. 1cl.	Higbee, Mo. C Co. 4th Mo. OS-MA-HE.
Dupree, Wallace	Pvt. 1cl.	Kirksville, Mo. C Co. 4th Mo. OS-MA-HE.
Ellzey, Wesley	Pvt. 1cl.	Junction City, Kans. C Co. 3rd Kans. OS-MA.

I COMPANY

Finney, Frank A.	Pvt. 1cl.	Junction City, Kans. C Co. 3rd Kans. OS-MA-HE.
Ford, Glee L.	Pvt. 1cl.	Emporia, Kans. Repl. OS-MA.
Ford, Lloyd E.	Pvt. 1cl.	Junction City, Kans. C Co. 3rd Kans. OS-MA-GSW.
Fisher, John R.	Pvt. 1cl.	Repl. MA.
Flatland, Andrew O.	Pvt. 1cl.	Repl. MA.
Folck, Lilburn T.	Pvt. 1cl.	Junction City, Kans. C Co. 3rd Kans. OS-MA-GSW.
Frerk, Edward	Pvt. 1cl.	Repl. MA.
Grear, Ora E.	Pvt. 1cl.	Kirksville, Mo. C Co. 4th Mo. OS-MA-HE.
Glenn, Arthur D.	Pvt. 1cl.	Junction City, Kans. C Co. 3rd Kans. OS-MA.
Gormley, Earl C.	Pvt. 1cl.	Junction City, Kans. C Co. 3rd Kans. Died at Camp Doniphan, Okla.
Gratton, William M.	Pvt. 1cl.	Junction City, Kans. C Co. 3rd Kans.
Garrard, Clyde A.	Pvt. 1cl.	Junction City, Kans. C Co. 3rd Kans. OS-MA-GSW.
Gardner, Lloyd	Pvt. 1cl.	Kirksville, Mo. C Co. 4th Mo. OS-MA.
Green, George	Pvt. 1cl.	Repl.
Hadden, William	Pvt. 1cl.	Junction City, Kans. C Co. 3rd Kans. OS-MA.
Horton, James L.	Pvt. 1cl.	Kirksville, Mo. C Co. 4th Mo. Trans. to supply Co. 139th Inf.
Hanes, Harry	Pvt. 1cl.	Millard, Mo. C Co. 4th Mo. OS-MA.
Hayes, Brice L.	Pvt. 1cl.	Kirksville, Mo. C Co. 4th Mo. OS-MA. Gass.
Hilt, Byrl J.	Pvt. 1cl.	Kirksville, Mo. C Co. 4th Mo. OS-MA. Comm. 1st Lt. 35th Division.
Hayes, Harlen W.	Pvt. 1cl.	Kirksville, Mo. C Co. 4th Mo. OS-MA.
Hultquist, Frederick L.	Pvt. 1cl.	Repl. MA.
Hartung, William H.	Pvt. 1cl.	Junction City, Kans. C Co. 3rd Kans. OS-MA.
Hines, William D.	Pvt. 1cl.	Junction City, Kans. C Co. 3rd Kans. OS-MA.
Holterman, Emil J.	Pvt. 1cl.	Junction City, Kans. C Co. 3rd Kans. OS-MA. Gassed.
Hein, Daniel	Pvt. 1cl.	Minot, N. D. Repl. MA.
Hagerty, James H.	Pvt. 1cl.	Detroit, Mich. Repl.
Harbin, Ernest C.	Pvt. 1cl.	Repl.
Kneer, Clare F.	Pvt. 1cl.	Junction City, Kans. C Co. 3rd Kans. OS-MA.
Kidd, James E.	Pvt. 1cl.	Kirksville, Mo. C Co. 4th Mo. Trans. at Ft. Sill, Okla.
Kazmucha, Andrew M.	Pvt. 1cl.	Chicago, Ill. Repl. MA.
Kissling, John	Pvt. 1cl.	Junction City, Kans. C Co. 3rd Kans. OS-MA.
Little, Lewis	Pvt. 1cl.	Kirksville, Mo. C Co. 4th Mo. OS-MA-HE.
Lindell, Lloyd	Pvt. 1cl.	Repl. MA.

Leach, Thomas	Pvt. 1cl.	Junction City, Kans. C Co. 3rd Kans. OS.
Lovgren, Harry M.	Pvt. 1cl.	Chicago, Ill. Repl. MA.
McIntyre, Harry A.	Pvt. 1cl.	Junction City, Kans. C Co. 3rd Kans. OS-MA.
Miller, Henry O.	Pvt. 1cl.	Junction City, Kans. C Co. 3rd Kans. OS-MA-GSW.
Montgomery, Earl	Pvt. 1cl.	Kirksville, Mo. C Co. 4th Mo. OS-MA-HE.
Nelson, Gerald	Pvt. 1cl.	Junction City, Kans. C Co. 3rd Kans. Trans. at Ft. Sill, Okla.
Nixon, Guy L.	Pvt. 1cl.	Junction City, Kans. C Co. 3rd Kans. OS-MA.
O'Meara, Charles J.	Pvt. 1cl.	Junction City, Kans. C Co. 3rd Kans. Trans. at Ft. Sill, Okla.
Phillips, Ora	Pvt. 1cl.	Kirksville, Mo. C Co. 4th Mo. OS-MA.
Palmer, Ewart G.	Pvt. 1cl.	Junction City, Kans. C Co. 3rd Kans. OS-MA.
Powers, Lewis	Pvt. 1cl.	Kalamazoo, Mich. Repl.
Peterson, Albert V.	Pvt. 1cl.	Junction City, Kans. C Co. 3rd Kans. OS-MA-GSW.
Rathert, Lewis R.	Pvt. 1cl.	Junction City, Kans. C Co. 3rd Kans. OS-MA.
Reynolds, George	Pvt. 1cl.	Laplata, Mo. C Co. 4th Mo. OS-MA. Killed in action.
Shumake, Gerald	Pvt. 1cl.	Kirksville, Mo. C Co. 4th Mo. OS-MA. Killed in action.
Saterlee, Fred	Pvt. 1cl.	Junction City, Kans. C Co. 3rd Kans. OS-MA-HE-GSW.
Schraag, Willie S.	Pvt. 1cl.	Junction City, Kans. C Co. 3rd Kans. Trans. at Ft. Sill, Okla.
Shafer, Andrew J.	Pvt. 1cl.	Junction City, Kans. C Co. 3rd Kans. OS-MA-HE.
Shipley, Harry	Pvt. 1cl.	Harrington, Kans. C Co. 3rd Kans. OS-MA.
Skaggs, Roy P.	Pvt. 1cl.	Kirksville, Mo. C Co. 4th Mo. OS-MA-GSW.
Sexton, Dixon	Pvt. 1cl.	Repl.
Thompson, Elmer	Pvt. 1cl.	Repl. MA.
Thompson, Betloff	Pvt. 1cl.	Repl. Killed in action.
Upham, Ralph	Pvt. 1cl.	Junction City, Kans. C Co. 3rd Kans. Trans. at Ft. Sill, Okla.
Vetsch, George	Pvt. 1cl.	Junction City, Kans. C Co. 3rd Kans. Trans. at Ft. Sill, Okla.
Weaver, Ben	Pvt. 1cl.	Kirksville, Mo. C Co. 4th Mo. OS-MA. Trans. ambulance Co. 35th Division.
Wyatt, John O.	Pvt. 1cl.	Green City, Mo. C Co. 4th Mo. OS-MA. Trans. to Hdq. Co. 139th Infantry.
White, Ralph P.	Pvt. 1cl.	Kirksville, Mo. C Co. 4th Mo. OS-MA.
Welbaum, Freddie O.	Pvt. 1cl.	Kirksville, Mo. C Co. 4th Mo. OS-MA-GSW.
Welzel, George C.	Pvt. 1cl.	Saginaw, Mich. Repl.
Whiteoak, Earl	Pvt. 1cl.	Repl. MA.
Young, Farron G.	Pvt. 1cl.	Kirksville, Mo. C Co. 4th Mo. OS-MA-HE.
Akers, James W.	Private	Mound City, Kans. Repl. OS-MA.

I COMPANY

Albertillia, Massimo Private Indiana, Penn. Repl.
Andrews, Ira Private Mason, Michigan. Repl.
Adams, Frank Private Kirksville, Mo. C Co. 4th Mo. Trans. at Ft. Sill, Okla.
Abbott, Avery Private Kirksville, Mo. C Co. 4th Mo. OS-MA.
Beldon, George Private Caro, Michigan. Repl.
Blong, William A. Private Gaylord, Michigan. Repl.
Baettcher, Earl F. Private Ortinville, Michigan. Repl. MA-HE.
Barth, Robert C. Private Leland, Michigan. Repl.
Bavin, Leo J. Private Hillsdale, Michigan. Repl.
Bowling, Worthy G. Private Kirksville, Mo. C Co. 4th Mo. OS-MA-HE.
Bostrom, William Private Repl. MA-HE.
Barnes, Newton Private Repl. MA-HE.
Bryson, Warren V. Private Repl. MA-HE.
Bassham, James C. Private Junction City, Kans. C Co. 3rd Kans. Trans. at Ft. Sill, Okla.
Brady, Raymond L. Private Junction City, Kans. C Co. 3rd Kans. Trans. at Ft. Sill, Okla.
Bookhout, Henry Private Kirksville, Mo. C Co. 4th Mo. OS. Trans. to SOS.
Clark, Howard C. Private Junction City, Kans. C Co. 3rd Kans. OS-MA. Gassed.
Chapman, William A. Private Kirksville, Mo. C Co. 4th Mo. OS-MA. Gassed.
Clancy, Michael Private Jackson, Michigan. Repl.
Cooley, Lloyd D. Private Adrian, Michigan. Repl.
Christensen, Thomas Private Repl. MA-GSW.
Cornell, Victor Private Watertown, Minn. Repl. Killed in action.
Caswell, Albert Private Kirksville, Mo. C Co. 4th Mo. OS. Trans. at Romsey, England.
Collins, Pat Private Junction City, Kans. C Co. 3rd Kans. Trans. at Ft. Sill, Okla.
Daines, James W. Private Kirksville, Mo. C Co. 4th Mo. OS-MA. Gassed.
Dixon, Edgar N. Private Watseka, Ill. Repl.
Duda, Antyony L. Private Badaxe, Michigan. Repl.
Duncan, Fresrick Private Badaxe, Michigan. Repl.
Darnell, Purl Private Kirksville, Mo. C Co. 4th Mo. OS-MA. Trans. to 110 Motor Supply Train.
England, Glen W. Private Kirksville, Mo. C Co. 4th Mo. Trans. at Ft. Sill, Okla.
Foster, Orrin L. Private Green City, Mo. C Co. 4th Mo. OS-MA-GSW.
Francis, Eugene Private Stewartsville, Mo. Repl. OS-MA-HE.
Froehlich, Harry F. Private Sheboygan, Michigan. Repl.
Flogsdad, Oscar Private Repl. MA-GSW.
Freise, Ferdinand Private Repl. MA. Gassed.
Gardner, Orvil Private Kirksville, Mo. C Co. 4th Mo. OS-MA.
Green, William H. Private Detroit, Michigan. Repl.
Garver, Joseph Private Monticello, Ill. Repl. MA-GSW.
Garhardt, Bern Private Repl. MA. Gassed.
Gatts, Chester A. Private Lancaster, Mo. C Co. 4th Mo. Died at Ft. Sill, Okla.

Hauber, Joseph M. Private St. Joseph, Mo. G Co. 4th Mo. OS-MA.
Herman, Henry Private Peoria, Ill. Repl.
Hotchkiss, Roy C. Private Pekin, Ill. Repl.
Humphreys, James F. Private Ozena, Texas. Repl.
Hugo, John Private Repl. MA-HE.
Hatfield, Marcus Private Connelsville, Mo. C Co. 4th Mo. OS-MA. Killed in action.
Insley, William E. Private Junction City, Kans. C Co. 3rd Kans. OS-MA-HE.
Jetton, Erwin H. Private Greenville, Texas. Repl.
Jewett, Leon E. Private Caro, Michigan. Repl.
Kendzierski, Anton Private Springvalley, Ill. Repl.
Krause, Joe Private Chicago, Ill. Repl.
Kondrochi, Frank E. Private Grand Rapids, Mich. Repl.
Kelley, Hubert Private Repl. MA-HE.
Klein, Nichlos Private Repl. MA. Gassed.
Knapp, Olaf Private Repl. MA-GSW.
Knudson, Servin Private Repl. MA-GSW.
Kipple, Ray G. Private Junction City, Kans. C Co. 3rd Kans. Trans. at Ft. Sill, Okla.
Lindow, Harry A. Private Sheboygan, Mich. Repl.
Leitritz, Elmer A. Private Spokane, Washington. Repl.
Luoma, John Private Gogebic County, Mich. Repl.
Larson, Nels R. Private Repl. MA-GSW.
Lowe, Robert Private Repl. MA-HE.
Lucak, Mike Private Repl. MA-HE.
Lucak, George Private Repl. MA-HE.
Lindell, Lindow Private Repl. MA. Gassed.
Lokken, John Private Repl. MA-HE.
Landers, Carl E. Private Kenmore, N. D. Repl. MA. Killed in action.
Makowski, John Private Milwaukee, Wis. Repl.
Menke, George Private Lancaster, Wis. Repl.
Michna, Adolph Private Wichita Falls, Texas. Repl.
Motal, Frank Private Halltesville, Texas. Repl.
Melland, Edward Private Marquette, Mich. Repl.
Messmore, James T. Private Flint, Mich. Repl.
Mix, Leroy Private Monroe, Mich. Repl.
Marlatt, Esel Private Repl. MA. Gassed.
Morris, Earnest Private Repl. MA-HE.
McNalley, George Private Repl. MA. Gassed.
Midgarden, Gulbrand Private Repl. MA. Gassed.
Marcy, Fred Private Junction City, Kans. C Co. 3rd Kans. OS-MA. Killed in action.
Momonie, Tony Private Repl. MA. Killed in action.
Marshell, Clore Private Repl. MA.
McDowell, Tomy Private Kirksville, Mo. C Co. 4th Mo. Trans. at Ft. Sill, Okla.
Nelson, Carl A. Private Peoria, Ill. Repl.
Nillsen, William R. Private Repl. MA-HE.
Nichol, Harry Private Kahoka, Mo. C Co. 4th Mo. OS-MA. Killed in action.
Nunn, Roy Private Junction City, Kans. C Co. 3rd Kans. Deserted at Camp Doniphan, Okla.

I COMPANY

Otnes, John	Private	Junction City, Kans. C Co. 3rd Kans. OS-MA.
Oland, John	Private	Repl. MA-HE.
Olsen, Emil G.	Private	Repl. MA-HE.
Paske, Walter F.	Private	Sheboygan, Wis. Repl.
Parcell, Wayne	Private	Nevada, Mo. C Co. 4th Mo. Trans. at Ft. Sill, Okla.
Putman, Alvin W.	Private	Junction City, Kans. C Co. 3rd Kans. Trans. at Ft. Sill, Okla.
Radloff, Charles J.	Private	Waukesha, Wis. Repl.
Reidhenbach, Carl	Private	Allegan, Mich. Repl.
Reed, Charles	Private	Repl. MA-GSW.
Reilly, John J.	Private	Junction City, Kans. C Co. 3rd Kans. Trans. at Ft. Sill, Okla.
Strayer, Bertie A.	Private	Ft. Collins, Colorado. Repl.
Saaman, Cornelious	Private	Sheboygan, Wis. Repl.
Saccone, Anyhony J.	Private	Cook County, Ill. Repl.
Saunders, William R.	Private	Chicago, Ill. Repl.
Smith, Willard N.	Private	Ottowa, Ill. Repl.
Szemanis, Jonas	Private	Eagle River, Wis. Repl.
Shinafelt, O. K.	Private	Kirksville, Mo. C Co. 4th Mo. OS-MA.
Stordlem, Oscar J.	Private	Williston, N. D. Repl.
Smith, Charles L.	Private	Junction City, Kans. C Co. 3rd Kans. Trans. at Ft. Sill, Okla.
Sanford, Millard W.	Private	Sentre, Ala. Repl.
Shelton, Erwin	Private	Kirksville, Mo. C Co. 4th Mo. OS-MA.
Shirley, Ferda	Private	Rosscommon, Mich. Repl.
Spriggs, Ray	Private	Kirksville, Mo. C Co. 4th Mo. Trans. at Ft. Sill, Okla.
Smith, Frank	Private	Waukeshem, Michigan. Repl.
Styles, Harold D.	Private	Kirksville, Mo. C Co. 4th Mo. Trans. to Base Hospital.
Sweet, Paul	Private	Haughton, Mich. Repl.
Sutton, Earnest	Private	Pure air, Mo. C Co. 4th Mo. Discharged at Ft. Sill, Okla.
Smith, Oscar B.	Private	Grayling, Mich. Repl.
Salsbery, David	Private	Novinger, Mo. C Co. 4th Mo. OS-MA.
Schultz, Walter	Private	Junction City, Kans. C Co. 3rd Kans. OS-MA-HE.
Scott, Walter	Private	Junction City, Kans. C Co. 3rd Kans. Trans. at Ft. Sill, Okla.
Shaffer, Samuel	Private	Repl. MA-HE.
Shaner, William	Private	Junction City, Kans. C Co. 3rd Kans. OS-MA.
Steinbruick, Adolph	Private	Junction City, Kans. C Co. 3rd Kans. OS-MA-HE.
Sass, William	Private	Repl. MA-HE.
Schilling, Otto	Private	Repl. MA. Killed in action.
Stephens, Norman R.	Private	Junction City, Kans. C Co. 3rd Kans. OS-MA. Gassed.
Snyder, Otto	Private	Repl. MA-HE-GSW.
Supernant, Carl	Private	Junction City, Kans. C Co. 3rd Kans. OS-MA. Killed in action.
Talbott, Aubert	Private	Kirksville, Mo. C Co. 4th Mo. OS-MA.
Treacy, Philip	Private	Chicago, Ill. Repl.
Talbott, Hubert	Private	Kirksville, Mo. C Co. 4th Mo. Discharged at Ft. Sill, Okla.
Thomas, Cornelius C.	Private	Burlington, Iowa. Repl.
Tibbling, Victor M.	Private	St. Paul, Minn. Repl. MA-GSW.
Thompson, Edgar	Private	Kirksville, Mo. C Co. 4th Mo. OS. Killed in action.
Taylor, Clifford	Private	Repl. MA-GSW.
Trssin, Morgan	Private	Junction City, Kans. C Co. 3rd Kans. OS. Trans. at Romsey, England.
Veltkamp, Berand	Private	Lenton, N. D. Repl.
Vandermeer, Albert	Private	Repl. MA. Killed in action.
Vetsch, Charles	Private	Junction City, Kans. C Co. 3rd Kans. Trans. at Ft. Sill, Okla.
White, Floyd	Private	Junction City, Kans. C Co. 3rd Kans. OS-MA.
Wigent, Ross C.	Private	Whitefish Point, Mich. Repl.
Ware, George E.	Private	Junction City, Kans. C Co. 3rd Kans. Trans. at Ft. Sill, Okla.
Winn, William C.	Private	Junction City, Kans. C Co. 3rd Kans. OS-MA-HE.
Wold, Peter	Private	Repl. MA-HE.
Wunnenburg, Hubert	Private	Repl. MA-HE.
Wrakestraw, George A.	Private	Junction City, Kans. C Co. 3rd Kans. Trans. at Ft. Sill, Okla.
Whitley, Frank	Private	Junction City, Kans. C Co. 3rd Kans. OS-MA-GSW.
Whalen, Charley	Private	Repl. MA-HE.
Whitmore, Arthur F.	Private	Parma, Mich. Repl.
Zimmerman, Ora	Private	Kirksville, Mo. C Co. 4th Mo. Discharged at Ft. Sill, Okla.

I COMPANY

ROSTER OF COMPANY D, 139th INFANTRY

NAME AND RANK	EMERGENCY ADDRESS
William C. Williamson Captain	Mrs. Grace Williamson, wife, Trenton, Mo.
Charles E. Munn 1st Lt.	Mrs. C. E. Munn, wife, Mound City, Mo.
Jesse H. Wilson 1st Lt.	Mrs. Frances Wilson, wife, Caney, Kans.
Homer B. Loman 1st Lt.	Mrs. H. B. Loman, wife, 1611 E. 9th St., Trenton, Mo.
Guy Hobgood 2nd Lt.	Mrs. Guy Hobgood, wife, Landers, Wyo. a-c W. P. Haines.
Lawrence O'Kelley 2nd Lt.	C. W. O'Kelley, father, 1006 E. 6th St., Pueblo, Colo.
McArtor, Paul 1st Sgt.	Mr. Ervin Dunlap, uncle, 804 E. 17th St., Trenton, Mo.
Rinehart, Stephen R. Mess Sgt.	Mr. Stephen Rinehart, father, Caney, Kans.
Grider, Roy N. Supply Sgt.	Mr. Robert E. Grider, father, Toronto, Kans.
Witten, James M. Sergeant	Mr. Tom M. Witten, father, Trenton, Mo.
Axtell, Dale Sergeant	Mr. C. D. Axtell, father, Trenton, Mo.
Mitchell, Lesley H. Sergeant	Mrs. Mary E. Mitchell, mother, 1215 W. Howard St., Caney, Kans.
Taylor, Benjamin Sergeant	Mrs. Myrtle M. Taylor, mother, 716 N. 17th St., Independence, Kans.
Belscamper, Floyd W. Sergeant	Mr. Sylvester E. Belscamper, father, La Fountaine, Kans.
Ogram, Hoyt R. Sergeant	Mr. R. D. Ogram, father, 324 Sheridan Ave., Whiting, Ind.
Bradley, Charles H. Sergeant	Mr. James T. Bradley, father, National Bank of Commerce, Kansas City, Mo.
Davis, Ralph A. Sergeant	Mrs. M. H. Davis, mother, Green City, Mo.
Millett, Samuel Sergeant	Mrs. H. L. Hersberger, mother, 1433 Lulu St., Trenton, Mo.
Moss, Wilbur D. Sergeant	Mrs. Wilbur D. Moss, wife, Trenton, Mo.
Evans, Ferrol E. Sergeant	Mr. Robert M. Evans, father, Trenton, Mo.
Crain, Frank Sergeant	Mr. Ernest Crain, father, Trenton, Mo.
Wise, Zina L. Corporal	I. O. O. F. Lodge No. 669, Tindall, Mo.
Mapes, William M. Corporal	Mr. George E. Mapes, father, Trenton, Mo.
Hemmingway, William B. Corporal	Mr. Emmett Hemmingway, father, 1425 Norton Ave., Trenton, Mo.
Bofman, James E. Corporal	Mr. George W. Bofman, father, RR No. 3, Trenton, Mo.

NAME AND RANK	EMERGENCY ADDRESS
McLaughlin, Floyd F. Corporal	Mrs. Lula Bell McLaughlin, mother, Trenton, Mo.
Tittsworth, Lemuel M. Corporal	Mr. William S. Tittsworth, father, Tindall, Mo.
Ingersoll, Hulett P. Corporal	Mrs. Fannie E. Ingersoll, mother, Gallatin, Mo.
Crandall, Clarence L. Corporal	Dr. Charles T. Crandall, father, Peru, Kans.
Nance, Ward D. Corporal	Mrs. A. D. Nance, mother, Niotaze, Kans.
Rogers, Charles A. Corporal	Mr. W. E. Rogers, father, Caney, Kans.
Leatherock, Wesley K. Corporal	Mrs. Rilla Leatherock, mother, Cherryvale, Kans.
Bowen, Chester J. Corporal	Mr. Charles C. Bowen, father, Caney, Kans.
Pettibon, Edgar H. Corporal	Rev. Washington M. Pettibon, father, 137 Robard St., Brookfield, Mo.
Walton, Edward Corporal	Mrs. Nellie Walton, mother, Trenton, Mo.
Belscamper, Earl B. Corporal	Mr. Sylvester E. Belscamper, father, La Fountaine, Kans.
Coate, Frank D. Corporal	Mrs. Emily C. Coate, mother, Trinity, Tex.
Husted, Earl H. Corporal	Mrs. Sarah Husted, mother, 1811 Baltimore St., Trenton, Mo.
Brown, Ernest B. Corporal	Mrs. Sidney M. Brown, mother, R R 1, Caney, Kans.
Gullic, Jesse Corporal	Mrs. Alonzo Gullic, mother, Koshkonong, Mo.
Miller, Frank O. Corporal	Albert L. Milan, step-father, Box 488, Drumright, Okla.
Tomlinson, Jo C. Corporal	Lena E. Proctor, cousin, 1203 Main St., Trenton, Mo.
Burrill, Forrest C. Corporal	Mr. Fred D. Burrill, father, 1000 W 13th St., Trenton, Mo.
Nelson, John E. Corporal	Mr. Nels Nelson, father, Trenton, Mo.
Reynolds, Ernest E. Corporal	Mrs. Sarah A. Reynolds, mother, Cedarvale, Kans.
Webster, Alva E. Corporal	Mr. William A. Webster, father, 510 E 10th St., Trenton, Mo.
Jones, William J. Corporal	Mr. Henry D. Jones, father, Tyro, Kans.
Miller, Claude E. Corporal	Mrs. Lena Miller, mother, 404 Monroe St., Trenton, Mo.
Craig, Lloyd Corporal	Mr. Sherman Craig, father, 1333 Shanklin Ave., Trenton, Mo.
Witten, Ralph Corporal	Mr. Dave Witten, father, RR 8, Trenton, Mo.
Fox, Homer D. Corporal	Mrs. Etta Fox, mother, RR 1, Vann, Penn.

I COMPANY

Smith, Robert H. Corporal — Mrs. Minnie Smith, mother, Prior, Mo.

Branson, William E. Mechanic — James Kieth, brother-in-law, 1716 Lulu St., Trenton. Mo.

Snyder, James R. Mechanic — Mr. Ben Snyder, father, Princeton, Mo.

Butler, Fred Mechanic — James E. Butler, father, Laredo, Mo.

Lucas, Homer D. Mechanic — William E. Lucas, father, 1200 Harris Ave., Trenton, Mo.

Payne, Robert H. Cook — Mr. Edward Payne, father, Princeton, Mo.

Prall, Joseph N. Cook — Mrs. Etta R. Jones, mother, Sterling, Kans.

Schweppe, Edward L. Cook — Mr. F. L. Schweppe, father, Regan, Mo.

McCoy, Martin G. Cook — Mr. Jim C. McCoy, father, 194 Main St., Trenton, Mo.

Sperry, Clifford F. Bugler — Mr. Lewis Brown, grandfather, 909 Avalon St., Trenton, Mo.

Kirk, Norman Bugler — Mrs. Martha Kirk, mother, Trenton, Mo.

Allen, Dewey W. Pvt. 1cl. — Mr. O. N. Allen, father, Havana, Kans.

Bland, Arthur Pvt. 1cl. — Mr. Albert E. Bland, father, Larve, Ark.

Boles, Edward J. Pvt. 1cl. — Mrs. Dora Boles, mother, Koshkonong, Mo.

Booker, Harry C. Pvt. 1cl. — Mrs. Elizabeth Booker, mother, Caney, Kans.

Boon, Audry D. Pvt. 1cl. — Mr. Gus Boon, father, Hickory, Mo.

Bowen, Charles R. Pvt. 1cl. — Mr. Charles C. Bowen, father, Caney, Kans.

Brewster, Willard O. Pvt. 1cl. — Mrs. Anny S. Glen, mother, Sedan, Kans.

Bridges, Hubert C. Pvt. 1cl. — Arthur M. Bridges, father, Laredo, Mo.

Burns, Monroe C. Pvt. 1cl. — Mr. L. A. Burns, father, Lelia, Mo.

Buster, Roy F. Pvt. 1cl. — Mr. John I. Buster, father, Tyro, Kans.

Carson, John L. Pvt. 1cl. — Mr. James T. Carson, uncle, Caney, Kans.

Collins, Alva R. Pvt. 1cl. — Mr. Elerado L. Collins, father, Trenton, Kans.

Corbitt, Joseph W. Pvt. 1cl. — Mrs. James W. Ostrander, mother, 203 5th St., Cherryvale, Kans.

Cottom, Ira L. Pvt. 1cl. — Mr. Henry R. Cottom, father, Cherryvale, Kans.

Cottrell, Harry L. Pvt. 1cl. — Mr. William Cottrell, father, Princeton, Mo.

Cram, Harry H. Pvt. 1cl. — Mrs. Fannie H. Cram, mother, Trenton, Mo.

Culver, James E. Pvt. 1cl. — Mr. Henry Culver, father, Gallatin, Mo.

Darnaby, Harold M. Pvt. 1cl. — Mrs. Adolph Pharis, sister, 201 W. 11th St., Trenton, Mo.

Day, Vane S. Pvt. 1cl. — Mrs. Vane S. Day, wife, 511 E. 9th St., Trenton, Mo.

Dragoo, Leonard R. Pvt. 1cl. — Mr. Ed Dragoo, father, R R 1, Princeton, Mo.

Drybread, McKinley Pvt. 1cl. — Mr. John T. Drybread, father, 531 S. 3rd St., Independence, Kans.

Dunn, Wilbur E. Pvt. 1cl. — Mr. George H. Dunn, father, 2112 Lulu St., Trenton, Mo.

Edmundson, Morrill H. Pvt. 1cl. — Mr. Hudson Edmundson, brother, Caney, Kans.

Ellington, Earl J. Pvt. 1cl. — Mrs. Emity Ellington, mother, 1218 Franklin Ave., Trenton, Mo.

Evans, Joe O. Pvt. 1cl. — Mr. Jim Evans, father, 203 S. 5th St., Fredonia, Kans.

Foster, Roy Pvt. 1cl. — Mr. George W. Whorton, friend, Gumlog, Ark.

Franklin, Roy E. Pvt. 1cl. — Mr. William M. Franklin, father, Natural Dam, Ark.

George, Hubert H. Pvt. 1cl. — Mr. Albert George, father, 2101 Lulu St. Trenton, Mo.

Gillen, Glen C. Pvt. 1cl. — Mrs. Elizah C. Gillen, mother, RR 7, Independence, Kans.

Harrelson, Clarence Pvt. 1cl. — Mr. Lee Harrelson, father, Milan, Mo.

House, Roy F. Pvt. 1cl. — Mr. Frank House, father, RR 1, Hickory, Mo.

Koons, Frank W. Pvt. 1cl. — Mr. Emanuel Koons, father, RR 1, Wann, Okla.

Kunz, Lawrence W. Pvt. 1cl. — Mrs. Lena Kunz, mother, Cherryvale, Kans.

Lage, James Pvt. 1cl. — Mrs. Fred Lage, mother, Gladbrook, Iowa.

Lindquist, Svante J. Pvt. 1cl. — Mr. Bendard Lindquist, father, RR 1, Hiteman, Ia.

McCoy, Floyd G. Pvt. 1cl. — Mr. Jim C. McCoy, father, 194 Main St., Trenton, Mo.

McAfee, William A. Pvt. 1cl. — Mr. E. L. McAfee, father, Sedan, Kans.

McClelland, George W. Pvt. 1cl. — Mrs. F. T. Wilkin, sister, 408 Westminster Ave., Independence, Ks.

McGhee, Clarence O. Pvt. 1cl. — Mrs. Sam M. McGhee, mother, Tyro, Kans.

Nelson, Sidney T. Pvt. 1cl. — Frank T. Nelson, father, Tagus, N. D.

Powell, John J. Pvt. 1cl. — Mrs. John Powell, mother, Elgin, Kans.

Raymond, Roy B. Pvt. 1cl. — Mr. David B. Raymond, father, Mullenville, Kans.

Rooks, Glen Pvt. 1cl. — Mr. Ezekiel G. Rooks, father, Laredo, Mo.

Ross, William W. Pvt. 1cl. — James M. Ross, father, Walnut, Kans.

Ryan, Floyd Pvt. 1cl. — Mr. C. K. Ryan, father, Angalo, Kans.

Sandlin, Cleo L. Pvt. 1cl. — Mrs. Emma Sandlin, mother, Millgrove, Mo.

Simpson, Robert E. Pvt. 1cl. — Mr. Robert A. Simpson, father, 805 Harris Ave., Trenton, Mo.

Snyder, William H. Pvt. 1cl. — Mrs. Bert Ellis, sister, RR 1, Trenton, Mo.

Stevenson, Herbert L. Pvt. 1cl. — Mr. James W. Stevenson, father, RR 7, Trenton, Mo.

Straight, Albert E. Pvt. 1cl. — Mr. John F. Straight, father, Sedan, Kans.

THEY TRAINED THE REGIMENT

Brig. Gen. Harvey C. Clark

Col. John D. McNeely

Brig. Gen. Charles I. Martin

K COMPANY

Summers, Servly S. Pvt. 1cl.   Mr. William A. Summers, father, Caney, Kans.

Taylor, Earl   Pvt. 1cl.   Mr. W. G. Taylor, father, 1504 Kensington Ave., Kansas City, Mo.

Thickstun, Lovell J.   Pvt. 1cl.   Mr. H. O. Thickstun, father, Spickard, Mo.

Thompson, Jesse E. Pvt. 1cl.   Mr. John F. Thompson, father, Sharpsburg, O.

Thrasher, Sibert A. Pvt. 1cl.   Mrs. Rosalie Thrasher, mother, Sedan, Kans.

Tittsworth, James J.   Pvt. 1cl.   Mrs. Margaret Tittsworth, mother, Tindall, Mo.

Trimble, Chester F. Pvt. 1cl.   Mrs. Armina Trimble, mother, Caney, Kans.

Veerkamp, Franz L.   Pvt. 1cl.   Mrs. Franz L. Veerkamp, wife, 408 E. Hickory St., Neosho, Mo.

Whorton, Cleo   Pvt. 1cl.   John C. Whorton, father, Hickory, Mo.

Wilson, Homer C. Pvt. 1cl.   Mr. W. R. Wilson, father, Caney, Kans.

Berg, Hans C.   Private   Mrs. Petra Fossum, sister, 3641 39th Ave. S., Minneapolis, Minn.

Black, Roy C. C.   Private   Elza Black, father, Stuartsville, Mo.

Bonnes, Olaf E.   Private   Mrs. Lars Bonnes, mother, Hendricks, Minn.

Booher, Charles T. Private   Mr. Jim Booher, father, Trenton, Mo.

Borg, Glenn F.   Private   Mr. Martin Borg, father, RR 5, Parkers Prairie, Minn.

Brandt, Oscar   Private   Mr. Anton Brandt, father, RR 3, Argyle, Minn.

Brandt, Martin   Private   Mrs. Martin Brandt, mother, Malvinia, Ia.

Brandt, Carroll J.   Private   John Brandt, father, Nye, Wis.

Brown, Clarence I. Private   Mrs. David Brown, mother, Caney, Kans.

Burlingame, Alton W.   Private   Mr. Albert Burlingame, father, Kenmore, N. D.

Callaway, Craven S. Private   Mr. Richard K. Callaway, father, 720 Arnold Ave., Thief River Fall, Minn.

Campbell, Earl W. Private   Mrs. Hannah Campbell, mother, Ponca, Nebr.

Cochran, Arden C. Private   William A. Cochran, father, Blue Grass, N. D.

Cochrane, William M.   Private   Mrs. Ed Cochrane, mother, Caney, Kans.

Cover, Joseph   Private   Mrs. C. A. Batham, mother, 2224 Cedar Ave. S., Minneapolis, Minn.

Cooley, Harry S.   Private   Mrs. Dora Cooley, mother, Maquoketa, Ia.

Cox, William P.   Private   Mrs. M. E. Carr, mother, Wichita, Kans.

Crepps, Glen M.   Private   Mr. J. W. Crepps, father, Sedan, Kans.

Davidson, Martin   Private   Mr. Alex Davidson, father, 956 Forest St., St. Paul, Minn.

Dennis, Henry D.   Private   Mrs. Anna Dennis, mother, Richville, Mo.

Dumond, Albert W.   Private   Mrs. Mary Dumond, mother, RR 2, Minot, N. D.

Dummer, Theodore   Private   Herman Dummer, father, New Germany, Minn.

Egermeier, Arbor J. Private   Mrs. J. C. Egermeier, mother, RR 7, Oklahoma City, Okla.

Elk, John   Private   Mr. Jerome Elk, father, Cannonball, N. D.

Fields, Charles W.   Private   Mrs. C. F. Ruettel, sister, a-c Ruettell Clo. Co., St. Cloud, Minn.

Fields, Frank L.   Private   Mr. John C. Fields, father, RR 1, Tyro, Kans.

Franklin, William J. Private   Chester Franklin, father, RR 2, Princeton, Mo.

Garrison, Ralph H.   Private   William E. Garrison, father, Barnesville, Minn.

Garvey, John J.   Private   Mrs. E. J. Hagen, mother, Main St., Williston, N. D.

Gillett, Orrie A.   Private   Mrs. M. Gillett, mother, 808 4th St. SE., Minneapolis, Minn.

Gray, William G.   Private   Mrs. Mary Williams, sister, Sardis, Miss.

Graybull, Thomas   Private   Charles Graybull, father, Cannonball, N. D.

Griggs, Floyd E.   Private   Miss Ida Marie Griggs, sister, Albion, Ia.

Grimsley, Henry D. Private   Mrs. Safronia Grimsley, mother, Bonaparte, Ia.

Griffin, Delbert   Private   Mr. Charles Griffin, father, RR 2, Spickard, Mo.

Hall, William H.   Private   Mrs. Edith Hall, mother, 501 Grundy St., Trenton, Mo.

Hagen, Ole H.   Private   Mr. Liguard Hagen, father, RR 1, Jackson, Minn.

Hanson, Chester   Private   Carl Hanson, father, New Golden, Minn.

Hanson, Henry A.   Private   Mr. Andrew Hanson, father, 4224 30th Ave. S., Minneapolis, Minn.

Hardman, Ralph W. Private   Mrs. Frank W. Hardman, mother, Caney, Kans.

Harp, Clyde E.   Private   Mrs. Ida M. Bright, mother, RR 1, Niotaze, Kans.

Hemphill, Loyd   Private   Mrs. J. T. Hemphill, mother, Caney, Kans.

Hicks, Ralph E.   Private   Mrs. Mabel Hicks, mother, Park St., Hamburg, Ia.

Hofstad, Louis A.   Private   Mr. Alfred Hofstad, father, Madison, Minn.

Hustad, Peter   Private   Mr. Erick Hustad, father, Minot, N. D.

Karlen, Ernest F.   Private   Mr. Alfred Karlen, father, 147 Iglehart Ave., St. Paul, Minn.

Kunz, George   Private   Mr. Fred Kunz, father, Judson, N. D.

Killion, Fred   Private   Mr. Jim Killion, father, Houston, Mo.

Koppel, Joseph L.   Private   Mr. Joseph Koppel, father, Waverly, Minn.

Kneeland, Earl   Private   Mr. H. E. Kneeland, father, RR 1, Medina, N. D.

K COMPANY

Larson, Ludvig	Private	Mr. L. J. Larson, father, RR 4, Waukon, Ia.
Loftus, Thomas	Private	Mr. S. T. Loftus, father, Banks, N. D.
Mason, Otis A.	Private	Mrs. Johanna Mason, mother, 1115 Summit Ave., Hancock, Mich.
Mackley, Guy E.	Private	Mr. Claude Mackley, father, Trenton, Mo.
Maiden, George A.	Private	Mrs. Ada Maiden, mother, Stafford, Kans.
Marek, George	Private	Mrs. Anna Marek, mother, 919 N. Elm St., Owatonna, Minn.
Medlen, Charley A.	Private	William A. Medlen, father, Copan, Okla.
McConachie, Theodore	Private	Mr. Nathaniel McConachie, father, RR 4, Perham, Minn.
McKinley, Roy R.	Private	Mrs. B. McKinley, mother, Homer, Neb.
Midstokke, Einar P.	Private	Einar Midstokke, father, RR 1, Arnegard, N. D.
Mil, William J.	Private	John Peter Mil, father, 912 W. 49th St., Seattle, Wash.
Mikkelson, Harry	Private	Mrs. Lena Mikkelson, mother, South Park, Minn.
Miller, Edward	Private	Mrs. Magdalena Miller, mother, W. Summit St., Monroe, Wis.
Miller, Curtis W.	Private	Mrs. Anna Miller, mother, 404 Monroe St., Trenton, Mo.
Millett, George	Private	Mrs. H. L. Hershberger, mother, 1433 Lulu St., Trenton, Mo.
Minota, Thomas	Private	Mr. Raymond Golebricky, friend, Depue, Ill.
Miller, Milton R.	Private	Mr. C. M. Miller, father, Trenton, Mo.
Morehouse, Harry	Private	Leslie Morehouse, father, Sanish, N. D.
Mulville, Joe	Private	Mrs. Mary Mulville, mother, Darwin, Minn.
Murphy, James C.	Private	Mrs. Frances P. Murphy, mother, Shields, N. D.
Nelson, Nels U.	Private	R. N. Jorgenson, friend, RR 1, Kenmore, N. D.
Norris, Walter D.	Private	J. W. Norris, father, RR 2, Havana, Kans.
O'Neil, Emmett	Private	Mrs. W. L. Lussenhop, friend, Morton, Minn.
Olson, Paul	Private	Mr. Hans Olson, father, Ringebu, Norway.
O'Donohue, John	Private	Coley Mullen, friend, 413 W. 3rd St., Anaconda, Mont.
Olson, George C.	Private	Mrs. Anna Nelson, mother, 2626 S. Bloomington Ave., Minneapolis, Minn.
Ostrander, Cecil H.	Private	Mrs. John W. Ostrander, stepmother, 304 W. Clark St., Cherryvale, Kans.
Parsons, Charles C.	Private	Mrs. C. W. Parsons, mother, 808 N. 6th St., Fredonia, Kans.
Pearson, Edmund W.	Private	Mr. Aron Grant, friend, RR 2, Braham, Minn.
Pettegrew, John R.	Private	Mrs. John R. Pettegrew, mother, 1611 9th St. Trenton, Mo.
Prosser, Albert N.	Private	Mrs. Anna Gusta Prosser, mother, 653 Fox St., Denver, Colo.
Robertson, Martin E.	Private	Mr. W. L. Robertson, brother, Caney, Kans.
Rodness, Martin	Private	Hans P. Rodness, father, Clarkefield, Minn.
Rupprecht, Bert A.	Private	Mr. George T. Rupprecht, father, 813 S. 3rd St., North Yakima, Wash.
Sanerud, Christian G.	Private	Mr. Alfred Anderson, friend, Hazel Run, Minn.
Savelkoul, Harry C.	Private	Mrs. Elizabeth Savelkoul, mother, Chaska, Minn.
Shafer, William F.	Private	Mr. Augusta Shafer, friend, RR 3, Postville, Ia.
Shane, James C.	Private	Mrs. Sarah Shane, mother, Caney, Kans.
Shelton, Frank M.	Private	Mrs. W. H. Shelton, mother, Trenton, Mo.
Snyder, Clarence	Private	Mr. C. W. Snyder, father, Trenton, Mo.
Stewart, James W.	Private	Mrs. Bertha Stewart, mother, Niotaze, Kans.
Steele, Jefferson H.	Private	Mr. Millard Steele, father, Trenton, Mo.
Steindel, Mat	Private	Mr. Joseph Steindel, father, Philbrook, Minn.
Storms, Everett E.	Private	Mrs. Mary E. Storms, mother, Pleasant Hill, Mo.
Storm, Leonard	Private	Mr. Otto Storm, father, Hartley, Iowa.
Streed, Daniel	Private	Mr. Carl Streed, father, Grandy, Minn. RR 2.
Stowers, Walter C.	Private	Mr. J. C. Stowers, father, Felton, Minn.
Stringer, Clyde L.	Private	Mrs. Ida Stringer, mother, Trenton, Mo.
Sundvall, Carl W.	Private	Mr. C. O. Sundvall, friend, 2813 Grand Ave. S., Minneapolis, Minn.
Swiger, Fred O.	Private	Mrs. Ida Swiger, mother, 620 E. 9th St., Cherryvale, Kans.
Trowbridge, Archie S.	Private	Horace S. Trowbridge, father, RR 3, Wellestown, N. D.
Vane, John H.	Private	Mrs. Mary Vane, mother, 1009 10th St. W., Cedar Rapids, Ia.
Woken, Peder L.	Private	Paul Woken, father, North Wood, N. D.
Waller, Alfred J.	Private	Mr. John Waller, father, Wegdall, Minn.
Ward, Charles H.	Private	Mr. Charley Ward, father, Monett, Kans.
Wheeler, Fred	Private	Mrs. Bears Arm, mother, Ellwood, N. D.
Whelan, Edward P.	Private	Mrs. Anna Hewitt, sister, 423 Tompkins, Syracuse, N. Y.
Webb, Henry C.	Private	Mr. Charles Owen, uncle, Caney, Kans.

K COMPANY

Welker, Carl M.   Private   Mort Welker, father, Bowman, N. D.

Westby, John   Private   Mr. Ole Bgornstead, friend, Couby, Minn.

Wenstrom, John J.   Private   William Wenstrom, father, 1219 W. Olive St.,

Western, Charles W.   Private   Mrs. Emmie Western, mother, Fountain City, Tenn.

Wujek, Martin F.   Private   Thomas Wujek, father, RR 23, La-Salle, Ill.

Zamor, Felix   Private   Mrs. Frances Zamor, mother, New Brighton, Minn.

Schulte, Henry A.   Private   Anton Schulte, father, 471 Rice St. St. Paul, Minn.

Hanson, Charles O.   Private   Mr. William Modendricker, friend, RR 34, Peoria, Ill.

Johnson, Albert   Private   Laurtz Larson, friend, RR 1, Vining, Minn.

Williams, Hiram M.   Private   Louis J. Williams, father, Sedan, Kans.

Rottke, Edward A.   Private   Wm. Rottke, father, RFD 5, bx 3, Waseca, Minn.

K COMPANY

ROSTER OF COMPANY E, 139th INFANTRY

NAME AND RANK	HOME ADDRESS AND REMARKS	NAME AND RANK	HOME ADDRESS AND REMARKS
George E. Klinkerfuss Captain	Overland, Mo., Box 180a. OS-St.M-MA. Pres.	Smith, Otto C. Sergeant	120 E. 8th St., Abilene. Kansas. OS. Trfd. Ser. US Aug. 19/19.
Charles H. Browne Captain	Horton, Kans. OS. Tr. service in U. S. Aug. 1918.	Lake, Stephen Sergeant	4418 Station Ave., Cincinnati, Ohio. OS-St.M-MA. Killed in action, Sept. 26 to Oct. 1/18.
Herbert C. Smith 1st Lt.	Detroit, Mich. Pres.	Coleman, Don. P. Sergeant	611 6th St., Leavenworth, Kansas. OS-St.M-MA-W-S. Trfd. to B. Hosp. October, 1918.
James B. Martin 1st Lt.	Hamilton Club, Chicago, Ill. Pres.	Douglas, William J. Sergeant	R.F.D. No. 6, Leavenworth, Kansas. OS-St.M-MA-W-S. Trfd. to B. Hosp. Oct. 1918.
Paul C. Radford 1st Lt.	Leavenworth, Kans. OS-St.M-MA-G. tr. 5th Div. Jan. 1919.	Piper, Clifford Sergeant	1921 Broadway St., Hannibal, Mo. OS-St.M-MA-W-S. Trfd. to B. Hosp. Oct., 1918.
Wm. H. McDonald 1st Lt.	Barry, Ill. OS. tr. to U. S. Aug. 1919.	Cochran, Walter H. Sergeant	R.F.D. No. Jarbalo, Kansas. OS-St.M-MA-WS. Trfd. to B. Hosp. Oct., 1918.
Wm. J. Oakes 1st Lt.	Columbia, Tenn. St.M-MA. tr. to Field and Staff.	Dodd, Ray E. Sergeant	Esbon, Kansas. OS-St.M-MA. Pres.
Alvin G. Steier 2nd Lt.	Union Hill, New Jersey, Pres.	Sloan, Jesse P. Sergeant	Roff, Okla. Pres.
Clarence B. Connell 2nd Lt.	Detroit, Minn. Pres.	Branstetter, Jean O. Corporal	509 N. 4th St., Hannibal, Mo. OS-St.M-MA. Pres.
Joseph M. Darst 2nd Lt.	St. Louis, Mo. OS. tr. to U. S. Aug. 1918.	Paulus, Lester W. Corporal	717 Union St., Hannibal, Mo. OS-St.M-MA. Pres.
James Bray 2nd Lt.	St. Louis, Mo. OS. tr. to U. S. July 1918.	Harding, Geo. E. Corporal	231 Walnut St., Leavenworth, Kan. OS-St.M-MA. Pres.
Welker, Glenn D. 1st Sgt.	Shelbina, Mo. OS-St.M-MA. Pres.	Sparks, Lee Corporal	1109 Lyon St., Hannibal, Mo. OS-St.M-MA. Pres.
Radloff, Henry W. 1st Sgt.	607 Osage St., Leavenworth, Kans. OS-St.M-MA.	Perkins, William H. Corporal	1313 S. Broadway, Leavenworth, Kan. OS-St.M-MA. Pres.
Kelsey, Harry R. 1st Sgt.	Easton, Kan. OS-St.M-MA. Killed in action Sept. 27, 1919.	Winner, Jesse B. Corporal	Appleton, Mo. OS-St.M-MA-G. Pres.
Gould, Jesse R. 1st Sgt.	Hannibal, Mo. OS. Transferred to Headquarters Co. June, 1919.	Renner, Fred Corporal	1906 Ervin St., Hannibal, Mo. OS-St.M-MA. Trfd. to B. Hosp. Dec. 1918.
Noble, Burl N. Mess Sgt.	Shelbina, Mo. OS-St.M-MA. Pres.	Porter, Clifford A. Corporal	616 N. Monroe St., Mason City, Ia. OS-St.M-MA. Pres.
Griggs, Walter Mess Sgt.	Hannibal, Mo. OS. Trans. to B. Hosp. June, 1919.	Bauer, John A. Corporal	Perry, Mo. OS-St.M-MA-W-M-G-F. Pres.
Yheulon, Harry Sup. Sgt.	Hannibal, Mo. St.M-OS-MA. Pres.	Mitchell, Sidney B. Corporal	Limit and Girard Sts., Leavenworth, Kan. OS-St.M-MA-G. Pres.
Moss, LeRoy Sergeant	100 Minnow St., Hannibal, Mo. OS-St.M-MA. Pres.	Sykes, John Corporal	1402 W. 5th St., Coffeyville, Kan. OS-St.M-MA. Pres.
Sigler, Bryan Sergeant	R. F. D. No. 2, River Road, Hannibal, Mo. OS-St.M-MA. Pres.	Glasgow, Robert Corporal	300 Lynn St., Leavenworth, Kan. OS-St.M-MA. Pres.
Slaughter, Albert Sergeant	Hannibal, Mo. OS-St.M-MA-W-GS. Pres.	Belz, Gus C. Corporal	R.F.D. No. 1, Leavenworth, Kan. OS-St.M-MA. Pres.
Mason, Emmet Sergeant	R. F. D. No. 3, Hannibal, Mo. OS-St.M-MA. Pres.	Harris, Edwin M. Corporal	R.F.D. No. 2, Leavenworth, Kan. OS-St.M-MA. Pres.
Jones, Howard Sergeant	2514 Chestnut St., Hannibal, Mo. OS-St.M-MA-G. Pres.	Cole, William T. Corporal	2124 Market St., Hannibal, Mo. OS-St.M-MA. Pres.
Perkins, Harry A. Sergeant	1313 S. Broadway St., Leavenworth, Kansas. OS-St.M-MA. Pres.	McAdams, William Corporal	213 S. 7th St., Hannibal, Mo. OS-St.M-MA. Pres.
Taylor, Raymond Sergeant	1212 Colfax Ave., Hannibal, Mo. OS-St.M-MA. Pres.		
Woodyard, Wesley M. Sergeant	1508 Broadway St., Hannibal, Mo. OS-St.M-MA. Pres.		
Cooper, Robert E. Sergeant	Sta. B, Route 28, Topeka, Kansas. OS-St.M-MA. Pres.		
Bursch, George W. Sergeant	519 N. Manhattan Ave., Manhattan, Kansas. OS-St.M-MA. Pres.		
Chambers, Ernest F. Sergeant	Leavenworth, Kansas. OS-St.M-MA-G. Pres.		
Johnson, Chas. J. Sergeant	Mohall, N. Dak. St.M-MA. Pres.		

88

CAPTAINS ALL

1. Capt. John F. Coffman
2. Capt. Matt Guilfoyle
3. Capt. Charles Haftle
4. Capt. C. A. Lusk
5. Capt. George C. Brewster

6. Capt. William Gilligan
7. Capt. R. W. Cater
8. Capt. F. D. Mathias
9. Capt. Henry F. Halverson
10. Capt. Brown Dyer

11. Capt. C. E. Munn

L COMPANY

Moody, Charles A. Corporal — R.F.D. No. 1, Hannibal, Mo. OS-St.M.-MA. Pres.

Settles, Oscar L. Corporal — Oakwood, Mo. OS-St.M.-MA. Pres.

Phillipps, Clifford Corporal — 322 N. 4th St., Hannibal, Mo. OS-St.M.-MA. Pres.

Wilson, George T. Corporal — R.F.D. No. 2, Leavenworth, Kan. OS-St.M.-MA. Pres. Trfd. to B. Hosp. March 1919.

Agee, Miles H. Corporal — R.F.D. No. 3, Nocoma, Texas. OS-St.M.-MA.

Ashley, Melvin B. Corporal — Douglas, Mo. OS-St.M.-MA. Pres.

Hillis, Gordon N. Corporal — 1347 N. 32nd St., Kansas City, Kan. OS-St.M.-MA. Pres.

Briscoe, Orval B. Corporal — 209 E. Gordon St., Hannibal, Mo. OS-St.M.-MA. Pres.

Miner, Henry E. Corporal — R.F.D. No. 4, Ebina, Mo. OS-St.M-MA. Pres.

Melby, Carney M. Corporal — Stanley, N. Dak. St.M.-MA. Pres.

Broughton, Lloyd D. Corporal — Bronson, Kansas. OS-St.M.-MA. Pres.

Given, Raymond Corporal — 213 S. 7th St., Hannibal, Mo. OS-St.M.-MA. Pres.

Harder, Fred P. Corporal — 1044 Winslow Ave. W., St. Paul, Minn. St.M.-MA. Pres.

Ninemire, George F. Corporal — Weston, Mo. OS-St.M.-MA. Pres.

Ohman, Frank H. Corporal — R.F.D. No. 4, Albany, Minn. Pres.

Doman, John R. Corporal — 454 Milwaukee St., Milwaukee, Wis. Pres.

Godoshiam, Dajad M. Corporal — 19 W. Wilson Ave., Pontiac, Mich. Pres.

Faulkner, Howard G. Corporal — Leavenworth, Kansas. OS. Trfd. to Isolation Camp, Romsey, Eng., May 1918.

Meister, Paul E. Corporal — 214 Ohio St., Leavenworth, Kan. OS. Trfd. to U. S. Ser. July 1918.

Hageman, Harry D. Corporal — 1306 Grand Ave., Leavenworth, Kan. OS. Killed in action, Aug. 26/1918.

Marshall, George R. Corporal — 2016 Hope St., Hannibal, Mo. OS. Killed in action Aug. 26/18.

Riley, George R. Corporal — 106 John St., Hannibal, Mo. OS. Killed in action Sept. 27/18.

Graham, Tolbert P. Corporal — R.F.D. No. 3, Fayetteville, Ark. OS. Killed Sept. 27/18.

Curtis, Samuel D. Corporal — 423 S. 6th St., Hannibal, Mo. OS. Killed in action Sept. 27/18.

Skinner, Jos. W. Corporal — Thayer, Kans. OS-St.M.-MA-W-M-G-F. Trfd. to B. Hosp. Oct. 1918.

Peters, Wallace J. Corporal — R.F.D. No. 3, Leavenworth, Kansas. OS-St.M.-MA-W-S. Trfd. to B. Hosp. Oct. 1918.

Roach, Delbert D. Corporal — Briggsville, Ill. OS-St.M.-MA-W-MGF.

Stout, Henry H. Corporal — 608 Summer St., Hannibal, Mo. OS-St.M.-MA. Killed in action Sept. 26 to Oct. 1/1918.

Clancy, George Corporal — W. Market St., Hannibal, Mo. OS-St.M.-MA-W-MGF.

Blockberger, Edward R. Corporal — 5th and Chestnut Sts., Leavenworth, Kansas. OS-St.M.-MA. Killed in action Sept. 26 to Oct. 1/1918.

Peters, Leslie L. Corporal — R.F.D. No. 3, Leavenworth, Kansas. OS-St.M.-MA. Captured by enemy Sept. 26 to Oct. 1/1918.

Fox, Layton V. Corporal — LaGrange, Mo. OS-St.M.-MA. Trfd. to B. Hosp. December 1918.

Crook, Marion F. Corporal — 9th and Walnut Sts., Leavenworth, Kan. OS-St.M.-MA. Trfd. to B. Hosp. Dec. 1918.

Foerstner, George Corporal — Hannibal, Mo. Pres.

Davis, Frank M. Cook — Leavenworth, Kan. OS-St.M.-M. Pres.

Baxter, Frank W. Cook — Sheffield, Iowa. OS-St.M.-MA. Pres.

Dunklin, Clarence Cook — Cambell, Mo. OS-St.M.-MA. Trfd. to M.PC. Mar. 1919.

Ginder, Roy F. Cook — R.F.D. 2, Belvue, Kan. OS-St.M-MA. Trfd. M.PC. Mar. 1919.

O'Conner, John W. Mechanic — Leavenworth, Kan. OS-St.M.-MA. Pres.

Greenwood, George Mechanic — Shellsburg, Iowa. OS-St.M.-MA. Pres.

Welker, Harry D. Mechanic — Shelbina, Mo. OS. Pres.

Wood, Norman W. Mechanic — Applegate, Mich.

Yate, Edward C. Mechanic — Leavenworth, Kan. OS. Trfd. to Hq. Co. 139th Inf. May, 1918.

Cornelius, Arthur Mechanic — Hannibal, Mo. OS-. Trfd. to B. Hosp. May 1918,

Gist, Walter M. Mechanic — Leavenworth, Kan. OS. Trfd. to 110th San. Train June 1918.

Nelson, Nels T. Mechanic — Hannibal, Mo. OS-St.M.-MA Killed in action Sept. 26 to Oct. 1, 1918.

Leach, Elwood M. Bugler — 104 Third Ave., Leavenworth, Kan. OS-St.M.-MA-G. Pres.

Abott, Lloyd E. Bugler — 25 F. West St., Hutchinson, Kan. OS-St.M.-MA. Trfd. to MP March 1919

Bagwell, Ernest M. Bugler — Tonganoxie, Kansas. OS-St.M.-MA. Killed in action Sept. 28/1918.

Aasen, Ole Pvt. 1cl. — Watford City, N. Dak. St.M.-MA. Pres.

Barrett, Carl F. Pvt. 1cl. — 904 Ely St., Hannibal, Mo. OS-St.M.-MA. Pres.

Broxton, Geo. V. Pvt. 1cl. — 509 Bluff St., Hannibal, Mo. OS-St.M.-MA. Killed in action Sept. 27/1918.

Ashurst, Raymond Pvt. 1cl. — 703 Olive St., Kansas City, Mo. OS-St.M.-MA-W-H-E. Sept. 29/1918.

Brenneman, Perry L. Pvt. 1cl. — 125 N. 2nd St., Leavenworth, Kan. OS-St.M.-MA. Trfd. to MPC March 1919.

Basley, Patrick Pvt. 1cl. — Fenton, Mich. Pres.

Bates, Eaf Pvt. 1cl. — 2019 Irvin St., Hannibal, Mo. OS-St.M.-MA. Pres.

Bell, Hugh M. Pvt. 1cl. — Akerland, Kan. OS-St.M.-MA. Pres.

90

L COMPANY

Berg, Alfred C. Pvt. 1cl.

Blackburn, Guy R. Pvt. 1cl.

Borrendame, Conreau H. Pvt. 1cl.

Brassell, Benj. F. Pvt. 1cl.

Briere, Ligaurie Pvt. 1cl.

Buchanan, James L. Pvt. 1cl.

Burton, Farris Pvt. 1cl.

Casselman, Gideon Pvt. 1cl.

Clifton, Clyde Pvt. 1cl.

Connelly, James E. Pvt. 1cl.

Craft, John M. Pvt. 1cl.

Curtis, Robt. R. Pvt. 1cl.

Daniels, Allan J. Pvt. 1cl.

Douglas, Lewis F. Pvt. 1cl.

Courtney, Guy H. Pvt. 1cl.

Charlesworth, Geo. H. Pvt. 1cl.

Downing, Robert A. Pvt. 1cl.

Dubbert, Louis R. Pvt. 1cl.

Dunkin, George R. Pvt. 1cl.

Dunphy, William F. Pvt. 1cl.

Douglas, Oscar L. Pvt. 1cl.

Eaton, Homer Pvt. 1cl.

Epley, Roy E. Pvt. 1cl.

Edwall, Theo M. Pvt. 1cl.

Francois, George J. Pvt. 1cl.

Froemke, Dan Pvt. 1cl.

Haggerty, James W. Pvt. 1cl.

Franklin, Marley Pvt. 1cl.

Hitzman, Clarence A. Pvt. 1cl.

Hofflinger, Sam A. Pvt. 1cl.

Kanell, Louis Pvt. 1cl.

King, William A. Pvt. 1cl.

Kuhlmann, Otto D. H. Pvt. 1cl.

Klatt, Adolph Pvt. 1cl.

Larson, Carl N. Pvt. 1cl.

Courtney, N. Dak. St.M-MA-G. Pres.

Vine St. S. S., Hannibal, Mo. OS-St.M-MA-W-S. Pres.

Grand Rapids, Mich. Pres.

704 Webb St., Hannibal, Mo. OS-St.M-MA. Pres.

Strong, Mich. Pres.

Hannibal, Mo. OS-St.M-MA. Pres.

Wesleyville, Ky. Pres.

St. Joseph, Mo. OS-St.M-MA. Pres.

2016 Irvin St., Hannibal, Mo. OS-St.M-MA. Pres.

Bowling Green, Mo. OS-St.M-MA. Pres.

Paris, Mo. OS-St.M-MA. Pres.

Indianapolis, Ind. Pres.

Ontanogan, Mich. Pres.

Columbia, Mo. OS-St.M-MA. Pres.

Ackerland, Kansas. OS. Trfd. 110th M.S. Trfd. June 1918.

Clarion, Iowa. OS-St.M-MA-W-S. Trfd. to B. Hosp. Oct. 1918.

Lowemont, Kansas. OS-St.M-MA-W-S. Pres.

Maquoketa, Iowa. OS-St.M. Pres.

R.F.D. No. 4, Hannibal, Mo. OS-St.M-MA. Pres.

184 Canfield Ave., Detroit, Mich. Pres.

Wallula, Kansas. OS-St.M-MA-W-S. Trfd. to B. Hosp. Oct. 1918.

R.F.D. No. 3, Bowling Green, Mo. OS-St.M-MA. Pres.

Hannibal, Mo. OS-St.M-MA. Pres.

St. Paul, Mo. OS-St.M-MA. Trfd. to M.P.C. March 1919.

Maquoketa, Iowa. OS-St.M-MA. Trfd. to 1st Repl. Depot Apr. 13, 1919.

Lisbon, N. Dak. OS-St.M-MA. Pres.

Canton, Mo. OS-St.M-MA. Pres.

Hannibal, Mo. OS-St.M-MA. Pres.

Ackerland, Kansas. OS-St.M-MA-W-H-E.

Garrison, Kansas. OS-St.M-MA. Killed in action Sept. 26/1918.

Laurel, Mont. St.M-MA. Trfd. to 1st Repl. Depot Apr. 13/1919.

Hannibal, Mo. OS-St.M-MA. Pres.

Charteroak, Iowa. St.M-MA. Pres.

California, Mo. OS-St.M-MA. Killed in action. Sept. 26 to Oct. 1/1918.

Scanville, Iowa. OS-St.M-MA. Pres.

Lee, Greenleaf W. Pvt. 1cl.

Long, William H. Pvt. 1cl.

Lowe, Ray Pvt. 1cl.

Landes, Roy E. Pvt. 1cl.

McCusic, John C. Pvt. 1cl.

Miller, Edward J. Pvt. 1cl.

Moody, Hugh A. Pvt. 1cl.

Marrow, Roland Pvt. 1cl.

Pettitt, Harvey R. Pvt. 1cl.

Pullos, Harry Pvt. 1cl.

Reed, Cecil J. Pvt. 1cl.

Olson, John P. Pvt. 1cl.

Reid, Covey Pvt. 1cl.

Robb, Cecil Pvt. 1cl.

Robertson, Irwin B. Pvt. 1cl.

Root, Harvey O. Pvt. 1cl.

Spidahl, Ben J. Pvt. 1cl.

Stevenson, Frank G. Pvt. 1cl.

Stewart, Joe Pvt. 1cl.

Swart, Archie H. Pvt. 1cl.

Tarkowski, Walter J. Pvt. 1cl.

Trackwell, Ernest E. Pvt. 1cl.

Via, Melvin B. Pvt. 1cl.

Walters, Joe H. Pvt. 1cl.

Webb, Roscoe Pvt. 1cl.

Wilcox, Frank E. Pvt. 1cl.

Wilson, Andy B. Pvt. 1cl.

Wilson, Chas. N. Pvt. 1cl.

Worley, Ellis O. Pvt. 1cl.

Wizorek, Frank H. Pvt. 1cl.

Ward, Chas. P. Pvt. 1cl.

Warren, Ben. C. Pvt. 1cl.

Watters, Chas. J. Pvt. 1cl.

Alexander, Claude Private

Anderson, Arthur F. Private

Burnaugh, Mo. OS-St.M-MA. Pres.

Hannibal, Mo. OS-St.M-MA-W-S. Pres.

Griggsville, Ill. OS-St.M-MA. Trfd. to 1st Repl. Depot Apr. 13/1919.

Wheaton, Kansas. OS-St.M-MA-W-S.

Detroit, Mich. Pres.

R.F.D. No. 4, Leavenworth, Kan. OS-St.M-MA.

Hannibal, Mo. OS-St.M-MA. Pres.

Leavenworth, Kansas. OS. Trfd. to Isolation at Romsey, Eng., May, 1918.

Hannibal, Mo. OS-St.M-MA. Pres.

Mohall, N. Dak. OS-St.M-MA. Pres.

Douglas, Mo. OS-St.M-MA. Pres.

Boyd, N. Dak. OS-St.M-MA-W-M-G. Pres.

OS-St.M-MA. Pres. Hannibal, Mo.

Hannibal, Mo. OS-St.M-MA-W-G. Pres.

Hannibal, Mo. OS-St.M-MA. Pres.

Leavenworth, Kansas. OS-St.M-MA. Pres.

Rothsay, Minn. St.M-MA. Pres.

Leavenworth, Kansas. OS-St.M-MA. Pres.

711 Lyon St., Hannibal, Mo. OS-St.M-MA. Pres.

Platville, Wisconsin. Pres.

Bay City, Mich. Pres.

Ackerland, Kansas. OS-St.M-MA-W-S. Pres.

Hannibal, Mo. OS-St.M-MA. Pres.

St. Bernard, La. Pres.

1821 Patchen St., Hannibal, Mo. OS-St.M-MA. Pres.

Fergus Falls, Minn. OS-St.M-MA-W-S. & G. Pres.

R.F.D. No. 2, Leavenworth, Kan. OS-St.M-MA. Pres.

R. F. D. No. 2, Leavenworth, Kans. OS-St.M-MA. Pres.

Tonganoxie, Kansas. OS-St.M-MA. Pres.

272 24th St., Detroit, Mich. Pres.

Tonganoxie, Kansas. OS. Trfd. to Isolation Camp, Romsey, Eng., May 1918.

Linwood, Kansas. OS-St.M-MA-W-S.

Greely, Iowa. OS-St.M-MA. Killed in action Sept. 26 to Oct. 1/1918.

Tracy, Minn. OS-St.M-MA. Pres.

Honeyford, N. Dak. St.M-MA. Pres.

L COMPANY

Anderson, Charles — Private — Matheville, Ill. OS-St.M-MA. Trfd. to MPC March 1919.

Balliet, Adam, Jr. — Private — Harvey, N. Dak. St.M-MA. Pres.
Barkhau, Earl C. — Private — Covington, Ky. Pres.
Beckley, Sherman D. — Private — Sedalia, Mo. OS-St.M-W-H-E. Pres.
Bell, Ernest L. — Private — 2606 Chestnut St., Hannibal, Mo. OS-St.M-MA. Pres.
Bellowes, Everett — Private — Laurey, Mo. OS-St.M-MA-G. Pres.
Bender, Jos. — Private — Williston, N. Dak. OS-St.M-MA. Pres.
Bennetti, Valentine — Private — Bay City, Mich. Pres.
Berg, Oscar R. — Private — LaMaure, N. Dak. OS-St.M. Pres.
Berskow, Thos. — Private — Elbow Lake, Minn. OS-St.M-MA. Pres.
Bills, Thos. S. — Private — Ionia, Mich. Pres.
Bistoff, Morris — Private — Underhill, Wisconsin. Died 3/17/19.
Bowen, Clarence M. — Private — Hannibal, Mo. OS-St.M-MA-W-H-E. Pres.
Bratcher, David — Private — Lafayette, Ind. Pres.
Brown, Lester G. — Private — Milca, Minn. OS. Pres.
Brown, Wm. J. — Private — Bay City, Mich. Pres.
Brumback, David — Private — Tarkio, Mo. OS-MA. Pres.
Bunke, Herman N. — Private — Racine, Wisc. Pres.
Burass, Casper — Private — Northwood, N. Dak. St.M-MA. Pres.
Busse, Samuel E. — Private — Amboy, Minn. OS-St.M-MA. Pres.
Butler, James W. — Private — LaGrange, Mo. OS-St.M-MA. Pres.
Benninger, Fred — Private — St. Jose, Ill. OS. Trfd. to B. Hosp. July 1918.
Bjarnson, Hilgif — Private — Mountain, N. Dak. Trfd. B. H. Oct. 1918.
Brelsford, Harry L. — Private — St. Joseph, Mo. OS-St.M-MA. Trfd. to B. Hosp. Oct. 1918.
Brown, Clarence — Private — Hope St., Hannibal, Mo. OS-St.M-.MA-G. Trfd. to B. H. Oct. 1918.
Blair, Wm. J. — Private — Langdon, N. Dak. St.M-MA. Died Jan. 25/1918.
Carlson, Melker V. — Private — Bowman, N. Dak. W-HE. Pres.
Chapman, Joseph — Private — Ft. Yates, N. Dak. St.M-MA. Pres.
Chounard, Frederick — Private — Mohall, N. Dak. St.M-MA. Trfd. 1st Repl. Dep. Mar. 1919.
Christensen, Edward A. — Private — Racine, Wisc. Pres.
Comer, Ray S. — Private — N. Branch, Mich. Pres.
Collins, Ray L. — Private — Topeka, Kans. OS-St.M-MA-G. Trfd. B. Hosp. Oct. 1918.
Dalen, Theodore J. — Private — Sargeant, Minn. OS-St.M-MA-W-HE. Pres.
Davis, Leo — Private — 608 Hawkins Ave., Hannibal, Mo. OS-St.M-MA. Pres.
DeLaGardella, Rene — Private — New York, N. Y. Pres.
Douglas, John J. — Private — Caruthersville, Mo. OS-MA. Pres.
Dales, Martin H. — Private — Climax, Minn. OS-St.M-MA. Killed in action Sept. 26 to Oct. 1/1918.
Dudlin, Alphonse — Private — Fargo, N. Dak. St.M-MA-W-HE. Trfd. B. H. Oct. 1918.

Dwight, Arley S. — Private — R. F. D. No. 2, Gilman, Iowa. OS-St.M-MA-W-HE. Trfd. to B. H. Oct. 1918.
Eurove, Isaac — Private — Paris, Ky. Pres.
Falcone, Paul R. — Private — Portland, Ore. Pres.
Ford, Louis — Private — 4th & Sheridan Sts., Leavenworth, Kans. OS-St.M-MA. Pres.
Fullhart, Lawrence E. — Private — Cincinnati, Iowa. OS-St.M-MA. Pres.
Fullerton, Charles R. — Private — 327 Beardsley St., Winnipeg, Canada. St.M-MA. Pres.
Fessenden, Harry A. — Private — LaGrange, Mo. OS-St.M-MA-W-S. Trfd. B. H. Oct. 1918.
Garvey, Harry O. — Private — Bain City, Kans. OS-St.M-MA-G. Pres.
Glasgow, Leslie M. — Private — Midland, Mich. Pres.
Green, Robert — Private — Atchison, Kans. OS-MA-St.M. Killed in action Sept. 27/1918.
Guenther, Louis W. — Private — R.F.D. No. 1, Leavenworth, Kans. OS-St.M-MA. Pres.
Gordon, Ray — Private — Bowling Green, Mo. OS-St.M-MA. Pres.
Hall, George S. — Private — South Boardman, Mich. Pres.
Hampton, Everette L. — Private — Canton, Mo. OS-St.M-MA. Pres.
Hansen, Oscar — Private — Braddock, N. Dak. Pres.
Harper, Arthur J. C. — Private — Chicago, Ill. Pres.
Harrison, Guy M. — Private — R.F.D. No. 1, Leavenworth, Kans. OS-MA-St.M. Pres.
Haug, Martin K. — Private — Downer, Minn. OS-St.M-MA. Trfd. B. H. April 13/19.
Heckathorn, David L. — Private — Galien, Mich. Pres.
Hoatson, Lester — Private — 128 Iroquois St., Laurium, Mich. Pres.
Hogue, John G. — Private — Terre Haute, Ind. Pres.
Holwell, Wm. J. — Private — Wallhalla, N. Dak. St.M-MA. Pres.
Hornung, Albert — Private — Grand Forks, N. Dak. St.M-MA. Pres.
Hoskins, Willie A. — Private — Canton, Mo. OS-St.M-MA. Trfd. 1st Repl. Dep. April 1/1919.
Hovland, Hans — Private — Nome, N. Dak. St.M-MA. Pres.
Hutchinson, Thurman D. — Private — Princeton, Mo. OS-St.M-MA. Pres.
Hogan, John — Private — Northwood, Minn. OS. Trfd. 130th M.G. Bn. May 1918.
Hagerman, Wm. F. — Private — Hannibal, Mo. OS-St.M-MA-W-HE. Trfd. B. H. 10/18.
Hyler, Norman — Private — Hannibal, Mo. OS-St.M-MA-G. Trfd. B. H. Oct. 1918.
Iverson, Gunwald — Private — Grand Forks, N. Dak. St.M-MA. Pres.
Johnson, Edvin — Private — Litchville, N. Dak. St.M-MA. Pres.
Johnson, Gustaf H. — Private — Garfield, Minn. St.M-MA. Pres.
Kehoe, Charles — Private — St. Louis, Mo. OS-St.M-MA. Pres.
Kelling, Paul E. — Private — New England, N. Dak. St.M-MA-W-GS. Pres.
Kelly, Edward L. — Private — Englevale, N. Dak. St.M-MA. Pres.
Klefier, George — Private — Kensal, N. Dak. St.M-MA. Pres.
Knight, Harrell — Private — Calumet, Mich. Pres.

92

L COMPANY

Knoch, Arthur J.   Private   New York, N. Y. Pres.
Kowalski, Clarence F.   Private
Kroeger, Arnold H.   Private   Merrill, Iowa. OS-St.M-MA-W-S. Pres.
Kruschke, Alexander F.   Private   Lavina, Montana. St. M-MA-W-HE. Pres.
Kuehl, Charles F.   Private   Melvin, Ill. OS-MA-St.M-W-S. Pres.
Kostelecky, Harry   Private   Mukwanago, Wisc. Pres.
Kerr, Len D.   Private   Dickson, N. Dak. St.M-MA-W-S. Trfd. B H Oct 1918.

Lampach, Isaac   Private   Leavenworth, Kans., OS-St.M-MA-W-HE. Trfd B.H. Oct. 1918.
Larkin, James F.   Private   New York City. Pres.
Larsen, John L.   Private   Abilene, Kans., OS-St.M-MA. Pres.
Lassher, Alferd   Private   Duluth, Minn. OS-St.M-MA. Pres.
Laukkala, Eli   Private   McClusky, N. Dak. St.M-MA. Pres.
Leaton, George   Private   Beldon, N. Dak. St.M-MA. Pres.
Liebowitz, Jacob   Private   Holton, Mich. Pres.
Long, Glen C.   Private   New York City. Pres.
Lewis, Milton H.   Private   Corydon, Iowa. Pres.
Lubeno, Lawrence J.   Private   Canton, Mo. OS-St.M MA. Pres.
Larmer, Clifford A.   Private   New Munster, Wis. Pres.

Johns, Angus G.   Private   Laurens, Iowa. OS-St.M-KIA. Sept. 29, 1918.

Landsphere, James   Private   Wenatchee, Wash. St.M-KIA. Sept. 28. 1918.
   Burlington, N. Dak. St.M-MA. Missing in action. Sept. 26 to Oct. 1, 1918.
Linnel, Russell J.   Private   Sebaka, Minn. OS-St.M-MA-W-HE. Trfd. BH. 10-18.
Logan, Tracy   Private   Regina, Canada. St.M-MA-KIA. Sept. 26 to Oct. 1, 1918.
McDonald, Charles J.   Private   Topeka, Kans. St.M-G. Trfd. BH. Oct. 1918.
McInnes, Hugh   Private   Fargo, N. Dak. St.M-MA. Pres.
Manks, John   Private   Ionia, Mich. Pres.
Mapes, Charles   Private   Charles City, Iowa. St.M-MA. Pres.
Martin, Thereon   Private   Harlem, Montana. St.M. Pres.
Mastropietro, Lorenzo   Private   Sioux City, Iowa. Pres.
Metzler, Edwill J.   Private   Nicholson, N. Dak., St.M-MA. Pres.
Meuler, Carl K.   Private   Oshkosh, Wisc. Pres.
Miller, Joseph J.   Private   Linton, N. Dak. St.M-MA. Pres.
Miske, August L.   Private   Herington, Kans. OS-St.M-MA-W-S. Pres.
Monkvold, Eddie   Private   Irene, S. Dak. St.M-MA-G. Pres.
Moore, George H.   Private   Plano, Iowa. Pres.
Morris, Ernest   Private   Pomeroy, Iowa. Pres.
Meinson, Irwin   Private   St. Joseph, Mo. OS-St.M-MA-W-S. Trfd. BH. Oct. 1918.
Mentzer, Paul F.   Private   Neosho Falls, Kans. OS-W-HE. Trfd. BH. August 1918.
Mosely, Dewey   Private   Leavenworth, Kans. OS. Trfd. July 1918 to BH.
Naeher, Stephen A.   Private   Leavenworth, Kans. OS-St.M. Pres.
Nelson, Gullai N.   Private   Ambrose, N. Dak. St.MA-G. Pres.
Newcombe, Charles H.   Private   Mt. Pleasant, Mich. Pres.

Nielson, Carl F.   Private   Tripoli, Iowa. Pres.
Nieni, Edgar F.   Private   Calumet. Mich. Pres.
Nagel, Albert A.   Private   New Ulm, Minn. OS-St.M-MA. Trfd. BH. 10-18.
Nessit, Arthur B.   Private   Austin, Minn. OS-St.M-MA. Trfd. BH. Nov. 1918.
Nitz, Edward   Private   Cummings, Kans. OS-St.M. Trfd. to MPC. 3-19.
Norman, Clyde C.   Private   St. Joseph, Mo. OS-St.M. Trfd. MPC. 3-19.
Oldfield, Charles W.   Private   Three Rivers, Mich. Pres.
Orbeck, Hans   Private   Surrey, N. Dak. St.M. Pres.
Oien, Joseph J.   Private   Boyd, Minn. OS-St.M-MA. Captured Sept. 26 to Oct. 1, 1918.
Oswald, Wm. H.   Private   Fertile, Minn., OS-St.M-MA-KIA. Sept. 26, to Oct. 1, 1918.
O'Hearn, George E.   Private   Hannibal, Mo. OS-St.M-MA-G. Trfd. BH. 10-18.
Perman, Christ   Private   Blue Grass, N. Dak. St.M. Pres.
Perrella, Luci   Private   Jenners, Penn. Pres.
Phelan, Harrol   Private   Oshkosh, Wisc. Pres.
Porter, Wm. D.   Private   Hannibal, Mo. OS-St.M-MA. Pres.
Pederson, Koldjorn   Private   Chicago, Ill. Missing in action. Sept. 26 to Oct. 1, 1918.
Praether, Finis B.   Private   Huntsville, Mo. OS-St.M-MA. Trfd. MPC. 3-19.
Riebel, Charlie   Private   West Point, Iowa. OS-St.M-MA. Pres.
Robb, Aschel   Private   Hannibal, Mo. OS-St.M-MA. Pres.
Rosenkrantz, Ike   Private   Leavenworth, Kans. MA-KIA. Sept. 26 to Oct. 1, 1918.
Robbins, Lawrence   Private   Perry, Kans. OS-St.M-MA-W-MGW Trfd. MPC. 3-19.
Scott, Jesse I.   Private   Tonganoxie, Kans. OS-St.M-MA-W. Pres.
Shobe, Audrey   Private   Chillicothe, Mo. OS-St.M-MA-W-S. Pres.
Smith, Robert D.   Private   Kansas City, Mo. OS-St.M-MA-MGW. Pres.
Stiencipher, Robert H.   Private   Paris, Mo. Pres.
Salisbery, Edgar R.   Private   Overbrook, Kans. OS-St.M-MA-W-HE. Trfd. BH. Oct. 1918.
Saylor, Grover C.   Private   Hannibal, Mo. OS-St.M-MA-G. Trfd. BH. 10-18.
Simms, Joseph D.   Private   Hannibal, Mo. OS-St.M-MA-W-MG. Trfd. BH. Oct. 1918.
Timola, Charles   Private   Odanah, Wisc. Pres.
Waddle, Crady   Private   Hindman, Ky. Pres.
Wagner, David   Private   Sheboygan, Wisc. Pres.
Way, Albert W.   Private   Ionia, Mich. Pres.
Webb, Harrell R.   Private   Leavenworth, Kans. OS-St.M-MA. Pres.
Webster, Wesley M.   Private   Douglas, Mo. OS-St.M-MA. Pres.
West, Harvey   Private   Hannibal, Mo. OS-St.M-MA. Pres.
Wiggins, Dannie C.   Private   Beech Grove, Ky. Pres.
Wilkinson, Calvin   Private   Dows, Iowa. OS-St.M-MA. Pres.
Willett, Robert N.   Private   Hannibal, Mo. OS-St.M-MA-W-S. Pres.
Witzel, Roy   Private   Ionia, Mich. Pres.

93

L COMPANY

ROSTER OF COMPANY F, 139th INFANTRY

Name and Rank	Home Address and Remarks
Edgar H. Dale Captain	Coffeyville, Kans. OS-K-MA-MGF.
George H. Klinkerfuss 1st Lt.	St. Louis, Mo. OS-MA.
Richard O. Worrell 2nd Lt.	Mexico, Mo. OS-MA-W-MGF.
John A. Hoffman 1st Lt.	St. Louis, Mo. OS-MA.
Glenn W. Davis 2nd Lt.	Reading, Mich.
Byrl J. Hilt 1st Lt.	Kirksville, Mo. MA-OS.
Perry A. Coker 1st Lt.	Hattiesburg, Miss. MA-G.
Raymond M. Reese 2nd Lt.	Los Angeles, Calif., 240 West Santa Barbara Avenue. OS.
George W. Mackey 2nd Lt.	Charleston, S. Car. MA.
Rice, Fred L. 1st Sgt.	Augusta, Kans. OS.
Bell, Beverly R. 1st Sgt.	RFD 2, Cuba, Mo. OS.
Gaumnitz, Walter H. Mess Sgt.	Rice, Minn. OS-MA-W.
Dyer, Roy E. Mess Sgt.	Box 188, Moline, Kans. OS-MA.
Griggs, Louis C. Sup. Sgt.	495 Oyma St., Columbia, Mo. OS-MA.
Wallace, Roy D. Sup. Sgt.	1641 Laurel Avenue, St. Paul, Minn. OS-MA-W-MGF.
Frederick K. Fisher 2nd Lt.	Edina, Mo.
Arnold, Lonzo B. Sergeant	Agua Dulce, Tex. OS-MA.
Brown, Joe O. Sergeant	RFD 2, Boicourt, Kans. OS-MA-W-MGF.
Calvert, John F. Sergeant	817 College Avenue, Columbia, Mo.
Correll, John L. Sergeant	Edna, Tex. OS-MA.
Goff, Manuel B. Sergeant	117 Settler Street, El Dorado, Kans. OS-MA.
Harmoh, Karl M. Sergeant	1218 College Avenue, Rosedale, Kans. OS.
Harris, Joe W. Sergeant	212 Third Avenue, Columbia, Mo. OS-MA.
Harshbarger, Ned P. Sergeant	403 Board of Commerce, Little Rock, Ark. OS-MA.
Hulen, Harold A. Sergeant	Route 10, Columbia, Mo. OS-MA.
Ingraham, Thomas C. Sergeant	Mountain Grove, Mo. OS-W-MGF-D.
Jones, Russell F. Sergeant	Cameron, Mo. OS-MA.
McCurdy, Walter R. Sergeant	119 North 8th Street, Wellington, Kans. OS-W-HE.
McGilton, George J. Sergeant	730 North Adams Street, Nevada, Mo. OS.
Norris, Henry T. Sergeant	3303 College Avenue, Kansas City, Mo. OS-MA-G.
Roberts, Frank F. Sergeant	Hallsville, Mo. OS-MA.
Rosegren, Alfred T. Sergeant	541 Melrose, Chicago, Ill. OS-MA.
Scofield, Benjamin F. Sergeant	1008 Maud Street, Poplar Bluff, Mo. OS.
Stratford, Ray A. Sergeant	504 Denver Street, El Dorado, Kans. OS.
Warden, Hubert P. Sergeant	Mexico, Mo.
Tipple, Franklin A. Sergeant	Knox City, Mo. OS-MA.

Name and Rank	Home Address and Remarks
Berkebile, Judson E. Sergeant	708 Rangeline, Columbia, Mo. OS-MA.
Daggs, Jackson A. Sergeant	Arbela, Mo. OS-MA-W-MGF.
McRae, Charles Sergeant	Fort Ogden, Fla. MA.
Alexander, Harlan A. Corporal	Medora, N. Dak. MA.
Barger, Jesse W. Corporal	810 Highland Avenue, Columbia, Mo. OS-MA.
Bloir, Charles E. Corporal	323 North Summit Street, El Dorado, Kans. OS-MA.
Brown, Allen L. Corporal	209 Mulberry Street, Jefferson City, Mo. OS-MA. (Captured by Germans.)
Brown, John L. Corporal	RFD 5, Columbia, Mo. OS-MA.
Bundy, Bert F. Corporal	807 Pannell Avenue, Columbia, Mo. OS-MA.
Butler, Roy E. Corporal	Knox City, Mo. OS.
Daniels, Robert E. Corporal	208 Kansas Avenue, El Dorado, Kans. OS-MA-W-MGF.
Daniels, William O. Corporal	Box 125, El Dorado, Kans. OS-MA.
Derrig, Thomas L. Corporal	Mapleton, N. Dak. MA.
Doyle, Delts W. Corporal	Harrison Street, Hillyard, Wash. OS-MA-K-MGF.
Dugan, Sherman Corporal	Red Rock, Okla. OS.
Fehland, George B. Corporal	216½ Ann Street, St. Paul, Minn. OS-MA.
Forristall, George C. Corporal	Box 16, Sulphur Springs, Ark. OS.
Grossman, Edmund A. Corporal	Box 37, Staples, Minn. MA-W-MGF.
Gordon, James Sergeant	Amarillo, Tex. OS-MA-K-MGF.
Halfhill, Noah Corporal	515 Star Street, El Dorado, Kans. OS-MA.
Harris, Earl Corporal	501 Mulberry Street, Murphysboro, Ill. OS.
Hennessey, John W. Corporal	Preston, Minn. OS-MA.
House, Carl W. Corporal	RFD 4, Columbia, Mo. OS-MA-W-MGF.
Hufford, Glenn F. Corporal	Latham, Kans. OS-MA.
Hunter, Floyd M. Corporal	Plainville, Kans. OS-MA.
Lindsay, Nat M. Corporal	RFD 1, Lawrenceville, Ill. OS-MA-K-MGF.
McCauley, Robert M. Sergeant	Clements, Kans. OS-MA-W-MGF.
McCullum, John L. Corporal	Steele, Mo. MA-W-MGF.
Melloway, Frank Corporal	504 West Broadway, Columbia, Mo. OS-MA-W-MGF.
Moore, Omer Corporal	Lincoln Center, Kans. MA.
Crow, Archie G. Corporal	Kimble, Mo. OS.
Neal, Andrew M. Corporal	RFD 1, Billet, Ill. OS-MA.
Osterud, Lars Corporal	Ostrander, Minn. OS-MA.

94

L COMPANY

Riggs, Young E. Corporal
RFD 7, Columbia, Mo. OS.
Sanders, Charles L.
Corporal
219 South 8th Street, Ponca City, Okla. OS-MA.
Sapp, Wilbur I. Corporal
Third Avenue, Columbia, Mo. OS-MA.
Sharp, Oliver S. Corporal
414 West Steele, Cushing, Okla. OS-MA.
Smith, Edward M. Corporal
Moundridge, Kans. OS-MA-G.
Smith, Marion W. Corporal
1219 West Delaware, Evansville, Ind. OS-MA.
Strickler, Dudley D.
Corporal
Knox City, Mo. OS.
Stratford, John R. Corporal
301 Clark Street, Augusta, Kans. OS-MA-W-MGF.
Tomlinson, Jo C. Corporal
1213 Main Street, Trenton, Mo. MA-W-MGF.
Vaughn, Lloyd E. Corporal
Fulton, Mo. OS-MA.
Waters, John J. Corporal
301 Hitt Street, Columbia, Mo. OS-MA.
Wilson, Charles H. Corporal
301 Orchard Street, El Dorado, Kans. OS-MA-W-MGF.
Mayes, Harrison H. Cook
Hallsville, Mo. OS-MA.
Oliver, Clyde W. Cook
Thompson, Mo. OS-MA.
Robnett, James O. Cook
1509 Broadway, Columbia, Mo. OS-MA.
Thomas, John W. Cook
Centerville, Iowa. OS-MA.
Adamson, Murl L. Mechanic
RFD 3, Guthrie, Mo. OS-MA.
Cooper, Frank J. Mechanic
Millersburg, Mo. OS-MA.
Hightower, Herbert H.
Mechanic
Star Street, El Dorado, Kans. OS-MA.
Foust, Benjamin E.
Mechanic
Columbia, Mo. OS-MA-W-MFG.
Oblander, Charles J.
Mechanic
Lehigh, Kans. OS-MA.
Thuma, Lester C. Mechanic
114 Vine Street, El Dorado, Kans. OS.
Ricord, Edwin O. Mechanic
Caldwell, Kans. OS-MA. (Missing in action.)
Biggs, Russell F. Cook
112 North Main Street, El Dorado, Kans. OS-MA-W-MGF.
Houchen, Thomas E. Bugler
Salem, Ill. OS-MA.
Oliver, Charlie L. Bugler
Thompson, Mo. OS-MA.
Aprille, William Pvt. 1cl.
Pulaski, Wis.
Benson, Anton J. Pvt. 1cl.
Lakota, N. Dak. OS-MA.
Bressell, Philip Pvt. 1cl.
RFD 4, El Dorado, Kans. MA-OS.
Brock, George H. Pvt. 1cl.
Wadena, Minn. OS-MA.
Brodbeck, Ernest A.
Pvt. 1cl.
RFD 1, Wichita, Kans. OS-MA-K-MGF.
Bruno, Michael Pvt. 1cl.
Province Cosenza, Maranomarchisato, Italy.
Bumgarner, Hubert J.
Pvt. 1cl.
Spring Valley, Minn. OS-MA.
Cain, Philip M. Pvt. 1cl.
Glen Beulah, Wis. OS-MA.
Christiansen, Herbert C.
Pvt. 1cl.
Ruthven, Iowa. OS-MA-K-MGF.
Cook, Andrew W. Pvt. 1cl.
Main Street, Sugar Notch, Pa.
Cookson, Harry B. Pvt. 1cl.
1128 South Main Street, Bellefontain, Ohio. OS-MA.
Connelley, George T.
Pvt. 1cl.
1414 South Kentucky, Sedalia, Mo. OS-MA.
Counts, John T. Pvt. 1cl.
Winslow, Ark. OS-MA.

Cremer, Thomas J. Pvt. 1cl.
West Frankfort, Ill.
Davenport, Floyd E.
Pvt. 1cl.
Simmons, Tex. OS-MA-W-MGF.
Doores, Forrest L. Pvt. 1cl.
Bronaugh, Mo. OS.
England, Kenton J. Pvt. 1cl.
Box 696, Casper, Wyo. OS-MA.
Fall, Albert Pvt. 1cl.
Neodesha, Kans. MA.
Feingold, Fred Pvt. 1cl.
690 9th Street, Milwaukee, Wis.
Ferguson, Harold E.
Pvt. 1cl.
RFD 10, Columbia, Mo. OS-MA.
Foster, Roy E. Pvt. 1cl.
Caney, Kans. OS-MA.
Gilliland, Claude K. Pvt. 1cl.
Leon, Kans. OS-MA.
Graves, John F. Pvt. 1cl.
Douglass, Kans. OS-MA. Captured.
Green, Harry B. Pvt. 1cl.
317 South Topeka Street, El Dorado, Kans. OS-MA.
Hailey, George W. Pvt. 1cl.
Brinkley, Ark. OS-MA.
Harrington, Birt Pvt. 1cl.
Edwardsport, Ind.
Hiffner, Carl M. Pvt. 1cl.
Ithaca, Mich.
Hood, George W. Pvt. 1cl.
Washington, Kans. OS-MA-K-MGF.
Hoffman, Walter Pvt. 1cl.
Detroit, Mich.
Holmquist, Carl C. Pvt. 1cl.
Allegan, Mich.
Hounshell, Fred Pvt. 1cl.
317 South Clinton Avenue, Middletown, Ohio.
Jackson, John M. Pvt. 1cl.
726 Bluff Street, Fulton, Mo. OS-MA-W-MGF.
Jensen, Soren T. Pvt. 1cl.
RFD 4, Paullana, Iowa. OS-MA.
Kassaros, Jim Pvt. 1cl.
Metsovon, Hyperos, Greece. OS-MA-W-MGF.
Klein, John M. Pvt. 1cl.
Strausburg, N. Dak. OS-MA.
Kolbu, Aslak Pvt. 1cl.
Van Hook, N. Dak. MA.
Krauser, Earle E. Pvt. 1cl.
709 South Bend Avenue, South Bend, Ind.
Kurtz, William E. Pvt. 1cl.
216 Logan Avenue, Waterloo, Ia. OS.
LaCroix, Tracy M. Pvt. 1cl.
Boyne City, Mich.
Larson, Arthur E. Pvt. 1cl.
RFD 6, Muskegon, Mich.
Lewis, Clarence Pvt. 1cl.
Everton, Mo. OS-MA-W-MGF.
Love, Rama S. Pvt. 1cl.
RFD 1, Odin, Ill. OS-MA-K-MGF.
Lynch, Clarence Pvt. 1cl.
Plummer, Minn. OS-MA.
McCaskey, Russell D.
Pvt. 1cl.
6718 East End Avenue, Chicago, Ill. OS-MA
McDonald, Millington L.
Pvt. 1cl.
Owendale, Mich.
McDorman, Scott Pvt. 1cl.
West Plains, Mo. OS-MA.
McKivett, James C. A.
Pvt. 1cl.
224 West Avenue, Grand Junction, Col. OS-MA.
Montague, Harry A.
Pvt. 1cl.
4180 Enright Street, St. Louis, Mo. OS.
Marback, Mike Pvt. 1cl.
1310 South Street, Bismark, N. Dak. MA.
Merritt, Henry P. Pvt. 1cl.
Coopersville, Mich.
Morrissey, Thomas M.
Pvt. 1cl.
New Richland, Minn. OS-MA-W-MGF.
Mullins, Oscar B. Pvt. 1cl.
205 South Waters Street, Robinson, Ill. OS-MA.
Neal, Leonard F. Pvt. 1cl.
RFD 6, Columbia, Mo. OS-MA-G.
Noonan, John P. Pvt. 1cl.
Elma, Iowa. OS-MA-W-MGF.
Peffley, Elba B. Pvt. 1cl.
719 South Star Street, El Dorado, Kans. OS-MA-W-MGF. (Reported later as missing.)
Pierce, Herschel W.
Pvt. 1cl.
601 Wheeling Avenue, Muncie, Ind. OS-MA.

L COMPANY

Pottorf, Vertis S. R.
Pvt. 1cl. Plaza, N. Dak. OS-MA.
Ree, Ingwald J. Pvt. 1cl.
753 Rainery Street, St. Paul, Minn.
OS-MA.
Reeder, Stuart H. Pvt. 1cl.
117 Westwood Avenue, Columbia,
Mo. OS-MA-W-MGF.
Richardson, Oliver S.
Pvt. 1cl. El Dorado, Kans. OS-MA.
Robinson, Harold S.
Pvt. 1cl. Stady, N. Dak. OS-MA.
Schrader, Hans Pvt. 1cl.
Schmidt, Harry J. Pvt. 1cl. Carlos, Minn. OS-MA.
317 Broadway, Fort Worth, Tex.
OS-MA-W-MGF.
Sheen, Joe R. Pvt. 1cl.
617 Star Street, El Dorado, Kans.
OS-MA.
Smith, Joe J. Pvt. 1cl. Box 44, Grange, Pa.
Smith, Millard Pvt. 1cl. Corydon, Iowa.
Stanfield, Howard B.
Pvt. 1cl. 412 Olive Street, Peabody, Kans.
OS-MA-G.
Stoltz, Ray L. Pvt. 1cl. RFD 4, El Dorado, Kans. OS-MA.
Tillery, Lewis W. Pvt. 1cl. California, Mo. OS-MA-W-MGF.
Tyliski, Joseph R. Pvt. 1cl. 2421 Pattie Street, St. Joseph, Mo.
OS-MA.
Young, Herbert O. Pvt. 1cl. Rocheport, Mo. OS-MA.
Vaughan, Otis P. Pvt. 1cl. RFD 4, Fulton, Mo. OS-MA-W-
MGF.
Watson, Earnest F. Pvt. 1cl. Winfield, Mo. OS-MA-W-MGF.
Whalen, John P. Corporal Great Valley, New York. OS-MA.
(Missing in action.)
Whitner, Kent O. Pvt. 1cl. Oblong, Ill. OS.
Williams, Herbert C. 101 Sexton Road, Columbia, Mo.
Pvt. 1cl. OS-MA-K-MGF.
Wilson, Karl F. Pvt. 1cl. Gurdon, Ark. OS-MA-W-MGF.
Woods, John F. Pvt. 1cl. 509 Moss Avenue, Columbia, Mo.
OS.
Zumalt, Martin W. Pvt. 1cl. Fulton Gravel, Columbia, Mo. OS-
MA.
Zumalt, Roy P. Pvt. 1cl. Fulton Gravel, Columbia, Mo. OS-
MA-W-MGF.
Gunsell, Fred D. Pvt. 1cl. Carroll, Mich.
Abels, Conrad Private Holland, Iowa. MA.
Albrecht, Harry Private RFD 5, Battle Creek, Mich.
Alsheimer, Andrew J. 1141 St. Vincent Street, Utica, New
Private York.
Anderson, Albert S. Private Harmony, Minn. OS-MA.
Anderson, John A. Private Ryenbergv, Christinia, Norway. OS-
D.
Allphin, William E. Private Wyaconda, Mo. OS.
Barron, Roy I. Private Route 1, Newport, Mich.
Barnes, Henry H. Private Route 2, Columbia, Mo. OS-MA-
W-MGF.
Bartel, Walter F. Private Route 5, Austin, Minn. OS-MA-W-
MGF.
Benit, Charles R. Private RFD 5, Columbia, Mo. MA-W-
MGF.
Becker, Charles Private 934 16th Street, Milwaukee, Wis.
Berry, James H., Jr. Hallsville, Mo. OS-MA-W-MGF.
Private
Borgen, Christ J. Private New Richland, Minn. OS-MA-W-
MGF.

Bowles, Jay G. Private Mokee, Ky.
Browning, Fred A. Private Edgar, Mont. MA.
Braun, William J. Pvt. 1cl. 912 West Churchhill, Stillwater,
Minn. OS.
Carnes, Albert H. Private Plattsmouth, Neb.
Casbeer, William B. Private Box 264, Lampasas, Tex.
Cherry, Elmer E. Private 409 Bates Avenue, St. Paul, Minn.
Cichon, Thomas J. Private 125 Popular, Ironwood, Mich.
Clark, Frank M. Private 313 East Central Avenue, El Do-
rado, Kansas. OS-MA.
Cline, Charles Private 29 North 11th Street, Phoenix, Ariz.
Coliton, William Private Moorehead, Minn.
Collins, Clarence Private Yale, Okla. OS-MA.
Crum, Lonnie H. Private Box 338 Seneca, Ill. MA.
Cronin, Peter T. Private 717 State Street, Lincoln, Ill. OS-
MA-W-MGF. Later reported miss-
ing.
Crist, Angelo Private Columbia, Mo. OS-D.
Daak, Otto J. Private RFD 4, Hutchinson, Minn. OS-MA-
W-MGF.
Dickson, Frederick H. 461 Hamilton, Detroit, Mich.
Private
Duchovney, Heyman Private 1412 Columbus Avenue, Bay City,
Mich.
Eilertson, Peder K. Private State Farm, Crookston, Minn.
Elliott, Floyd E. Private RFD 4, Osage, Iowa. OS-MA.
Emery, William H. Private 117 North 11th Street, Enid, Okla.
OS.
English, Thomas P. Private 114 Palm Street, Detroit, Mich.
Erickson, Mike Private McNally, Iowa. MA.
Erickson, George Private Winger, Minn. OS.
Ekre, Selmer T. Private RFD 4, McIntosh, Minn. OS-MA.
(Missing)
Faulkner, Harry B. Private Marceline, Mo. OS-MA.
Fay, James C. Private Christian College Avenue, Colum-
bia, Mo. OS-MA.
Feyed, Mike Private 1929 Mahoney Road, Canton, Ohio.
Fisher, Roy E. Private Boonesboro, Missouri.
Fitzpatrick, Edmund W. Langdon, N. Dak. MA.
Private
Fonk, Adolph Private Harvey, N. Dak. MA.
Forsberg, Otto T. Private 1014 7th Avenue, South, Fargo, N.
Dak.
Foss, Elmer P. Private Hatton, N. Dak. MA.
Froehlich, Walter F. Private Crystal, N. Dak. MA-G.
Gardner, Robert Private RFD 2, Bonfield, Ill. MA-K-
MGF.
Getz, Peder D. Private 1309 Bell Avenue, Grand Fork, N.
Dak. K-HE. (At Camp Picard
Alsace.)
Gilmore, Harrison H. Richland, Mo.
Private
Gist, Ernest C. Private Remsen, Iowa. OS-MA.
Gnadt, Walter Private 829 Highland Avenue, Detroit,
Mich.
Groth, Harry Private Box 369, Fulda, Minn. OS-MA-W-
MGF (reported later as missing).
Grahek, Paul A. Private Mora, Minn. OS-MA.
Guthrie, Justus W. Private Box 55, Colon, Mich.
Haftorson, Silas S. Private RFD 4, Fertile, Minn. OS-MA-G.

LIEUTENANTS OF MARK

1. Lieut. W. S. Gray
2. Lieut. Ralph W. Martin
3. Lieut. W. H. Ellenburg

4. Lieut. Edward Johnson
5. Lieut. Homer Yale
6. Lieut. William J. Oakes

M COMPANY

Hall, Lon O. Private RFD 2, Northville, Mich.
Hamack, Thomas W. Private Thomas, Okla. OS-MA-W-MGF.
Hanson, Halvean E. Private RFD 5, Maddock, N. Dak. MA-W-MGF.
Hansen, Alfred E. Private Crystal Lake, Ill. MA. (Reported as missing, later as captured, wounded in German prison camp)
Harden, Milton J. Private Route 1, Stella, Mo. OS-MA-W-MGF.
Hart, Harry S. Private 614 Pasadena, Whittier, Calif.
Haas, John Private McCluskey, N. Dak. OS-MA.
Hays, George W. Private 422 Elmwood Avenue, Traverse City, Mich.
Herrington, Curtis C. Private Ponca City, Okla. OS-MA-G.
Howard, Joseph S. Private 609 State Street, Marshalltown, Ia. OS.
Howell, Percy E. Private Wahalla, N. Dak. MA.
Hoven, Camiel Private Laverne, N. Dak. MA-W-MGF.
Hoyt, Harry L. Private Alamo, N. Dak. MA.
Hulen, Amos B. Private 207 College Avenue, Columbia, Mo. OS-MA.
Hunt, Frank B. Private Emmet, Idaho. OS-MA.
Ingberg, John Private Fooston, Minn. OS-MA-W-G.
Jossi, Louis Private Emporia Street, El Dorado, Kans. OS-MA-W-MGF. (Taken prisoner.)
Johnson, Earl Milan Private 204 Clark Street, Augusta, Kans. OS-MA.
Johnson, Harold Private Crystal Springs, N. Dak. OS-MA.
Johnson, Ingbert H. Private RFD 5, Walhalla, N. Dak.
Johnson, Ole Private Route 2, Carpio, N. Dak. OS-MA.
Johnson, Paul Private Belden, N. Dak. OS-MA.
Johnson, Theodore S. Private Rhame, N. Dak. OS-MA.
Johnson, Willis R. Private RFD 3, Princeton, Minn. MA.
Jorgenson, Carl W. Private Kensal, N. Dak. MA.
Kachidlow, John Private Carpio, N. Dak. MA.
Kappus, Thomas J. Private 336 Michigan Street, Eauclaire, Wis.
Kelsey, Benjamin H. Private 1630 South Jefferson Street, Hastings, Mich.
Kidd, Harry L. Private Mandan, N. Dak. MA. (Reported as missing.)
Kirby, William J. Private Seattle, Wash. MA-W-MGF.
Kite, John Private Rocheport, Mo. OS-MA-K-MGF.
Kiekbush, Charles F. Private Route 4, St. Charles, Mich.
Koch, Franklin B. Private Chatsworth, Iowa. MA.
Kotila, Arthur E. Private 622 Franklin Street, Hancock, Mich.
Kuhn, John Private McCluskey, N. Dak. MA-W-MGF.
Kurpius, Lawrence L. Private Staples, Minn. OS-MA-W-MGF.
Lackawitzer, Edward Private Perham, Minn. MA-G.
Larsen, Magens Private Route 2, Ludington, Mich.
Law, John H. Private El Dorado, Kans. OS-MA.
Layman, Ferris A. Private Berrien Center, Mich.

Lehman, Leonhardt Private 216 Des Plains Avenue, Park, Ill. MA.
Lindblom, Lawrence C. Private 325 East 58th Street, Chicago, Ill. OS-MA-W-MGF.
Lindblom, Albin B. Private Portland, Oregon.
Lemke, George Private Whitewater, Wis.
Lentz, Bernard Private 812 Harmon Street, Milwaukee, Wis.
Linden, Raymond D. Private RFD North St. Paul, Minn. OS-MA-W-MGF.
Lindquist, Edd Private Chisago City, Minn. MA-W-MGF.
Loran, Nicholas Private Mandan, N. Dak. MA-W-MGF.
McAndrews, Michael Private Dickinson, N. Dak. MA.
McDaniels, Baylis G. Private Steedman, Mo. OS.
McKay, Belmont M. Private Ironwood, Mich.
Mayew, Leslie J. Private 216 Cherry Street, Green Bay, Wis.
Michelson, John R. Private Belden, N. Dak. MA-W-MGF.
Mikulas, Frank Private New York City, N. Y.
Moe, Benjamin F. Private 259 Hilger Avenue, Detroit, Mich.
Murtovara, William R. Private Box 279, Atlantic Mine, Mich.
Ogren, Julius H. Private 633 Lake Street, Cadillac, Mich.
Olson, Hugo Private Route 2, Freesoil, Mich.
Olson, Olaf E. Private Vining, Minn. OS.
Omsted, Clifford P. Private Fooston, Minn. OS-MA-W-MGF.
Palmer, Harry H. Private Rockport, Ill. OS-MA.
Pawneshing, Willie Private East Jordan, Mich.
Peterson, Carey E. Private Clarks Grove, Minn. OS.
Peterson, Carl V. Private 287 Scott Street, Oshkosh, Wis.
Petty, Frank S. Private 513 South 6th Street, Columbia, Mo. MA-G.
Pirtle, Charles E. Private Oaktown, Ind.
Ransom, Daniel R. Private 348 Dix Avenue, Detroit, Mich. OS-MA-W-MGF.
Rapson, Carl H. Private Carp Lake, Mich.
Rasmussen, George W. Private 2682 Champlain Avenue, Chicago, Ill.
Rasmussen, Walter Private Hajbysjalland, Denmark
Reagan, Richard Private 166 Garnett, Houghton, Mich.
Reed, Arlie R. Private 808 North 7th Street, Columbia, Mo.
Reed, Carl E. Private Taylors Falls, Minn. OS-MA.
Reese, Howard T. Private 1327 Broadway Street, Brenerton, Wash. OS.
Renz, Herbert W. Private RFD 2, Donnelson, Iowa. OS-MA-W-MGF.
Rintzler, Abraham Private 1436 Trumble Avenue, Chicago, Ill.
Robbins, Ollie E. Private Buffalo, Okla. OS-MA.
Rogers, Homer M. Private RFD 2, Farewell, Mich.
Root, Willis S. Private Long Prairie, Minn. OS-MA.
Ross, Mervin G. Private Harrisburg, Mo. MA-W-MGF.
Richardson, Roy R. Private Route 1, Odin, Ill. OS-MA-W-MGF. (Died in hospital.)
Russell, Cecil Earl Private Wamego, Kans. OS-MA-W-MGF.
Qual, Robert Private Mahnomen, Minn. OS-MA-K.
Rogers, Forrest L. Private Route 9, Trenton, Mo. OS.

98

M COMPANY

Sandahl, Rudolph E. Private — 1236 Brookdale Avenue, Chariton, Iowa. OS-MA-K-MGF.
Schmieder, Fred Private — Minster, Ohio.
Segerstrom, Helge R. Private — Milaca, Minn. OS-MA-W-MGF.
Shepka, Leo Private — Iron Mountain, Mich.
Smith, Bernard F. Private — 501 Pallister Avenue, Detroit, Mich.
Springer, Frank B. Private — Linden, Mich.
Smith, George W. Private — 695 Cavalry Avenue, Detroit, Mich.
Shultz, Vernie H. Private — Hedrick, Iowa. OS-MA-W-MGF.
Somers, Thomas A. Private — Red Lake Falls, Minn. OS-MA. (Reported as missing, later as W-MGF.)
Spiegel, Abraham Private — 4859 Champlain Avenue, Chicago, Ill.
Spindler, Adolph Private — Browns Valley, Minn. OS-MA-W-MGF.
Steine, Norman H. Private — Luverne, Mich.
Straw, Walter V. Private — Ray, Ind.
Sussex, Floyd W. Private — Route 1, Edson, Kans. OS-MA-K. (Died in German Prison Camp.)
Takes, Leo P. Private — Box 33, Walker, Iowa. OS-MA.
Tantow, Maynard A. Private — Manley, Iowa. OS.
Terrell, William C. Private — Bluford, Ill. OS-MA.
Thede, Herman R. Private — Reinbeck, Iowa. OS-MA-W-MGF.
Thomas, Glen W. Private — Welcome, Minn. OS.
Trana, Elmer H. Private — Henning, Minn. OS-MA.
Valos, Gust Private — East Moline, Ill.
Vernon, Earnest F. Private — Oblong, Ill. OS.
Walcott, Henry Private — Zeeland, Mich.

Walling, Charles E. Private — Redman, Oklahoma. OS-MA.
Walden, Carl G. A. Private — Tracy, Minn.
Welliver, Delbert M. Private — 1133 35th Street, Rock Island, Ill. OS-MA-K-MGF.
Wells, John R. Private — 3901 Gilbert, Latonia, Ky.
Williams, Benjamin F. Private — 605 North 6th Street, Columbia, Mo. OS-MA-W-MGF.
White, Roscoe Private — Savage, Ky.
Windsor, Fred Private — Spokane, Washington. OS-MA-W-MGF.
Winterrowd, Guy P. Private — Washington, Kans. OS-MA-W-G.
Erickson, John E. Private — 46 McGrath Street, Muskegon, Mich.
Letcher, Fred Private — St. Joseph, Mo. MA.
Davisson, Curtis L. Private — Clarksburg, W. Va. MA-W-MGF.
Gant, Tracy L. Private — Morris, Okla.
Lumm, Earl L. Private — 917 East Virmy Street, Colorado Springs, Colo. MA-W-MGF. (Reported as prisoner.)
Mahlum, Christian Private — RFD 2, Palermo, N. Dak. MA-W-MGF.
Marden, Earl C. Private — Kenmar, N. Dak. MA.
Mars, Truman G. L. Private — Bentley, N. Dak. OS-MA-W-MGF. (Reported later as missing.)
Marvin, John E. Private — Brooks, Wis.
Morgan, Vard M. Private — Dewey, Okla. OS-MA-W-MGF.
Oblander, Rhiney Private — Lehigh, Kans. OS.
Gus S. Gehlbach Captain — Trenton, Mo. OS-MA.
Edgar A. Miller, 1st Lt. — Ohio.
Norwood K. Lillybridge, 2nd Lt. — 149 Broadway, New York City, N. Y.

99

M COMPANY

ROSTER OF COMPANY G, 139th INFANTRY

NAME AND RANK	EMERGENCY ADDRESS	NAME AND RANK	EMERGENCY ADDRESS
Randall Wilson Captain	James C. Wilson, father, Bethany, Mo.	Turner, Carl W. Corporal	F. Turner, father, Cawker City, Kans.
Carlisle Wilson 1st Lt.	James C. Wilson, father, Bethany, Mo.	Yardley, Marshal G. Corporal	Alex. Yardley, father, Boynton, Mo.
Hugh B. Dudley 1st Lt.		Meek, Byron Corporal	C. A. Meek, father, Bethany, Mo.
Thomas Hopkins 2nd Lt.	Mrs. Edna I. Hopkins, wife, 1124 Bitting Ave., Wichita, Kans.	Allen, Vivian S. Corporal	D. E. Allen, father, Downs, Kans.
John A. Hoffman 2nd Lt.		Bottorff, Glen W. Corporal	J. W. Bottorff, father, Downs, Kans.
Richard P. McDonald Attached 2nd Lt.		Maize, John Corporal	W. R. Maize, father, Bethany, Mo.
Cowley, Richard P. 1st Sgt.	Edward Cowley, brother, Downs, Kans.	Mathews, Raymond Corporal	Alice Mathews, mother, Dora, Kans.
Moore, Ora G. Mess Sgt.	George Moore, father, Eagleville, Mo.	Smith, Frank Corporal	Kate Smith, mother, Montrose, Mo.
Blanke, Dean T. Sup. Sgt.	Earon Blanke, father, Downs, Kans.	Sexton, Joseph C. Corporal	H. G. Sexton, father, RFD 3, Norris City, Ill.
Dillon, Oscar N. Sergeant	Mrs. Oscar Dillon, wife, Bethany, Mo.	Meyers, Richard L. Corporal	Emma Meyers, wife, RFD 3, Cincinnati, Ia.
Bryant, George W. Sergeant	Mrs. George Bryant, wife, Bethany, Mo.	Hull, Laurel W. Corporal	F. B. Hull, father, Downs, Kans.
Walker, Jackson E. Sergeant	R. L. Walker, father, Bethany, Mo.	Jones, Ralph H. Corporal	E. B. Jones, father, Downs, Kans.
Henry, Harley Sergeant	Mrs. T. F. Henry, mother, Weatherby, Mo.	Odam, Wilber C. Corporal	William G. Odam, father, Unionville, Mo.
Murray, Charles F. Sergeant	Mrs. James Murray, mother, Whitemore, Kans.	Strait, Noel Corporal	William Strait, father, Bethany, Mo.
Crum, Raymond H. Sergeant	A. M. Crum, father, Downs, Kans.	Sellee, Earnest Corporal	W. A. Sallee, father, Mt. Moriah, Mo.
Arend, Harold D. Sergeant	Frank S. Arend, father, Downs, Kans.	Bowers, Arthur W. Corporal	W. F. Bowers, father, Downs, Kans.
Stansbury, Vaughn L. Sergeant	E. M. Stansbury, father, Cawker City, Kans.	Talbot, Richard W. Corporal	W. G. Talbot, father, Downs, Kans.
Hollar, Everitt R. Sergeant	J. E. Hollar, father, Ovando, Mont.	Edwards, Harry Corporal	Alfred Edwards, father, Downs, Kans.
Smith, Wren Sergeant	E. J. Smith, brother, Bethany, Mo.	Stuart, Pearson D. Corporal	Mrs. Pearson D. Stuart, wife, Albany, Mo.
Fisher, William F. Sergeant	Joe Nutter, friend, Hollenburg, Kans.	McDaniel, Cecil G. Corporal	J. D. McDaniel, father, Cainsville, Mo.
Scott, Robert D. Corporal	Mrs. Robert D. Scott, wife, Bethany, Mo.	Hardy, Lloyd E. Corporal	J. A. Hardy, father, Bethany, Mo.
Tobias, John B. Corporal	J. W. Tobias, father, Bethany, Mo.	Bryant, George L. Cook	F. T. Bryant, father, Downs, Kans.
Fruit, Orval Corporal	Mrs. Maude Carr, mother, Bethany, Mo.	Baker, Lou E. Cook	W. M. Baker, father, New Hampton, Mo.
Wightman, Edwin S. Corporal	Mrs. W. S. Wightman, mother, Bethany, Mo.	Gorham, Arthur Cook	Blorence Gorham, mother, Cawker City, Kans.
Flint, Paul O. Corporal	A. J. Flint, father, Bethany, Mo.	Stevenson, Floyd E. Cook	R. M. Stevenson, father, Bethany, Mo.
Sutton, Cecil A. Corporal	Mrs. Cecil A. Sutton, wife, Cawker City, Kans.	Johnson, Ercelle W. Bugler	Charles E. Johnson, father, Bethany, Mo.
White, John N. Corporal	F. S. White, father, Litchfield, Neb.	Burch, Roscoe E. Bugler	Mrs. Bertha E. Burch, mother, Kensington, Kans.
Williams, Albert J. Corporal	Mrs. Anna Williams, mother, Downs, Kans.	King, Ben Mechanic	Mrs. Roda Carroll, mother, Bethany, Mo.
Remick, Glenn W. Corporal	E. H. Remick, father, Downs, Kans.	Killinger, LeRoy Mechanic	W. H. Killinger, father, Portis, Kans.
Gale, Russell K. Corporal	Joe Gale, father, Bethany, Mo.	White, Dan Mechanic	Theodore Hodge, friend, Gen. Del. Detroit, Mich.
Wilkinson, Levi C. Corporal	J. B. Wilkinson, father, Bethany, Mo.	Akens, Frank M. Pvt. 1cl.	W. H. Akens, father, Portis, Kans.
VanCleave, Clifford M. Corporal	J. W. VanCleave, father, Lynville, Tenn.	Baker, Orval Pvt. 1cl.	Fannie Baker, mother, Ford City, Mo.
		Creamer, Forest H. Pvt. 1cl.	W. H. Creamer, father, Portis, Kans.

M COMPANY

Creek, Thomas	Pvt. 1cl.	Mattie Wilson, sister, Darlington, Mo.
Cordle, William M.	Pvt. 1cl.	John B. Cordle, father, Downing, Mo.
Covert, Louis L.	Pvt. 1cl.	Harve Covert, father, Glen Elder, Kans.
Davis, George M.	Pvt. 1cl.	J. W. Davis, father, New Hampton, Mo.
Dinsmore, Herman L.	Pvt. 1cl.	W. M. Dinsmore, father, Mt. Moriah, Mo.
Earles, Gordon L.	Pvt. 1cl.	J. H. Earls, father, Downs, Kans.
Elliott, Anderson	Pvt. 1cl.	W. A. Elliott, father, Rogers, Ark.
Finley, Harold A.	Pvt. 1cl.	Albert J. Finley, father, Cawker City, Kans.
Fowler, Clyde L.	Pvt. 1cl.	W. L. Fowler, father, Eagleville, Mo.
Fowler, David B.	Pvt. 1cl.	Mrs. Thomas Fowler, mother, Industry, Ill.
Franklin, Gohn H.	Pvt. 1cl.	Mrs. Ira Markley, sister, Leon, Ia.
Garrett, Ray B.	Pvt. 1cl.	Mrs. Louis R. Garrett, mother, Milan, Mo.
Goss, William G.	Pvt. 1cl.	Carrie Weymier, aunt, 715 6th Ave. S. E., Minneapolis, Minn.
Greenman, Benjamin E.	Pvt. 1cl.	J. J. Greenman, father, Downs, Kans.
Harris, James H.	Pvt. 1cl.	Mrs. Enos Harris, mother, Cora, Mo.
Hauber, Joseph M.	Pvt. 1cl.	John R. Hauber, father, RFD 7, St. Joseph, Mo.
Harris, Otto P.	Pvt. 1cl.	J. F. DeLong, uncle, Lamoni, Ia.
Hauptli, August J.	Pvt. 1cl.	J. H. Hauptli, father, Glen Elder, Kans.
Harrellson, George R.	Pvt. 1cl.	Catherine Harrellson, mother, Boynton, Mo.
Henderson, Arthur W.	Pvt. 1cl.	W. P. Henderson, father, Downs, Kans.
Henderson, Walter P.	Pvt. 1cl.	W. P. Henderson, father, Downs, Kans.
Hobbs, Roy V.	Pvt. 1cl.	C. B. Hobbs, father, Eagleville, Mo.
Hull, Floyd E.	Pvt. 1cl.	Ed Hull, father, Downs, Kans.
Irey, John M.	Pvt. 1cl.	S. G. Irey, father, Downs, Kans.
Jones, John	Pvt. 1cl.	Homer Minenthaler, uncle, Portis, Kans.
Ladow, Aubrey L.	Pvt. 1cl.	Mrs. Charles Ladow, mother, Cawker City, Kans.
Lovering, Earl W.	Pvt. 1cl.	Waldo Lovering, father, Hector, Minn.
Larson, Edwin E.	Pvt. 1cl.	Jane Ballew, mother, Princeton, Mo.
Leslie, Joseph P.	Pvt. 1cl.	W. T. Leslie, father, Milan, Mo.
Marzolf, Milton J.	Pvt. 1cl.	J. H. Marzolf, father, Glen Elder, Kans.
Morgan, Joseph D.	Pvt. 1cl.	Mrs. W. I. Morgan, mother, Pollock, Mo.
Moyer, Harry E.	Pvt. 1cl.	Frank Moyer, father, Portis, Kans.
Mullenix, Gurney F.	Pvt. 1cl.	John C. Mullenix, father, Unionville, Mo.
Parks, Lemiel A.	Pvt. 1cl.	M. E. Parks, father, New Hampton, Mo.
Poe, Clarence C.	Pvt. 1cl.	Vina Poe, mother, Albany, Mo.
Payne, Cail	Pvt. 1cl.	Sarah Payne, mother, Milan, Mo.

Reeder, Carl W.	Pvt. 1cl.	H. L. Reeder, father, 2813 S. 22nd St., St. Joseph, Mo.
Reddick, Earl E.	Pvt. 1cl.	N. E. Reddick, father, Downs, Kans.
Robinson, Charley L.	Pvt. 1cl.	J. W. Robinson, father, Downs, Kans.
Rogers, William M.	Pvt. 1cl.	J. A. Rogers, father, Boynton, Mo.
Sharp, Chester	Pvt. 1cl.	William Sharp, father, Cawker City, Kans.
Sharp, Gordon	Pvt. 1cl.	Lulu B. Sharp, mother, Lynnville, Tenn.
Shipps, Thomas C.	Pvt. 1cl.	Frank Shipps, father, Princeton, Mo.
Smothers, Ward M.	Pvt. 1cl.	Grant Smothers, mother, Eagleville, Mo.
Stufflebean, Dewey A.	Pvt. 1cl.	Ellen Stufflebean, mother, Milan, Mo.
Tipton, Albert	Pvt. 1cl.	Alfred Tipton, father, Milan, Mo.
Tipton, James E.	Pvt. 1cl.	Minnie Tipton, mother, North Salem, Mo.
Treaster, Oscar N.	Pvt. 1cl.	H. D. Treaster, father, Glen Elder, Kans.
Ward, Paul	Pvt. 1cl.	Mrs. Limje Ward, mother, Downs, Kans.
Wilson, Charley C.	Pvt. 1cl.	Tom Simpson, uncle, Boynton, Mo.
Wright, William	Pvt. 1cl.	Irwin J. Wright, father, Clifton, Kans.
Williams, Carl	Pvt. 1cl.	Benjamin Williams, father, Beloit, Kans.
Yeater, Glen	Pvt. 1cl.	E. R. Yeater, father, Ridgeway, Mo.
Aasved, Jesse I.	Private	Mrs. H. C. Aasved, mother, Wannaski, Minn.
Adamson, Gernie B.	Private	B. J. Adamson, father, Tabor, Ia.
Addams, Irwin	Private	G. A. Addams, father, Downs, Kans.
Akens, Charley R.	Private	W. H. Akens, father, Portis, Kans.
Anderson, Frank E.	Private	Orin Anderson, father, Eagle Bend, Minn.
Anderson, Glen	Private	A. C. Anderson, father, Bethany, Mo.
Welch, Jesse	Private	Zalus Welch, father, Dallas City, Ill.
Welch, Preston	Private	Zalus Welch, father, Dallas City, Ill.
Wells, Donald K.	Private	E. W. Wells, father, Downs, Kans.
Wideman, Fred E.	Private	Marrete Wideman, mother, Cawker City, Kans.
Wilke, Albert A.	Private	Louisa Wilke, mother, 2402 Broadway Ave., Everett, Wash.
Winters, Andrew F.	Private	Edward Winters, father, Portis, Kans.
Wood, Lemiel	Private	Mrs. Wood, mother, Denver, Mo.
Yoakum, Louie G.	Private	J. W. Yoakum, father, Brookfield, Mo.
Neifort, Jesse G.	Private	J. F. Neifort, father, Glen Elder, Kans.
Dial, Lawrence E.	Private	Isaac Dial, father, Cawker City, Kans.
Wolters, Bastaan J.	Private	Mrs. C. H. Wolters, mother, Downs, Kans.

101

M COMPANY

Shubert, Borthold G. Private

Haverty,

Arends, Harm Private — Teddo Arends, father, Watford City, N. Dak.

Becker, Joe P. Private — Maggie Becker, mother, Osborne, Kan.

Birkland, Halvor Private — Ola Birkland, father, Oklee, Minn.

Brayley, Elige Private — Mrs. S. V. Brayley, mother, Milan, Mo.

Brooks, Albert L. Private — Mrs. C. Brooks, mother, 417 No. 8th St., St. Joseph, Mo.

Campbell, Howard L. Private — Fannie Campbell, mother, Mt. Sterling, Ill.

Carmer, Roy C. Private — Cage Carmer, father, Boynton, Mo.

Casey, Philip Private — B. F. Casey, father, Glen Elder, Kans.

Casina, Sam Private — Angella Casina, mother, Patterson Road, Joliet, Ill.

Carmody, Thomas Private — Miss Mable Carmody, sister, Tarkio, Mo.

Cushing, Roy W. Private — G. W. Cushing, father, Downs, Kans.

Coble, Glen C. Private — Julia E. Coble, mother, Glen Elder, Kans.

Cope, James H. Private — Anna F. Swanson, mother, Mineola, Minn.

Cowan, Robert H. Private — Elizabeth Cowan, mother, Bethany, Mo.

Cox, Robert D. Private — Mrs. E. B. Cox, mother, Vermont, Ill.

Cox, LaRose Private — John W. Cox, father, Downs, Kans.

Duncan, Frank E. Private — Ed Duncan, father, Bloomington, Ind.

Dunn, Jesse I. Private — Florence Rogers, mother, 23 W. 4th St., Hutchinson, Kans.

Florea, Glen E. Private — Elizeberth Florea, mother, Republic, Kans.

Fuson, Richard D. Private — T. J. Fuson, father, 3416 Lafayette St., St. Joseph, Mo.

French, Minor E. Private — O. B. French, father, 1415 High St., Keokuk, Ia.

Free, Howard O. Private — James Free, father, Parker, Ind.

Glidewell, Lee S. Private — Mary Glidewell, mother, Milan, Mo.

Goheen, Maurice S. Private — John Goheen, father, Downs, Kans.

Green, Ralph P. Private — Oklay R. Green, father, Beloit, Kans.

Griffin, John J. Private — J. J. Griffin, father, 427 Thompson Ave., Hoopeston, Ill.

Harris, Cecil Private — George W. Hammonds, uncle, Bethany, Mo.

Hiatt, John D. Private — Orlando Hiatt, father, Bethany, Mo.

Holton, Sigurd Private — O. J. Holton, father, Langdon, N. Dak.

Holland, Raymond E. Private — E. C. Holland, father, Milan, Mo.

Hanson, Albert E. Private — Ole Hanson, father, Milaca, Minn.

Horne, Arthur B. Private — Lizzie Kaup, mother, Downs, Kans.

Cheesman, Theodore Private — Charles Cheesman, father, Rock Port, Mo.

Hoyt, James O. Private — Dora Hout, mother, 315 N. Penn St., Independence, Kans.

Humphrey, Everitt R. Private — Dora E. Humphrey, mother, Beaver Creek, Minn.

Ingvaldson, Peter Private — Thore Ingvaldson, father, Starbuck, Minn.

Iserman, William F. Private — Minnie Iserman, mother, Dakota, Ill.

Johnson, Carl Private — Ole Johnson, father, Kildeer, N. D.

Johnson, Leonard L. Private — J. P. Johnson, father, 432 Haines St., Kane, Pa.

Johnson, Phillip R. Private — Helen Johnson, mother, 2625 1st. St. Ave. S., Minneapolis, Minn.

Johnson, Nicholas W. Private — Tom Johnson, father, Bethany, Mo.

Johnson, Vearl V. Private — H. N. Johnson, father, Cawker City, Kans.

Kicker, Gustav Private

Kirshbaum, Henry Private — Mrs. K. Kirshbaum, mother, Downs, Kans.

Kling, John W. Private — P. C. Kling, father, 700 Blend St., Canton, Mo.

LaRock, Roy Private — Bert LaRock, father, Felton, Minn.

Larsen, Joe M. Private — Mrs. J. Larsen, mother, 2300 E. 35th St., Minneapolis, Minn.

Larson, Ole J. Private — Lars Lee, uncle, Manfred, N. D.

Leibenow, Paul G. Private — Mrs. Gust Haney, mother, Durbin, N. D.

Lemburg, Edward D. Private — Henry Lemberg, father, Lynd, Minn.

Locke, Velma G. Private — H. W. Locke, father, DeLean, Tex.

Lyson, Arthur Private — L. O. Lyson, father, Parshall, N. Dak.

Lynch, Harvey W. Private — J. C. Lynch, father, Beloit, Kans.

McCarty, William A. Private — Mrs. William McCarty, wife, 903 9th Ave. So., St. Cloud, Minn.

McCullough, Tello B. Private — J. H. McCullough, father, Milton, N. D.

Malcolm, Ollie M. Private — I. J. Keeney, uncle, Braymond, Ia.

Manor, John D. Private — Belle Manor, mother, Eagleville, Mo.

Markfort, Joseph F. Private — Anna Flory, sister, Princeton, Minn.

Marsh, Willie Private — W. N. Marsh, father, Ridgeway, Mo.

Marvanic, Frank P. Private — F. P. Marvanic, father, Downs, Kans.

Mattson, Mathews Private — Elias Mattson, father, Stanchfield, Minn.

Maxwell, Ray Private — Ben W. Maxwell, father.

Mew, George W. Private — J. H. Mew, father, West Cowes, Isle of Wight, England.

Micheals, Elmer A. Private — O. M. Micheals, father, Bethany, Mo.

Miller, Jess Private — Mrs. Clements, friend, Regent, N. D.

Montgomery, Earl Private — Minnie Montgomery, mother, Ridgeway, Mo.

Morrell, John S. Private — Joseph Morrell, father, Beloit, Kans.

Morris, Edward G. Private — Mrs. Lou Morris, mother, 201 Hellem St., Brookfield, Mo.

M COMPANY

Mortensen, Harry T. Private — Louis A. Mortensen, father, 2329 N. Keeler Ave., Chicago, Ill.

Murphy, William P. Private — Mrs. William Murphy, mother, 538 Pearl St., Benton Harbor, Mich.

Nasman, Elmer V. Private — Emma Nasman, sister, Clay Center, Kan.

Nasman, Eddie L. Private — Lillie Nasman, sister, 308 Clark, Clay Center, Kans.

Neal, Harry Private — Luther Propes, friend, Fairfax, Mo.

Nedoff, Mike Private — Ed Nedoff, father, Milliston, N. D.

Nelson, Arthur T. Private — Thos. A. Nelson, father, Tracy, Minn.

Nichols, Bernie E. Private — Ray Nichols, father, Berthold, N. D.

Okland, Thomas Private — Hans Okland, father, Walford City, N. D.

Olson, Oscar A. Private — Adolph Tolgen, uncle, Sanish, N. D.

Olson, Walter A. Private — Gust Olson, father, Irvin Valley, Minn.

Paucineau, Dave Private — Guy Packineau, father, Elbowood, N. D.

Paul, John Private — Joe Paul, father, Glen Ullin, N. D.

Parmelee, Dickinson L. Private — Lynhmp Parmelee, father, Osborne, Kans.

Peterson, Oscar A. Private — Howard F. Peterson, father, Ada, Minn.

Phillips, Harry Private — Daisy Jeffreys, friend, Portis, Kans.

Poppler, Edward T. Private — John Poppler, father, Frazee, Minn.

Rachuy, Samuel A. Private — Ernest Rachuy, father, West Hook, Minn.

Randall, James R. Private — Serah I. Randall, mother, Webster, Kans.

Ray, Ralph P. Private — Chas. G. Ray, father, Downs, Kans.

Reddick, William J. Private — N. E. Reddick, father, Downs, Kans.

Redenbo, William J. Private — David Redenbo, father, Smithbou, Ill.

Reiter, August C. Private — Louise Reiter, mother, 3047 W. Courtland St., Chicago, Ill.

Richardson, Wayne J. Private — Zell Richardson, father, Clay Center, Kans.

Renolds, James H. Private — Chas. E. Renolds, father, Winnebago, Minn.

Rosenberg, Edward H. Private — Mrs. S. Rosenberg, mother, Sobeski, Wisc.

Rollins, Vern Private — H. P. Atkins, uncle, Cawker City, Kans.

Roth, Chas. T. Private — H. C. Roth, father, 2518 Mullberry St., St. Joseph, Mo.

Sadowsky, Benjamin Private — Mrs. Chosha Sadowsky, mother, 223 E. Chicago Ave., St. Paul, Minn.

Seashore, Harry A. Private — J. A. Seashore, father, Buffalo, Minn.

Sears, Claude Private — Anna Sears, mother, Milan, Mo.

Sheets, Rudolph F. Private — Dewey Sheets, father, Cawker City, Kans.

Six, Willie Private — Dan C. Six, father, La Plata, Mo.

Slette, Oscar C. Private — Lauritz Slette, father, Mahnomen, Minn.

Swinson, Charley Private — Neri Swinson, father, Elbowlake, Minn.

Smith, Carl T. Private — John O. Smith, father, Bowen, Ill.

Smith, Frank H. Private — John W. Smith, father, St. Cloud, Minn.

Smith, Harold C. Private — Clarence W. Smith, father, Downs, Kans.

Smith, Orval J. Private

Smith, Zeb Private — J. W. Smith, father, Osborne, Kans.

Spake, James Private — Edward Spake, father, Brookfield, Mo.

Stanton, John T. Private — Mrs. A. W. Stanton, mother, Unionville, Mo.

Strickler, Omar N. Private — L. F. Strickler, father, Centerville, Ia.

Swanson, Selby J. Private — C. L. Swanson, father, Slayton, Minn.

Sztuk, John F. Private — Nellie Sztuk, sister, New Brighton, Minn.

Thompson, John T. Private — John Thompson, father, Princeton, Minn.

Thrasher, Robert Private — R. E. Thrasher, father, Downs, Kans.

Tobias, Vernon H. Private — J. W. Tobias, father, Bethany, Mo.

VanVeghel, William A. Private — Cecilia VanVeghel, mother, 724 10th Ave. N., Fargo, N. D.

Virak, Elias Private — Nels Virak, father, Harmony, Minn.

Wahlstrand, Harry L. Private — J. A. Wahlstrand, father, Willmar, Minn.

Wattenbarger, Verna E. Private — T. E. Wattenbarger, father, Milan, Mo.

Weingartner, Andrew P. Private — Margret Weingartner, mother, Wabasha, Minn.

Walker, Earl E. Private — I. M. Walker, father, Downs, Kan.

SHOCK TROOPS

1. Sergt. J. J. Kirkpatrick
2. Sergt. Earl A. Morgan
3. Bugler Kenneth M. Robinson
4. Chauncey E. Tipton
5. Corp. Wilber C. Odam

6. Joe S. Simpich
7. Albert E. Steele
8. Cecil L. Smith
9. Sergt. Albert E. Suess
10. Sergt. Hubert P. Warden, Jr.

11. William Plank

SIGNAL PLATOON OF HEADQUARTERS COMPANY

ROSTER OF COMPANY H, 139th INFANTRY

NAME AND RANK	HOME ADDRESS AND REMARKS
Edward S. Axline 2nd Lt.	Weona, Ill., joined Org. 11-1-18.
Charles H. Brown Captain	Horton, Kans., 3rd Kans. Trfd. to 60th Depot Brigade when 3rd Kans. and 4th Mo. were consolidated.
Ralph H. Cox 2nd Lt.	Carrollton, Mo., 4th Mo. Discharged at Camp Doniphan, Okla.
Brown Dyer Captain	Carrollton, Mo., 4th Mo. Retd. to States as instructor. A.
Donald A. Eskridge 2nd Lt.	Joined Org. 11-12-18. A.
William S. Gray 1st Lt.	Yankton, S. Dak., joined Org. at Camp Doniphan, Okla. St.M-A-G-P.
Charles W. Graham 2nd Lt.	Gardner, Kans., joined Org. 5-1-18. St.M. Wounded in Argonne. A.
Theodore Hunt 2nd Lt.	St. Louis, Mo., Joined Org. 7-5-18. St.M-W-Argonne. A.
Coburn Hull 1st Lt.	Joined Org. 11-17-18. St.M-W-Argonne. Trfd. to 12-11-18.
Clarence T. Johnson 1st Lt.	Baltimore, Md., 4th Mo. Retd. to States as instructor. A.
Rodney J. Ludlow Captain	Chicago, Ill., 5th Mo. St.M and Argonne. Joined Org. 1-16-18.
Charles F. Lynch 2nd Lt.	Columbia, Penn., joined Org. 10-6-18. Trfd. Camp Dodge Det.
Ralph F. Lucier Captain	Abilene, Kans., 3rd Kans. Hq. Co. this Regt.
Richard P. McDonald 2nd Lt.	Joined Org. at Camp Doniphan.
John W. McManigal 1st Lt.	Horton, Kans., 3rd Kans. St.M. Wounded in Argonne. A.
Joe W. McQueen Captain	Carrollton, Mo., 4th Mo. St.M. Wounded in Argonne. A.
Harry Ross 2nd Lt.	Joined Org. 10-8-18. Trfd. Co. 2nd Bn. Staff.
Todd 2nd Lt.	
Francis Wall 1st Lt.	Joined Org. 11-11-18. Retd. to States as instructor.
Adkins, Oliver P. Cook	Hardin, Mo., 4th Mo. St.M-MA. Sent to hospital. A.
Adkins, Robert O. Pvt. 1cl.	Wakenda, Mo., 4th Mo. St.M-MA-GSW. Argonne. P.
Adkins, Charley Private	Hardin, Mo., 4th Mo. Left in casual camp, Camp Doniphan, Okla.
Adkins, Ira Corporal	Carrollton, Mo., 4th Mo. St.M-MA. Sent to hospital. A.
Allgire, Ray R. Corporal	Wakefield, Kans. St.M-MA-P.
Alstrom, Carl W. Corporal	Enterprise, Kans. St.M-MA. Sent to hospital. A.
Anderson, Arvid H. Corporal	Enterprise, Kans. 3rd Kans. St.M-MA-P.

NAME AND RANK	HOME ADDRESS AND REMARKS
Anderson, William J. Private	Grand Rapids, Mich., 85th Repl. Joined 10-20-18. P.
Andres, Albert Pvt. 1cl.	Abilene, Kans., 3rd Kans. Trfd. to 110th Supply Train. A.
Aplin, Robert Private	Abilene, Kans., 3rd Kans. Trfd. to Co. B 139th Inf. A.
Appel, Albert B. Private	85th Repl. Trfd. to Hq. Co. 139th Inf.
Armstrong, Harry A. Pvt. 1cl.	Abilene, Kans., 3rd Kans. Trfd. to General Hq. 7-23-18. A.
Arnold, George W. Mess Sgt.	1233 Oak St., Kansas City, Mo., 4th Mo. St.M-MA-P.
Aspley, Roscoe R. Private	Abilene, Kans., 3rd Kans. St.M. Sev. Shrapnel in Argonne. A.
Auckland, John H. Private	Detroit, Mich., 85th Repl. J. 10-20-18. P.
Bly, Frank H. Private	Detroit, Mich., 85th Repl. J. 10-20-18. P.
Boehmke, Edwin G. Pvt. 1cl.	Velva, N. Dak., 88th Repl. J. 5-25-18. St.M-GSW in Argonne. P.
Boschert, Leo Sergeant	Norborne, Mo., 4th Mo. St.M-MA-P.
Boyd, John Private	Abilene, Kans., 3rd Kans. Discharged at Camp Doniphan, Okla. A.
Branch, Irving Private	Port Huron, Mich., 85th Repl. J. 10-20-18. P.
Bradbury, Cyril H. Pvt. 1cl.	New Ulm, Minn., 88th Repl. J. 5-25-18. St.M-GSW. Argonne. P.
Brenner, Sydney C. Bn. Sgt. Maj.	Wakefield, Kans., 3rd Kans. St.M-MA-A.
Brinkmeyer, John A. Pvt. 1cl.	Navarre, Kans., 3rd Kans. St.M-GSW Argonne. A.
Brinkmeyer, William F. Pvt. 1cl.	Enterprise, Kans., 3rd Kans. St.M-MA-P.
Brotherton, Lewis F. Corporal	Wakenda, Mo., 4th Mo. St.M. Killed in Argonne.
Buchanan, Dewey H. Pvt. 1cl.	Abilene, Kans., 3rd Kans. St.M. Killed in Argonne.
Buchanan, Frank L. Private	Abilene, Kans., 3rd Kans. St.M-GSW. Argonne. P.
Buchanan, Harry W. Bugler	Abilene, Kans., 3rd Kans. St.M-MA-P.
Buchanan, Paul Private	Abilene, Kans., 3rd Kans. St.M-MA-P.
Buchanan, Ward Private	Abilene, Kans., 3rd Kans. St.M-MA-P.
Burroughs, Charles Pvt. 1cl.	Holden, Mo., 4th Mo. St.M-MA-P.
Burton, Simeon S. Pvt. 1cl.	Abilene, Kans., 3rd Kans. St.M-MA-P.
Baarsgaard, Carl J. Private	Rochert, Minn., 88th Repl. J. 5-25-18. St.M-MA-P.

SIGNAL PLATOON OF HEADQUARTERS COMPANY

Bales, Charles G. Corporal
Norborne, Mo., 4th Mo. St.M-GSW. Argonne. A.

Ballweg, Clarence Private
Abilene, Kans., 3rd Kans. Trfd. to 110th Amm. Train. A.

Bankers, Arnold M. Pvt. 1cl.
Ghent, Minn., 88th Repl. 5-25-18. St.M-MA-A.

Bargabas, Ralph J. Pvt. 1cl.
Royalton, Minn., 88th Repl. 5-25-18. St.M-GSW in Argonne. P.

Barkley, Elmer W. Private
Abilene, Kans., 3rd Kans. St.M. Sent to Hospital. A.

Barrier, Hugh A. Private
Carrollton, Mo., 4th Mo. St.M-MA. Trfd. Hq. Co. 138th Inf.

Bates, Murl L. Pvt. 1cl.
Hale, Mo., 4th Mo. St.M-MA. Sent to hospital. A.

Beck, George J. Private
Norborne, Mo. 4th Mo. St.M-MA-P.

Berry, Robert C. Private
Royal Oak, Mich., 85th Repl. 10-20-18. P.

Best, Earl P. Private
Bogard, Mo., 4th Mo. St.M. Sev. wounded in Argonne, died in hospital.

Bierle, Samuel Private
McClusky, N. Dak., 88th Repl. J. 5-25-18. St.M-MA-P.

Blair, Oberton J. Private
Abilene, Kans., 3rd Kans. Trfd. to Hdqrs. Co. 139th Inf. A.

Blomberg, Amil Private
85th Repl. J. 10-20-18. Trfd. to Hdqrs. Co. 139th Inf. A.

Cairns, Charles B. Pvt. 1cl.
Wakefield, Kans., 3rd Kans. St.M-MA-P.

Callahan, Holly W. Private
Abilene, Kans., 3rd Kans. St.M-GSW Argonne. A.

Callahan, Joe H. Private
Abilene, Kans., 3rd Kans. St.M-GSW Argonne. A.

Cameron, Harry Private
Langdon, N. Dak., 88th Repl. J. 5-25-18. St.M-MA-P.

Campbell, James Private
Abilene, Kans., 3rd Kans. Trfd. to Co. A, 139th Inf. A.

Camplen, Charles H. Private
Detroit, Mich., 85th Repl. J. 10-20-18. P.

Carter, George B. Corporal
Bogard, Mo., 4th Mo. St.M-MA-P.

Cashman, John L. Pvt. 1cl.
Okmulgee, Okla., 3rd Kans. St.M-GSW Argonne.

Caton, William J. Private
Carrollton, Mo., 4th Mo. St.M-MA-P.

Charles, Luther A. Pvt. 1cl.
Bogard, Mo., 4th Mo. St.M. Gassed in Argonne. A.

Chestnut, Raymond L. Pvt. 1cl.
Washington, Kans., 3rd Kans. Trfd. to 139th MC-A.

Clark, Homer L. Cook
Abilene, Kans., 3rd Kans. St.M-MA-P.

Cobbs, Elmer W. Private
Norborne, Mo., 4th Mo. St.M-MA-P.

Cochran, Robert A. Sergeant
Carrollton, Mo., 4th Mo. St.M-MA-P.

Conley, John W., Jr. Pvt. 1cl.
Carrollton, Mo., 4th Mo. St.M-GSW Argonne. A.

Conley, Everett L. Sergeant
Carrollton, Mo., 4th Mo. St.M-MA-P.

Correll, Elvin O. Corporal
Mildred, Kans., 4th Mo. St.M-MA-P.

Cox, Joseph J. Corporal
Abilene, Kans., 3rd Kans. St.M-MA-A.

Cravens, Guy D. Pvt. 1cl.
Carrollton, Mo., 4th Mo. St.M-MA-P.

Croke, Charles J. Private
Wyandott, Mich., 85th Repl. J. 10-20-18. P.

Crouse, Burnie D. Private
Murray, Ky., 85th Repl. J. 10-20-18. P.

Crumrine, Harvey W. Pvt. 1cl.
Abilene, Kans., 3rd Kans. St.M-MA-P.

Curran, Mark S. Private
Abilene, Kans., 3rd Kans. St.M. Killed in Argonne.

Currier, Frank B. Corporal
112 N. Prospect St., Rochester. Minn. 88th Repl. J. 4-20-18. St.M-MA-P.

Cole, Frank A. Corporal
Norborne, Kans., 4th Mo. St.M-GSW Argonne. P.

Coles, Harry E. Private
Marceline, Mo., 4th Mo. St.M-GSW Argonne. A.

Collins, Sammy Pvt. 1cl.
Bogard, Mo., 4th Mo. St.M. Killed in Argonne. A.

Cooper, James M. Corporal
Manson, Tenn., 3rd Kans. St.M-MA-P.

Conner, Walter Private
Norborne, Mo., 4th Mo. St.M-GSW Argonne. P.

Curtis, Joseph A. Private
88th Repl. J. 10-20-18. Trfd. to Hdqrs. Co. 139th Infantry.

Curtis, James O. Corporal
Carrollton, Mo., 4th Mo. St.M-GSW Argonne. A.

Cutler, James R. Corporal
Abilene, Kans., 3rd Kans. St.M. Killed in Argonne.

Cutler, Dale J. Corporal
Abilene, Kans., 3rd Kans. St.M-GSW in Argonne. P.

Dalton, Jess A. Private
Fort Thomas, Ky., 85th Repl. J. 10-20-18. P.

Daniels, Jesse Private
Abilene, Kans., 3rd Kans. Trfd. to 110th Amm. Train.

Davis, Arch W. 1st Sgt.
Abilene, Kans., 3rd Kans. Trfd. to Base Hosp. A.

Davis, Frank E. Corporal
Blue Rapids, Kans., 3rd Kans. St.-M-GSW in Argonne. P.

Dawson, Lee Roy Sergeant
Abilene, Kans., 3rd Kans. St.M-MA. Sent to Hospital.

Day, Williard L. Private
Abilene, Kans., 3rd Kans. St.M-GSW in Argonne.

Dayton, Howard E. Private
Abilene, Kans., 3rd Kans. Trfd. to General Headquarters.

Dean, Leslie Private
Pontiac, Mich., 85th Repl. J. 10-20-18. P.

Dederick, Howard E. Private
Battle Creek, Mich., 85th Repl. J. 10-20-18. P.

Deering, Richard Private
Pontiac, Mich., 85th Repl. J. 10-20-18. P.

DeHaven, Walter Private
Abilene, Kans., 3rd Kans. Left in Miami County Hosp. Peru. Ind.

Demagio, Sam Pvt. 1cl.
Abilene, Kans., 3rd Kans. St.M-GSW in Argonne. P.

Dettmers, William H. Sergeant
Edwardsville, Ill., 88th Repl.

Dixon, Wesley Private
85th Repl. J. 10-20-18. Trfd. to Troop L. 2nd Cal.

106

SIGNAL PLATOON OF HEADQUARTERS COMPANY

Dixon, Louie E.   Pvt. 1cl.   Bigsville, Ill., 88th Repl. J. 4-20-18. St.M. Gassed Argonne. P.

Dixon, Clarence E.   Private   Abilene, Kans., 3rd Kans. St.M-GSW in Argonne. P.

Dixon, Rodger F.   Private   Norborne, Mo., 4th Mo. Left in casual camp, Camp Doniphan. A.

Dobkins, John   Private   Abilene, Kans., 3rd Kans. Trfd. to Hdqrs. Co. 139th Inf. A.

Dockery, Elmer E.   Pvt. 1cl.   Hale, Mo., 4th Mo. St.M-GSW Argonne. A.

Donovan, Murl L.   Private   Abilene, Kans., 3rd Kans. SDD Camp Doniphan. A.

Dooley, Willie D.   Private   Lexington, Mo., 4th Mo. St.M-GSW Argonne. A. Sent to hospital.

Dooley, Carl   Corporal   Norborne, Mo., 4th Mo. St.M. Killed in Argonne.

Dower, Jess R.   Mechanic   Talmage, Kans., 3rd Kans. St.M-MA-P.

Dronenburg, Russel N.   Private   Norborne, Mo., 4th Mo. St.M-GSW Argonne. A. Sent to hospital.

Duckworth, William A.   Private   85th Repl. J. 10-20-18. Trfd. to 110th M. S.

Duffy, Issac   Pvt. 1cl.   Abilene, Kans., 3rd Kans. St.M-MA-P.

Durnell, Oscar K.   Pvt. 1cl.   Tina, Mo., 4th Mo. St.M. Gassed in Argonne. P.

Dyer, Vaughn   Private   Abilene, Kans., 3rd Kans. St.M-MA. Trfd. Hdqrs. 35th Div. P.

Eaves, Everett   Corporal   Manchester, Kans., 3rd Kans. St.M-MA. Trfd. B. Hospital 85. A.

Eckley, Charles T.   Pvt. 1cl.   Abilene, Kans., 3rd Kans. Trfd. to C. Hosp. 34, Romsey, Eng. Retd. to Co. 6-18-18. P.

Ehley, August A.   Pvt. 1cl.   Fort Washington, Wis., 85th Repl. 10-20-18. P.

Elwick, Fay A.   Pvt. 1cl.   Abilene, Kans., 3rd Kans. St.M-MA-P.

England, Robert J.   Pvt. 1cl.   Carrollton, Mo., 4th Mo. St.M. Killed in Argonne.

English, Byron A.   Private   Mason, Mich., 85th Repl. J. 10-20-18. P.

Erp, John B., Jr.   Corporal   Bogard, Mo., 4th Mo. St.M-GSW Argonne. A.

Etherington, Geo. W.   Private   Abilene, Kans., 3rd Kans. Trfd. to 110th MP.A.

Ewing, Rexford E.   Corporal   Birchtree, Mo., 3rd Kans. St.M-MA P.

Farley, William   Private   Fort Slocum. N. Y., 85th Repl. J. 10-20-18. P.

Farmer, Thomas R.   Private   Marinette, Wis., 85th Repl. J. 10-20-18. P.

Faulkner, Harry B.   Private   Marceline, Mo., 4th Mo. St.M-MA. Trfd. to F. Co. 139th Inf. A.

Fears, Hulbert O.   Private   Bosworth, Mo., 4th Mo. St.M-GSW Argonne. A.

Fisher, Grant H.   Private   Abilene, Kans., 3rd Kans. St.M-MA. Trfd. to 70th Brig. Hdqrs. Det.

Flanngin, Paul P.   Private   Bogard, Mo., 4th Mo. St.M-GSW Argonne. A.

Foltz, Edward J.   Corporal   Abilene, Kans., 3rd Kans. St.M-GSW Argonne. P.

Foltz, Carl H.   Private   Abilene, Kans., 3rd Kans. St.M-MA. Trfd to 70th Brig. Hdqrs. Det.

Foltz, John A.   Sergeant   Abilene, Kans., 3rd Kans. MA-P. 85th Repl. J. 10-20-18. Sent to hospital.

Franck, Oscar W.   Private   Carrollton, Mo., 4th Mo. St.M-MA. Sent to hospital.

Franke, August A.   Sup. Sgt.   Abilene, Kans., 3rd Kans. Trfd. to Hdqrs. Co. A.

Frazier, Leslie   Private   Wakenda, Kans., 4th Mo. St.M-GSW Argonne. A.

Frazier, John J.   Private   Wakenda, Kans., 4th Mo. Returned to States as instructor.

Frazier, Joseph L.   Corporal   Hardingsburg, Ky., 85th Repl. J. 10-20-18. P.

French, Proctor   Private   Abilene, Kans., 3rd Kans. St.M-MA-A. Trfd. to 130th M. G. Bn.

Frey, John   Sergeant   Carrollton, Mo., 4th Mo. St.M-MA-P.

Fugit, Rector E.   Private   Abilene, Kans., 3rd Kans. St.M-GSW Argonne. A.

Garton, William H.   Private   Abilene, Kans., 3rd Kans. Trfd. to 5th Army replacement bn. A.

Gibbs, Glenn I.   Private   4th Mo. Left in Base Hospital, Camp Doniphan, Okla.

Gibson, Eldon L.   Private   Abilene, Kans., 3rd Kans. St.M-MA-P.

Gish, Jacob M.   Corporal   Abilene, Kans., 3rd Kans. St.M-GSW Argonne. Trfd. to Base Hospital Port Debarkation Newport News. A.

Gish, Ray   Corporal   Bogard, Mo., 4th Mo. St.M-MA-P.

Glover, Daniel T.   Private   88th Repl. Trfd. to Base Hospital. A.

Goin, Roy E.   Private   New York City, N. Y., 85th Repl. J. 10-20-18. P.

Goldsmith, Samuel B.   Private   Centerville, Iowa., 88th Repl. J. 5-25-18. P-St.M-MA.

Grasso, Alfredo   Private   Dubuque, Ia., 88th Repl. J. 5-25-18. P-St M-MA.

Griffith, Lorenzo   Private   Braymer, Mo., 4th Mo., St.M-MA. Trfd. to Hdqrs. Co.

Gunby, William E.   Private   Abilene, Kans., 3rd Kans. Trfd. to Co. B, 139th Inf. A.

Hall, James E.   Private   Hardin, Mo., 4th Mo. St.M-MA-P.

Halterman, Willie J. B.   Pvt. 1cl.   Richmond, Mo., 4th Mo. St.M-MA-P

Halterman, William S.   Private   Litchfield, Minn., 85th Repl. J. 10-20-18. P.

Halverson, Harry B.   Private   705 E. 34th St., Kansas City, Kans., 3rd Kans. St.M-MA-P.

Hanna, Max   1st Sgt.   Wakefield, Kans., 3rd Kans. St.M-GSW Argonne. Trfd. to Hospital. A.

Harris, Ralph M.   Corporal   Ionia, Mich., 85th Repl. J. 10-20-18. P.

Harroun, Ben L.   Private

HEADQUARTERS COMPANY

Hatcher, Issac — Private
Rochester, Mich., 85th Repl. J. 10-20-18. P.

Hawthorne, Coe — Private
Abilene, Kans., 3rd Kans. Trfd. to 130th M. G. Bn. A.

Haynes, Quinn H. — Pvt. 1cl.
Abilene, Kans., 3rd Kans. St.M-MA-P.

Helm, Curtis S. — Bugler
Hale, Mo., 4th Mo. St.M. Killed in Argonne.

Herman, Walter R. — Corporal
Abilene, Kans., 3rd Kans. St.M-MA-P.

Herman, Carl J. — Private
Charles City, Ia., 88th Repl. J. 5-25-18. P-St.M-MA.

Heskitt, Alvin — Private
Abilene, Kans., 3rd Kans. Trfd. to Hdqrs. Co. A.

Hess, Edward J. — Private
Chicago, Ill., 85th Repl. J. 10-20-18. P.

Heston, Alfred A. — Private
Jamestown, Ark., 4th Mo. St.M-GSW Argonne. P.

Hoham, Fred B. — Private
Ft. Wayne, Ind., 85th Repl. J. 10-20-18. P.

Holloway, William R. — Private
Charlotte, Mich., 85th Repl. J. 10-20-18. P.

Horn, Walter B. — Corporal
Carrollton, 4th Mo. St.M-GSW Argonne. P.

Howe, George H. — Private
Hersey, Mich., 85th Repl. J. 10-20-18. P.

Hudson, David K. — Sergeant
Bogard, Mo., 4th Mo., St.M-MA-P.

Hummel, Frank W. — Private
Monroe, Mich., 85th Repl. J. 10-20-18. P.

Huss, Louis O. — Private
Makoti, N. Dak., 88th Repl. J. 5-25-18. St.M. Killed in Argonne.

Issitt, George — Private
Enterprise, Kans., 3rd Kans. Left in Camp Doniphan. A.

Ivaneck, Ignatz — Private
Mandan, N. Dak., 85th Repl. J. 10-20-18. Sent to hospital. A.

Jacobson, Knud — Private
Coules, N. Dak., 88th Repl. J. 5-25-18. St.M-MA-P.

James, David R. — Pvt. 1cl.
Carrollton, Mo., 4th Mo. St.M-GSW Argonne. P.

Jawerski, Joseph W. — Private
85th Repl. J. 10-20-18. A. Sent to hospital.

Jeffcoat, Melvin E. — Corporal
Abilene, Kans., 3rd Kans. St.M-GSW Argonne. A.

Jenson, Albert — Private
Cando, N. Dak., 88th Repl. St.M-MA-P.

Johnson, Arthur S. — Private
88th Repl. J. 4-15-18. A.

Johnson, Harry — Private
Lamberton, Minn., 88th Repl. 5-25-18. P-St.M-GSW Argonne.

Jones, Ralph E. — Private
Tina, Mo., 4th Mo. St.M-MA. Trfd. to 110th Amm. Train. A.

Jones, Aaron E. — Sergeant
Enterprise, Kans., 3rd Kans. St.M-GSW Argonne. A.

Jordan, Frank B. — Mechanic
Abilene, Kans., 3rd Kans. St.M-MA-P.

Jordan, Harold M. — Pvt. 1cl.
1244 Wash. St., Kansas City, Mo., 3rd Kans. St.M-GSW in Argonne died of wounds.

Jorgenson, Arthur O. — Private
Pilot, N. Dak., 88th Repl. J. 5-25-18. St.M-GSW Argonne. A.

Kahn, Bernard F. — Private
Milwaukee, Wis., 85th Repl. J. 10-20-18. P.

Kassen, Frank H. — Sergeant
Norborne, Mo., 4th Mo. Trfd. OTS. Assigned to 42nd Div. A.

Kauffman, Clyde — Sergeant
Abilene, Kans., 3rd Kans. Discharged to accept Com. as 2nd Lt. Assigned to 28th Div. A.

Kauffman, Clarence — Sergeant
Salina, Kans., 3rd Kans. Trfd. OTS. Assigned to 5th Div. A.

Keener, Orie — Private
85th Repl. 10-20-18, A. Trfd. to Hdqrs. Co. 139th Inf.

Kehler, Ward H. — Pvt. 1cl.
Abilene, Kans., 3rd Kans. St.M-MA-P.

Kellington, Charles A. — Private
88th Repl. J. 5-25-18. A. Sent to hospital. A.

Kelman, James C. — Pvt. 1cl.
85th Repl. J. 10-20-18. Trfd. to 1st replacement depot St. Agnieau. A.

Kemmerer, Birtrus — Corporal
Carrollton, Mo., 4th Mo. St.M-GSW Argonne, awarded D.S.C. P.

Kibby, Doe D. — Private
Cadillac, Mich., 85th Repl. J. 10-20-18. P.

Kirk, Charles G. — Sergeant
Abilene, Kans., 3rd Kans. Returned to states for service.

Klug, Henry — Private
Bad Axe, Mich., 85th Repl. J. 10-20-18. P.

Knoblock, Julius A. — Pvt. 1cl.
Allegan, Mich., 85th Repl. J. 10-20-18. P.

Knutson, Erling — Private
Williston, N. Dak., 88th Repl. J. 5-25-18. P-St.M-GSW Argonne.

Koontz, Sam F. — Pvt. 1cl.
Carrollton, Mo., 4th Mo. Trfd. to Hdqrs. 139th Inf. A.

Kooistra, Jacob J. — Private
Lake City, Mich., 85th Repl. J. 10-20-18. P.

Koost, Otis A. — Private
Carrollton, Mo., 4th Mo. St.M-GSW Argonne. Taken prisoner in Argonne. A.

Kotts, Robert B. — Private
Ypsilanti, N. Dak., 88th Repl. J. 5-25-18. A. St.M-GSW Argonne.

Koch, David — Private
New York City, N. Y., 85th Repl. J. 10-20-18. P.

Kugler, Henry Jr. — Private
Hardin, Mo., 4th Mo. Discharged at Doniphan.

Labadie, Clifford D. — Pvt. 1cl.
Manistique, Mich., 85th Repl. J. 10-20-18. P.

Lackey, Ray — Private
Abilene, Kans., 3rd Kans. Trfd. to 110th Amm. Train. A.

Lamb, Frank — Corporal
Bogard, Mo., 4th Mo. St.M-MA-P.

Langchoug, Emil O. — Private
Northwood, N. Dak., 88th Repl. J. 5-25-18. P-St.M-MA-P.

Larkin, James — Private
Abilene, Kans., 3rd Kans. Trfd. to Co. E, 139th Inf. A.

Lasser, Edward F. — Sergeant
Carrollton, Mo., 3rd Mo. St.M-MA-P.

Lautenschaeger, Henry J. — Private
Milwaukee, Wis., 85th Repl. J. 10-20-18. P.

Lee, Arthur S. — Private
White Earth, N. Dak., 88th Repl. J. 5-25-18. St.M. Killed in Argonne.

Leshley, Floyd — Private
Abilene, Kans., 3rd Kans. Discharged at Camp Doniphan.

Leshley, Blake — Private
Abilene, Kans., 3rd Kans. Trfd. to Co. I, 139th Inf. A.

Lewis, Robert R. — Private
Abilene, Kans., 3rd Kans. Trfd. to 110th Supply Train. A.

HEADQUARTERS COMPANY

Loader, George L. Pvt. 1cl.
Wakefield, Kans., 3rd Kans. St.M-GSW Argonne. P.

Loader, Robert K. Pvt. 1cl.
Wakefield, Kans., 3rd Kans. St.M-MA-P.

Lindberg, Harry W. Private
Scranton, N. Dak., 88th Repl. J. 5-25-18. St.M-Killed in Argonne.

Lonsdale, Arthur L. Private
Prestigo, Wis., 85th Repl. J. 10-20-18. P.

Lovell, John C. Private
Carrollton, Mo., 4th Mo. Killed in Vosges Mts. 1st man killed in action in 35th Div.

Lucier, Alcide H. Private
Abilene, Kans., 3rd Kans. St.M-GSW Argonne. A.

Luck, Charles J. Private
Solomon, Kans., 3rd Kans. Trfd. to Co. I, 139th Inf. A.

Lukas, Anthony Corporal
Racine, Wis., 88th Repl. J. 5-25-18. St.M. Gassed in Argonne.

Lutes, Olin S. Private
Coal Center, Penn., 88th Repl. J. 5-25-18. St.M-MA-Trfd. Aver. Uni.

Machen, John E. Sergeant
Solomon, Kans., 3rd Kans. St.M-GSW Argonne taken prisoner, later in American hospital.

Madden, John H. Private
Lansing, Mich., 85th Repl. J. 10-20-18. P.

Mancel, Barney L. Corporal
Williston, N. Dak., 88th Repl. J. 5-25-18. St.M-MA-P.

Mann, Allie Corporal
Abilene, Kans., 3rd Kans. Trfd. to 110th Amm. Train.

McClanahan, Albert Private
Brooksville, Ky., 85th Repl. J. 10-20-18. P.

McCormack, Wharton J. Sergeant
Carrollton, Mo., 4th Mo. St.M-MA-P.

McCosh, Harry Private
Abilene, Kans. 3rd Kans. Trfd. to Hq. Co. Wounded in Argonne.

McGran, Preston J. Pvt. 1cl.
Perham, Minn. 88th Repl. St.M. Gassed in Argonne. P.

McGuire, Dewey H. Pvt. 1cl.
Norborne, Mo. 4th Mo St.M-GSW. Argonne A.

McKerghan, Harry E. Private
Coleraine, Minn. 88th Repl. J. 5-25-18. St.M-GSW. Argonne. A.

McKibbin, Bryon D. Private
Hastings, Mich. 85th Repl. J. 10-20-18. P.

McNeal, Ellis A. Private
Abilene, Kans. 3rd Kans. Trfd. to Vet. Corp. 5th Unit. A.

Meier, Theodore Private
Hallottsville, Tex. 85th Repl. J. 10-20-18. P.

Melby, Emil J. Corporal
Williston, N. Dak. 88th Repl. J. 5-25-18. St.M-MA. P.

Merillat, Harve G. Pvt. 1cl.
Enterprise, Kans. 3rd Kans. St.M. Killed in Argonne.

Merkling, George Private
Pierz, Minn. 88th Repl. J. 5-25-18. St.M-GSW. Argonne. A.

Michaels, Elmer A. Private
Bethany, Mo. 4th Mo. St.M-MA. P.

Michelson, Frank J. Private
Mandan, N. Dak. 88th Repl. St.M-MA. J. 5-25-18. P.

Mill, Fred Private
Stanley, N. Dak. 88th Repl. St.M-MA. J. 5-25-18. P.

Mints, Robert J. Private
Vernon, Tex. 85th Repl. J. 10-20-18. P.

Moe, Herbert L. Pvt. 1cl.
St. Paul, Minn. 88th Repl. J. 5-25-18. St.M-GSW. Argonne. P.

Monroe, Elmer L. Pvt. 1cl.
Enterprise, Kans. 3rd Kans. St.M. Missing in action Argonne.

Monty, Floyd F. Private
Freyburg, N. Dak. 88th Repl. J. 5-25-18. St.M-GSW. Argonne. A.

Meyers, Frederick D. Private
Carrollton, Mo. 4th Mo. St.M-MA. P.

Neighbors, Chester B. Private
Lemonville, Mo. 4th Mo. St.M-GSW Argonne. A.

Neil, James H. Private
85th Repl. J. 10-20-18. Trfd. to Hq. 139th A.

Nelson, Oscar Private
Minot, N. Dak. 88th Repl. J. 5-25-18. St.M-MA-P.

Nelson, Nels E. Private
Kenmare, N. Dak. 88th Repl. J. 5-25-18. St.M-GSW Argonne. A.

Nemec, William N. Pvt. 1cl.
Abilene, Kans. 3rd Kans. Trfd. to BH No. 33 Portsmouth, Eng.

Newton, Herbert J. Sergeant
Carrollton, Mo. 4th Mo. St.M-MA. Sent to hospital. A.

Neibrugge, John Private
Bunston, Mo. 4th Mo. St.M-MA-P.

Nowland, Owen Pvt. 1cl.
Carrollton, Mo. 4th Mo. St.M-MA. P.

Olson, John G. Private
Vanhock, N. Dak. 88th Repl. J. 5-25-18. P-St.M-GSW Argonne. P.

Olson, Carl O. Private
Muland, Minn. 85th Repl. J. 10-20-18. P.

O'Neal, Willie H. Private
Abilene, Kans. 3rd Kans. St.M-MA-P.

O'Neil, Clarence F. Sergeant
Norborne, Mo. 4th Mo. St.M-GSW Argonne P.

Parcels, Lee W. Private
4th Mo. Sent to hospital at Camp Doniphan. A.

Parke, Ellis C. Private
Hillsdale, Mich., 85th Repl. J. 10-20-18. P.

Parkins, Ray W. Sergeant
Carrollton, Mo. 4th Mo. Comm. Lt. Camp Doniphan. Assigned to 138th Inf.

Parkins, William Sergeant
Carrollton, Mo. 4th Mo. St.M-GSW Argonne P.

Parkins, Charle B. Sergeant
Carrollton, Mo. 4th Mo. St.M-GSW Argonne. A.

Parsons, Clent Private
Trfd. to Co. I. 139th Inf.

Parks, Everett L. Corporal
Abilene, Kans. 3rd Kans. St.M-MA-P.

Paul, William H. Pvt. 1cl.
Abilene, Kans. 3rd Kans. St.M-MA-P.

Paynter, Byron H. Pvt. 1cl.
Darlington, Wis. 85th Repl. J. 10-20-18. P.

Pederson, Otto D. Private
Williston, N. Dak. 88th Repl. J. 5-25-18. P-St.M-GSW Argonne. P.

Perreton, Henry J. Pvt. 1cl.
Carrollton, Mo. 4th Mo. St.M-MA-P.

Pesel, Charles F. Private
Carrollton, Mo. 4th Mo. Discharged at Camp Doniphan, A.

Petry, Frank Private
108 Grant Ave., Dubuque, Iowa. 88th Repl. 5-25-18. P-St.M-MA-P.

Phillips, Edwin O. Private
Flint, Mich. 85th Repl. J. 10-20-18. P.

Phillips, Burl Private
Roy, Mo. 4th Mo. St.M-GSW Argonne. A.

109

HEADQUARTERS COMPANY

Pickett, Victor E. Pvt. 1cl.
Plymell, Charlie D. Private

Pomeroy, Vernon W.
  Pvt. 1cl.
Porter, Ray R. Sergeant

Prall, Eugene Pvt. 1cl.
Prebble, Milton Private
Price, Earl Private

Proffitt, Charles R. Private
Raines, Charles E. Pvt. 1cl.
Ray, James I. Pvt. 1cl.

Rector, Malhon R. Pvt. 1cl.

Reep, Elmer L. Pvt. 1cl.

Reese, Claude A. Private

Reid, George A. Private

Rice, Charles F. Corporal

Riley, Lovelle L. Private

Rinehardt, Charles Pvt. 1cl.
Rinkenbaugh, John R.
  Private
Robinson, George P. Private

Romberger, Roy Private

Roshau, Jacob Private

Rosell, Darrell R. Corporal

Russel, Roy R. Pvt. 1cl.

Shermack, James A. Private

Sagissor, George W.
  Pvt. 1cl.
Sampson, Clarence A.
  Sergeant
Sandberg, Frank L. Private

Savidge, Arthur Private

Savidge, Ernest Private

Schmidt, Edward Private

Schmidt, William J. Private

Schneider, August G.
  Private
Schneider, Kelen A.
  Pvt. 1cl.

Harris, Mo. 4th Mo. St.M-MA-P.
Coffeville, Mo. 4th Mo. St.M-GSW Argonne. A.
Lemmon, S. Dak. 88th Repl. J. 5-25-18. P-St.M-GSW Argonne. P.
Enterprise, Kans. 3rd Kans. Trfd. to SOS Hosp. A.
Joplin, Mo. 4th Mo. St.M-MA-P.
Paris, Ky. 85th Repl. J. 10-20-18. P.
Scranton, Ky. 4th Mo. St.M-GSW Argonne.
Norborne, Mo. 4th Mo. St.M-MA-P.
Versailles, Mo. 4th Mo. St.M-MA-P.
Gallatin, Mo. 4th Mo. St.M-GSW Argonne. P.
Abilene, Kans. 3rd Kans. St.M-MA-P.
Abilene, Kans. 3rd Kans. St.M-MA. Sent to Hosp. A.
Abilene, Kans. 3rd Kans. Trfd. to 110 Amm. Train. A.
Abilene, Kans. 3rd Kans. to MG BN. A.
Carrollton, Mo. 4th Mo. St.M-GSW Argonne. A.
Glenwood, Minn. 88th Repl. J. 5-25-18. St.M-GSW Argonne. A.
Hale, Mo. 4th Mo. St.M-MA-P.
Carrollton, Mo. 4th Mo. Trfd. to hospital Eng. A.
85th Repl. 10-20-18. A. Trfd. to hospital. A.
Abilene, Kans. 4th Kans. Trfd. to Co. M. 139th Inf. A.
Mandan, N. Dak. 88th Repl. J. 5-25-18. St.M-GSW Argonne. A.
Norborne, Mo. 4th Mo. St.M-GSW Argonne. P.
Abilene, Kans., 3rd Kans. St.M-GSW Argonne. A.
Buchanan, Mich., 85th Repl. J. 10-20-18. P.
Wabasha, Minn., 88th Repl. J. 5-25-18. St.M-MA-P.
Abilene, Kans., 3rd Kans. St.M-MA-P.
Kenosha, Wis., 85th Repl. J. 10-20-18. P.
Abilene, Kans., 3rd Kans. Trfd. to Hq. Co. 139th Inf. A.
Abilene, Kans., 3rd Kans. Trfd. to Hq. Co. 139th Inf. A.
Indianapolis, Ind., 85th Repl. J. 10-20-18. P.
Chicago, Ill., 85th Repl. J. 10-20-18. P.
Birchtree, Mo. 4th Mo. St.M-MA-P.
Birchtree, Mo. 4th Mo. St.M-MA-P.

Shum, Lawrence E. Private

Seeds, Robert Private

Seip, Howard L. Corporal

Servin, Albert E. Private

Seymour, George H. Private

Shannon, Clarence I. Cook

Sheridan, Patrick J. Private

Sherwood, Roy C. Pvt. 1cl.

Shingleton, Walter R.
  Pvt. 1cl.
Shirk, Lonze D. Private

Shockey, Fred Private

Shuey, John S. Private

Shook, Antony Pvt. 1cl.

Shook, Grover C. Private

Shook, Wilbur V. Private

Shoup, Clarence A. Private

Siimers, John F. Pvt. 1cl.

Simpich, Joseph S. Pvt. 1cl.

Simpson, Clarence A.
  Private
Singer, William L. Pvt. 1cl.

Skidmore, Everett E.
  Pvt. 1cl.
Smith, Burl W. Private
Smith, William Corporal

Smith, Otto B. Sergeant

Smith, Albert W. Corporal

Smithpeter, William L.
  Bugler
Sparwasser, Edward Private

Specht, Harry M. Private

Starr, John R. Mechanic

Greenleaf, Kans., 3rd Kans. St.M-GSW Argonne A.
Abilene, Kans., 3rd Kans. Discharged at Camp Doniphan. A.
Abilene, Kans., 3rd Kans. St.M-MA-P.
Litchfield, Minn., 88th Repl. J. 5-25-18. A-St.M-GSW Argonne. A.
Traverse City, Mich., 85th Repl. J. 10-20-18. P.
Abilene, Kans., 3rd Kans. St.M-MA-P.
Newhampton, Ia., 88th Repl. J. 5-25-18. St.M-GSW Argonne. A.
Abilene, Kans., 3rd Kans. St.M-GSW Argonne. A.
Nevada, Mo., 4th Mo. St.M-MA-P.

Abilene, Kans., 3rd Kans. St.M-GSW Argonne. Trfd. to Hq. Co. 139th Inf. A.
Abilene, Kans., 3rd Kans. Trfd. to I Co. 139th Inf. A.
Talmage, Kans., 3rd Kans. Trfd. to Hq. Co. 139th Inf. A.
Abilene, Kans., 3rd Kans. St.M. Killed in Argonne.
Abilene, Kans., 3rd Kans. St.M. Killed in Argonne.
Abilene, Kans., 3rd Kans. Trfd. to Hq. Co. 139th Inf. A.
Abilene, Kans., 3rd Kans. Trfd. to Co. K. 139th Inf. A.
Wakefield, Kans., 3rd Kans. StM-MA-P.
New Franklin, Mo., 4th Mo. St.M-GSW and taken prisoner in Argonne.
Abilene, Kans., 3rd Kans. Trfd. to Hq. Co. 139th Inf. A.
Winthrop, Ia., 88th Repl. J. 5-25-18. St.M-MA-P.
Carrollton, Mo., 4th Mo. St.M-MA-P.
Hale, Mo., 4th Mo. St.M-MA-P.
Carrollton, Mo., 4th Mo. St.M-MA-P. Sent to hospital.
Abilene, Kans., 3rd Kans. Trfd. to Co. E. 139th Inf. A.
Burdick, Kans., 3rd Kans. St.M. Died from wounds in Argonne.
Carrollton, Mo., 4th Mo. St.M. Killed in Argonne.
Abilene, Kans., 3rd Kans. Trfd. to Co. K. 139th Inf. A.
Saginaw, Mich., 85th Repl. J. 10-20-18. P.
Carrollton, Mo., 4th Mo. St.M-GSW Argonne. A.

110

HEADQUARTERS COMPANY

Staley, Will L.   Private   Lexington, Ky., 85th Repl. J. 10-20-19. P.

Stanley, Fred J.   1st. Sgt.   Carrollton, Mo., 4th Mo. St.M-GSW Argonne. Sent to hospital. A.

Steers, George E.   Private   85th Repl. J. 10-20-18. P.

Spotts, Edgar   Cook   Carrollton, Mo., 4th Mo. St.M-MA-P.

Stevenson, Henry J.   Pvt. 1cl.   Marceline, Mo., 4th Mo. St.M-GSW Argonne. Sent home. A.

Stick, Joseph J.   Private   St. Ignace, Mich., 85th Repl. J. 10-20-18. P.

Steinborn, George   Private   Abilene, Kans., 3rd Kans. Died at Camp Doniphan.

Stayer, Clark   Corporal   Abilene, Kans., 3rd Kans. St.M-MA. Sent to hospital. A.

Stith, Forest G.   Pvt. 1cl.   Norborne, Mo., 4th Mo. St.M-MA-P.

Strowig, Olin R.   Sergeant   Abilene, Kans., 3rd Kans. St.M-MA-P.

Stuck, William J.   Private   Abilene, Kans., 3rd Kans. Trfd. to Hq. Co. 139th Inf.

Stuck, Mervin   Private   Abilene, Kans., 3rd Kans. Trfd. to 110th Amm. Train. A.

Sutton, William S.   Private   Enterprise, Kans., 3rd Kans. Trfd. to Co. K. 139th Inf. A.

Szczygielski, Standley J.   Private   Chicago, Ill., 85th Repl. J. 10-20-18. P.

Tabbron, John W.   Mechanic   New York City, N. Y., 3rd Kans. St.M-GSW in Argonne. P.

Tate, William E.   Pvt. 1cl.   Enterprise, Kans., 3rd Kans. St.M-MA. Sent to hospital. A.

Templeton, William A.   Corporal   Carrollton, Mo., 4th Mo. St.M-MA-P.

Thelan, Victor A.   Private   Grand Rapids, Mich., 85th Repl. J. 10-20-18. P.

Thom, Victor   Private   Tiffin, O., 85th Repl. J. 10-20-18. P.

Tisron, Eugene   Private   Charlevoix, Mich., 85th Repl. J. 10-20-18. P.

Tober, Claude A.   Pvt. 1cl.   Abilene, Kans., 3rd Kans. St.M-MA-P.

Tomlin, James   Private   Catlettsberg, Mich., 85th Repl. J. 10-20-18. P.

Toupin, Albert   Pvt. 1cl.   Hancock, Mich., 85th Repl. J. 10-20-18. P.

Thomas, Frank P.   Pvt. 1cl.   Carrollton, Mo., 4th Mo. St.M-MA-P.

Tubbs, Earl C.   Private   88th Repl. J. 5-25-18. Trfd. 130th MG Bn. A.

Van Akin, Charles H.   Private   Adrian, Mich., 85th Repl. J. 10-20-18. P.

Vance, Earl   Corporal   Carrollton, Mo., 4th Mo. St.M-MA-P.

Vanderpool, Leo   Pvt. 1cl.   Norborne, Mo., 4th Mo. Trfd. to camp hospital at Camp Mills.

Vanderkooi, George   Private   Muskegon, Mich., 85th Repl. J. 10-20-18. P.

VanDoren, Chester G.   Private   Abilene, Kans., 3rd Kans. Trfd. to Hq. Co. 139th Inf. A.

Vinyard, Roscoe R.   Corporal   Carrollton, Mo., 4th Mo. St.M-GSW Argonne. Sent to hospital. A.

Viola, Ralph H.   Private   Abilene, Kans., 3rd Kans. St.M. Killed in action in Argonne.

Wade, Jess A.   Pvt. 1cl.   Norborne, Mo., 4th Mo. St.M-MA-P.

Wagner, Rudolph   Sergeant   Carrollton, Mo., 4th Mo. St.M-MA. Trfd. to OTS. A.

Walker, Alexander   Sergeant   Norborne, Mo., 4th Mo. St.M. Killed in action in Argonne.

Walters, Harry E.   Private   Abilene, Kans., 3rd Kans. Trfd. 130 MG Bn. A.

Ward, Fletcher T.   Private   Carrollton, Mo., 4th Mo. St.M-MA-P.

Weaver, Earl C.   Pvt. 1cl.   Carrollton, Mo., 4th Mo. St.M-GSW. Argonne. A.

Weaver, Robert S.   Cook   Carrollton, Mo. 4th Mo. St.M-MA-P.

White, Leslie S.   Pvt. 1cl.   Bogard, Mo., 4th Mo. Trfd. to hospital at Camp Doniphan. A.

White, Harry   Private   Carrollton, Mo., 4th Mo. Trfd. to 130 MG Bn 139th Inf. A.

Wiggins, Williams   Private   Abilene, Kans., 3rd Kans. Trfd. to Hq. Co. 139th Inf. A.

Wilke, David B.   Pvt. 1cl.   Abilene, Kans., 3rd Kans. St.M-MA-P.

Willett, Byron   Private   Big Rapids, Mich., 85th Repl. J. 10-20-18. P.

Williams, James P.   Private   Detroit, Mich., 85th Repl. J. 10-20-18. P.

Williams, Luther A.   Pvt. 1cl.   Bucklin, Mo., 4th Mo. St.M-MA-P.

Wilson, Clarence   Private   Carrollton, Mo., 4th Mo. Trfd. to hospital at Camp Doniphan. A.

Wilson, Russell   Corporal   Marceline, Mo., 4th Mo. St.M-MA-P. Sent to hospital St. Nazaire.

Woods, Charles J.   Corporal   Detroit, Kans., 3rd Kans. St.M-MA-P.

Wilson, Buck M.   Private   Ardmore, Okla., 3rd Kans. St.M-GSW Argonne. A.

Workman, Lewis   Private   Muskegon, Mich., 85th Repl. J. 10-20-18. P.

Wright, Weslie G.   Private   Marceline, Mo., 4th Mo. St.M. Died of wounds in hospital from Argonne offensive.

Wright, Cyrus H.   Corporal   Carrollton, Mo., 4th Mo. Sent to hospital A.

Wright, Thurman   Private   Detroit, Mich., 85th Repl. J. 10-20-18. P.

Wight, Lewis E.   Private   Flint, Mich., 85th Repl. J. 10-20-18. P.

Yeadon, Jay   Private   Abilene, Kans., 3rd Kans. Trfd. to Hq. Co. 139th Inf. A.

Yeadon, George W.   Corporal   Abilene, Kans., 3rd Kans. St.M-MA. Gassed in Argonne. P.

Yeadon, Henry   Private   Solomon, Kans., 3rd Kans. St.M-GSW Argonne. P.

York, Bradley   Private   Manchester, Ky., 85th Repl. J. 10-20-18. P.

York, Glenn O.   Pvt. 1cl.   Norborne, Mo., 4th Mo. St.M-GSW Argonne. P.

Young, Roscoe D.   Mechanic   Carrollton, Mo., 4th Mo. St.M-GSW Argonne. A.

Zukowski, John   Private   Kenosha, Wis., 85th Repl. J. 10-20-18. P.

111

HEADQUARTERS COMPANY

ROSTER OF COMPANY I, 139th INFANTRY

NAME AND RANK	HOME ADDRESS AND REMARKS
Ralph W. Martin Captain	Moran, Kans., OS-St.M-MA-P.
Alexander M. Elett Captain	Chillicothe, Mo., OS-K-G.
Henry F. Halverson Captain	Valley City, N. Dak., OS-St.M-MA-W-MG-A.
William D. Turnbull 1st Lt.	Detroit, Mich., OS-P.
Truman O. Pooler 1st Lt.	Burlington, Kans., OS-P.
Robert W. Roberts 1st Lt.	Chillicothe, Mo., OS-A.
Matthew Guilfoyle 1st Lt.	Herington, Kans., OS-St.M-MA-P.
William H. Morris 1st Lt.	Billings, Mont., OS-St.M-MA-W-MG-A.
Eugene A. Hirsch 1st Lt.	Little Rock, Ark., OS-A.
Oliver C. Underhill 1st Lt.	Schenectady, N. Y., OS-A.
James H. McCord, Jr. 1st Lt.	St. Joseph, Mo., OS-A.
Ross Diehl 1st Lt.	Chillicothe, Mo., OS-A.
Robert L. Lovern 2nd Lt.	Philadelphia, Penn., OS-A.
Joseph Glashow 2nd Lt.	New York City, N. Y., OS-A.
Edward S. Carmack 2nd Lt.	6325 Washington St., St. Louis, Mo., OS-St.M-MA-P.
Homer J. Henney 2nd Lt.	Horton, Kans., OS-St.M-MA-A.
Morgan S. Smith 2nd Lt.	Jonesville, Va., OS-A.
Irwin H. Miller 2nd Lt.	Shawano, Wis., OS-A.
Batta, Frank 1st Sgt.	Chillicothe, Mo., OS.
Kistler, John J. 1st Sgt.	Alta Vista, Kans., OS-MA.
Oldfield, Willie A. 1st Sgt.	Canton, Kans., OS-MA.
Glick, Vern R. Mess Sgt.	117 East Jackson, Chillicothe, OS-MA-K-HE.
Hopkins, Arthur B. Sup Sgt.	Grant City, Mo., OS-MA-W-HE.
Avery, Thomas E. Sup. Sgt.	Chillicothe, Mo., OS-MA.
Rowland, James H. Sergeant	Stover, Mo., OS-MA.
Foley, Claude Sergeant	217 E. 9th St., Chillicothe, Mo., OS-MA.
Blackburn, Clarence A. Sergeant	1304 Webster, Chillicothe, Mo., OS.
Calkins, Arthur Sergeant	Herington, Kans., OS-MA-W-MG.
Cramner, William S. Sergeant	Chillicothe, Mo., OS-MA.
Krause, John A. Sergeant	Woodbine, Kans., OS-MA-W-MG.
McWilliams, Earl J. Sergeant	Alta Vista, Kans., OS-MA-W-MG.
Ervin, William M. Sergeant	537 S. Main, Brookfield, Mo., OS-MA.
Reed, Alonzo L. Sergeant	Hope, Kans., OS-MA-G.
Danielson, Herbert E. Sergeant	1123 Clay St., Chillicothe, Mo., OS-MA.
Hoskins, Geo. A. Sergeant	Marceline, Mo., OS-MA.
Harris, Fred K. Sergeant	437 Cherry St., Chillicothe, Mo., OS-MA.
Love, Wesley O. Sergeant	Brookfield, Mo., OS-MA.
Sloan, William T. Sergeant	539 W. 144th St., N. Y., OS-MA.
Hoskins, Frank E. Sergeant	Marceline, Mo., OS-MA.
Doyle, Joseph L. Sergeant	Herington, Kans., OS-MA.

NAME AND RANK	HOME ADDRESS AND REMARKS
Barrett, Samuel Sergeant	Komalty, Okla., OS-MA-W-MG.
McMurry, Harold D. Corporal	1047 Quindaro Bvd., Kansas City, Kans., OS-MA.
Diegelman, John Sergeant	934 Remmonia Ave., Los Angeles, Cal., OS-MA.
McHolland, Joseph D. Sergeant	Chillicothe, Mo., OS.
Clark, Ora Corporal	Hamilton, Mo., OS-MA-K.
McClellan, Irl Corporal	1518 Calhoun, Chillicothe, Mo., OS-MA-W-MG.
McClaren, Carry R. Corporal	Culver, Kans., OS-MA-K.
Grouse, Charlie F. Corporal	1420 W. Calhoun, Chillicothe, Mo., OS-MA-G.
Sheehan, Francis W. Corporal	Herington, Kans., OS.
Burgard, Lester C. Corporal	Avalon, Mo., OS-MA-K.
Sturgis, George Corporal	Hamilton, Mo., OS-MA.
King, Pearcie Corporal	315 W. Helm St., Brookfield, Mo., OS-MA-G.
Thomas, Earl D. Corporal	Wheeling, Mo., OS-MA.
Rogers, Thomas R. Corporal	Granite, Okla., OS-MA.
Rader, Procter E. Corporal	Russell, Kans., OS-MA-W-MG.
Spidle, Forest L. Corporal	Gallatin, Mo., OS-MA-W-MG.
Volkman, Arthur W. Corporal	Woodbine, Kans., OS-MA.
Young, Leo H. Corporal	Milford, Kans., OS-MA.
Pottorf, Frank H. Corporal	Oskaloosa, Kans., OS-MA.
Sheridan, Delmar Corporal	412 N. 9th St., Herington, Kans., OS-MA.
Schrolick, Martin W. Corporal	906 W. Olive, Herington, Kans., OS-MA.
Wright, Earl Corporal	Bucklin, Mo., OS-MA-W-MG.
O'Niel, John J. Corporal	1653 Summit St., Kansas City, Mo., OS-MA.
Bently, Preston M. Corporal	Sawyer, Kans., OS-MA-W-MG.
Zimmerman, Harvey F. Corporal	802 S. Oak St., Pratt, Kans.
Ruyle, Lawrence R. Corporal	Lincoln, Kans., OS-MA.
Marble, Clinton D. Corporal	Ardath, Sask., Canada, OS-MA.
Strunk, Milton Corporal	Dillon, Kans., OS-MA.
Bratcher, Homer Corporal	Hamilton, Mo., OS-MA.
Kohler, Ervin F. Corporal	Woodbine, Kans., OS-MA.
Meyers, Thomas D. Corporal	Herington, Kans., OS-MA.
Ward, Isom R. Corporal	Tampa, Kans., OS-MA.
Carpenter, George W. Corporal	Cowgill, Mo., OS-MA.
Fisher, Elmer C. Corporal	Alta Vista, Kans., OS-MA.
Maddux, George Corporal	Hamilton, Mo., OS-MA-G.
Moore, Samuel H. Corporal	R.F.D. No. 3, Chillicothe, Mo., OS-MA.

HEADQUARTERS COMPANY

Morehead, Fred D. Corporal
Fort Scott, Kans., OS-MA.
Rauber, Floyd S. Corporal
Hamilton, Mo., OS-MA.
Wakefield, Fred Corporal
Alta Vista, Kans., OS-MA.
Schrader, Herbert C.
    Corporal
Council Groves, Kans., OS-MA.
Tomlinson, Jack Corporal
2110 S. 10th St., St. Joseph, Mo.,
    OS-MA.
Botimer, Lloyd Corporal
R.F.D. No. 1, Reese, Mich.
Wager, Claude H. Corporal
Leon, Kans., OS-MA-W-HE.
Seffen, George P. Corporal
506 E. Church St., Champaign, Ill.,
    OS-MA.
Longfofer, Godfrey Corporal
Woodbine, Kans., OS-MA-W-S.
Stone, Marion Corporal
Fowler, Ind., OS-MA-WHE.
Hicks, Carl Cook
Hamilton, Mo., OS-MA.
Oldfield, Lewis D. Cook
Canton, Kans., OS-MA.
Anderson, Clarence L. Cook
Herington, Kans., OS-MA.
Ireland, Fred Cook
Chillicothe, Mo., OS-MA.
Cardiani, Mike Cook
Racine, Wis.
Allen, Kanes Mechanic
R.F.D. No. 5, Chillicothe, Mo., OS.
Clark, Palmer Mechanic
Pittsburg, Mo., OS.
Lightner, James Mechanic
Chillicothe, Mo., OS-MA-W-MG.
Brown, William E.
    Mechanic
Chillicothe, Mo., OS-MA.
Nelson, Andrew A.
    Mechanic
411 Charlotte St., Escanaba, Mich.,
    OS-MA.
Chapman, Van Bugler
1021 W. Polk, Chillicothe, Mo., OS-
    MA-W-HE.
Johnson, Dolph C. Bugler
402 Maple St., Dowagiac, Mich.
Adam, Wilbur L. Pvt. 1cl.
Woodbine, Kans., OS-MA.
Anderson, Vivian C.
    Pvt. 1cl.
Herington, Kans., OS-MA.
Asling, Fred Pvt. 1cl.
Delavan, Kans., OS-MA.
Arnold, Percy H. Pvt. 1cl.
Latimer, Kans., D.
Bane, George E. Pvt. 1cl.
Herington, Kans., OS-MA-W-MG.
Blythe, Harold J. Pvt. 1cl.
White City, Kans., OS-MA-W-MG.
Boyd, Anderson J. Pvt. 1cl.
Independence, Ia., OS-MA.
Burkett, Roy L. Pvt. 1cl.
200 High St., Chillicothe, Mo., K.
Borchardt, Frank F.
    Pvt. 1cl.
Waconia, Minn., OS-MA.
Bower, James Pvt. 1cl.
R.F.D. No. 1, Kendall, Mich.
Braden, Monte C. Pvt. 1cl.
Sank Rapids, Minn., OS-MA.
Callahan, Charles T.
    Pvt. 1cl.
Herington, Kans., OS-MA-W-MG.
Carolan, Anthony D.
    Pvt. 1cl.
R.F.D. No. Gage Town, Mich.
Cashman, Clarence W.
    Pvt. 1cl.
Chillicothe, Mo., OS-MA-W-G.
Cameron, Robert S.
    Pvt. 1cl.
White City, Kans., OS.
Clark, George R. Pvt. 1cl.
Herington, Kans.
Culver, Harold E. Pvt. 1cl.
Fowler, Kans., OS-MA-W-HE.
Chalifoue, Edward F.
    Pvt. 1cl.
R.F.D. No. 2, Levering, Mich.
Chrisman, Earnest Pvt. 1cl.
Laredo, Mo., OS-MA.
Cook, Hugh P. Pvt. 1cl.
124 Prospect Ave., Marshall, Mich.
Costello, Joseph J. Pvt. 1cl.
Herington, Kans., OS-MA.
Cox, Roy B. Pvt. 1cl.
Brunswick, Mo., OS-MA.
Edens, Harry H. Pvt. 1cl.
Council Groves, Kans., OS-MA.
Fetter, Clyde T. Pvt. 1cl.
c/o Central Hotel, Three Rivers,
    Mich.
Goodwin, Charlie R.
Laclede, Mo., OS-MA-G.
Goodwin, Ray Pvt. 1cl.
Laclede, Mo., K-OS.

Grice, Wallace Pvt. 1cl.
Purdin, Mo., OS-MA.
Grouse, John A. Pvt. 1cl.
1420 W. Calhoun, Chillicothe, Mo.,
    OS-MA.
Hensel, Hugo E. Pvt. 1cl.
Bemidji, Minn., OS-MA.
Johnson, Arthur Pvt. 1cl.
R.F.D. No. 2, Box 4, Chanchard
    Ville, Wis.
Kahle, Frank W. Pvt. 1cl.
Eskridge, Kans., OS-MA.
Kahle, Harvey J. Pvt. 1cl.
Eskridge, Kans., OS-MA.
Knight, Lawrence R.
    Pvt. 1cl.
1248 Clay Ave., N. Y. City.
Koppelo, William G.
    Pvt. 1cl.
Delhi, Ia., OS-MA.
Krause, Erphine A.
    Pvt. 1cl.
Woodbine, Kans., OS-MA-W-MG.
Leigh, Arthur F. Pvt. 1cl.
Nettleton, Mo., OS-MA.
Leshley, Blake Pvt. 1cl.
R.F.D. No. 7, Abilene, Kans., OS-
    MA-W.
Lewis, Thomas M. Pvt. 1cl.
E. Lake, Minn., OS-MA-W-S.
Longhofer, Fred Pvt. 1cl.
Woodbine, Kans., OS-MA-W-MG.
Luck, Charles J. Pvt. 1cl.
Houston, Mo., OS-MA-W-HE.
Mahoney, Everett Pvt. 1cl.
Shellsburg, Wis.
McDandel, Earl O. Pvt. 1cl.
Laclede, Mo., OS-MA.
McDiffett, Larenzo W.
    Pvt. 1cl.
Alta Vista, Kans., OS-MA.
Metevier, Ludgier L.
    Pvt. 1cl.
R.F.D. No. 2, Sheboygan, Mich.
Michels, Herbert L.
    Pvt. 1cl.
Osage, Ia., OS-MA-W-MG.
Midkiff, Carl E. Pvt. 1cl.
Manchester, Ia., OS-MA-K.
Pio, Jess L. Pvt. 1cl.
R.F.D. No. 4, Eskridge, Mo., OS-
    MA-W-HE.
Pfiester, Semmie C. Pvt. 1cl.
Liberty, Mo., OS-MA.
Morris, Robert O. Pvt. 1cl.
White City, Kans., OS-MA-W-
    MGF.
O'Leary, Francis Pvt. 1cl.
Neche, N. Dak., OS-MA.
Owens, Barney E. Pvt. 1cl.
Tibbetts, Mo., OS-MA.
Pegorsch, Henry A.
    Pvt. 1cl.
Herington, Kans., OS-MA-W-MGF.
Penegor, Edward A.
    Pvt. 1cl.
Plato, Mich.
Plucinski, Stanislaw
    Pvt. 1cl.
8816 Exchange Ave., Chicago, Ill.
Parkman, Morris J. Pvt. 1cl.
Laredo, Mo., OS-MA.
Rauber, Ernest Pvt. 1cl.
Hamilton, Mo., OS-MA.
Remick, Louis M. Pvt. 1cl.
1219 Como Bvd., St. Paul, Minn.,
    OS.
Rupert, Evert Pvt. 1cl.
Springfield, Mo., OS-MA-W-S.
Schump, Joseph F. Pvt. 1cl.
White City, Kans., OS-MA.
Schump, Paul J. Pvt. 1cl.
White City, Kans., OS-MA.
Seaman, Elmer J. Pvt. 1cl.
Chillicothe, Mo., OS-MA-G.
Shultz, Elmer D. Pvt. 1cl.
Milan, Mo., OS-MA.
Shultz, Harry W. Pvt. 1cl.
Milan, Mo., OS-MA.
Silvey, Stokely O. Pvt. 1cl.
Nettleton, Mo., OS-MA.
Sisson, Haden H. Pvt. 1cl.
Benson, Minn., OS-MA.
Smith, Lloyd A. Pvt. 1cl.
Clay City, Ill., OS-MA.
Smith, Roy H. Pvt. 1cl.
Council Grove, Kans., OS-MA.
Staley, Henry H. Pvt. 1cl.
Kiowa, Tex., OS-MA.
Steckhoffer, Howard J.
    Pvt. 1cl.
Pontiac, Ill., OS-MA-W-S.
Stevens, William G.
    Pvt. 1cl.
Grand Forks, N. Dak., OS-MA.
Taylor, Lee R. Pvt. 1cl.
Chillicothe, Mo., OS-MA.

HEADQUARTERS COMPANY

Thompson, Jonnie F. Pvt. 1cl. Rockville, Mo., OS-MA.
Troutman, William J. Pvt. 1cl. Plattsburg, Mo., OS-MA.
Wilhelmsen, Joseph Pvt. 1cl. RFD No. 3, Argyle, Wisc.
Wilson, Mark E. Pvt. 1cl. Dunlap, Kans., OS-MA.
Trumblee, Roy O. Pvt. 1cl. Lamont, Iowa., OS-MA.
Walker, Earl R. Pvt. 1cl. Hope, Kans., OS-MA.
Wilde, Lavern F. Pvt. 1cl. White City, Kans., OS-MA.
Wilde, Teddy L. Pvt. 1cl. White City, Kans., OS-MA-K.
Annis, Edward C. Pvt. 1cl. Woodbine, Kans.. OS-MA.
Alvord, Joseph O. Private Jewell, Kans., OS-MA-K.
Arnold, John W. Private Latimer, Kans., OS-MA.
Anderson, John L. Private OS-MA.
Anderson, William C. Private
Bankowsky, Charlie Private Mt. Carmel, N. D.
Barrett, Daniel Private Komalty, Okla., OS-MA-W-HE.
Baxter, Homer G. Private 688 Lincoln Ave., Detroit, Mich.
Behring, Harry E. Private Council Groves, Kans., OS-MA.
Benton, Charles Private
Brons, Iver K. Private Crookston, Minn. OS-MA.
Brown, Tom Private 403 Princeton, W. Va.
Burns, Archie H. Private RFD No. 1, Kingston, Mich.
Busse, Ben E. Private RFD No. 5, Amboy, Minn.
Black, Henry W. Private Wilsey, Kans., OS-MA-W-S.
Barber, Jerome E. Private Trenton, Mo., OS-MA-W-MGF.
Brees, Charles W. Private Council Groves, Kans., OS-MA.
Burns, Aubra Private Council Groves, Kans., OS-MA-K.
Carney, James Private Plattsburg, N. Dak., OS-MA-W-HE.
Chester, Charles R. Private Drayton, N. Dak., OS-MA-W-MGF.
Cialdiani, Alfreda Private 265 St. Clair St., Milwaukee, Wis.
Cockburn, Keith D. Private Esterville, Iowa, OS-MA.
Cook, Clarence C. Private 527 Freeman Ave.. Kansas City, Kans. OS-MA-W-HE.
Cravens, Tinsley Private Hamilton, Mo., OS.
Crisp, Edgar E. Private Cambridge, Nebr., OS.
Davis, Edwin Private 833 South 10th Street, St. Joseph, Mo., OS-St.M-MA-P.
Detgen, William A. Private Port Hope, Mich.
Donovan, James J. Private 101 Monroe St., New York, N. Y.
Dutter, George C. Private Minot, N. Dak., OS-MA-P-St.M.
Dwyer, Norman Private 99 Elizabeth St., Detroit, Mich.
Elliott, Worley H. Private Herington, Kans., OS-St.M-MA-A-W-MGF.
Forbes, Walter M. Private Chillicothe, Mo., OS-St.M-MA-WHE-A.
Falen, Martin R. Private Carlton, Kans., St.M-MA-W-MGF-P.
Falk, Helmuth Private 1141 25th St., Milwaukee, Wis.
Farris, John Private Fairfax, Mo., OS-St.M-MA-P.
Fatout, William R. Private 220 East King St., Franklin, Ind.
Fetting, Edward W. Private Sandusky, Mich.
Finiak, Stanislaus Private 758 Lincoln Ave., Milwaukee, Wis.
France, Clyde D. Private Chillicothe, Mo., OS-St.M-MA-P.
Frey, Frederick Private 543 West 160th St., New York City, N. Y.
Gage, Frank D. Private Ahran, Mich.
Galetto, Ralph Private New York City, N. Y.

Galloway, Frank Private Council Grove, Kans., OS-St.M-MA-P.
Garrow, Joseph Private Sheboygan, Mich.
Gibson, Fred E. Private Neuvetle, N. Dak., OS-St.M-MA-P.
Grimsley, Henry D. Private Keosauqua, Ia., OS-St.M-MA-P.
Gross, Walter M. Private Breckenridge, Mo., OS-St.M-MA-P.
Gullick, Russel H. Private Brookfield, Mo., OS-St.M-MA-P.
Hagen, Peter Private Darlington, Wis.
Harthun, Otto R. Private Dent, Minn., OS-St.M-MA-P-W-MG.
Harvey, Wayne W. Private Ford City, Mo. OS-St.M-MA-WHE-A.
Haverstock, Dewey G. Private Herington, Kans., OS-St.M-MA-WHE-A.
Hicks, Henry W. Private Chillicothe, Mo., OS-St.M-MA-P.
Jaakola, Uno Private Virginia, Minn.
Johnson, Fred Private Sault Ste. Marie, Mich.
Johnson, Peter A. Private Grand Meadow, Minn., OS-St.M-MA-WMG-P.
Kage, Heinrich K. Private Wausau, Wis.
Keefer, Samuel B. Private Tampa, Kans., OS-St.M-MA-P.
Klassen, Math A. Private Ionia, Ia., OS-St.M-MA-WG-P.
Kermode, John Private Washington, Ind.
Kozlowski, Anton Private Wausau, Wis.
Kranzler, Henry Private Ashley, N. Dak., OS-St.M-MA-P.
Kuempel, Jacob Private Ionia, Mich.
Larson, Edgar A. Private Woodward, N. Dak., OS-St.M-MA-P.
Leitzau, Rudolph Private Chicago, Ill.
Lojewski, Joseph Private Chicago, Ill.
Lundine, Arthur G. Private Hope, Kans., OS-St.M-MA-A.
Maack, Ernest L. Private Charter Oak, Ia., OS-St.M-MA-P.
Mutter, Leroy Private Grandview, Ill., OS-MA-St.M-WMG-A.
McCullock, Roy L. Private Saskatoon, Sask. Ca., OS-St.M-MA-WMGF-A.
McArthur, Upton B. Private Backoo, N. Dak., OS-St.M-MA-P.
McCaleb, Ernest T. Private Brookfield, Tenn., OS-St.M-MA-P.
McCulla, Sam A. Private Sutherland, Ia., OS-St.M-MA-P.
McCurdy, Howard V. Private Mason, Mich.
McDaniel, Wilbur L. Private Hamilton, Mo., OS-St.M-MA-P.
Mellum, Gustav O. Private Tinsley, N. Dak., OS-St.M-MA-P-WHE.
Metcalf, Albert L. Private Dunlap, Kans.. OS-St.M-MA-P.
Meyers, Roy F. Private Sedalia, Mo., OS-St.M-MA-P.
Mullinix, Leonard C. Private New Cambria, Mo., OS-St.M-MA-P.
Mason, Sidney E. Private Broadway, Va., OS-St.M-MA-WMGF-A.
Mazzarano, Joseph Private Springvalley, Ill., OS-St.M-MA-WNYD-A.
Moen, Uldrick Private Shawnee, N. Dak., OS-St.M-MA-M-A.
Nichols, Thomas J. Private Potomac, Ill., OS-St.M-MA-WMG-P.
Nilson, Bernard Private Park River, N. Dak., OS-St.M-MA-P.

FIGHTING MEN

1. Sergt. Frank C. Spargur
3. Sergt. Wesley O. Love
4. Calvin Wilkinson
5. Sergt. Dean T. Beaneke
6. Walter, Harry and Charley Buffington

7. Russell M. Dudley
8. Herbert F. Stoffle
9. Conrad Mogan
10. Frank J. Kilfoyle
11. Loran Conkin

SUPPLY COMPANY

Normandin, William H. Private — Council Grove, Kans., OS-St.M-MA-WMG.
Neil, Arthur — Private — Bucklin, Mo., OS-St.M-MA-WHE-A.
Nichols, Harold C. — Private — Carlton, Kans., OS-MA-St.M-S.
Norton, William F. — Private — Otsego, Mich., OS-St.M-MA.
Novak, Frank A. — Private — Chicago, Ill.
Oaks, Curtis L. — Private — New Market, Tenn., OS-St.M-MA-P.
Oakland, Alfred B. — Private — Tinsley, N. Dak., OS-St.M-MA-P.
Olson, Alfred — Private — Mayville, N. Dak., OS-StM-MA-P.
Paquet, Cornelius I. — Private — Chicago, Ill.
Peacock, Frank — Private — Morris, Ill., OS-St.M-MA-P.
Porsch, Arthur T. — Private — Leeds, Ia., OS-St.M-MA-A.
Porter, William R. — Private — Grandforks, N. Dak., OS-St.M-MA-P.

Potts, Albert S. — Private — Hope, Kans., OS-St.M-MA-P.
Polk, John O. — Private — Seymour, Ill., OS-St.M-MA-WMG-A
Passalacqua, Ross — Private — St. Louis, Mo., OS-St.M-MA-WMG-A.

Quamme, Clarence N. Private — Northwood, N. Dak., OS-St.M-MA-P.
Rauber, Ed. — Private — Hamilton, Mo., OS-St.M-MA-WM GF-P.

Rauber, Henry — Private — Hamilton, Mo., OS-St.M-MA-WM GF-P.

Richards, George F. — Private — Denison, Ia., OS-St.M-MA-WMG-P.
Rittel, August — Private — Herington, Kans., OS-St.M-MA-P.
Richie, Leonard C. — Private — Versailles, Mo., OS-St.M-MA-WM GF-A.

Roepke, August C. T. Private — Kenosha, Wis., OS-St.M-MA-P.
Russel, Delbert C. — Private — Chillicothe, Mo., OS-St.M-MA-G.P.

Renier, Joseph C. — Private — Jamestown, N. Dak., OS-St.M-MA-WHE-A.

Reed, Daniel W. — Private — Beaukiss, Tex., OS-A.
Sailor, Arthur H. — Private — Marion, Kans., OS-St.M-MA-P.
Sainsbury, Edward — Private — Madison, Wis.
Saltamacchia, Mariano Private — Chicago, Ill., OS-St.M-MA-WMG-P.

Schrader, Robert C. — Private — White City, Kans., OS-P.
Seavey, Charles A. — Private — Unionville, Mo., OS-St.M-MA-WH E-P.

Seigenthal, Albert — Private — Marion, Kans., OS-St.M-MA-P.
Semler, Anthony D. — Private — Kenosha, Wis.
Shappard, Abe — Private — Des Moines, Ia., OS-St.M-MA-WII E-P.

Sheehan, Thomas — Private — Williston, N. Dak., OS-St.M-MA-P.
Shepperd, John R. — Private — Pekin, Ill., OS-St.M-MA-P.
Shust, Alexander — Private — Kalamazoo, Mich.
Seims, Herbert — Private — Baudette, Minn., OS-St.M-MA-P.
Signarini, Dominico — Private — Grandville, Ill., OS-St.M-MA-P.
Smith, Herbert J. — Private — Tokio, N. Dak., OS-St.M-MA-P.
Smith, Joseph E. — Private — Monticello, Ill., OS-St.M-MA-P.
Smith, Cecil E. — Private — Lost Springs, Kans., OS-St.M-MA-WHE-A.

Smith, Joseph T. — Private — Jamestown, N. Dak., OS-A.
Smith, Lewis L. — Private — Dunlap, Ia., OS-St.M-MA-WHE-A.
Sandbeck, Harold M. Private — Williams, Minn., OS-St.M-MA-WII E-A.
Sorenson, Selmer — Private — Reynolds, N. Dak., OS-St.M-MA-W HE-P.
Stevenson, Luther C. Private — Herington, Kans., OS-St.M-MA-P.
Statton, Adolphus A. Private — Hinton, W. Va.
Sticayecues, Peter — Private — Kenosha, Wis.
Stone, William M. — Private — Sampsell, Mo., OS-St.M-MA-WG-P.
Stryjewski, Wladyslaw Private — New York City, N. Y.
Swanson, William M. Private — Utica, Ill., OS-St.M-MA-P.
Shirek, Tom A. — Private — Lankin, N. Dak., OS-St.M-MA-G-A.
Sopher, Frank W. — Private — Dwight, Ill., OS-St.M-MA-D.
Sorenson, Robert N. — Private — Grafton, N. Dak., OS-St.M-MA-K.
Sparks, James H. — Private — Avalon, Mo., OS-St.M-MA-K.
Spady, Alex P. — Private — Herington, Kans.
Torgeson, Gilbert — Private — Preston, Minn., OS-St.M-MA-P.
Thompson, Thomas H. Private — Chicago, Ill., OS-St.M-MA-WMG-A.
Traub, William — Private — Tarkio, Mo., OS-St.M-MA-P.
Tullis, Harvey W. — Private — Hope, Kans., OS-St.M-MA-WIIE-A.
Trosper, Roy C. — Private — Breckenridge, Mo., OS-St.M-MA-P.
Turner, Edward — Private — Chillicothe, Mo., OS-St.M-MA-P.
Trumble, Roy O. — Private — Independence, Ia., OS-St.M-MA-P.
Van Hoozer, LeRoy Private — Chillicothe, Mo., OS-St.M-MA-G-P.
Walters, Claude W. — Private — Chillicothe, Mo., OS-St.M-MA-K.
Winegar, Trace — Private — Laclede, Mo., OS-St.M-MA-WMG-P.

Wobschall, Edward — Private — Waseca, Minn., OS-St.M-MA-G-A.
Wollom, Gustav O. — Private — Minneapolis, Minn., OS-St.M-MA-WMG-A.
Wilkison, Ray — Private — Avalon, Mo., OS-St.M-MA-A.
Waylan, Harold E. — Private — Lost Springs, Kans., OS-St.M-MA-A.
Walker, Earl R. — Private — Hope, Kans., OS-St.M-MA-P.
Wilde, Lavern F. — Private — White City, Kans., OS-St.M-MA-P.
Cox, Floyd C. — Mess Sgt. — Laredo, Mo., OS-St.M-MA-P.
Ostrander, Clarence Sergeant — Chillicothe, Mo., OS-St.M-MA-G-P.
McCourt, John W. — Sergeant — Atchison, Kans., OS-St.M-MA-P.
Sage, Orpha E. — Corporal — Chillicothe, Mo., OS-St.M-MA-A.
Sterling, Joseph A. — Private — Dayton, Kans., OS-St.M-MA-WMG-A.

Zincak, Frank — Private — Chicago, Ill.
Zwiebel, Leo J. — Private — Burlington, Wis.
Kardiani, Mike — Cook — Milwaukee, Wis.
Darling, John — Private — Herington, Kans.
Lund, Axel — Private — Florence, Wis.
Rowe, Earl W. — Private — Jamestown, N. Dak., OS-St.M-MA-P.

116

SUPPLY COMPANY

ROSTER OF COMPANY K, 139th INFANTRY

NAME AND RANK	HOME ADDRESS AND REMARKS
John E. Wells Captain	Weston, Mo., OS.
Marcus J. Morgan Captain	Coffeyville, Kans., OS-MA.
William H. Ellenburg 1st Lt.	Corvallis, Ore., MA-W-MGF.
Coburn Hull 1st Lt.	Weston, Mo., OS-MA-W-MGF.
George C. Brewster 1st Lt.	Newton, Kans., OS.
Oliver F. Crockett 1st Lt.	Weston, Mo., OS-MA.
Charles M. Flynn 1st Lt.	Bluefield, W. Va., OS-MA.
Burr A. Davison 1st Lt.	(?) MA.
Trumen O. Pooler 1st Lt.	Burlington, Kans.
Frederick E. Swanson 1st Lt.	(?)
Homer J. Henney 1st Lt.	Herington, Kans., OS-MA.
Andrew T. Kirk 2nd Lt.	Conway Springs, Kans., OS-MA-K.
John D. Cosgrove 2nd Lt.	St. Louis, Mo., OS-MA-K.
John W. Frazier 2nd Lt.	Lexington, Mo., OS.
Stanislaus Lafond 2nd Lt.	Kankakee, Ill.
James M. Brown 2nd Lt.	
Frazer, Eldon M. 1st Sgt.	Weston, Mo., OS-MA-W-G.
Stultz, Percy Mess Sgt.	Weston, Mo., OS-MA.
Roddy, James Jr. Sup. Sgt.	Newton, Kans., OS-MA.
West, Frank Sergeant	Weston, Mo., OS-MA.
Timmons, Franklin P. Sergeant	Newton, Kans., OS.
Miller, Welty A. Sergeant	Weston, Mo., OS.
Huey, Frank G. Sergeant	Newton, Kans., OS.
Arnold, Irvin Sergeant	Marysville, Kans., OS.
Swearingen, Charlie E. Sergeant	Weston, Mo., OS-MA-W-S.
Arnold, Milford Sergeant	Weston, Mo., OS.
Smith, Carlton S. Sergeant	Newton, Kans., OS.
Donovan, Thomas W. Sergeant	Weston, Mo., OS-MA-W-G.
Wing, Norris N. Sergeant	Newton, Kans., OS-MA.
Hill, Al P. Sergeant	Weston, Mo., OS.
Helman, Charles H. Sergeant	Weston, Mo., OS-MA.
Adams, Carl E. Sergeant	Newton, Kans., OS-MA.
Barnett, Carl D. Sergeant	1213 Park Ave., Kansas City, Kans., OS-MA.
Plummer, Frank B. Sergeant	Newton, Kans., OS-MA-W-MGF.
Duncan, Charles M. Sergeant	Dearborn, Mo., OS-MA-K.
Wilson, Coburn Sergeant	Weston, Mo., OS-MA-W-G.
Wolter, Fred W. Sergeant	Newton, Kans., OS-MA.
Chambers, Walter F. Sergeant	407 E. 1st St., Newton, Kans., OS-MA-W-S.
Hampson, Thomas C. Sergeant	Tulare, Calif., OS-MA.
Hill, James W. Sergeant	Weston, Mo., OS-MA.
Smith, Emmett E. Sergeant	Newton, Kans., OS-MA.

NAME AND RANK	HOME ADDRESS AND REMARKS
Shepard, John W. Sergeant	3805 W. Pine St., St. Louis, Mo., OS-MA-W-MGF.
Spinner, Richard C. Sergeant	Weston, Mo., OS-MA.
Derby, Harry Sergeant	1258 Broadway, Quincy, Ill., OS-MA.
Barker, Roy B. Corporal	Newton, Kans., OS-MA.
Arnold, Armstrong Corporal	Weston, Mo., OS.
Raines, Clarence M. Corporal	Clinton, Mo., OS-MA-K.
Purcell, Miles Corporal	Edgerton, Mo., OS-MA-W-G.
Simpson, Duke B. Corporal	Salina, Kans., OS-MA.
Hill, Neely Corporal	Weston, Mo., OS-MA-W-MGF.
Starrett, Royce E. Corporal	Scott City, Kans., OS-MA-W-G.
Fuller, Ellis B. Corporal	Peabody, Kans., OS-MA-W-S.
Roberts, Erskine Corporal	Farwell, Tex., OS-MA.
Moberly, Harry F. Corporal	1345 S. 25th St., Kansas City, Kans., OS-MA-W-S.
Reeder, William A. Corporal	1016 S. Locust St., Ottawa, Kans., OS-MA.
Snyder, John R. Corporal	Newton, Kans., OS-MA-W-S.
Daily, Allen H. Corporal	205 Indiana Ave., St. Joseph, Mo., OS-MA-W-G.
Daily, Lee Corporal	205 Indiana Ave., St. Joseph, Mo., OS-MA.
Wright, Robert M. Corporal	Weston, Mo., OS-MA.
Stone, Edward A. Corporal	Burrton, Kans., OS-MA-W-MGF.
Geer, John W. Corporal	East Leavenworth, Mo., OS-MA.
Hankins, James L. Corporal	Syracuse, Kans., OS-MA-W-MGF.
Pletcher, Paul Corporal	Newton, Kans., OS-MA-W-S.
Tinder, Robert L. Corporal	1529 Locust St., Kansas City, Mo., OS-MA-W-MGF.
Duncan, John S. Corporal	Dearborn, Mo., OS-MA-W-HE.
Kennedy, Arthur T. Corporal	Clay Center, Kans., OS-MA-W-S.
Wilson, Otis E. Corporal	Rushville, Mo., OS-MA-W-MGF.
Mitchell, Thomas W. Corporal	Weston, Mo., OS-MA-W-G.
Heavelow, Clarence E. Corporal	Augusta, Kans., OS-MA. (W-S-Alsace)
La Foe, Laurence Corporal	Peabody, Kans., OS-MA-W-HE.
Renick, Harry H. Corporal	Garden City, Kans., OS-MA-K.
Shertz, George R. Corporal	Newton, Kans., OS-MA-W-HE.
Wilson, William B. Corporal	Camden Point, Mo., OS-MA-W-MGF.
Zimmerman, Harvey F. Corporal	Burrton, Kans., OS-MA.
Branum, Roy F. Corporal	Weston, Mo., OS-MA.
Hartman, Joseph W. Corporal	Sedgwick, Kans., OS-MA.
Kinard, Fred F. Corporal	Newton, Kans., OS-MA.
Rogers, Harold A. Corporal	Newton, Kans., OS-MA.
Pace, William L. Corporal	Garden City, Kans., OS-MA.

SUPPLY COMPANY

Nincmire, George W.
    Corporal — Weston, Mo., OS-MA.
Simmons, Lester L.
    Corporal — Weston, Mo., OS-MA.
Kerby, Earl L. Corporal — Centerville, Ia., OS-MA.
Harder, Fred P. Corporal — 1044 Wislow Ave., West St. Paul, Minn., OS-MA.
Ohman, Frank M. Corporal — Albany, Minn., OS-MA.
Tapscott, Silas W. Corporal — Laclede, Mo., OS-MA.
Wallis, Delmer L. Corporal — Platte City, Mo., OS-MA.
Freiwald, Elmer A.
    Corporal — 1213 Helen Ave., Detroit, Mich.
Duncan, Ben F. Corporal — Dearborn, Mo., OS-MA.
Dally, Ray M. Corporal — Laporte, Minn., OS-MA.
Paulson, Gustav Corporal — More Springs, Ia., OS-MA.
Armstrong, Earl D.
    Corporal — 2737 S. 18th St., St. Joseph, Mo., OS-MA-W-G.
Palmer, Alva, W. Corporal — Braddyville, Ia., OS-MA.
Krick, Albert A. Corporal — 3223 N. Lyndale Ave., Minneapolis, Minn.

Blaylock, Herbert J.
    Corporal — Newton, Kans., OS-MA.
Smallwood, Harry A.
    Corporal — Hopkins, Mo., OS-MA-W-MGF.
Melton, Louis W. Cook — Muskogee, Okla., OS-MA.
Morelan, Bone A. Cook — Clinton, Mo., OS-MA.
Slaymaker, Charles E. Cook — Peabody, Kans., OS-MA.
Clemens, Hardy L. Cook — Weston, Mo., OS-MA.
Morrison, George E. Cook — Weston, Mo., OS-MA.
McMillian, James W.
    Mechanic — New Market, Mo., OS-MA-Missing.
Hall, Harry L. Mechanic — 24th and Lincoln St., Topeka, Kans. OS.

Denzer, Albert E. Mechanic — Weston, Mo., OS-MA.
Simpson, Oren S. Mechanic — Ulysses, Kans., OS.
Bauer, John Mechanic — Ney, Ohio., RFD 1.
Quinley, Pete J. Bugler — Weston, Mo., OS-MA-W-MGF.
Fowler, Clarke D. Bugler — Lost Springs, Kans., OS-MA.
Adkins, Ira Pvt. 1cl. — (No records.)
Agee, Milard T. Pvt. 1cl. — 151 S. Main. Trenton, Mo., OS-MA-W-G.
Albrecht, Henry G. Pvt. 1cl. — Newton, Kans., OS-MA-W-G.
Armstrong, Lloyd H.
    Pvt. 1cl. — Salina, Kans., OS-MA-W-MGF.
Arnold, Gay Pvt. 1cl. — Weston, Mo., OS-MA.
Arnold, Hobart Pvt. 1cl. — Weston, Mo., OS-MA.
Ashburn, Robert A.
    Pvt. 1cl. — Camden Point, Mo., OS.
Barchus, William Pvt. 1cl. — Wathena, Kans., OS.
Berens, Martin Pvt. 1cl. — Gray Eagle, Minn., OS-MA.
Berknes, John O. Pvt. 1cl. — Sedan, Minn., MA.
Blough, Vernon L. Pvt. 1cl. — Garden City, Kans., OS.
Bowdre, Harry F. Pvt. 1cl. — 544 S. 11th St., Kansas City, Kans., OS-MA-W-HE.
Boyd, Hugh J. Pvt. 1cl. — RFD 5, Maysville, Mo., OS-MA.
Brogdon, John I. Pvt. 1cl. — Peabody, Kans., OS.
Burgener, Leo I. Pvt. 1cl. — 125 E. 14th St., Newton, Kans., OS-MA-W-S.
Campbell, Earl W. Pvt. 1cl. — Ponca, Nebr.
Carter, James L. Pvt. 1cl. — Iatan, Mo., OS-MA-W-G.
Carter, Milo O. Pvt. 1cl. — Newton, Kans., OS-MA.

Cavanaugh, Earnest
    Pvt. 1cl. — Platte City, Mo., OS-MA.
Cheesman, Theodore
    Pvt. 1cl. — Rock Port, Mo., OS-MA.
Coots, James M. Pvt. 1cl. — Platte City, Mo., OS-MA.
Currie, Donald H. Pvt. 1cl. — Prescott, Mich., MA-W-MGF.
Davniero, Anthony Pvt. 1cl. — 17 Saint Edward St., Brooklyn, N. Y.
Delehanty, Howard R.
    Pvt. 1cl. — Fenton, Mich.
Deets, Stanton E. Pvt. 1cl. — Camden Point, Mo., OS-MA-K.
Deschner, Walter H.
    Pvt. 1cl. — Newton, Kans., OS-MA.
Duncan, George E. Pvt. 1cl. — Dearborn, Mo., OS-MA.
Duncan, Robert L. Pvt. 1cl. — Dearborn, Mo., OS-MA.
Dunn, Frank Jr. Pvt. 1cl, — (?)
Dyvig, Edward S. Pvt. 1cl. — Gilmore City, Iowa., OS-MA.
Ecton, Wiley J. Pvt. 1cl. — Osborn, Mo., OS-MA-W-HE.
Egan, William D. Pvt. 1cl. — Covington, Ky.
Fieth, Milton E. Pvt. 1cl. — Higginsville, Mo., OS-MA.
Finnell, Lauren Pvt. 1cl. — Newton, Kans., OS-MA-K.
Flinn, Evert L. Pvt. 1cl. — Stewartsville, Mo., OS-MA.
Freeburne, Clarence L.
    Pvt. 1cl. — Peabody, Kans., OS.
Fulk, William A. Pvt. 1cl. — Weston, Mo., OS-MA. (Missing.)
Griffin, Michael P. Pvt. 1cl. — (?)
Grisham, Jesse D. Pvt. 1cl. — Platte City, Mo., OS-MA.
Griswold, Oberly A.
    Pvt. 1cl. — Newton, Kans., OS-MA.
Groh, Earl C. Pvt. 1cl. — 847-17th St., Detroit, Mich.
Hamilton, Thomas D.
    Pvt. 1cl. — Newton, Kans., OS-MA.
Hanson, Elmer S. Pvt. 1cl. — Platte City, Mo., OS-MA.
Hartman, William L.
    Pvt. 1cl. — Sedgwick, Kans., OS-MA.
Hegle, Martin Pvt. 1cl. — Wolverton, Minn., OS-MA.
Hopperstad, Louis Pvt. 1cl. — Calmar, Ia., OS-MA.
Howard, Arthur L. Pvt. 1cl. — Burrton, Kans., OS-MA.
Hull, Wilson E. Pvt. 1cl. — Weston, Mo., OS-MA-WG.
Hutton, LeRoy J. Pvt. 1cl. — Langley, Kans., OS-MA.
Johnson, Charles V.
    Pvt. 1cl. — Ludington, Mich.
Johnson, Elmer R. Pvt. 1cl. — Bruce Crossing, Mich., D.
Kaith, Claude Pvt. 1cl. — Woodruff, Mo., OS-MA.
Karnick, Milton J. Pvt. 1cl. — Hastings, Minn., OS-MA.
Kenney, David T. Pvt. 1cl. — 3434 School St., Chicago, Ill.
Kessler, Harold H. Pvt. 1cl. — Spickard, Mo., OS-MA-W-HE.
Koller, Jacob E. Pvt. 1cl. — Stillwater, Minn., OS-MA-W-MGF.
Knutson, Peter G. Pvt. 1cl. — 3923 W. 4th St., Duluth, Minn., OS-MA.
Lantz, Chauncy M. Pvt. 1cl. — Newton, Kans., OS-MA.
Liggett, Austin A. Pvt. 1cl. — Peabody, Kans., OS-MA.
Linch, George I. Pvt. 1cl. — Norborne, Mo., OS-MA-K.
Livingston, Arthur D.
    Pvt. 1cl. — (?)
Loubey, Louis A. Pvt. 1cl. — Rushville, Mo., OS-MA.
Masters, Orville L. Pvt. 1cl. — Brunswick, Mo., OS-MA.
Matthews, Samuel D.
    Pvt. 1cl. — Fridley, Minn., OS-MA.
McDaniel, Hillary F.
    Pvt. 1cl. — (?)

SUPPLY COMPANY

McDonald, Harvey Pvt. 1cl.	Newton, Kans., OS-MA-W-MGF.	Benson, Bernard Private	(?)
McGinn, Thomas Pvt. 1cl.	(?)	Berry, Luther Private	Weston, Mo., OS.
Miller, Wilbe F. Pvt. 1cl.	Burrton, Kans., OS-MA-W-MGF.	Blumhagen, Willie Private	Kief, N. Dak., MA.
Minnick, Donald C. Pvt. 1cl.	524 E. Missouri Ave., St. Joseph,	Boderski, Wtyatlaw Private	Joliet, Ill., MA-W-HE.
Moffett, Charles C. Pvt. 1cl.	Mo., OS-MA-K.	Boje, Edward Private	424½ Brown St., Davenport, Iowa,
Nolan, Frank L. Pvt. 1cl.	Peabody, Kans., OS.	Bolen, Jesse T. Private	Bessemer, Mich.
	50 Wegman Parkway, Jersey City,	Bollum, Edward W. Private	(?)
Park, Loyd D. Pvt. 1cl.	N. J.	Bounds, Eugine F. Private	Knoxville, Tenn., MA-W-HE.
Payne, Charles H. Pvt. 1cl.	RFD 3, Galena, Kans., OS-MA.	Bragg, Pearl Private	Kirksville, Mo., OS-MA.
	1536 Potter Ave., Wichita, Kans,	Brennen, Chester F. Private	(?) Detroit, Mich.
Phillips, Ora Pvt. 1cl.	OS-MA.	Brown, Thomas F. Private	Marmarth, N. Dak.
Quigley, Edward D.	Kirksville, Mo.	Brummond, Charles F.	713 Vliet St., Milwaukee, Wis.
Pvt. 1cl.	1715 S. Market St., Wichita, Kans.	Private	
Rainey, Leslie Pvt. 1cl.	OS-MA-W-MGF.	Burrock, John A. Private	Hatton, N. Dak., MA.
Reed, William J. Pvt. 1cl.	(?)	Campbell, Carl F. Private	341 N. Hydraulic Ave., Wichita,
Rein, Will Pvt. 1cl.	Newton, Kans., OS-MA-W-MGF.		Kans.
Rhoades, Marvin E.	Ponca City, Okla., OS-MA-W-MGF.	Card, Richard D. Private	(?)
Pvt. 1cl.	Tucumcari, N. M., OS.	Caron, William H. Private	Fort Francis, Ontario, Canada., OS-
Richards, Roy Pvt. 1cl.			MA.
Royse, Elbert Pvt. 1cl.	(?)	Chabot, Ovila A. Private	Malta, Mont., OS-MA.
Russell, George L. Pvt. 1cl.	Sweetwater, Ill., OS-MA-K.	Clemens, Roy H. Private	Weston, Mo., OS-MA-W-MGF.
Sands, Ewart W. Pvt. 1cl.	Iatan, Mo., OS-MA-W-HE.	Clothier, Alba Private	Woodsville, Wis., MA.
Sawyer, Gordon W.	Eldorado, Kans., OS-MA.	Coleman, Virgil H. Private	Ithaca, Mich.
Pvt. 1cl.	Newton, Kans., OS-MA-W-MGF.	Coppock, Charlie Private	Garden City, Kans., OS-MA.
Sellers, Merle D. Pvt. 1cl.		Crockett, Charlie A. Private	Weston, Mo., OS-MA-K.
Smith, Albert Pvt. 1cl.	Syracuse, Kans., OS-MA.	Cox, Alphonsus C. Private	313 Townsend Ave., Detroit, Mich.
Sorrell, Leslie Pvt. 1cl.	Marceline, Mo., OS.	Cummings, Milton J.	32 Allen St., Rochester, N. Y.
Steeno, Ralph Pvt. 1cl.	Midway, Ky., OS-MA-W-MGF.	Private	
Still, Clyde W. Pvt. 1cl.	814 Kellog St., Green Bay, Wis.	Curtis, George W. Private	McEwen, Tenn.
Thronson, Joseph Pvt. 1cl.	Trenton, Mo., OS-MA.	Dally, Donald H. Private	La Porte, Minn., OS.
Torgerson, Kimpton C.	Emerado, N. Dak., OS-MA.	Dean, Clinton D. Private	Nora Springs, Iowa., OS-MA.
Pvt. 1cl.	Faredale, N. Dak., MA.	Delavergne, Nelson W.	Oberon, N. Dak.
Tritt, James E. Pvt. 1cl.		Private	
Vig, Alfred V. Pvt. 1cl.	Smithville, Mo., OS-MA.	Doberstein, Frank W.	(?) OS.
Wagle, John H. Pvt. 1cl.	Sharon, N. Dak., MA-W-MGF.	Private	
Warner, John C. Pvt. 1cl.	Platte City, Mo., OS-MA-K.	Dokkesven, Clarence Private	(?) OS.
Warner, Merle B. Pvt. 1cl.	Burrton, Kans., OS-MA.	Dugall, Paul F. Private	(?)
Wasrick, Edward Pvt. 1cl.	Burrton, Kans., OS-MA-W-MGF.	Dupras, William Private	481 Elizabeth St., Kenosha, Wis.
Weber, Theodore Pvt. 1cl.	514 Park St., Kenosha, Wis.	Duranto, Antonio Private	635 Elizabeth St., Utica, N. Y.
West, Paul L. Pvt. 1cl.	Independence, Iowa, OS-MA.	Dutcher, Raymond Private	(?)
White, John S. Pvt. 1cl.	McCracken, Kans., OS-MA-K.	Dybdal, Olaf Private	McLeod, N. Dak., OS-MA-W-HE.
Wilcox, James M. Pvt. 1cl.	Sedgwick, Kans., OS-MA.	Dykstra, Albert Private	Hudsonville, Mich.
Woodworth, James R.	Chili, Wis., OS-MA.	Enns, George Private	Unich, N. Dak.
Pvt. 1cl.	20 Nesbit St., Providence, R. I.	Erickson, Mannie H.	Cambridge, N. Dak., OS.
Aase, Albert Private	OS-MA-K.	Private	
Abbott, Lloyd E. Private	Ross, Minn., OS-MA-W-MGF.	Einarson, Carl E. Private	(?)
Absher, Roy Private	(?) OS.	Fahnestock, Harry A.	211 E. Locust St., Mechanicsburg,
Ackerman, Alger E. Private	Anderson, Ind., OS-MA-W-G.	Private	Pa., OS-MA.
Anderson, George A. Private	Gaines, Mich.	Farr, James Private	623 St. Paul St., Burlington, Va.,
Anderson, Joe Private	Newton, Kans., OS-MA-W-HE.		OS-MA-K.
Anderson, Roy A. Private	405 1st St., Sioux Falls, S. Dak.	Field, Ole E. Private	Cummings, N. Dak., MA.
Bailard, Jay L. Private	310 Scott St., Milwaukee, Wis.	Fisher, Clarence Private	(?)
Bailey, Harrison Private	(?)	Francis, Eugene Private	Stewartsville, Mo., OS.
	New Rockford, N. Dak., MA-W-	Friel, Roy Private	(?) OS-MA-W-?
	MGF.	Garland, Joseph E. Private	Lamorn, Iowa, OS-MA.
Barnes, Harry Private	127 W. Oak St., Ironwood, Mich.	George, Henry J. Private	(?)
Barr, Harry R. Private	Abilene, Kans., OS-MA.	Giesick, Henry Private	Leota, Kans., OS-MA.
Becker, Ralph E. Private	(?)	Gillespie, James F. Private	Abervale, W. Va.
Bengston, Eli F. Private	Rush City, Minn., OS-MA.	Giroux, Hector, O. Private	Buchanan, N. Dak., MA.
Bennett, Charles A. Private	McClusky, N. Dak., MA.		

119

SUPPLY COMPANY

Grace, Riley G.	Private	112 E. D St., Pueblo, Colo., MA-W-MGF.
Gratton, Hubert J.	Private	(?)
Gray, Harold J.	Private	53 Printic St., Lockport, N. Y.
Grochowsky, Jacob	Private	Aulne, Kans., OS-MA-W-MGF.
Gustavson, David A.	Private	Vifing, Minn., OS-MA. (Missing.)
Haberman, William F.	Private	1091 Wakefield Ave., St. Paul, Minn., OS-MA.
Hall, Decatur B.	Private	Weston, Mo., OS-MA.
Hall, Thomas H.	Private	1955 Portland Ave., St. Paul, Minn.
Hanson, Walter	Private	Athens, Wis.
Harden, Ellis I.	Private	Syracuse, Kans., OS-MA-K.
Harris, Weston V.	Private	Newton, Kans., OS-MA-W-G.
Heller, George H.	Private	2439 Madison Ave., Granite City, Ill.
Highley, Elmer N.	Private	Coffeyville, Kans., OS-MA.
Hire, Frank T.	Private	1018 Jenks St., St. Paul, Minn., OS-MA-W-MGF.
Hodges, Edgar	Private	577 Ellen St., Milwaukee, Wis.
Holle, Frank J.	Private	Newton, Kans., OS-MA.
Holt, Lester H.	Private	Oconomowoc, Wis.
Horwitz, Jake M.	Private	172 Garfield Ave., Milwaukee, Wis.
Houfer, Henry F.	Private	Fairmont, Minn., OS.
Huntsinger, Eddie	Private	Forest City, N. C.
Huseman, Ernst C.	Private	(?)
Hutchinson, Otis	Private	Princeton, Mo., OS-MA-W-MGF.
Iverson, Elwin P.	Private	Englevale, N. Dak.
Jensen, Eddie	Private	Alta, Iowa, OS-MA.
Johnson, Andrew H.	Private	Tracy, Minn., OS-MA-W-MGF.
Kelley, Herbert T.	Private	(?) OS.
Kleine, Richard	Private	Scotts Express Co., Minneapolis, Minn., OS-MA-W-MGF.
Kline, Bert D.	Private	Weber, Kans., OS-MA.
Koeppen, Hancel G.	Private	Attica, Kans., OS-MA-W-HE.
Krause, Carl	Private	RFD 2, Station D, Milwaukee, Wis.
La Croix, Archie D.	Private	(?)
Lane, George	Private	1929 Elm St., Milwaukee, Wis.
Larson, Albert H.	Private	Gluckeen, Minn., OS-MA-W-MGF.
Leigh, Lee	Private	Tarkio, Mo., OS-MA.
Letcher, Fred	Private	(?) OS-MA.
Lindquist, Kaleb E.	Private	Rosean, Minn., OS-MA-W-MGF.
Linville, David E.	Private	Weston, Mo., OS-MA.
Linville, Vernard V.	Private	Weston, Mo., OS-MA-W-MGF.
Loeffler, Frank G.	Private	Hampton, Minn., MA.
Loing, Oliver	Private	Reynolds, N. Dak., MA.
Lokken, John	Private	(?)
Loveland, Floyd	Private	Oskaloosa, Kans., OS.
Lower, Fred W.	Private	(?) OS.
Lukes, Joseph F.	Private	Long Prairie, Minn., OS.
Lundeen, Hjalmer	Private	Adams, N. Dak., MA-W-MGF.
Lundgren, Ernest H.	Private	Grafton, N. Dak., MA.
Madrigal, Lorenzo	Private	Lyons, Ill.
Maki, Eric V.	Private	Newberry, Mich.
Marcussen, Lucius H.	Private	(?)
Marolf, William E.	Private	Rushville, Mo., OS-MA-K.
Marshall, Chester B.	Private	Platte City, Mo., OS.
Martin, Raymond F.	Private	Cumberland, Wis.
Mash, Ervin	Private	St. James, Mo.

Masten, Jesse W.	Private	(?)
McClellan, Henry W.	Private	Manitowoc, Wis., D.
McIntyre, Alexander	Private	Newberry, Mich., D.
McMillen, Ralph E.	Private	Peabody, Kans., OS-MA-K.
McNeal, Joe	Private	Tarkio, Mo., OS-MA.
McNutt, George W.	Private	107 W. 7th St., Sedalia, Mo.
Miller, Peter	Private	Lorato, Minn., OS-MA.
Miller, William F.	Private	Mount Rose, Mo., OS-MA-K.
Milmine, John H.	Private	Sheboygan, Mich.
Miranda, Herbert	Private	(?)
Moeling, Benjamin W.	Private	3916 Harrison St., Kansas City, Mo.
More, Lawrence D.	Private	Ionia, Kans., OS-MA-K.
Mortenson, Richard E.	Private	Farmington, Minn., OS-MA (Missing.)
Mosher, Grant F.	Private	Cassopolis, Mich.
O'Connor, Joseph H.	Private	390 Linwood Ave., Detroit, Mich., D.
Orphan, Nick	Private	12 Broadway, Milton, Pa.
Ozzello, Emil	Private	Durango, Colo.
Palmer, Magnus	Private	Foxholm, N. Dak.
Parsons, James H.	Private	Boyne City, Mich.
Peterson, Oscar E.	Private	3940-12th Ave., S. Minneapolis, Minn., OS.
Pillatzki, Robert B.	Private	Nassau, Minn., OS-MA-W-MGF.
Plettl, Otto J.	Private	Little Falls, Minn., OS-MA-W-HE.
Post, Raymond	Private	Bridgmen, Mich.
Quinn, Michael W.	Private	Gen. Del., Minneapolis, Minn., OS-MA.
Raffauf, Charles B.	Private	(?) OS.
Rasler, Lawrence	Private	Liberal, Kans., OS-MA.
Reed, Elmer.	Private	Logan, W. Va., OS-MA-W-MGF.
Reed, Mansie	Private	(?)
Reinwand, Alie A.	Private	2422 W. 6th St., Sheboygan, Wis.
Renfro, Earl E.	Private	Hopkins, Mo., OS.
Revira, Ventura	Private	Las Cruces, N. M.
Rix, Max W.	Private	Oshtemo, Mich.
Rogaski, Stanley	Private	312 N. Division Ave., Grand Rapids, Mich.
Rogers, William L.	Private	Newton, Kans., OS-MA-K.
Royer, Paul	Private	RFD 1, Newton, Kans., OS.
Scanlon, Thomas J.	Private	320 E. North Ave., Pittsburg, Pa.
Schmarzo, August G.	Private	Osage, Iowa, OS-MA-W-S.
Schmidt, Edwin G.	Private	48 Union St., Hillsdale, Mich.
Schofield, Rufus F.	Private	1244 13th St., Des Moines, Iowa, OS.
Schrader, Herman	Private	6601 National Ave., West Allis, Wis.
Schreiber, William P.	Private	531 2nd St., Milwaukee, Wis.
Schuessler, Albert W.	Private	947 N. St. Louis Ave., Chicago, Ill.
Scott, Leon C.	Private	Prosper, Minn., OS.
Scully, Edward	Private	Blue M. D. Road, Wauwatosa, Wis.
Sedlack, Rudolph	Private	Mishicot, Wis.
Sewell, Ole E.	Private	Liberal, Kans., OS-MA-W-HE.
Sharp, James P., Jr.	Private	Merkel, Texas.

SUPPLY COMPANY

Shellhorn, Hubert P. Private (?) OS.
Shinn, Thomas Private Laurel, Miss.
Shirley, Charlie C. Private (?) OS-MA.
Shockey, Rudolph R. Private N. St. Paul, Minn., OS-MA-K.
Sisson, Alvin E. Private Courtland, Kans., OS-MA-K.
Slivensky, Joseph Private 318 S. Lowell St., Ironwood, Mich.
Smart, Wyatt S. Private Wheeler, Texas.
Smith, Frank W. Private Portage, Pa.
Sorensen, Soren B Private 132 Nassou St, New York, N. Y.
Sparwasser, Edward W. Private Glasco, Kans., OS-MA-W-MGF.
Sperry, Frank L. Private Scott City, Kans., OS-MA-W-MGF.
Starkovitch, Charles Private 1405 Melen St., Lincoln, Ill.
Stephens, Clyde G. Private Mt. Ayr, Iowa.
Stephenson, William E. Private Snider, Mo.
Stevens, Edson C. Private 52 Adams St., Ashtabula, Ohio.
Stoleson, Howard Private Tigerton, Wis.
Stufflebeam, Ray Private Lewistown, Ill.
Susewic, August Private 335-33rd St., Detroit, Mich.
Sward, Henry W. Private Graceton, Minn., OS-MA-W-MGF.
Tangen, Andy O. Private Morehead, Minn. OS-MA-K.
Taylor, George W. Private 692-4th Ave., Detroit, Mich.
Taylor, Warren A. Private (?)
Thimmesch, Fred J. Private Windsor, N. Dak.

Thompson, Martin Private Lisbon, N. Dak., MA-W-HE.
Thorvilson, Barney Private Adams, N. Dak., MA-W-MGF.
Tollifson, Harry Private Warwick, N. Dak., MA.
Trimirka, Adam Private 1076 Wabash Ave., Detroit, Mich.
Truitt, Cecil T. Private Osewathamie, Kans., OS-MA-W-HE.
Volpatti, Christ Private 46 Franklin St., Grand Rapids, Mich.
Walter, Clarence U. Private Berlin, N. Dak., MA.
Ward, Oscar G. Private Piedmont, Mo.
Weber, Charles Private Independence, Iowa, OS-MA-W-MR.
Weber, John F. Private Independence, Iowa, OS.
Weisner, Arthur J. Private Sauk Center, Minn., OS-MA.
Westby, Einar P. Private Fairdale, N. Dak., MA.
Wichman, Max Private 386 Adelaide St., Detroit, Mich.
Wiggins, Richard T. Private Trenton, Mo., OS-MA.
Williams, Claude F. Private Weston, Mo., OS-MA-W-HE.
Winter, Math G. Private Albany, Minn., MA.
Whale, Earl G. Private 631 17th St., Detroit, Mich.
Whitesell, Arthur P. Private RFD 4, Newton, Kans., OS-MA-K.
Wheeler, William W. Private Oskaloosa, Kans., OS-MA.
Wolf, Fredrick, L. Private Rowell Ave., Joliet, Ill., MA-W-HE.
Wood, Dueber R. Private Panama, Ill., MA. (PW)
Wooley, Burt G. Private Grand Junction, Mich.
Worthingham, Thornton K. Private La Crescent, Minn., MA-W-S.

DO YOU REMEMBER THESE TWO DAYS?

The upper picture was taken on September 30 in the trenches dug by the Engineers. The enemy had just started a counter attack which was promptly beaten off.

The lower picture was taken October 1, at the rendezvous in the open field near Cheppy. Surely you remember that day?

MACHINE GUN COMPANY

ROSTER OF COMPANY L, 139th INFANTRY

Charles Haftle, Captain
Spencer Otis, Jr., 1st Lt.
George C. Walters, 1st Lt.
Lonnie N. Young, 2nd Lt.
George A. Gleason, 2nd Lt.
Schoonover, Orville 1st Sgt.
Bridgmon, Orville L.
    Sup. Sgt.
Gibson, Hugh J. Sergeant

Cardinell, John H. Sergeant

Netherton, Charles E.
    Sergeant
McJunkins, John R.
    Sergeant
Montgomery, William S.
    Sergeant
Bickel, Fred E. Sergeant

Roberts, Jack A. Sergeant

Weightman, Ray Sergeant

Zook, Russel A. Sergeant

Renn, George S. Sergeant

Sunderland, Roscoe Sergeant

Casselman, Phillip J.
    Sergeant
Browning, Frost A.
    Sergeant
Halcomb, John S. Corporal

Hopper, Frank C. Corporal

Beattie, James I. Corporal

Ostrander, Roy Corporal

Anderson, Archie N.
    Corporal
Ward, Harold C. Corporal

Hill, Roy D. Corporal

Rerick, Charles A. Corporal

Gomel, Lois Corporal
Scott, Francis E. Corporal

Baker, Mont., St.M-MA.
Chicago, Ill.
Saurata, Tex.
Anna, Ky.
Jacksonville, Fla.
Bigelow, Mo., OS-P-4th Mo.
Bigelow, Mo., OS-MA-P-St.M-4th
Mo.
Mound City, Mo., OS-MA-P-St.M-
4th Mo.
Mound City, Mo., OS-MA-P-St.M
4th Mo.
Wellington, Kans., OS-MA-P-St.M-
3rd Kans.
Mound City, Mo., OS-MA-P-St.M-
4th Mo.
Maitland, Mo., OS-MA-P-St.M-4th
Mo.
Mound City, Mo., OS-MA-P-St.M-
4th Mo.
Horton, Kans., OS-MA-G-P-St.M-
4th Mo.
Mound City, Mo., OS-MA-P-St.M-
4th Mo.
Milan, Kans., OS-MA-P-St.M-3rd
Kans.
Wellington, Kans., OS-MA-P-St.M-
3rd Kans.
Belle Plaine, Kans., OS-MA-P-St.M-
3rd Kans.
Wellington, Kans., OS-MA-P-St.M-
3rd Kans.
Mound City, Mo., OS-MA-W-S-P-
St.M-3rd Kans.
Wellington, Kans., OS-MA-P-St.M-
3rd Kans.
Wellington, Kans., OS-MA-P-St.M-
3rd Kans.
Wellington, Kans., OS-MA-P-St.M-
3rd Kans.
Wellington, Kans., OS-MA-P-St.M-
3rd Kans.
Wellington, Kans., OS-MA-P-St.M-
3rd Kans.
Mound City, Mo., OS-MA-G-P-St.M-
4th Mo.
Fortescue, Mo., OS-MA-P-St.M-4th
Mo.
Wellington, Kans., OS-MA-P-St.M-
3rd Kans.
Craig, Mo., OS-MA-P-St.M-4th Mo.
Mound City, Mo., OS-MA-P-St.M-
4th Mo.

Winsor, Glenn H. Corporal

Dyste, Percy H. Corporal

Wilson, Roscoe Corporal

Meredith, Warren A.
    Corporal
Cook, Charlie Corporal

Overby, Jesse M. Corporal

Blanchard, Floyd Corporal

Allison, Albert Corporal

Potucek, Charles Corporal

Reynolds, Floyd Corporal

Tucker, Robert B. Corporal

Caples, Russel B. Corporal

Spahr, Orville Corporal

Anderson, Carl E. Corporal

Wilson, Julian Corporal

Robinson, Ronald Corporal

Myers, William Corporal

Brown, Fawn D. Corporal

Curtin, Joseph Corporal

McFarland, Oral Corporal

Cardinell, Roy G. Cook

Collins, Claude H. Cook

Couts, Clyde S. Cook

Rives, George W. Cook
Noll, Jacob S. Mechanic

McKee, Nelson Mechanic

Wilson, Ray Mechanic

Wellington, Kans., OS-MA-P-St.M-
3rd Kans.
Foreman, N. D., OS-MA-P- St.M-4-
20-18.
Argonia, Kans., OS-MA-P-St.M-3rd
Kans.
Wellington, Kans., OS-MA-P-St.M-
3rd Kans.
Mound City, Mo., OS-MA-P-St.M-
4th Mo.
Callio, Mo., OS-MA-P-St.M-3rd
Kans.
St. Joseph, Mo., OS-MA-P-St.M-4th
Mo.
Mound City, Mo., OS-MA-P-St.M-
4th Mo.
Portland, Kans., OS-MA-P-St.M-
3rd Kans.
Maryville, Mo., OS-MA-P-St.M-4th
Mo.
Wellington, Kans., OS-MA-G-P-St.-
M-3rd Kans.
Wellington, Kans., OS-MA-P-St.M-
3rd Kans.
Wellington, Kans., OS-MA-P-St.M-
3rd Kans.
22 North Sarah, Escanaba, Mich.,
P-joined Oct. 5, 1918.
Mound City, Mo., OS-P-St.M-4th
Mo.
Wellington, Kans., OS-MA-P-St.M-
3rd Kans.
307 Colo. Ave., St. Joseph, Mo., OS-
MA-P-St.M-4th Mo.
Wellington, Kans., OS-MA-P-St.M-
3rd Kans.
824 Parker St., St. Joseph, Mo., OS-
MA-P-St.M-4th Mo.
Wellington, Kans., OS-MA-P-St.M-
3rd Kans.
Mound City, Mo., OS-MA-P-St.M-
4th Mo.
Wellington, Kans., OS-MA-P-St.M-
3rd Kans.
Bigelow, Mo., OS-MA-P-St.M-4th
Mo.
Colorene, Ala., OS-MA-P-10-5-18.
Mound City, Mo., OS-MA-P-St.M-
4th Mo.
Bigelow, Mo., OS-MA-P-St.M-4th
Mo.
Mankato, Kans., OS-MA-P-St.M-
joined 2-15-17.

123

MACHINE GUN COMPANY

Ogden, Lafe — Mechanic — Mound City, Mo., OS-MA-P-St.M-4th Mo.

Hadden, Harry — Bugler — Mound City, Mo., OS-MA-G-P-St.M-4th Mo.

Litts, Charles, — Bugler — 3029 Prospect Ave., Kansas City, Mo., OS-MA-G-P-St.M-4th Mo.

Adams, George W. Pvt. 1cl. — Mound City, Mo., OS-MA-P-St.M-4th Mo.

Anno, Trevor G. Pvt. 1cl. — Fortescue, Mo., OS-MA-P-St.M-4th Mo.

Ballinger, James R. Pvt. 1cl. — Mound City, Mo., OS-MA-P-St.M-4th Mo.

Banghart, Merle Pvt. 1cl. — Oxford, Kans., OS-MA-W-S-P-St.M-3rd Kans.

Barlow, Harry Pvt. 1cl. — Moline, Ill., 418-19th St.M-A-P-joined 10-5-18.

Bauckle, Frank F. Pvt. 1cl. — Brewster, Minn., OS-MA-W-HE-in left arm. P. Joined 10-5-18.

Bertram, William E. Pvt. 1cl. — Mound City, Mo., OS-MA-P-St.M-4th Mo.

Bose, Charles W. Pvt. 1cl. — Detroit, Mich., 142 Palmer Ave., P. Joined 10-5-18.

Braukman, Harry H. Pvt. 1cl. — 709 Craig St., Covington, Ky., joined 10-5-18. P.

Brickey, Henry G. Pvt. 1cl. — Mound City, Mo., OS-MA-St.M-P-4th Mo.

Buckles, Carl R. Pvt. 1cl. — Nodaway, Mo., OS-MA-P-St.M-4th Mo.

Crimmons, Leo M. Pvt. 1cl. — Port Huron, Mich., 828 Erie St., P. Joined 10-5-18.

Cross, Lemmie Pvt. 1cl. — Muncie, Mich., 30155 Jefferson St., P. Joined 10-5-18.

Denny, Martin R. Pvt. 1cl. — Pellston, Mich., P. Joined 10-5-18.

Donan, Francis B. Pvt. 1cl. — Mound City, Mo., OS-MA-P-4th Mo., St.M.

Edmondson, Dale E. Pvt. 1cl. — Wellington, Kans., OS-MA-P-St.M-3rd Kans.

Eklund, Ralph L. Pvt. 1cl. — McPherson, Kans., OS-MA-P-St.M-3rd Kans.

Fitzmaurice, Michael P. Pvt. 1cl. — Forest City, Mo., OS-MA-P-St.M-3rd Kans. Trfd. to Hosp.

Hatch, Alfred Pvt. 1cl. — 4th Mo. P-St.M. St. Joseph, Mo., Gen. Delivery, OS-MA-W-S-in leg.

Hunt, Clarence M. Pvt. 1cl. — Spottsville, Ky., P-10-5-18.

Johnson, LeRoy Pvt. 1cl. — Glencoe, Mich., P.Apr. 20, 1918.

Kinsella, Thomas J. Pvt. 1cl. — 143 West 115th St., Chicago, Ill., P-10-5-18.

Kraeszig, Adam Pvt. 1cl. — Louisville, Ky., P-10-5-18.

Lane, Edward J. Pvt. 1cl. — 7403 St. Lawrence Ave., Chicago, Ill., P-10-5-18.

Lavengood, Earl J. Pvt. 1cl. — Elsie, Mich., P-10-5-18.

Manning, Charles H. Pvt. 1cl. — Stambaugh, Mich., P-10-5-18.

McLees, Walter R. Pvt. 1cl. — Sanborn, N. D., OS-MA-P-Apr. 20, 18 St.M.

Miller, Jacob W. Pvt. 1cl. — 164 William St., Louisville, Ky., P-10-5-18.

Moore, Delmer O. Pvt. 1cl. — Bigelow, Mo., OSP-4th Mo.

Nauman, Robert Pvt. 1cl. — Craig, Mo., OS-MA-St.M-P-4th Mo.

Nye, Elmer Pvt. 1cl. — Forest City, Mo., OS-MA-P-St.M-4th Mo.

Ostrowski, Joseph Pvt. 1cl. — Plymouth, Mich., P-Oct. 5, 1918.

Perryman, William H. Pvt. 1cl. — Greenland, Mich., 10-5-18. Trfd. to Hosp.

Quinby, Albert M. Pvt. 1cl. — Wellington, Kans., OS-MA-P-St.M-Trfd. to Hosp. 4-18-19.

Riesburg, Elmer O. Pvt. 1cl. — Moorland, Mich., P-Oct. 5, 1918.

Rohliff, John A. Pvt. 1cl. — Denver, Colo., P-Oct. 5, 1918.

Rybacki, Michael Pvt. 1cl. — 889-10th Ave., Milwaukee, Wis., P-10-5-18.

Scherhaufer, Thomas Pvt. 1cl. — 1427 South 12th St., Sheboygan, Wis. P-10-5-18.

Schoonover, Tot Pvt. 1cl. — Bigelow, Mo., OS-MA-G-P-4th Mo. St.M.

Schultz, William C. Pvt. 1cl. — Aldrich, Mich., OS-MA-W-S-Right shoulder. St.M-P. 4-20-18.

Sinclair, Glen Pvt. 1cl. — Mound City, Mo., OS-MA-St.M-4th Mo., Trfd. to Hosp.

Skotland, Jason Pvt. 1cl. — Willow City, N. D., OS-MA-P-St.M-May 21, 1918.

Smith, Walter E. Pvt. 1cl. — St. Joseph, Mo., 2004 Boyd St., OS-MA-P-St.M-4th Mo.

Small, John J. Pvt. 1cl. — 7601 Champlaign Ave., Chicago, Ill., P-10-5-18.

Sparks, George A. Pvt. 1cl. — Otterville, Mo., OS-MA-P-St.M-4th Mo.

Stevenson, Godfred P. Pvt. 1cl. — Wakefield, Mich., P-10-5-18.

Stewart, Hiram Pvt. 1cl. — Petoskey, Mich., P-10-5-18.

Stokes, Don D. Pvt. 1cl. — Craig, Mo., OS-MA-P-St.M-4th Mo.

Story, Earnest G. Pvt. 1cl. — Craig, Mo., OS-MA-P-St.M-4th Mo.

Story, Thomas M. Pvt. 1cl. — Craig, Mo., OS-MA-G-P-St.M-4th Mo.

Thomas, Claude F. Pvt. 1cl. — Flushing, Mich., P-10-5-18.

Vanslyke, William J. Pvt. 1cl. — Oregon, Mo., OS-MA-P-St.M-4th Mo.

Verscheuron, Gust Pvt. 1cl. — Hart, Mich., P-10-5-18.

Walker, Earl B. Pvt. 1cl. — Ashland, Wis., P-10-5-18.

Watters, Clarence G. Pvt. 1cl. — Craig, Mo., OS-MA-G-P-St.M-4th Mo.

Williams, James Pvt. 1cl. — Fortescue, Mo., OS-P-St.M-4th Mo. Trfd. to Hosp.

Yount, Clyde C. Pvt. 1cl. — Bigelow, Mo., OS-MA-P-St.M-4th Mo.

Anderson, James W. Private — Mt. Pulaski, Ill., OS-MA-P-St.M. May 21, 1918.

Andrews, Irwin F. Private — Altantic, Ill., OS-MA-P-St.M-May 21, 1918.

Barner, Lee M. Private — Wellington, Kans., OS-MA-P-St.M-3rd Kans.

Booton, Wesley J. Private — Knapp, Wis., P-10-5-18.

Botkins, Elmo Private — Wellington, Kans., OS-MA-P-St.M-3rd Kans.

Boyd, John Private — Tingley, Ia., OS-MA-P-St.M-April 20, 1918.

Bragg, Jake Private — Squires, Mo., OS-MA-HE. Shell shocked. P-St.M-4th Mo.

MACHINE GUN COMPANY

Brokamp, William J. Private — 1215 Scott St., Covington, Ky., P-10-5-18.

Card, Joseph E. Private — Gibson, Ill., P-May 21,1918.

Cavanaugh, Vincent Private — Madison, N. J., 75 Park Ave., MA-St.M-P-Jan. 15, 1919.

Coleman, Charles C. Private — Ludington, Mich., 322 North William St., P-10-5-18.

Connett, Carrol H. Private — 2511 Faron St., St. Joseph, Mo., OS-MA-P-St.M-4th Mo.

Coyle, William T. Private — Maitland, Mo., OS-MA-P-St.M-4th Mo.

Darrow, Clair L. Private — Cross Village, Mich., P-10-5-18. Trfd. to Hosp.

Dege, Adolph Private — Craig, Mo., OS-MA-St.M-P-4th Mo.

Doering, Richard Private — Goodrich, N.D., MA-St.M-P-May 20, 1918.

Donoho, Pat Private — Alma, Mich., MA-St.M-P-Jan. 15, 1919.

Dugar, Sidney L. Private — 125 East 57 Ave., Chicago, Ill., P-10-5-18.

Duncan, Thomas H. Private — Mound City, Mo., OS-MA-W-MGF in right ear. P-St.M-4th Mo.

Elbert, Mathew A. Private — St. Bonifacius, Minn., MA-St.M-Apr. 20, 1918. Trfd. to Hosp.

Ellis, Emmons B. Private — Williston, N. D., MA-St.M-P-May 21, 1918.

Everett, Roy Private — Mound City, Mo., OS-MA-St.M-P-4th Mo.

Fettig, Leo J. Private — Petoskey, Mich., P-10-5-18.

Fischer, Arthur E. Private — 3623 Greenfield Ave., Milwaukee, Wis., P-10-5-18.

Fitzmaurice, Francis Private — Mound City, Mo., OS-MA-P-St.M-4th Mo.

Flesch, John Private — 430 Bridgewater Ave., Chippewa Falls, Wis., MA-OS-P-St.M-joined 4-20-18.

Ford, Mayo F. Private — 18 East 114th St., Chicago, Ill., MA-P-joined Oct. 5, 1918.

Fritzm, Charles P. Private — 234 14th Ave., St. Cloud, Minn., OS-MA-P-Oct. 5, 1918.

Frosch, Loyd Private — Alma, Mich., OS-MA-P-Oct. 5, 1918.

Gnesin, Phillip Private — 262 Elliot St., Detroit, Mich., P-Oct. 5, 1918.

Grabler, Emil E. Private — Milwaukee, Wis., Hosp.-Jan. 13, 1919. Joined Oct. 5, 1919.

Gracewski, William Private — 207 Wash. St., St. Hibbing, Minn., P-Oct. 5, 1918.

Gray, Veress Private — Norwalk, Ia., Hosp. Dec. 12, 1918, joined Oct. 5, 1918.

Gutherie, Robert N. Private — Mound City, Mo., OS-MA-P-St.M-4th Mo.

Hainsworth, Ralph B. Private — Wellington, Kans., OS-MA-W-MGF-right hand.

Hering, Richard F. Private — 6247 3rd Ave., Milwaukee, Wis., P-joined Oct. 5, 1918.

Hicks, Luther Private — Tarkio, Mo., OS-MA-P-St.M-4th Mo.

Huck, Casper Private — New Salem, N. D., P-joined 10-5-18.

Hunt, Clarence M. Private — Spottsville, Ky., P-joined 10-5-8.

Janik, Albert A. Private — Lena, Wis., Hosp. Jan. 18, 1918, joined 10-5-18.

Johnson, Angus M. Private — Wellington, Kans., OS-MA-P-St.M-3rd Kans.

Johnson, LeRoy Private — Glencoe, Mich., OS-MA-P-joined 10-5-18.

Johnson, Nathen Private — 11930 Parnel Ave., Chicago, Ill., P-joined 10-5-18.

Jones, Sumber Private — Perth, Kans., OS-MA-P-St.M-3rd Kans.

Kalman, Edward Private — Melrose, Minn., OS-MA-P-St.M-5-21-18.

Kauth, Raymond Private — Potosi, Wis., P-joined 10-5-18.

Kelley, Michael J. Private — Buford, N. D., OS-MA-G-P-St.M-April 5, 1918.

Knapp, Olof Private — Massena, Ia., OS-MA-P-St.M-April 4, 1918.

Krauth, Edward F. Private — Mound City, Mo., OS-MA-P-St.M-4th Mo.

Kreek, John Private — Spring Grove, Minn., OS-MA-P-St.M-May 21, 1918.

Kvelve, Rudolph Private — Wellington, Kans., OS-MA-P-St.M-3rd Kans.

Marshall, Thomas B. Private — Mason, Mich., P-joined 10-5-18.

Mattice, Roy D. Private — Craig, Mo., OS-MA-P-St.M-4th Mo.

Maudlin, James W. Private — Wellington, Kans., OS-MA-P-St.M-3rd Kans.

Maxon, Emery L. Private — Wichita, Kans., OS-MA-P-St.M-3rd Kans.

Mayes, Curtiss L. Private — Wellington, Kans., OS-MA-St.M-P-3rd Kans.

McCabe, Delbert E. Private — Douglas, Okla., OS-MA-G-P-St.M-3rd Kans.

McCombs, Nathanial G. Private — Flint, Mich., P-joined 10-5-18.

McGlinchey, Hugh J. Private — Merrill, Mich., P-joined 10-5-18.

McNier, William E. Private — 1244 North Wood St., Chicago, Ill., P-joined 10-5-18.

Michaelson, Morris Private — 164 William St., Louisville, Ky., P-joined 10-5-18.

Miller, Jacob W. Private — Minneapolis, Minn., OS-MA-P-St.M-Apr. 4, 1918.

Mostu, Arthur Private — Pawnkee, Wis., RFD 14, P-joined 10-5-18.

Mueller, Alex C. Private — Craig, Mo., OS-MA-P-St.M-4th Mo.

Nauman, Clarence G. Private — Craig, Mo., OS-MA-P-St.M-4th Mo.

Nelly, Glen Private — Anamosa, Ia., OS-MA-P-St.M-Apr. 4, 1918.

Neville, Maichael T. Private — 771 7th St., Milwaukee, Wis., P-joined 10-5-18.

Nyka, Frank L. Private — Parkersburg, Ia., P-joined 10-5-18.

Ogline, Earl H. Private — Starbuck, Minn., OS-MA-G-P-St.M-May 21, 1918.

Opdahl, Albert Private — Plymouth, Mich., P-joined 10-5-18.

Ostrowski, Joseph A. Private — Trenton, Mich., P-joined 10-5-18.

Parker, Elijah E. Private — 1598 Barr St., Detroit, Mich., P-joined 10-5-18.

Pagano, Phillip Private — New Castle, Wyo., OS-MA-St.M-P-4th Mo.

Phillips, Thomas Private —

MACHINE GUN COMPANY

Piper, Paul E.   Private   Pittsford, Mich., P-joined 10-5-18.

Poirier, Victor G.   Private   Wellington, Kans., OS-MA-W-MGF-in left hip. St.M-P-3rd Kans.

Privratski, Alexander   Private   Dickinson, N. D., P-Trfd. to Co. Jan. 18, 1918.

Reed, Clifford F.   Private   Chesaning, Mich., P-joined 10-5-18.

Reese, Francis   Private   Blandburg, Penn., P-joined 10-5-18.

Riesburg, Elmer O.   Private   Moreland, Mich., P-joined 10-5-18.

Riner, Howard   Private   Wellington, Kans., OS-MA-P-St.M-3rd Kans.

Ronnington, Albert   Private

Root, Elzer   Private   Spring Valley, Minn., P-joined 10-5-18.

Roth, Charles T.   Private   3317 Duncan St., St. Joseph, Mo., OS-MA-P-St.M-4th Mo.

Russel, Floyd I.   Private   Velva, N. D., OS-MA-P-St.M-Apr. 4, 1918.

Rybacki, Michael   Private   889 10th Ave., Milwaukee, Wis., P-joined 10-5-18.

Sarbacker, Bernert   Private   Kenosha, Wis., 436 Lyman Ave., P-joined 10-5-18.

Savage, Charles   Private   Velva, N. D., OS-MA-W-S-left arm. P-St.M-Apr. 5, 1918.

Scanlon, Francis,   Private   Harmony, Mich., P-joined 10-5-18.

Scheflo, Rudolph   Private   Alanda, N. D., OS-MA-St.M-to Hosp. 12-10-18-joined 4-4-18.

Schantz, George L.   Private   304 Hampshire St., Quincy, Ill., P-joined 10-5-18.

Schiebel, Albert W.   Private   Ellendale, N. D., P-joined 10-5-18.

Shaffer, Charles   Private   Milan, Kans., OS-MA-St.M-Trfd. to Hosp. 3rd Kans.

Shinafelt, O. K.   Private   (Unknown) Joined Jan. 12, 1919 Trfd. to Hosp.

Simmons, Rolla E.   Private   Granada, Minn., OS-MA-St.M-P-joined Apr. 5, 1919.

Smith, Charles   Private   Owosso, Mich., P-joined 10-5-18.

Smith, Clarence   Private   Takota, N. D., OS-MA-St.M-P-Apr. 4, 1918.

Solin, John A.   Private   Heimdal, N. D., OS-MA-St.M-P-Apr. 4, 1918.

Souter, Arthur   Private   Paris, Mich., P-joined 10-5-18.

Sparks, George A.   Private   Otterville, Mo., OS-MA-St.M-P-4th Mo.

Stephens, Norman   Private   Brunswick, Mo., OS-MA-St.M-P-4th Mo.

Stoller, Henry   Private   Carson, N. D., OS-MA-St.M-P-joined Apr. 4, 1918.

Suholalski, Joseph   Private   Detroit, Mich., 236 Haslet St., P-joined 10-5-18.

Sullivan, Ambrose F.   Private   Sears, Mich., P-joined 10-5-18.

Sweeter, John   Private   Rice, Minn., P-joined 10-5-18.

Swift, Claude J.   Private   Wellington, Kans., OS-MA-St.M-P-3rd Kans.

Timmons, Olin J.   Private   Stanton, Mich., P-joined 10-5-18.

Torfin, Adrian D.   Private   Aneta, N. D., OS-MA-W-MGF-in chest. St.M-P. 5-21-18.

Tooley, Chester M.   Private   Wellington, Kans., OS-MA-P-St.M-3rd Kans.

Turner, Ray   Private   Ellis, Kans., OS-MA-P-St.M- 3rd Kans.

Uphouse, Loyd T.   Private   Mound City, Mo., OS-MA-P-St.M-4th Mo.

Vanzandt, Benjamin   Private   Fortescue, Mo., OS-MA-P-St.M-4th Mo.

Varvel, Luther   Private

Vaughn, Warren Z.   Private   Wallingford, Vt., OS-MA-G-P-St.M-3rd Kans.

Vogt, John   Private   Detroit, Mich., P-joined 10-5-18.

Walker, Earl B.   Private   Ashland, Wis., P-joined 10-5-18.

Webster, Ray B.   Private   Sturgis, Mich., 202 West Maple St., P-joined 10-5-18.

Weck, Albert O.   Private   Reed City, Mich., P-joined 10-5-18.

Wilds, Fred H.   Private   Chesaning, Mich., P-joined 10-5-18.

Williams, Claude D.   Private   Wellington, Kans., OS-MA-P-St.M-3rd Kans.

Winters, Harry M.   Private   Barlow, Ky., P-Trfd. Oct. 5, 1918.

Worel, James L.   Private   2230 Kedzie Ave., Chicago, Ill., P-joined 10-5-18.

Young, John E.   Private   Oxford, Kans., OS-MA-W-S-in right leg. P-St.M-3rd Kans.

Zavitniewicz, Peter   Private   266 Exchange St., Kenosha, Wis., P-joined 10-5-18.

Hopkins, Jesse

Rock, Waldo   Sergeant   Mound City, Mo., Trfd. for duty in the U. S. SO No. 201 Hq. 35th Div. OS. 4th Mo.

Werner, Nathian   Private   McIntyre, Ia., OS. Dropped from rolls per joined G O No. 111 GHQ A. E. F. 18. Apr. 20, 1918.

Mathews, Whit O.   Pvt. 1cl.   Oxford, Kans., OS. Dropped from rolls per G. O. No. 111 GHQ A. E. F. 18. 3rd Kans.

Berndt, Frederick,   Private   Balfour, N. D., OS. Dropped from rolls as admitted to BH May 21, 1918.

Christenson, Cornell   Private   Trfd. to Hq. Co. this Regt. OS Apr. 20, 1918.

Stuart, Vernon   Private   Fortescue, Mo., OS. Trfd. to 130th Machine Gun Bn. 4th Mo.

Shutts, Paul P.   Sergeant   Mound City, Mo., OS-MA-K-St.M-4th Mo.

Elkins, Orville   Corporal   Lexington, Mo., OS-MA-K-St.M-4th Mo.

Chuning, Edwin F.   Corporal   Bigelow, Mo., OS-MA-K-St.M-4th Mo.

Dovel, Tassel   Pvt. 1cl.   Mound City, Mo., OS-MA-K-St.M-4th Mo.

Benoit, Guy V.   Private   Verona, N. D., OS-MA-K-St.M-Apr. 24, 1918.

Botkins, Jay   Private   Wellington, Kans., OS-MA-K-St.M-3rd Kans.

Collins, Glen   Private   Wellington, Kans., OS-MA-K-St.M-3rd Kans.

Fleming, Claude   Private   Maitland, Mo., OS-MA-K-St.M-4th Mo.

Holt, Elmer M.   Sergeant   Wellington, Kans., OS-MA-Trfd. to 41st Div. for attendance A. C. S. St.M-3rd Kans.

MACHINE GUN COMPANY

Tibbets, Roy	Sergeant	Mound City, Mo., OS-MA-W-HE-severely wounded in back, dropped from rolls admitted to SOS BH. St-M.-4th Mo.
Elton, Fred E.	Corporal	Mound City, Mo., OS-MA-W-MGF-in leg; dropped from rolls. St.M-4th Mo.
Black, Guy	Corporal	Wellington, Kans., OS. Dropped from rolls as admitted to SOS BH 3rd Kans.
Tennant, Warren A.	Corporal	Wellington, Kans., OS-MA-G. Dropped from rolls as admitted into SOS BH. St.M-3rd Kans.
Stewart, Harry L.	Corporal	Wellington, Kans., OS-MA-W-S-in leg, dropped from rolls. St.M-3rd Kans.
Crowdus, William W.	Corporal	Wellington, Kans., OS-MA-W-MGF-in neck. Dropped from rolls. St.M-3rd Kans.
Bradley, David E.	Pvt. 1cl.	St. Joseph, Mo., Gen. Delivery, OS-MA-W-S-in face. St.M-4th Mo.
Horn, Edward R.	Pvt. 1cl.	134 Hutton St., Jersey City, N. J. OS-MA-G-St.M-4-20-18.
Walker, Joseph E.	Pvt. 1cl.	Martinsburg, Va., 709 Va. Ave., OS-MA-St.M-3rd Kans. Dropped from rolls as admitted to SOS BH.
Weddle, Carl	Pvt. 1cl.	Shubert, Neb., OS-MA-G-St.M-4th Mo.
Simmons, Delbert E.	Pvt. 1cl.	Trfd. to Hq. Co. OS-MA-G-St.M-4th Mo., Holt, Mo.
Beattie, Charles L.	Private	Wellington, Kans., OSMA-W-S-in leg. St.M-3rd Kans.
Brummett, Glen E.	Private	Skidmore, Mo., OS. Dropped from rolls as admitted to SOS BH 4th Mo.
Buron, Ray E.	Private	Wellington, Kans., OS-MA-W-MGF-in ankle. St.M-3rd Kans.
Campbell, Enos C.	Private	Oxford, Kans., OS-MA-G-St.M-3rd Kans.
Englebart, John	Private	Pekin, Ill., OS-MA-G-St.M-May 21, 1918.
Fletcher, Warren T.	Private	Heyworth, Ill., OS-MA-W-HE-both legs were mangled and he died on way to the hosp. St.M-4-4-18.
Foster, Alfred E.	Private	Wellington, Kans., OS-MA-K-St.M-3rd Kans.
Garton, William	Private	1010 North Elm, Bloomington, Ill., OS-MA-W-MGF.St.M-4-4-18.
Hald, Marinus	Private	Buchanan, N. D., OS-MA-W-S-St.M May 21, 1918.
Hollingsworth, Ralph	Private	Trfd. to Hq. Co. this Regt. OS-MA-G-St.M-3rd Kans.
McGreavey, Thomas W.	Private	Wellington, Kans., OS-MA Trfd to Hq. Co. this regt. St.M-3rd Kans.
Morrel, Floyd B.	Private	Wellington, Kans., OS-MA-W-S-St.M-3rd Kans.
Mosby, Harry	Private	Wellington, Kans., OS-MA-W-S-St.M-3rd Kans.
Muchvitch, Lee M.	Private	Wahpeton, N. D., OS-MA-K-St.M-4-4-18.
Mycue, Earl A.	Private	(Not known) OS-MA-G-St.M-4-4-18.
Robinson, Albert R.	Private	Forest City, Mo., OS-MA-W-MGF-St.M-4th Mo.
Sandve, Simon	Private	Tioga, N. D., OS-MA-W-MGF-in left arm. St.M-5-21-18.
Thompson, Albert S.	Private	Farwell, Minn., OS-MA-W-MGF-in leg. St.M-5-21-18.
Wolf, Joe	Private	Zeeland, N. D., OS-MA-W-MGF in right hip. St.M-4-4-18.
Woods, Earl	Private	Mound City, Mo., OS-MA-W-MGF-St.M-4th Mo.
Everhart, William	Private	Corpus Christi, Tex., OS-MA-W-MGF in hand. St.M-4th Mo.
Curtin, Henry P.	Mechanic	St. Joseph, Mo., OS-MA-W-S-St.M-4th Mo.
Bayha, Richard	Private	Skidmore, Mo., OS-MA-K-St.M-4th Mo.
Scrivens, Rolla E.	Private	Perth, Kans., OS-MA-K-St.M-3rd Kans.
Balliet, Leonard	Private	Harvey, N. D., OS-MA-W-MGF-St.M-5-21-18.
Balster, Frank	Private	Jamestown, N. D., OS-MA-W-S-St.M-5-21-18.
Bell, Port	Private	New Holland, Ill., OS-MA-K-St.M-5-21-18.
Doyle, Joseph	Private	Goodrich, N. D., OS-MA-St.M-4-20-18.
Gift, Floyd W.	Private	Wellington, Kans., OS-MA-W-S-St.M-3rd Kans.
Schwartz, Charlie F.	Private	Suverne, N. D., OS-MAK-St.M-5-21-18.
Christofferson, Peter	Private	Homballton, Iowa, OS-MA-St.M-5-21-18.
Schindler, John J.	Private	Tappen, N. D., OS-MA-K-St.M-4-20-18.
Fountain, William H.	Corporal	6123 Champlaigh Ave., Chicago, Ill., 10-5-18.
Bull, Arthur	Private	(Unknown) to Hosp.
Burns, Velma L.	Private	Ravenwood, Mo., OS-MA-St.M-4th Mo.
Clark, William C.	Private	Brashear, Mo., OS-MA-G-St.M-3rd Kans.
Holmes, Cecil	Private	Wellington, Kans., OS-MA-Trfd. to 1st Replacement Bn. St. Aignan. St.M-3rd Kans.
Hopkins, Zachariah	Private	Craig, Mo., OS-MA-St.M-4th Mo.
Williams, James	Private	Fortescue, Mo., OS-4th Mo.
Byersdorf, James	Private	(Unknown) Trfd. to Hq. Co. this Regt.
Cook, William H.	Private	Mound City, Mo., OS-MA-W-MGF in foot. St.M-4th Mo.
Devitt, John D.	Private	(Unknown) MA-Trfd. to Hq. Co. this Regt.
Heubregtsa, Donnis	Private	(Unknown) 10-5-18-Trfd. to Hosp.
Jennings, Carl	Private	(Unknown) MA-Trfd. to E Co. this Regt. 10-5-18.
Saxton, Raphael	Private	Cardy, Ia., OS-MA-St.M-joined 4-20-18.
Semrau, Fred T.	Private	(Unknown)
Tunem, Jack	Private	Halstead, Minn., OS-MA-Trfd. to Hq. Co., this regt. St.M-5-21-18.

127

MACHINE GUN COMPANY

Tyson, James — Private — Skidmore, Mo., OS-MA-W-MGF-in foot St.M-4th Mo.

White, Gilbert — Private — (Unknown) Trfd. to M Co. this regt.

Wilson, Russel — Private — Mound City, Mo., OS-MA-Trfd. to MP. Co. 35th Div. St.M-4th Mo.

Gehringer, Verne O. — Sergeant — Mound City, Mo., admitted to SOS Hosp. OS-MA-St.M-4th Mo.

Burscough, Guy — Cook — Wellington, Kans., OS-MA-admitted to SOS Hosp. St.M-3rd Kans.

Ziesmer, Charles — Cook — (Unknown) OS-MA-admitted to SOS Hosp.

Hainsworth, Avery — Private — Wellington, Kans., OS-MA-Trfd. to 1st Rep. Bn. St. Aignan. St.M-3rd Kans.

Patterson, Richard — Pvt. 1cl. — Wellington, Kans., OS-MA-Trfd. to 110th Supply Train Dec. 28, 1918 St.M-3rd Kans.

Webster, Ray B. — Pvt. 1cl. — Admitted to SOS Hosp. Dec. 21, 1918. OS-MA-St.M-3rd Kans.

Oldenburg, Walter R. — Private — Flint, Mich., admitted to SOS Hosp. Dec. 3, 1918.

Seeley, William A. — Private — Onotoma, Minn., OS-MA-St.M-Trfd. to Hq. Co. 139th 4-20-18.

Strauss, Orville F. — Private — Not known. Admitted to SOS Hosp 10-5-18.

Eads, David R. — Corporal — Wellington, Kans., OS-MA-St.M-Trfd. to 35th M. P. 1-6-3rd Kans.

Gaines, Wilber S. — Corporal — Wellington, Kans., Trfd. to G. Co. Jan. 6, 1919. OS-MA-St.M-3rd Kans.

Cowherd, William — Pvt. 1cl. — Wellington, Kans., OS-MA-Trfd. to Hq. Co. 1-17-19. St.M-3rd Kans.

Wilms, Emil — Pvt. 1cl. — Indianapolis, Ind., Died in BH No. 91 about Jan. 5, 1919, joined 10-15-18.

Hollingsworth, Ralph — Pvt. 1cl. — Wellington, Kans., OS-MA-Trfd. to Hq. Co., this regt. 1-25-19-St.M-3rd Kans.

Green, William — Pvt. 1cl. — (Unknown) Trfd. to MP 35th 1-13-19. (not known)

Scheffer, Joseph E. — Pvt. 1cl. — Rockwood, Mich. Dropped from rolls as admitted to SOS Hosp. 1-3-19. 10-5-18.

Beattie, Harold — Private — Wellington, Kans., OS-MA-Trfd. to Sup. Co., this Regt. 1-25-19. St.M-3rd Kans.

Hamel, Melvin A. — Private — Wellington, Kans., OS-MA-Trfd. to Sup. Co. this Regt. 1-25-19 St.M-3rd Kans.

Lawrence, Earl A. — Sergeant — Mound City, Mo., OS-MA-Trfd. to 372 MP. 2-9-4th Mo.

Bell, Cecil V. — Corporal — Wellington, Kans., OS-MA-Trfd. to 372 MP 2-3rd Kans.

Bentz, Albert — Corporal — St. Joseph, Mo., OS-MA-St.M-Trfd. to 372 MP-1-31-4th Mo.

Bohart, Ora — Pvt. 1cl. — Mound City, Mo., OS-MA-Trfd to 372 MP-4th Mo.

Hintz, Anthony F. — Pvt. 1cl. — Detroit, Mich., Trfd to Hq. Co. 140th Inf.-2-11-19-10-5-18.

Hopkins, Emmitt — Pvt. 1 cl. — Mound City, Mo., OS-MA-Trfd. to 372 MP-1-31-19 St.M-4th Mo.

Miller, Paul K. — Pvt. 1cl. — Mound City, Mo., OS-MA-Trfd to 273 MP. 1-31-19-St.M-4th Mo.

Woodard, Jesse M. — Private — Mound City, Mo., OS-MA- Trfd. to 273 MP-2-8.

Grenway, Raymond — Mess Sgt. — Wellington, Kans., Trfd. to 1st Rep. Bn.-OS-MA-St.M.-3rd Kans.

Robertson, Walter — Private — Mound City, Mo., Trfd. to 1st. Rep. Bn.-OS-MA-St.M-4th Mo.

HUMOR BY
AN INTELLIGENCE
DEPARTMENT
ARTIST

GOING UP?

THOSE MILITARY HAIR CUTS.

TRENCH MORTAR

ROSTER OF COMPANY M, 139th INFANTRY

Name and Rank	Home Address and Remarks	Name and Rank	Home Address and Remarks
Asbury Roberts, Captain	Unknown. OS-MA-W-HE.	Neiderhauser, Charles C. Sup. Sgt.	Marion, Kans., OS-MA.
Charles E. Holt Captain	St. Joe, Mo., OS.	Newcomb, Wayne C. Sergeant	Fossland, Ill., OS-MA-D.
James B. Garrett Captain	Unknown, OS.		
John E. Ray, Captain	Seattle, Wash., OS-MA.	Clemens, Orval E. Sergeant	Weston, Mo., OS-MA-W-S.
George C. Brewster 1st Lt.	Litchfield, Conn., OS.	Kilfoyle, Frank J. Sergeant	1015 Henry St., St. Joe, Mo., OS-MA.
Walter C. Dickey 1st Lt.	804 Harmon St., St. Joe, Mo., OS.	Zane, Waldo C. Sergeant	Revere, Mo., OS-MA.
James H. McCord, Jr., 1st Lt.	McCord Merc. Co., St. Joe, Mo., OS-MA-MGF.	Swenson, Paul T. Sergeant	1203 Corby St., St. Joe, Mo., OS-MA.
Ross Deal 1st Lt.	Chillicothe, Mo., OS-MA.	Grace, John S. Sergeant	St. Joe, Mo., OS-MA.
Edwin V. Burkholder 1st Lt.	Marion, Kans., OS-MA.	Loveless, Paul C. Sergeant	Marion, Kans., OS-MA.
Robert R. Rink, 1st Lt.	Unknown.	Houlton, Carroll V. Sergeant	Florence, Kans., OS-MA.
Milo C. Teeter 1st Lt.	Unknown.	Rickets, Charlie O. Sergeant	1602 Sav. Ave., St. Joe, Mo., OS-MA.
John P. Cosgrove 2nd Lt.	St. Louis, Mo., OS-MA-K.	Jacka, Alfred F. Sergeant	Arnold, Kans., OS-MA.
Reilly, Lester F. Sergeant	Amazonia, Mo., OS-MA.	Grimes, Bruce H. Sergeant	Marion, Kans., OS-MA.
Whalen, John R. Sergeant	311 S. 20th St., St. Joe, Mo. OS-MA.	Yardley, Marshall G. Sergeant	Boynton, Mo., OS-MA.
Lauder, James R. Sergeant	513 Blake St., St. Joe, Mo., OS.	Singley, Rilley E. Sergeant	Kirksville, Mo., OS-MA.
McKinnis, Warren R. Sergeant	1704 S. 10th St., St. Joe, Mo., OS-MA.	Weihl, George C. Corporal	611 N. 11th St., St. Joe, Mo., OS-MA.
Schuder, Rollie M. Sergeant	708 Shady Ave., St. Joe, Mo., OS.	Christian, George A. Corporal	Larned, Kans., OS-MA.
Raney, George W. Sergeant	RFD No. 5, St. Joe, Mo., OS.	McAllister, James D. Corporal	Seneca, Kans., OS-MA-W-G.
McCallan, Clarence Sergeant	2601 Duncan St., St. Joe, Mo., OS-MA.	Weinmeister, Henry, Jr. Corporal	Hillsboro, Kans., OS-MA.
Vadakin, Athol G. Sergeant	1423 W. Maine St., Enid, Okla. OS.	McClellan, John I. Corporal	Bazaar, Kans., OS-MA-W-G.
Caswell, Arthur B. Sergeant	Shoreborn, Vt., OS.	Friesen, William Corporal	Hillsboro, Kans., OS-MA.
Noll, Archie R. Sergeant	Marion, Kans., OS.	Mackie, Frank J. Corporal	Bushong, Kans., OS-MA.
Miller, Harold A. Sergeant	25 Krug Apts., Walnut Hill, Cincinnati, O., OS.	Carbry, Vincent N. Corporal	2015 Highly St., St. Joe, Mo., OS-MA-W-MGF.
Pritchard John S. Corporal	Grant, Ia., OS.	Guinn, Estel E. Corporal	RFD 4, Savanna, Mo., OS-MA.
Blackburn, Russel W. Corporal	Cottonwood Falls, Kans., OS-MA-W-HE-K.	Stuart, Foster F. Corporal	St. Joe, Mo., OS-MA.
Castle, Roy C. Corporal	Marion, Kans., OS-MA-G.	Wikus, Julius L. Corporal	Marion, Kans., OS-MA.
Shahan, Winfield F. Corporal	Marion, Kans., OS-MA-MGF.	Brott, James W. Corporal	2317 S. 4th St., St. Joe, Mo., OS MA.
Suess, Albert E. Corporal	Brookfield, Mo., OS-MA-K.	Mullendore, Lloyd C. Corporal	Dearborn, Mo., OS-MA-W-MGF.
Holmberg, Charles H. Corporal	Florence, Kans., OS-MA-MGF.	Noll, Charles Corporal	912 N. 13th St., St. Joe, Mo., OS-MA.
Seifert, Fred H. Corporal	St. Joe, Mo., OS-MA-K.	Bray, Francis E. Corporal	Bazaar, Kans., OS-MA.
Musser, Steve C. Corporal	Weatherby, Mo., OS-MA-HE.	Wight, Ollie O. Corporal	Lincolnville, Kans., OS-MA.
Elwin L. McCormick, 1st Lt.	Muskegon, Mich.	Fawley, Wilbur O. Corporal	Peabody, Kans., OS-MA.
Walter A. Ruch, 1st Lt.	Chaffee, Mo.	Babcock, Eltee Corporal	1511 Seymour St., St. Joe, Mo., OS MA.
William R. Carpenter, 1st Lt.	Marion, Kans., OS-MA.	Lovelace, Joseph Corporal	Hillsboro, Kans., OS-MA.
Howard N. Frizzell, 1st Lt.	D-S. with Div. Hdqrs.	Keltner, Neal H. Corporal	Peabody, Kans., OS-MA.
Thomas J. MacMahon, 2nd Lt.	Holyoke, Mass., MA-G.	Buffington, Harry W. Corporal	Cottonwood Falls, Kans., OS-MA.
Isaac F. Morrison 2nd Lt.	Chicago, Ill.	Doron, Arthur W. Corporal	Creal Spgs., Ill., OS-MA.
Kirkpatrick, John J. 1st Sgt.	1610 Sav. Ave., St. Joe, Mo., OS-MA.		
Otten, George W. Mess Sgt.	205 W. Ind. Av., St. Joe, Mo., OS-MA.		

130

TRENCH MORTAR

Honn, Calvin R. Corporal
Schmidt, Alvin Corporal
Torbert, Mark Corporal
Swiercinski, Leo H.
    Corporal
Spencer, George W.
    Corporal
Rosenauer, Christ Corporal
Bowen, Isaiah F. Corporal

Tipton, Chauncey E.
    Corporal
Gindra, George F. Corporal
Motley, Frank L. Corporal
Larson, Robert A. Corporal
Smith, Roy Cook

Sherry, Benjamin J. Cook

Searcy, Orvan O. Cook

Schmitz, John J. Cook

Landers, William E.
    Mechanic
Bowlby, Harry H. Mechanic
Reiswig, Dave Mechanic
May, Alexander J. Mechanic
Robison, Edward Bugler

Wagenknecht, Raymond
    Bugler
Applegate, Oscar C.
    Pvt. 1cl.
Bahr, Gustoff V. Pvt. 1cl.
Bath, Charles Pvt. 1cl.
Benick, Albert Pvt. 1cl.

Bibler, Meade O. Pvt. 1cl.
Booth, Ernest L. Pvt. 1cl.
Bray, Earl W. Pvt. 1cl.
Brunner, Henry Pvt. 1cl.
Buffington, Charles H.
    Pvt. 1cl.
Buffington, Walter O.
    Pvt. 1cl.
Cameron, Cecil B. Pvt. 1cl.
Carpenter, Henry C.
    Pvt. 1cl.
Clift, Cecil W. Pvt. 1cl.

Cooper, Milbourn M.
    Pvt. 1cl.
Dehner, Frank W. Pvt. 1cl.
Dodge, William J. Pvt. 1cl.
Edmonson, Will Pvt. 1cl.
Fisher, Frank Pvt. 1cl.
Grace, Grant F. Pvt. 1cl.

Marion, Kans., OS-MA.
Nashville, Kans., OS-MA.
St.M-OS-MA.
2406 Lafayette St., St. Joe, Mo.,
    OS-MA.
6205 Brown St., St. Joe, Mo., OS-
    MA.
718 Noyes Ave., St. Joe, Mo., OS-
    MA.
419 N. 18th St., St. Joe, Mo., OS-
    MA.
Aulne, Kans., OS-MA.

Two Rivers, Wis., OS-MA.
Sharps, Va., OS-MA.
Peabody, Kans., OS-MA-W-MGF.
2823 S. 23rd St., St. Joe, Mo., OS-
    MA.
1504 Highland Ave., St. Joe, Mo.,
    OS-MA.
1510 St. Joe Ave., St. Joe, Mo., OS-
    MA.
1907 Bartlett St., St. Joe, Mo., OS-
    MA.
RFD 7, St. Joe, Mo., OS-MA.

Marion, Kans., OS-MA-G.
Hillsboro, Kans., OS-MA.
Lehigh, Kans., OS-MA.
1012 N. Jackson St., Topeka, Kans.,
    OS-MA-G.
St. Joe, Mo., OS-MA.

Ramona, Kans., OS-MA.

Cottonwood Falls, Kans., OS-MA.
Hamilton, Ia., OS-MA.
1018 Felix St., St. Joe, Mo., OS-
    MA.
Florence, Kans., OS-MA.
Marion, Kans., OS-MA.
Bazaar, Kans., OS-MA.
Lost Springs, Kans., OS-MA.
Cottonwood Falls, Kans., OS-MA.

Cottonwood Falls, Kans. OS-MA.

1561 Beaubin, Detroit, Mich.
Summersville, Mo., OS-MA.

757 Prospect Ave., Springfield, Mo.,
    OS-MA-W-S.
Bazaar, Kans., OS-MA.

Madison Pike, Covington, Ky.
Marion, Kans., OS-MA.
Tabernash, Colo., OS-MA.
Lincolnville, Kans., OS-MA-W-S.
McIntire, Ia., OS-MA.

Groomes, James L. Pvt. 1cl.

Hall, Freddie Pvt. 1cl.
Hannaman, Abraham
    Pvt. 1cl.
Haynes, Bert. L. Pvt. 1cl.

Heschong, Ernest R.
    Pvt. 1cl.
Hurt, Harold H. Pvt. 1cl.
Hyman, Arthur J. Pvt. 1cl.
Johnson, Walter G.
    Pvt. 1cl.
Lane, Roy W. Pvt. 1cl.
Martin, Henry S. Pvt. 1cl.
Martinson, Oscar M.
    Pvt. 1cl.
McDowell, Alvin L.
    Pvt. 1cl.
McKinney, George A.
    Pvt. 1cl.
Meister, Carl P. Pvt. 1cl.
Miller, Joseph E. Pvt. 1cl.
Morgan, Harold L. Pvt. 1cl.

Raley, Frank O. Pvt. 1cl.
Revo, Clyde Pvt. 1cl.
Salisbury, Bryan Pvt. 1cl.

Scott, Albert B. Pvt. 1cl.

Severson, Edward Pvt. 1cl.
Severson, Hans Pvt. 1cl.

Shaffer, Charles O. Pvt. 1cl.
Shorts, Roy Pvt. 1cl.
Shoup, Norman Pvt. 1cl.

Sims, Robert D. Pvt. 1cl.
Smith, John E. Pvt. 1cl.
Swenson, Hjlmer A.
    Pvt. 1cl.
Taylor, Lonnie M. Pvt. 1cl.
Trear, Barney H. Pvt. 1cl.
Truit, James E. Pvt. 1cl.
Walker, Lilburn J. Pvt. 1cl.

Wilcox, Harry M. Pvt. 1cl.
Arseneau, Howard J.
    Private
Baker, John F. Private
Baker, Orval Private
Berger, Herman Private

Berlin, Bennie F. Private

Boehme, Bert Private
Burgogonone Telesforo
    Private
Brannan, Sam Private

631 Albemarley St., St. Joe, Mo.,
    OS-MA.
Cedarville, Ky.
Hillsboro, Kans., OS-MA.

1404 Bellevue St., St. Joe, Mo., OS-
    MA.
2022 N. Main St., St. Joe, Mo., OS-
    MA.
Romona, Kans., OS-MA.
Chicago, Ill.
Paw Paw, Mich.

Gentry, Ark., OS-MA.
Utica, Kans., OS-MA.
Everest, Kans., OS-MA.

401 Prindle St., St. Joe, Mo., OS-
    MA-W-HE.
1124 Church St., St. Joe, Mo., OS-
    MA.
Middleton, Wisc.
Faucett, Mo., OS-MA.
2704 Osage St., St. Joe, Mo., OS-
    MA.
Wellsville, Kans., OS-MA.
Marion, Kans., OS-MA.
511 Thompson Ave., St. Joe, Mo.,
    OS-MA.
4527 8th Ave. N. E., Seattle, Wash.,
    MA-OS.
Alexander, Minn., OS-MA.
411 E. Green St., Champaign, Ill.,
    OS-MA.
Wyoming, Ia., OS-MA.
1313 Kingley Court, Lansing, Mich.
2305 Cedar St., St. Joe, Mo., OS-
    MA.
Schenectady, N. Y., OS-MA.

Harris, Minn., OS-MA.

Agency, Mo., OS-MA-W-HE.
Madison, Kans., OS-MA.
Osowatomie, Kans., OS-MA.
2023 S. 20th St., St. Joe, Mo., OS-
    MA.
Cottonwood Falls, Kans., OS-MA.
3802 A Ave., Milwaukee, Wis.

Florence, Kans., OS-MA-MGF.
Ford City, Mo., OS-MA.
1504½ Buchanan Ave., St. Joe, Mo.
    OS-MA.
414 S. Walnut St., Cameron, Mo.,
    OS-MA.
Ozawkie, Kans., OS-MA.
Highland Park, Mich.

Coodys Bluff, Okla., OS-MA-G.

TRENCH MORTAR

Brown, Clarence O. Private 2718 Locust St., St. Joe, Mo., OS-MA-HE.
Burrough, Newton Private St. Joe, Mo., OS-MA-MGF.
Chambard, Everett T. Private 1501 Park Ave., Minneapolis, Minn., OS-MA.
Cook, Edward E. Private 39 W. Sycamore St., St. Paul, Minn. OS-MA.
Covillo, Joseph Private Newark, N. J.
Dawson, Benjamin H. Private Mayfield, Kans., OS-MA.
Downey, Elmer G. Private Danville, Kans., OS-MA-G.
Druse, Martin F. Private Marion, Kans., OS-MA.
Egler, John V. Private Suttons Bay, Mich.
Eikum, John Private 1716 7th Ave., Lewiston, Ida.
Erickson, John J. Private 1010 Ridenbaugh St., St. Joe, Mo. OS-MA.
Evans, Ernest R. Private Plymouth, Kans., OS-MA-G.
Ferry, Alphai P. Private St. Louis, Mo.
Fitch, Charles L. Private Florence, Kans., OS-MA.
Flock, Herman E. Private Marion, Kans., OS-MA-W-HE.
Fox, Bert Private Bethany, Mo., OS-MA.
Fultz, John D. Private Alba, Mo., OS-MA.
Gatewood, Raymond C. Private Joplin, Mo., OS-MA.
Gaunce, Charles J. Private 708 Shady Ave., St. Joe, Mo., OS-MA.
Geidt, Theodore H. Private Kulm, N. D., MA-OS.
Good, Weslev P. Private 1910 24th St., St. Joe, Mo., OS-MA.
Hall, Jasper N. Private Covington, Ky.
Hammer, Park S. Private Lincolnville, Kans., OS-MA.
Hansen, Fred H. Private 1522 Savannah Ave., St. Joe, Mo., OS-MA-W-S.
Hargrave, Glenn N. Private Chillicothe, Mo., OS-MA.
Hawkins, Floyd Private McLouth, Kans., OS-MA.
Hayes, Morris Private St. Louis, Mo., OS-MA.
Haynes, Harry F. Private Mackville, Kans., OS-MA.
Hemann, Anton J. Private Staceyville, Ia., OS-MA.
Henry, Ernest R. Private 602 S. 10th St., St. Joe, Mo., OS-MA.
Herndon, Charles D. Private Marion, Kans., OS-MA.
Hively, Albert F. Private Turner, Mich.
Hunt, Blaine A. Private Cottonwood Falls, Kans., OS-MA-W-MGF.
Kaminski, Izydore Private Grand Rapids, Mich.
Krause, Isaac Private Hillsboro, Kans., OS-MA.
Lawrence, Edward Private Cottonwood Falls, Kans., OS-MA.
Leonard, Dewey B. Private Burlington Jct., Mo., OS-MA.
Lindell, Oscar G. Private Rock Elm, Wis., OS-MA.
Loose, Fred J. Private 813 6th St., Milwaukee, Wis.
Luehrs, Edward M. Private Flint, Mich.
Marion, Guy D. Private Clinton, Mich.
Marshall, Chester B. Private Platte City, Mo., OS-MA.
Marshall, Oscar Private Dana, Ill., OS-MA.
Mason, Andrew A. Private Thor, Ia.
Matthews, Clarence L. Private Marion, Kans., OS-MA.
Mayall, Claude Private Newman, Kans., OS-MA.
McClelland, Lester L. Private 3017 Gardner Ave., St. Joe, Mo., OS-MA.

Milbourne, Orville Private Amazonia, Mo., OS-MA.
Miller, Walter J. Private Lincolnville, Kans., OS-MA.
Milota, Albert M. Private Cresco, Ia., OS-MA-W-S.
Neiherz, John Private 733 K K Ave., Milwaukee, Wis.
Newton, Forrest Private Natoma, Kans., OS.
Patterson, Harry O. Private Marion, Kans., OS-MA.
Piper, William O. Private Florence, Kans.,
Porter, Cecil R. Private Fairmont, Okla., OS-MA.
Porter, James C. Private 428 Madison St., Minneapolis, Minn. OS-MA-W-HE.
Porter, John H. Private 914 Oak Wood Blvd., Chicago, Ill.
Quirk, Arthur, M. J. Private 1314 Saginaw St., Flint, Mich.
Ray, George W. Private Budcah, Tex.
Reese, Hamilton G. Private Edinburg, N. D., OS-MA.
Reichart, Fred Private 3rd and Lake Ave., Racine, Wis.
Riley, Charles E. Private Amazonia, Mo., OS-MA.
Rollins, James C. Private Cottonwood Falls, Kans., OS-MA-W-MGF.
Ronde, Paul Private Sharon, N. D., OS-MA.
Rupp, Milo R. Private Ross, N. D., OS-MA-W-G.
Rush, Earl Private Marion, Kans., OS-MA.
Russel, Howard C. Private Spruce, Mo., OS-MA-W-MGF.
Rustad, Sever Private Rudd, Ia., OS-MA-W-HE.
Samen, Peter Private St. Francis, Wis.
Sanven, Randall B. Private Deer Field, Wis., OS-MA.
Schaedlich, Max Private 45 Orlando St., Springfield, Mass.
Scheuffele, Christ Private Hebron, N. D., OS-MA.
Schiller, Carl J. Private Sweet Brier, N. D. OS-MA.
Schleck, Arthur L. Private 319 Arbor St., St. Paul, Minn., OS-MA.
Schmierer, William A. Private Trachs, Alta. Canada, OS-MA.
Schuessler, Peter, Private Fryberg, N. D., OS-MA-G.
Schultz, Fred Private Williford, Ark., OS-MA.
Seeley, Charles B. Private Tonganoxie, Kans., OS-MA.
Seghreri, Dante Private 589 Mississippi St., St. Paul, Minn. OS-MA.
Sellars, August Private Florence, Kans., OS-MA.
Septon, Arthur B. Private Palmero, N. D., OS-MA.
Shaver, Elmer J. Private 406 S. Pine St., Lansing, Minn.
Shelley, Albert O. Private 1807 Pen St., Minneapolis, Minn., OS.
Shimic, Albert Private Lincolnville, Kans., OS-MA.
Schmidt, Richard M. Private Nashville, Kans., OS-MA-W-HE.
Schmitz, Thomas Private Eden Valley, Minn., OS-MA-K-HE.
Scoggin, John R. Private Gardner, Ill., OS-MA-MGF.
Shafer, Ernest W. Private Marstonnoor, N. D., OS-MA.
Simmons, Dana C. Private Fort Worth, Tex.
Simonson, Hartvig M. Private 1329 Adams St., Minneapolis, Minn. OS-MA.
Sinnot, James H. Private Osceola, Wis., OS-MA.
Sivertson, Lars Private Carpio, N. D., OS-MA.
Sharkey, William J. Private Fairmont, Minn., OS-MA-W-MGF-K.
Shields, Albert J. Private Antelope, Kans., OS-MA-W-S.
Sjoberg, Oscar C. Private 2553 Humbolt Ave., Minneapolis, Minn., OS-MA.
Sjolset, Andrew J. Private Ambrose, N. D., OS-MA.

TRENCH MORTAR

Skarpa, Gilbert	Private	Lakota, N. D., OS-MA.
Smith, Cecil L.	Private	Portland, N. D., OS-MA-G.
Smith, Kennith L.	Private	Ross, N. D., OS-MA.
Smith, Roy W.	Private	Dickinson, N. D., OS-MA.
Sorenson, Hans P.	Private	Williston, N. D., OS-MA-W-MGF.
Steeber, George A.	Private	2406 Lyndal Ave., Minneapolis, OS-MA-G.
Stich, Charles J.	Private	Dannybrook, N. D., OS-MA-G.
Stockwell, Grover R.	Private	2559 Delman St., Terre Haute, Ind., OS-MA.
Stone, Hans H.	Private	Rice Lake, Wis., OS-MA.
Strand, Henry	Private	Halstead, Minn., OS-MA-G.
Strand, Olif P.	Private	709 Oak St., Fargo, N. D., OS-MA.
Strauhs, Heron S.	Private	Elmdale, Kans., OS-MA.
Strehlow, Arthur H.	Private	Odessa, Minn., OS-MA.
Tancre, Alvin E.	Private	Towner, N. D., OS-MA.
Thomas, Claude	Private	3507 Lafayette St., St. Joe, Mo., OS-MA.
Thomas, Roy	Private	2216 S. 10th St., St. Joe, Mo., OS-MA-W-MGF.
Trammell, William A.	Private	205 Harvard St., St. Joe, Mo., OS-MA-G.
Tommlinson, Jack	Private	1421 S. 10th St., St. Joe, Mo., OS-MA.
Thorsen, Thomas	Private	Cooperston, N. D., OS-MA.
Thurber, Charles W.	Private	Glendale, W. Va., OS-MA-W-HE.
Tressin, Morgan	Private	Milford, Kans., OS-MA.
Troseth, Selmer B.	Private	Newbrighten, Minn., OS-MA.
Turner, Peder J.	Private	Spring Grove, Minn., OS-MA.
Urbanek, Phillip M.	Private	Lincolnville, Kans., OS-MA.
Valentine, Howard R.	Private	5641 S. 2nd St., St. Joe, Mo., OS.
Vogan, Orval C.	Private	Utica, Kans., OS-MA.
Vanduzer, John S.	Private	Chatham, Mich.
Wheeler, Lewis H.	Private	Bazaar, Kans., OS-MA.
Wilhite, Desmond R.	Private	Cottonwood Falls, Kans., OS-MA-W-S.
Wilson, Dessie T.	Private	Perth, Kans., OS-MA.
Wolfingberger, Willard		Marion, Kans., OS-MA-W-MGF.
Zeaske, Carl G.	Private	2103 Crosat St., LaSalle, Ill., OS-MA.
Zeih, Jacob, Jr.	Private	Aulne, Kans., OS-MA.
Zeih, Henry	Private	Aulne, Kans., OS-MA-W-MGF.

Reiner, Earl S.	Private	Ramona, Kans., OS-MA.
Bullock, Clyde	Pvt. 1cl.	Wilsey, Kans., OS-MA-W-S.
Roth, Jona	Pvt. 1cl.	Hillsboro, Kans., OS-MA.
Kline, Henry	Pvt. 1cl.	Marion, Kans., OS.
Lovelace, Herbert	Pvt. 1cl.	Hillsboro, Kans., OS-MA-W-HE.
Martin, Tolbert S.	Pvt. 1cl.	Utica, Kans., OS-MA-G.
Riddle, John	Pvt. 1cl.	Marion, Kans., OS-MA-W-HE.
Wineland, Clare	Pvt. 1cl.	725 S. 14th St., St. Joe, Mo., OS-MA-W-HE.
Bengston, Axel S.	Private	342 Goodrich Ave., St. Paul, Minn., OS-MA.
Brown, William J.	Private	Cottonwood Falls, Kans., OS-MA-W-MGF.
Buechler, Mark A.	Private	Kulm, N. D., OS-MA-G.
Crist, Morris,	Private	Glasgow, Mont., OS-MA-W-HE.
Goodman, Nolan G.	Private	Utica, Kans., OS-MA.
Hamill, Alexander H.	Private	Earlsville, Ill., OS-MA.
Hanrahan, John J.	Private	Prole, Ia., OS-MA.
Hickman, Clarence	Private	2919 Webster Ave., Pittsburg, Pa., OS.
Hyde, Ray J.	Private	Alexander, N. D., OS.
Keener, Arthur F.	Private	1202 N. 12th St., St. Joe, Mo., OS.
Keazer, Kennith	Private	Marion, Kans., OS-MA-W-MGF.
Keeling, James A.	Private	Oskaloosa, Kans., OS-MA.
Lowe, Jesse L.	Private	Gilman, Mo., OS.
Michel, Frank J.	Private	916 S. Lucas St., Iowa City, Ia., OS-MA-W-S.
Miesse, James W.	Private	Marion, Kans., OS-MA-K.
Moore, Roger L.	Private	Amazonia, Mo., OS-MA-MGF.
Plummer, Charles	Private	Graham, Mo., OS-MA.
Ray, Harold A.	Private	312 6th Ave., Des Moines, Ia.
Shauver, Howard T.	Private	614 S. 18th St., St. Joe, Mo., OS-MA-G.
Sowden, Earl G.	Private	1515 Oakdale St., Burlington, Ia., OS.
Johnson, Nels E.	Private	Fargo, N. D., OS-MA.
Romberger, Roy V.	Private	Abilene, Kans., OS.
Hall, Jasper N.	Private	Cincinnati, O.
Andrews, John M.	Private	200 12th St., Jersey City, N. J.
Aniswitz, Jacob	Private	37 Clinton St., New York City, N. Y.
Gertzfeld, Sam	Private	1327 40th St., Brooklyn, N. Y.
Templin, George A.	Private	Alga, Mich.

SANITARY DETACHMENT

ROSTER SANITARY DETACHMENT WITH REGIMENTAL HEADQUARTERS

NAME AND RANK		EMERGENCY ADDRESS
Henry D. Smith	Major	Mrs. Marjorie W. Smith, wife, Washington, Kans.
Richard P. Lewis	1st Lt.	Miss Helene Lewis, daughter, 4220 Highland Ave., Kansas City, Mo.
Wayne Allphin,	Sgt. 1cl.	Mrs. Edith S. Allphin, wife, 818 Kentucky St., Lawrence, Kans.
Dudley, Russel M. Pvt. 1cl.		Mr. Peter Winston Dudley, father, Louisiana, Mo.

NAME AND RANK		EMERGENCY ADDRESS
Duer, Alva O.	Pvt. 1cl.	Mr. Elmer O. Duer, father, Washington, Kans.
Schropp, Martin A. Pvt. 1cl.		Mr. William Schropp, father, Washington, Kans.
Allen, William H.	Private	Mr. Daniel S. Allen, father, Washington, Kans.,
Swan, Bradford L.	Private	Mrs. Claire A. Swan, wife, Washington, Kans.
Lokes, Wm. H.	Private	Mrs. Ellen J. Lokes, 1116 S. 52nd St., Philadelphia, Penn.

SANITARY DETACHMENT

ROSTER MACHINE GUN COMPANY, 139th INFANTRY

NAME AND RANK	EMERGENCY ADDRESS
Albert E. Cooper, Captain	Agnes Cooper, wife, Fowlerville, Mich.
Walter A. Wood, 1st Lt.	Mrs. Nannie B. Wood, mother, 620 E. Broadway, Sedalia, Mo.
Lewis O. Northrup 2nd Lt.	Del P. Northrup, father, 502 East St., Iola, Kans.
Boyd Inman, 2nd Lt.	Mr. Otis O. Inman, father, 1635 North College St., Decatur, Ill.
Harry H. Fleming, 2nd Lt.	Daniel H. Fleming, father, Willow Springs, Mo.
Meriwether, Philip S. 1st Sgt.	Fontaine Meriwether, father, Broadway and Barrett, Sedalia, Mo.
Coman, James G. Mess Sgt.	Elizabeth Coman, mother, 912 East St., Iola, Kans.
Schneider, Charley H. Stable Sgt.	Samuel Schneider, father, R.F.D. No. 7, Sedalia, Mo.
Nelson, William A. Sergeant	Mayme Herring Nelson, wife, 210 East Second St., Sedalia, Mo.
McCabe, Russell E. Sergeant	Mrs. Elizabeth McCabe, mother, 320 N. Quincy St., Sedalia, Mo.
Barnett, Lawrence Sergeant	George W. Barnett, father, Sedalia, Mo.
Jared, Marvin W. Sergeant	Minnie Lucile Jared, wife, 211 Clark Ave., Warrensburg, Mo.
Dickerson, James G. Sergeant	William S. Dickerson, father, Carlyle, Kans.
Holland, Carl E. Sergeant	Mrs. Alice Holland, mother, 623 E. Tenth St., Sedalia, Mo.
Telford, Allen F. Sergeant	Edward A. Telford, father, 20th and Warren Sts., Sedalia, Mo.
Elkins, Walter E. Sergeant	Benjamin V. Elkins, father, 923 E. Third St., Sedalia, Mo.
Hair, James L. Sergeant	James M. Hair, father, Lock Box No. 41, Mildred, Kans.
Urban, Carl F. Sergeant	Sebastian Urban, father, 900 West Second St., Sedalia, Mo.
Pierce, Frank O. Corporal	William J. Pierce, father, Bronson, Kans.
Dewey, William M. Corporal	Minnie L. Finley, mother, Leroy, Kans.
Codding, Almeron B. Corporal	Mrs. May Bell Codding, mother, 321 West Tenth St., Sedalia, Mo.
Cunningham, William D. Corporal	Gertrude Cunningham, mother, 1507 East Seventh St., Sedalia, Mo.
O'Flaherty, John F. Corporal	Mrs. Julia O'Flaherty, mother, 3105 East Twenty-seventh St., Kansas City, Mo.
Kirkpatrick, Jesse H. Corporal	Mrs. Anna E. Kirkpatrick, mother, 624 North Chestnut, Iola, Kans.
Croy, Harold B. Corporal	John A. Croy, father, 1611 S. Lamine St., Sedalia, Mo.

NAME AND RANK	EMERGENCY ADDRESS
Greene, Albert L. Corporal	Jennie Greene, mother, 1806 South Harrison, Sedalia, Mo.
Walker, George S. Corporal	Willis C. Walker, father, Moran, Kans.
Creegan, Marvin J. Corporal	Mark L. Creegan, father, 4640 Cote Brilliante Ave., St. Louis, Mo.
Franklin, Forrest C. Corporal	Joseph Franklin, father, R.F.D. No. 11, Knobnoster, Mo.
Long, Chester S. Corporal	Joseph Long, father, 1202 East Thirteenth St., Sedalia, Mo.
Nicholson, Jay Corporal	Mrs. Ella Nicholson, mother, 212 Thirteenth St., Sedalia, Mo.
Smith, Luther M. Horseshoer	A. J. Crews, friend, 1600 S. Park Ave., Sedalia, Mo.
Cone, Albert B. Mechanic	John L. Cone, father, 1523 S. Harrison St., Sedalia, Mo.
Ballard, Roy G. Saddler	Mrs. Guy Roberts, sister, Gas City, Kans.
Smith, James E. Cook	Preston B. Smith, father, Moran, Kans.
Kennedy, Carl S. Cook	Mrs. Ova Kennedy, wife, 410 West Madison, Iola, Kans.
Hoffman, George S. Cook	George T. Hoffman, father, Harrisburg, Penn.
Newton, Herbert F. Bugler	Thomas E. Newton, father, 13 S. Jefferson, Iola, Kans.
Starr, Joseph A. Bugler	Mrs. Ella A. Starr, mother, 500 E. Twelfth St., Sedalia, Mo.
Ard, David Private	Mrs. Theba Ard, mother, Elsmore, Kans.
Anderson, Earl O. Private	Carry Anderson, mother, 238 East Eighth St., Cherryvale, Kans.
Baker, Barney Private	Ida Baker, mother, 2118 Mullanphy St., St. Louis, Mo.
Baker, Walter J. Private	John W. Baker, father, La Harpe, Kans.
Baum, Leonard H. Private	Mrs. Clara Baum, mother, R.R. No. 4, Sedalia, Mo.
Beaudine, Chester C. Private	Mrs. Josephine Beaudine, mother, R.R. No. 1, Kent, Minn.
Bennett, Ray E. Private	Eugene H. Bennett, father, 18th and Limit Sts., Sedalia, Mo.
Bjornson, Menom Private	Martha Bjornson, Humboldt, Ia.
Bothyl, Anthony Private	Dan Hurd, friend, Ida Grove, Ia.
Bourdelais, James L. Private	Mrs. Fedelia Bourdelais, mother, 4021 Van Buren St., Sioux City, Ia.
Bowman, Hezekiah K. Private	John Bowman, father, Wickliffe, Ky.
Braffettl, Melvin Private	Dave Baker, grandfather, Princeton, Mo.

SANITARY DETACHMENT

Briggs, Carl S.   Private   Philip D. Briggs, uncle, Sedan, Kans.

Brouillard, Albert L. Private   Mrs. Emma B. Brouillard, mother, Moran, Kans.

Brouillard, Charles E. Private   Mrs. Emma B. Brouillard, mother, Moran, Kans.

Broyles, Jesse R.   Private   William G. Broyles, father, Chetopa, Kans.

Bushie, Alexander W. Private   Mrs. Clara Bushie, wife, Hallock, Minn.

Clark, Homer J.   Private   Frank L. Clark, father, Trenton, Mo.

Crisswell, John T. Private   John Crisswell, father, 1112 E. Sixth St., Winfield, Kans.

Crochet, Wilton A. Private   Victoria Crochet, father, Loreauville La.

Cummins, Charles C. Private   Luther G. Cummins, father, 624 N. Elm St., Iola, Kans.

Dean, Virgil   Private   William R. Dean, father, 2405 Chestnut St., Trenton, Mo.

Dow, William H.   Private   John Riley Dow, father, Easton, Ill.

Doyle, Vander   Private   Daniel B. Doyle, father, Eldridge, Mo.

Duncan, Roy P.   Private   Richard P. Duncan, father, Stansbury, Mo.

Dyck, John E.   Private   Peter B. Nichols, uncle, Aulne, Kans.

Englund, Lawrence N. Private   Mrs. Leona Englund, mother, 620 E. Eleventh St., Sedalia, Mo.

Eschbach, Charles Private   John W. Eschbach, brother, Meppen, Ill.

Fisher, Charles   Private   Mrs. Isabell Fisher, mother, Bronson, Kans.

Ford, Roy V.   Private   James S. Ford, father, 612 N. Quincy St., Sedalia, Mo.

Foster, Hopestill Private   Ben R. Foster, Globe Democrat Bldg., St. Louis, Mo.

Fox, Bert   Private   Mrs. Edna Williams, sister, General Delivery, Bethany, Mo.

Freeman, Pearl F. Private   Thomas Freeman, father, 59 O. St., Hoquian, Wash.

Gillett, Donnie W. Private   Mrs. Joehanna Gillett, mother, Princeton, Mo.

Glabes, Ruben   Private   Mary Glabes, mother, Weskan, Kans.

Glover, Charles C. Private   Mr. Charles T. Glover, father, R.F.D. No. 4, Sedalia, Mo.

Gooding, George   Private   John Gooding, father, Lisbon, N. Dak.

Grandstaff, Lowell Private   Lotty Shaley, mother, Winclota, Mo.

Grinde, Selmer C. Private   Mr. Peter R. Grinde, brother, 3848 Twenty-seventh Ave. So., Minneapolis, Minn.

Gromer, Ernest S. Private   Alva Gromer, father, Glenn Allen, Mo.

Haller, Yngolfur   Private   Dewey H. Haller, brother, Bassett, Nebr.

Hayes, Everett F. Private   Frances A. Hayes, father, Virgil, Kans.

Heaton, Claude L.   Private   Elmer E. Heaton, father, Bronson, Kans.

Henderson, Bert E. Private   George M. Henderson, father, 304 West Pettis St., Sedalia. Mo.

Henderson, Robert C. Private   George M. Henderson, father, 1202 South Montgomery Ave., Sedalia. Mo.

Hilton, Theodore E. Private   Mrs. Martha Hilton, mother, Nave, Mo.

Holden, Raymond T. Private   Anna L. Holden, mother, R.R. No. 6, Independence, Kans.

Hoover, Charlie E. Private   Mrs. Emma Hoover, mother, Osborn, Mo.

Howard, Lewis   Private   Albert J. Howard, father, Sedan. Kans.

Huber, Frank R.   Private   Mr. Florian Huber, father, R.R. No 2, Hopkins, Minn.

Jeffries, William M. Private   Mrs. Johana Jeffries, mother, R.R. No. 1, Zulch, Tex.

Johnson, George C. Private   Nels P. Johnson, father, R.R. No. 1. Russell, Minn.

Johnston, Harold   Private   Mr. William H. Johnston, father, Kipp, Kans.

Jordan, Olin L.   Private   Ruth L. Brown, aunt, 306 N. Cottonwood, Iola, Kans.

Kenney, Le Roy L. Private   Dr. W. F. Kenney, father, 2407 Doniphan Ave., St. Joseph, Mo.

Kinyon, Clayton G. Private   William H. Kinyon, father, Adaza. Ia.

Knudsen, Knud M. Private   Mrs. Petrine Knudsen, mother, Agersbolgaard pr. Brorup, Denmark.

Kranzler, Henry   Private   Jacob Kranzler, father, Aberdeen, N. Dak.

Krog, Oscar F.   Private   Mary C. Krog, mother, R.R. No. 7, Girard, Kans.

Kunz, Hirum A.   Private   Mrs. Marie Kunz, wife, 1700 S. Sixteenth St., Burlington, Ia.

Lambirth, Harry N. Private   George T. Lambirth, father, 616 Wilkerson St., Sedalia, Mo.

Latimer, Bernie F. Private   Mr. Robert Latimer, father, R.R. No. 2, Iola, Kans.

Lee, Elmer   Private   Emily Lee, mother, 624 East Madison, Iola, Kans.

Lessley, John T.   Private   Nora Curts, mother, 1048 South Twenty-fifth St., Argentine, Kans.

Lien, Ole   Private   Knut O. Lien, father, Langdon, N. Dak.

Lindsly, Charles H. Private   Frank H. Lindsly, father, 104½ N. Washington, Iola, Kans.

MacCurdy, Clyde E. Private   Martha L. MacCurdy, mother, R.R. No. 13, Knobnoster, Mo.

Malcom, Canby H. Private   Mrs. Nancy Jane Malcom, mother, 607 South St., Iola, Kans.

Mall, Truman A.   Private   Mattie I. Mall, mother, Clay Center, Kans.

Mason, Andrew A. Private   Andrew Mason, father, Thor, Ia.

McCaffrey, John F. Private   Patrick H. McCaffrey, father, Verdi, Minn.

136

SANITARY DETACHMENT

McKinney, Henry — Private — Mrs. Bettie Jackson, sister, Milan, Mo.

Meyer, August W. — Private — John A. Meyer, father, Farnhamville, Ia.

Middleton, Carl S. — Private — John Middleton, father, Bluemound, Kans.

Miles, Marvin C. — Private — Mrs. Mattie Miles, mother, 1321 S. Moniteau St., Sedalia, Mo.

Miller, Claude — Private — (Service record at 70th Brig. Hdq. Detachment.)

Milne, Dell P. — Private — Mrs. Agnes Milne, mother, 822 N. Jefferson St., Iola, Kans.

Mitchell, Frederick S. — Private — Lydia K. Mitchell, mother, 417 E. Seventh St., Sedalia, Mo.

Mogan, Conrad — Private — Olaf Mogan, father, R.R. No. 3, Lake Mills, Ia.

Moll, Matt — Private — Jacob Moll, father, Modoc, Ill.

Moravek, Frank B. — Private — George Moravek, father, Otego, Kans.

Morris, Clarence E. — Private — Edward Morris, father, Pattonsburg, Mo.

Morrison, Lenard T. — Private — George C. Morrison, father, Moran, Kans.

Moss, Eugene R. — Private — Mrs. Margaret Moss, mother, 920 McPherson, Trenton, Mo.

Muedeking, Frederick L. — Private — Miss Louise Muedeking, sister, R.R. No. 1, Tracy, Minn.

Munn, Carroll B. — Private — Jesse Scott, half-brother, Pollock, Mo.

Nelson, William K. — Private — Andrew J. Nelson, father, R.F.D. No. 3, Anita, Ia.

Nickels, Lloyd O. — Private — John C. Nickels, father, Colony, Kans.

Nielsen, Carl E. — Private — Christense Nielsen, wife, Tripoli, Ia.

Noble, Donald J. — Private — James Noble, father, Bronson, Kans.

Norris, Willard M. — Private — Clara J. Norris, mother, 217 E. Fifth St., Sedalia, Kans.

Norton, Everette C. — Private — Joseph C. Norton, father, Moran, Kans.

Olein, Clarence A. — Private — Andrew P. Olein, father, R.R. No. 2, Turtle Lake, N. Dak.

Parvey, Jalmar — Private — Jack Parvey, brother, Gockle, N. Dak.

Pauley, Edgar A. — Private — Ollie S. Wickham, uncle, Osage, Io.

Price, Howard L. — Private — George Price, father, Ellston, Ia.

Quinnt, Carroll — Private — Mrs. Estella Quinnt, mother, 659 W. Saratoga St., Baltimore, Md.

Reimler, Charles W. — Private — William H. Reimler, father, Lupus, Mo.

Richardson, Arthur B. — Private — Mary E. Richardson, mother, 712 Lincoln St., Liberal, Kans.

Ritter, Archie D. — Private — Mrs. Delania Ritter, mother, Bronson, Kans.

Robinson, Kenneth M. — Private — Mrs. Ida M. Robinson, 201 S. First St., Iola, Kans.

Russell, Benjamin C. — Private — Rev. James M. Russell, father, 1817 S. Stewart, Sedalia, Mo.

Seals, Lionel A. — Private — Mr. Barney Seals, father, R.R. No. 2, Iola, Kans.

Selveit, Halvor A. — Private — Mrs. Halvor A. Selveit, wife, Turtle Lake, N. Dak.

Shallop, Fred — Private — Mrs. Mary Bellish, aunt, Scobey, Mont.

Sibert, Ernest L. — Private — M. Harvey Sibert, father, 1220 S. Barrett, Sedalia, Mo.

Sibert, Harvey L. — Private — M. Harvey Sibert, father, 1220 S. Barrett, Sedalia, Mo.

Sicks, Elza C. — Private — Mrs. Mary Sicks, mother, Iola, Kans.

Shipley, Will — Private — Robert Thomas, uncle, Batesville, Ark.

Spafford, Hugh A. — Private — Christina Spafford, mother, Chester, Nebr.

Stallsmith, Emery D. — Private — Amelia Stallsmith, wife, Morganville, Kans.

Strain, Edgar D. — Private — John W. Strain, father, 19th and Engineer Sts., Sedalia, Mo.

Talbot, Nathan A. — Private — William A. Talbot, father, 104 Maron St., Marshalltown, Ia.

Tippie, Leroy — Private — William A. Tippie, father, Carlyle, Kans.

Tordsen, George C. — Private — William Tordsen, father, R. F. D. No. 2, Belleview, Minn.

Tripp, John D. C. — Private — Grace Tripp, wife, Clay Center, Kans.

Ulmer, John R. — Private — George Ulmer, father, Fullerton, N. Dak.

Wagner, Antone F. — Private — W. Harry Wagner, brother, 501 W. Second St., Sedalia, Mo.

Waugh, William F. — Private — John Waugh, father, Elsmore, Kans.

Wennes, Edgar R. — Private — Louis O. Wennes, father, R.R. No. 4, Spring Grove, Minn.

Wheeler, Frederick H. — Private — Edward J. Wheeler, father, 107 S. Prospect St., Sedalia, Mo.

Winge, Oscar H. — Private — Cris A. Winge, father, Ryder, N. Dak.

Witte, William M. — Private — Frank A. Witte, father, 1900 S. Harrison St., Sedalia, Mo.

Wilson, Earl K. — Private — Frank Wilson, father, Windsor, Mo.

Wood, Clarence R. — Private — Mrs. Nannie B. Wood, mother, 620 E. Broadway, Sedalia, Mo.

Wright, Benjamin C. — Private — Mrs. Elizabeth Wright, mother, 800 N. Prospect St., Sedalia, Mo.

Young, Floyd, — Private — Mrs. Katherine Young, mother, 211 E. Fifth St., Junction City, Kans.

Young, John F. — Private — Benjamin F. Young, father, Randall, Kans.

Finkelson, Nels E. — Private — Gilbert N. Finkelson, father, RFD 1, North Branch, Minn.

Gann, Harvey C. — Private — John Gann, father, Trenton, Mo.

Hoke, Oscar F. — Private — Frank Hoke, father, 306 N. Buckeye St., Iola, Kans.

Johnson, Axel F. — Private — John Ericksonm, friend, Stratcona, Minn.

Ledin, Archie — Private — Ida Ledin, mother, R. F. D. No. 1, North Branch, Minn.

BAND

Lien, Hans	Private	Ragna Hansen, sister, Granite Falls, Minn.
Lien, Jacob	Private	Knute Lien, father, Langdon, N. Dak.
Myers, John R.	Private	Pearl Myers, sister, Oswego, N. Y.
Paulson, David W.	Private	Andrew C. Paulson, R.F.D. No. 4, Dassell, Minn.
Redding, Dennie W.	Private	Walter Redding, brother, Clay Center, Kans.
Shackles, Pete	Private	Charles C. Shackles, father, 609 S. Lafayette St., Sedalia, Mo.
Thomas, Lea Roy	Private	Minnie Thomas, mother, Centerview, Mo., R.F.D. No. 3.

Warren, John W.	Private	John C. Warren, father, 400 East Fourteenth St., Sedalia, Mo.
Raisch, John M.	Private	Daniel A. Raisch, father, 414 North St., Iola, Kans.

CASUALS ATTACHED

Jaakola, Uno	Private	Isaac Jaakola, father, Pomarkku, Finland.
Olson, Oscar	Private	A. Ferdinand Olson, father, R.F.D. No. 1, North Branch, Minn.
Rohlik, Anthony T.	Private	John F. Rohlik, father, Seaforth, Minn.

BAND

ROSTER OF HEADQUARTERS COMPANY, 139th INFANTRY

NAME AND RANK	EMERGENCY ADDRESS
James B. Garrett, Captain	Mrs. James B. Garrett, wife, 915 East 18th St., Cheyenne, Wyo.
Guss R. Ridge, 1st Lt.	Mrs. Guss B. Ridge, wife, Ilasco, Mo.
George J. Woodward, 1st Lt.	Mrs. George J. Woodward, wife, 1226 N. Market St., Wichita, Kans.
John D. Heiny 1st Lt.	B. F. Heiny, father, 703 N. Franklin St., Kirksville, Mo.
James R. Paynter 1st Lt.	Mrs. James R. Paynter, wife, R.F.D. 2, Hannibal, Mo.
F. A. Appenfelder 1st Lt.	W. H. Appenfelder, brother, 2142 Ravine St., Cincinnati, Ohio.
John S. Benningfield 2nd Lt.	Mrs. John S. Benningfield, wife, 1904 N. 3rd St., St. Joseph, Mo.
Albert D. Pitts, 2nd Lt.	Mrs. A. D. Pitts, wife, General Delivery, Lawton, Okla.
Alfred M. Miller, 2nd Lt.	A. H. Miller, father, Murray, Ia.
William E. Galligan, 1st Lt.	Mrs. P. J. Galligan, mother, Carterville, Mo.
Schmitz, Joseph O. Regtl. Sgt. Maj.	C. J. Schmitz, father, 615 S. 14th St., St. Joseph, Mo.
Morse, Theodore, Band Leader	Charles T. Morse, father, 1127 Quincy St., Topeka, Kans.
Gould, Jesse R. 1st Sgt.	Mrs. Jesse R. Gould, wife, R.R. No. 2, New London, Mo.
Pedigo, William R. Asst. Band Leader	Mrs. J. W. Pedigo, mother, 613 Monroe St., Topeka, Kans
Porter, George E. Sgt. Bugler	Harry M Porter, brother, Milan, Mo.
Ingold, Walter T. Color Sgt.	Mr. E. Ingold, father, 621 E. 7th St., Newton, Kans.
Good, Wesley F. Color Sgt.	Dr. Wesley Good, father, 409½ Monroe St., Topeka, Kans.
Fleming, James R. Sup. Sgt.	Mrs. Dorothy R. Fleming, wife, 429 College Ave., Topeka, Kans.
Gratton, William M. Mess Sgt.	Samuel Gratton, father, Wakefield, Kans.
McMahan, James R. Stable Sgt.	Mrs. J. M. McMahan, mother, Maryville, Mo.
Crouch, Alfred D. Band Sgt.	E. E. Crouch, father, 330 Green St., Topeka, Kans.
Abell, Robert E. Band Sgt.	Mrs. R. E. Abell, wife, 1206 E. 10th St., Topeka, Kans.
Lavelle, John J. Sergeant	Mrs. J. M. LaVelle, mother, 419 E. Edward St., Maryville, Mo.
McCord, Charles F. Sergeant	Howard McCutcheon, step-father, 121 W. 8th St., Kansas City, Mo.
King, Herman B. Sergeant	Mrs. C. C. King, mother, Coin, Ia.
Iliff, Theodore L. Sergeant	Dr. D. A. Iliff, father, Cherokee, Kans.
Wolfe, Eugene Sergeant	Mrs. L. D. Wolfe, mother, 921 Clay St., Topeka, Kans.

NAME AND RANK	EMERGENCY ADDRESS
Lange, Carl H. Sergeant	L. C. Lange, father, 3732 Prospect St., Kansas City, Mo.
Fiscus, Ray Sergeant	Mrs. F. S. Macklin, mother, 1016 E. Harrison St., Kirksville, Mo.
Meyres, Ferdinand W., Jr. Sergeant	F. W. Meyer, father, 607 N. 27th St., St. Joseph, Mo.
Johnson, Carl J. Sergeant	Louise Ericson, mother, Marielund, Sweden.
Gilbert, Clark O. Sergeant	H. L. Gilbert, father, Chillicothe, Mo.
Craig, Harry F. Sergeant	Luther C. Craig, father, Espiro, Okla.
Wilson, Willard E. Sergeant	Mrs. W. E. Wilson, wife, Chanute, Kans.
Morris, Harold G. Sergeant	Mrs. Edith Morris, mother, Hope, Kans.
Spargur, Frank C. Sergeant	W. M. Spargur, father, Burlington Jct., Mo.
Vermehren, William H. Sergeant	Mrs. Emma Cornelius, aunt, 1208 Maple St., Coffeyville, Kans.
Cole, Charles H. Sergeant	Mrs. C. A. Cole, mother, 511 Shady Ave., St. Joseph, Mo.
Hull, Ralph W. Sergeant	A. I. Hull, father, Valley Falls, Kans.
Hargis, DeWitt M. Sergeant	Mrs. Lena M. Hargis, mother, Lansing, Kans.
Van Brunt, Frederic C. Sergeant	J. H. VanBrunt, father, 639 N. 8th St., St. Joseph, Mo.
Bernauer, Raymond O. Sergeant	Mrs. James R. Bernauer, mother, Wellsborough, Penn.
Smith, Charles J. Band Corporal	Mrs. Clara Smith, mother, 511 Fillmore St., Topeka, Kans.
Haage, William R. Band Corporal	Mrs. William R. Haage, wife, 1631 Central Park Ave., Topeka, Kans.
Fleming, David W. Band Corporal	Mrs. Mary L. Fleming, mother, 323 Hancock St., Topeka, Kans.
Stafford, Robbins, Corporal	Mabelle H. Stafford, wife, 1121 N. 2nd St., St. Joseph, Mo.
Timmons, Harley M. Corporal	Mrs. E. DeWalt, mother, 306 W. 4th St., Newton, Kans.
Landis, Adolph H. Corporal	Mr. John Landis, father, Lucien, Okla.
Karnes, Frank L. Corporal	Mrs. Cora Karnes, mother, Overbrook, Kans.
Pickering, Ben C. Corporal	J. C. Pickering, father, 504 W. 5th St., Coffeyville, Kans.
Black, Rex R. Corporal	Mrs. Ida Black, mother, Newton, Kans.
Knee, James C. Corporal	Mrs. Jesse Knee, mother, Newton, Kans.
Pickerel, Archie B. Corporal	Mrs. J. H. Pickerel, mother, 5535 S. 2nd St., St. Joseph, Mo.
Loring, Elmer A. Corporal	Mrs. William Loring, mother, Scandia, Kans.

BAND

Morgan, Earl A. Corporal — Mrs. J. W. Morgan, mother, Newton, Kans.

Humphreys, John E. Corporal — E. J. Humphreys, father, Rock Island, Tex.

Reed, Nolan P. Corporal — Mrs. John Reed, mother, Otterville, Mo.

Chilcote, Ferrin H. Corporal — R. J. Chilcote, brother, Independence, Kans.

Gardner, John A. Corporal — F. B. Gardner, father, 1121 W. 7th St., Wellington, Kans.

Spiegel, Oscar Corporal — Mrs. George Moonan, cousin, 204 W. 1st St., Newport, Ky.

Updyke, Ted Corporal — Mrs. J. S. Updyke, mother, Ridgeway, Mo.

Yeaden, J. H. Corporal — Edward Yeaden, father, Abilene, Kans.

Louthan, Herman D. Corporal — Mrs. Helen R. Louthan, wife, Maynard, Minn.

Sutton, Herbert D. Corporal — Mrs. J. H. Sutton, mother, Bethany, Mo.

Phelps, William A. Corporal — Mrs. W. H. Phelps, mother, Wellington, Kans.

Hammond, Harry Corporal — Andrew Hammond, father, Johnson, Kans.

High, William A. Corporal — A. J. High, father, Milan, Mo.

Lynch, Claude L. Horseshoer — Mrs. Desse Lynch, wife, Webb City, Mo.

Brown, William M. Mechanic — Mrs. Mary H. Whaley, sister, 2428 S. 11th St., St. Joseph, Mo.

Lacy, John W. Mechanic — B. L. Lacy, father, Clay Center, Kans.

Hughes, Erwin, E. Mechanic — George F. Hughes, father, Mound City, Mo.

Tarpley, Carl H. Cook — Mrs. B. F. Tarpley, mother, Maryville, Mo.

Moffit, Callip J. Cook — C. F. Moffit, brother, Burlington Jct., Mo.

Rardin, Paul R. Cook — S. T. Rardin, father, Ridgeway, Mo.

Auwarter, Floyd D. Cook — Mrs. J. D. Auwarter, mother, Hale, Mo.

Savage, Arthur W. Cook — Mrs. Minnie Savage, mother, 326 Enterprise St., Abilene, Kans.

Boyd, Henry Cook — R. S. Boyd, father, Fortescue, Mo.

King, Ernest E. Cook — J. J. King, father, 525 Kansas Ave., Topeka, Kans.

Crans, Thurlow S. Musician 1cl. — Mrs. Margaret A. Crans, mother, 308 East 34th St., Kansas City, Mo.

Royer, Harold J. Musician 1cl. — Mrs. Emma C. Royer, mother, Abilene, Kans.

Ewan, Philip T. Musician 2cl. — Mrs. F. W. Ewan, mother, 432 W. Bdw'y. Newton, Kans.

Hartley, Minor Joe Musician 2cl. — Mrs. M. J. Hartley, wife, 433 Hickory St., Ottawa, Kans.

Hanstine, Paul H. Musician 2cl. — Mrs. G. B. Hanstine, Whitewater, Kans.

Bruner, James Musician 3cl. — Mrs. Tillie Bruner, mother, Eldon. Ia.

Cambern, Leon J. Musician 3cl. — L. S. Cambern, father, Erie, Kans.

Dutton, Lane A. Musician 3cl. — Mrs. C. C. Dutton, mother, Erie, Kans.

Greenlee, Samuel R. Musician 3cl. — J. N. Greenlee, father, Scott City, Kans.

Greenman, Loyd B. Musician 3cl. — Mrs. Loyd B. Greenman, wife, 514 Fruit St., Santa Ana, Calif.

Henderson, William R. Musician 3cl. — Lt. R. R. Henderson, father, Rock Island, Ill.

Knopf, Roby J. Musician 3cl. — Mrs. Frank Knopf, mother, Holton, Kans.

McCarter, Arthur W. Musician 3cl. — Mrs. W. E. McCarter, mother, 21st and Lime Sts., Topeka, Kans.

Mitchell, Ralph E. Musician 3cl. — W. Mitchell, father, Erie, Kans.

Nininger, Ora E. Musician 3cl. — Mrs. E. J. Nininger, mother, 309 Quincy St., Topeka, Kans.

Stitt, Earl D. Musician 3cl. — Mrs. J. E. Stitt, mother, 1931 Van Buren St., Topeka, Kans.

Stitt, Orby J. Musician 3cl. — Mrs. J. E. Stitt, mother, 1931 Van Buren St., Topeka, Kans.

Stocking, Clyde L. Musician 3cl. — Mrs. Sarah E. Stocking, mother, 1115 E. 7th St., Winfield, Kans.

Hackney, James A. Wagoner — A. J. Hackney, father, R.F.D. No. 2, St. Joseph, Mo.

Hogan, Jerdie Wagoner — Thomas Hogan, father, Shubert, Nebr.

Koontz, Sam F. Wagoner — Peter Koontz, father, Norborne, Mo.

Nelson, James V. Wagoner — J. L. Nelson, father, Bethany, Mo.

Stephenson, Roy V. Wagoner — Mrs. E. J. Stephenson, mother, Gallatin, Mo.

Abbott, Avery Pvt. 1cl. — W. M. Abbott, father, R.F.D. 6, Kirksville, Mo.

Bachtel, Fred J. Pvt. 1cl. — Mrs. W. W. Bachtel, mother, Clifton, Kans.

Ball, Clarence Pvt. 1cl. — Mrs. Annie Ball, mother, Mercer, Mo.

Beason, Henry M. Pvt. 1cl. — Mrs. R. J. Beason, mother, Fair Play, Mo.

Benedict, Myron D. Pvt. 1cl. — Mrs. F. Benedict, mother, Corning, Mo.

Bonjour, Ira S. Pvt. 1cl. — Mrs. Millie Bonjour, mother, Onaga, Kans.

Burgin, Bayard T. Pvt. 1cl. — Mrs. Etta Burgin, mother, Bethany, Mo.

Calvert, John W. Pvt. 1cl. — Mrs. Kate Calvert, mother, DeWitt, Mo.

Clinton, Arthur E. Pvt. 1cl. — Mrs. Nettie G. Clinton, wife, Madison, Kans.

Collier, James E. Pvt. 1cl. — Mr. J. W. Collier, father, Hardin, Mo.

Corley, Joe V. Pvt. 1cl. — Rev. Joe Corley, father, Alden, Kans.

Corley, John C. Pvt. 1cl. — Rev. Joe Corley, father, Alden, Kans.

Cowan, Clarence E. Pvt. 1cl. — Mr. R. M. Cowan, father, Hale, Mo.

140

BAND

Cox, Joseph H. Pvt. 1cl.
Mrs. Emma J. Cox, mother, 105 S. Buckeye, Abilene, Kans.

Daly, Everett E. Pvt. 1cl.
Mrs. Lucia E. Daly, mother, Huntsdale, Mo.

Duff, Allen E. Pvt. 1cl.
Thomas E. Duff, father, 1015 E. Bdwy, Sedalia, Mo.

Duff, Ernest M. Pvt. 1cl.
Thomas E. Duff, father, 1015 E. Bdwy, Sedalia, Mo.

Duffy, Clarence E. Pvt. 1cl.
Patrick H. Duffy, father, Downs, Kans.

Eichenour, John W. Pvt. 1cl.
Mrs. Laura Eichenour, mother, Durham, Kans.

Ennis, Everett B. Pvt. 1cl.
H. E. Ennis, father, 2317 Charles St., St. Joseph, Mo.

Ford, Glee L. Pvt. 1cl.
Frank W. Ford, father, Madison, Kans.

Foster, Corwin F. Pvt. 1cl.
D. M. Foster, father, Mercer, Mo.

Gains, Henry L. Pvt. 1cl.
E. O. Gains, father, Caruthersville, Mo.

Graham, Samuel P. Pvt. 1cl.
Mrs. Chloe Graham, mother, Gallatin, Mo.

Hartley, Luther A. Pvt. 1cl.
Mrs. Belle Hartley, mother, R.F.D. 5, Columbia, Mo.

Haslett, John L. Pvt. 1cl.
Miss Pearl H. Haslett, sister, R.F.D. 2, Frankfort, Kans.

Higgs, Arthur L. Pvt. 1cl.
Luther L. Higgs, father, Anderson, Mo.

Hodgson, George W. Pvt. 1cl.
John Hodgson, father, 701 E. Spruce, Herington, Kans.

Holloway, Lawrence W. Pvt. 1cl.
Mrs. Alice Holloway, mother, R.F.D. 5, Trenton, Mo.

Hull, George W. Pvt. 1cl.
A. I. Hull, father, Valley Falls, Kans.

Ishmain, Clarence Pvt. 1cl.
Mr. N. H. Ishmael, father, Greencastle, Mo.

Jones, Harry E. Pvt. 1cl.
E. B. Jones, father, Downs, Kans.

Kern, John C. Pvt. 1cl.
Thomas Kern, father, Avalon, Mo.

Krenzel, Lee H. Pvt. 1cl.
Henry Krenzel, father, Cheney, Kans.

Limbrey, George F. Pvt. 1cl.
Charles S. Limbrey, father, Clifton, Kans.

Lindensmith, Arthur S. Pvt. 1cl.
Ed. Lindensmith, father, R.F.D. No. 5, St. Joseph, Mo.

Martin, Leslie Pvt. 1cl.
Mr. F. L. Martin, father, Bogard, Mo.

Marshall, Edward Pvt. 1cl.
Mrs. C. C. Spalding, mother, Stoddard, Ariz.

McCormack, Alfred B. Pvt. 1cl.
Mrs. James McCormack, mother, Deckerville, Mich.

McDonald, Frank Pvt. 1cl.
Mrs. K. D. Meyers, mother, Marmaduke, Ark.

McIntire, Carmi L. Pvt. 1cl.
G. A. McIntire, father, 302 E. 5th, Cherryvale, Kans.

Miller, Charles C. Pvt. 1cl.
P. C. Miller, father, 20 S. Monroe St., Brookfield, Mo.

Mitchel, George L. Pvt. 1cl.
Mrs. C. W. Mitchel, mother, 1107 Bluehill Ave., Boston, Mass.

Morrison, Thomas L. Pvt. 1cl.
F. S. Morrison, father, Newton, Kans.

Nordgreen, Axel B. Pvt. 1cl.
H. Nordgreen, father, Olsburg, Kans.

Parrott, James D. Pvt. 1cl.
Mrs. H. E. Milsap, mother, 709 S. Campbell St., Springfield, Mo.

Poole, Fred Pvt. 1cl.
A. J. Poole, father, Jewell City, Mo.

Rainey, Leslie Pvt. 1cl.
S. L. Rainey, father, King City, Mo.

Ramsey, Garland A. Pvt. 1cl.
Mrs. C. P. Denning, sister, Larned, Kans.

Regester, Edgar M. Pvt. 1cl.
Mrs. Lizzie Regester, mother, 101 S. 6th St., Clay Center, Kans.

Rodarmel, Leroy Pvt. 1cl.
Mrs. H. Watton, mother, Longton, Kans.

Schnabel, Charles F. Pvt. 1cl.
L. J. Schnabel, father, Ionia, Mo.

Shelton, Sam Pvt. 1cl.
Sarah Shelton, mother, Memphis, Mo.

Sell, Vernon D. Pvt. 1cl.
Daniel D. Sell, father, 440 W. 16th St., Kansas City, Mo.

Stock, Emil Pvt. 1cl.
Mrs. Agnes Stock, mother, 2229 Messaine St., St. Joseph, Mo.

Tiers, Elwood E. Pvt. 1cl.
Ellsworth E. Tiers, brother, Clay Center, Kans.

Stuck, William J. Pvt. 1cl.
Erma Stuck, wife, Wakeeney, Kans.,

Valentine, Delbert A. Pvt. 1cl.
Mrs. Flora Valentine, mother, Overbrook, Kans.

Wiehl, Noel M. Pvt. 1cl.
Mrs. Cora V. Wiehl, mother, 611 N. 11th St., St. Joseph, Mo.

Zerbine, John Pvt. 1cl.
Mrs. Francea Zerbine, mother, Nocera-Umbrai, Italy.

Zook, John F. Pvt. 1cl.
Mrs. Jennie Zook, mother, Skidmore, Mo.

Abbott, Loyd E. Private
Mrs. Maude Abbott, mother, 25 F West, Hutchinson, Kans.

Anderson, James M. Private
Solomon R. Anderson, father, Rosalia, Kans.

Asher, Thomas L. Private
Mrs. W. B. Asher, mother, Bigelow, Mo.

Baldwin, James M. Private
Mrs. C. S. Hendrix, sister, Mich. Blk. and Stone, Detroit, Mich.

Barnhart, William C. Private
Mrs. Ora Barnhart, mother, Avalon, Mo.

Beal, Clarence E. Private
Oliver H. Beal, father, Hannibal, Mo.

Berry, Luther Private
Miss Ester Berry, sister, Branson, Mo.

Boes, Charles W. Private
Monia Boes, aunt, Larned, Kans.

Bouray, John H. Private
Mrs. Elizabeth Boehm, mother, Hardy, Neb.

Brelsford, Harry L. Private
Mrs. Eula Brelsford, wife, 704 Sacramento St., St. Joseph, Mo.

Brown, Ora E. Private
Arthur E. Brown, father, Milton, Ia.

Bowman, John L. Private
John Bowman, father, Glen Elder, Kans.

Butler, Clifford R. Private
Mr. T. W. Butler, father, Mediapolis, Ia.

Carlton, Guy Private
Mrs. Georgie Carlton, mother, 910 Ward Ave., Caruthersville, Mo.

Carr, Charles V. — Private — Mrs. Bessie Carr, wife, R.F.D. No. 3, Plymouth, Ill.

Cavanaugh, Ernest — Private — Miss Lena Cavanaugh, sister, Platte City, Mo.

Chamberlin, Carl W. — Private — Mrs. Delcie Ash, sister, Corbin, Kans.

Collins, Frank — Private — Mrs. Vergia Sinkhorn, sister, Straight Creek, Ky.

Colvin, Sam S. — Private — Mrs. E. L. Colvin, mother, 2606 Gilbert St., Marinette, Wis.

Connelly, Harry — Private — Mrs. Angeline Connelly, mother, St. Joseph, Mo.

Cope, Newton — Private — Mrs. Frank C. Cope, mother, 1516 New Hampshire, Lawrence, Kans.

Crashaw, William — Private — Miss Evelyn K. Hickey, friend, 709 Lawrence St., Topeka, Kans.

Crump, Claude C. — Private — Mrs. Zella V. Heizer, sister, Molino, Mo.

Davis, Tolbert J. — Private — Mrs. Nettie B. Davis, wife, Oxford, Kans.

Dayton, Howard — Private — William H. Dayton, father, 204 Pine St., Abilene, Kans.

Dobkins, John M. — Private — Mrs. Minnie Dobkins, mother, 412 East 8th St., Abilene, Kans.

Dokkesven, Clarence — Private — Bertha Dokkesven, mother, New London, Minn.

Duree, George W. — Private — Mr. Miles Duree, father, 3rd St. and Norton Ave., Bartlesville, Okla.

Elder, Lawrence S. — Private — Mrs. L. A. Elder, mother, 330 N. Main, Eldorado, Kans.

Emery, William H. — Private — Mrs. Bessie Emery, wife, 1817 S. Main St., Wichita, Kans.

Enslen, Roscoe — Private — Mrs. Fannie Enslen, mother, 1226 Market St., Hannibal, Mo.

Estep, James K. — Private — Mrs. M. Stephenson, mother, 610 N. 12th St., St. Joseph, Mo.

Farris, Fred W. — Private — Mrs. Julia Schaufler, mother, Troy, Kans.

Fowler, Leroy J. — Private — Mrs. Maggie Fowler, wife, R.F.D. 27, Topeka, Kans.

Garten, Robert — Private — Mrs. Robert Garten, wife, Maryville, Mo.

Gillespy, Walter A. — Private — Mrs. Arminta Gillespy, mother, 213 S. Pine St., Nowata, Okla.

Gist, Harold E. — Private — Joseph T. Gist, father, 618 N. Grand Ave., Enid, Okla.

Gordon, Sam — Private — Ben Finn, friend, Hibbing, Minn.

Gowers, George L. — Private — Mrs. Maude M. Gowers, mother, Thayer, Mo.

Green, Charles W. — Private — Mrs. Phoebe Green, mother, 926 W. 3rd St., Eldorado, Kans.

Gunby, William E. — Private — Mrs. Cathrine E. Wells, sister, Braymer, Mo.

Hall, John G. — Private — Jesse Hall, father, 1202 S. Ann St., Kirksville, Mo.

Hall, Claude — Private — Mrs. Emil Hall, wife, Wilson, Kans.

Harbert, Hugh P. — Private — Mrs. K. Harbert, mother, Hayti, Mo.

Harper, Thaddeus S. — Private — Mrs. Anna B. Harper, mother, 502 Lafayette St., Topeka, Kans.

Harrington, Lawnie E. — Private — M. J. Harrington, father, 819 Merchant St., Eldorado, Kans.

Hart, Donald R. — Private — Charles H. Hart, father, 1425 Boswell St., Topeka, Kans.

Holliday, George I. — Private — Mrs. Lizzie Holliday, wife, Spearville, Kans.

Holloway, Avillia — Private — Mrs. Martha Holloway, mother, Hardin, Mo.

Hoselton, Emerson — Private — Mrs. Sevina Hoselton, mother, Milan, Mo.

Howard, Carl C. — Private — Mrs. Maddie Howard, mother, Holcomb, Mo.

Hugo, John R. — Private — J. T. Hugo, father, Mulvane, Kans.

Hull, Warren — Private — Mrs. Ella Hull, mother, Clay Center, Kans.

Jacques, George L. — Private — Frank Jacques, father, 1535 N. Harrison, Topeka, Kans.

Jewell, Carl C. — Private — W. H. Jewell, father, Burrton, Kans.

Johnson, Donald W. — Private — Mrs. M. W. Johnson, mother, Beloit, Kans.

Jones, Fred R. — Private — Mrs. H. L. Jones, mother, 1031 Santa Fe St., Atchison, Kans.

Kehl, Willard B. — Private — Lewis Kehl, father, Valley Center, Kans.

Kehoe, Charles B. — Private — Mrs. Mary Kehoe, mother, 730 Carpenter Place, St. Louis, Mo.

Kuchera, Joseph C. — Private — John V. Kuchera, father, Cuba, Kans.

Larkin, James E. — Private — Mrs. Winifred Clark, sister, 19 Sackett St., Westfield, Mass.

Lower, Fred W. — Private — Mrs. Anna Scott, sister, Marceline, Mo.

Mason, Albert J. — Private — Albert Mason, father, 500 Buff St., Hannibal, Mo.

McArthur, James L. — Private — Mrs. Clara Hinds, mother, 1310 Lindle Ave., Hannibal, Mo.

McCosh, Harry P. — Private — Mrs. William McCosh, mother, Abilene, Kans.

McGlasson, John A. — Private — Mrs. S. E. McGlasson, mother, 500 W. 6th St., Newton, Kans.

Mericle, Joy — Private — Thomas Mericle, father, Noble, Ill.

Miles, Charles S. — Private — Miss May Miles, sister, 703 N. Main St., Garden City, Kans.

Morris, Earl B. — Private — Sam Morris, father, Mexico, Mo.

Morris, Thomas B. — Private — Mrs. Carrie Morris, mother, East 6th St., Trenton, Mo.

Murdock, Delbert — Private — Mrs. Laura M. Roberts, sister, Gladwin, Mich.

Mulkey, Myron M. — Private — Mrs. W. D. Mulkey, mother, 220 N. 1st St., Herington, Kans.

Moss, Daniel — Private — Mrs. Bessie Moss, mother, 1523 Bacon St., St. Louis, Mo.

Naslund, Clarence L. — Private — Miss Sylvia E. Naslund, sister, Clay Center, Kans.

Neville, Fred — Private — A. R. Neville, brother, 516 Harrison St., Topeka, Kans.

Norman, Clyde C. — Private — Frank Norman, father, R.F.D. 6, Columbia, Mo.

Patterson, Edward C. — Private — Mrs. Rosa Patterson, wife, Newton, Kans.

Poppe, Tobbe B. — Private — Mrs. Pauline Poppe, mother, Central City, Ia.

Prashaw, Cecil J. — Private — Mrs. Mina Prashaw, mother, Fulton, N. Y.

Reynolds, Henry O. — Private — Cyrus Reynolds, father, Maryville, Mo.

Robb, Ashel — Private — Mrs. Lue Robb, mother, 1011 Lalley St., Hannibal, Mo.

Root, George E. — Private — Mordecai O. Root, father, 2308 Davis St., St. Joseph, Mo.

Sanberg, Justus A. — Private — C. W. Sanberg, father, Taylors Falls, Minn.

Sandman, Earl W. — Private — Mrs. Gertrude Sandman, mother, 154 Lamartine St., Jamaica Plaine, Mass.

Schnabel, Loren J. — Private — Mrs. Loren J. Schnabel, wife, Maryville, Mo.

Scott, John E. — Private — Mrs. Vivian R. Scott, wife, Mankato, Kans.

Shaw, Wilburn T. — Private — Mrs. T. R. Shaw, mother, Coin, Ia.

Shaver, Arthur L. — Private — Millard F. Shaver, father, Randall, Kans.

Shellinger, William H. — Private — Edward Shellinger, father, Glen Elder, Kans.

Sherrow, Carl F. — Private — Mrs. Nora Sherrow, mother, Laredo, Mo.

Shirk, Alonzo D. — Private — David M. Shirk, father, 215 E. 5th St., Abilene, Kans.

Shirley, Charles C. — Private — J. A. Shirley, father, Syracuse, Kans.

Shook, Wilbur V. — Private — Margerite Shook, mother, Abilene, Kans.

Shuey, John S. — Private — James H. Shuey, father, Lemon, Penn.

Simpson, Clarence A. — Private — Laura M. Simpson, mother, 207 S. 2nd St., Abilene, Kans.

Salisbury, David — Private — William H. Salisbury, father, Novinger, Mo.

Spencer, Jack — Private — Mrs. Dela Spencer, mother, 1710 Faraon St., St. Joseph, Mo.

Spielman, Roy V. — Private — George Spielman, father, Ozawkie, Kans.

Steinberg, Shirley — Private — Mrs. George Vanorsdale, sister, Hope, Kans.

Steinman, Harry H. — Private — John H. Steinman, father, Republic, Kans.

Swager, Ed. — Private — Mrs. Agnes Swager, mother, Marceline, Mo.

Tingley, Edgar S. — Private — Marie Tingley, sister, 226 S. Front St., New Richmond, Ohio.

Varelman, George E. — Private — Jesse Varelman, mother, Hymer, Kans.

Wagner, Francis F. — Private — John E. Wagner, father, Burlington, Kans.

Watson, Vernice F. — Private — J. M. Watson, father, Hazelton, Ia.

Watts, Robert R. — Private — Gera Watts, father, Mount Morris, Ill.

Welch, Horace M. — Private — Mrs. Florence Briggs, mother, Marceline, Mo.

White, Lysle C. — Private — H. E. White, father, Wheling, Mo.

Wigham, William — Private — G. W. Wigham, father, Wellington, Tex.

Wise, Everett W. — Private — Mrs. Mary J. Wise, mother, 619 West St., Topeka, Kans.

Wood, William H. — Private — J. A. Wood, father, Oblong, Ill.

Woodley, Homer — Private — Benjamin J. Woodley, father, Syracuse, Kans.

142

ROSTER OF SUPPLY COMPANY, 139th INFANTRY

NAME AND RANK		HOME ADDRESS AND REMARKS
Charles J. Hall,	Major	Robidoux Hotel, St. Joseph, Mo., OS-MA, Sup. Co. 4th Mo. Assigned to 110th Supply Train Feb. 19.
Arthur F. Amick,	1st Lt.	St. Joseph, Mo., OS, 4th Mo. Sup. Co. Assigned to Railway work.
George T. Worthen,	1st Lt.	St. Joseph, Mo., 4th Mo. Co. M. OS Assigned to Co. H. 139th.
Charles W. Graham, Jr.,	2nd Lt.	Unknown, OS. Assigned to Remount service.
Harry E. Malloure,	1st Lt.	Caruthersville, Mo., 4th Mo. Co. B. OS-MA.
Edwin V. Burkholder,	1st Lt.	Marion, Kans., 3rd Kans. Co. M. OS-MA.
John L. Creech,	2nd Lt.	Kentucky, OS-MA.
Donnel, Calvin	Regtl. Sup. Sgt.	Okeene, Okla., 4th Mo. Sup. Co. OS-MA.
McCutchen, Robert J.	Regtl. Sup. Sgt.	414 Angelique St., St. Joseph, Mo., Sup. Co. 4th Mo., OS-MA.
Hall, Albert M.	Regtl. Sup. Sgt.	Robidoux Hotel, St. Joseph, Mo., 4th Mo. Sup. Co., OS-MA.
Dalton, Morris S.	1st Sgt.	717 Albermarle St., St. Joseph, Mo., Co. M. 4th Mo. OS-MA.
Robinson, Jasper C.	Sup. Sgt.	Oronogo, Mo., 4th Mo. Co. A., OS-MA.
Murnane, William M.	Mess Sgt.	621 6th St., Bismarck, N. D., Camp Dodge. MA.
Lowe, George	Stable Sgt.	1204 Boyd St., St. Joseph, Mo., Sup. Co., 4th Mo.
Cummings, Charles C.	Sergeant	912 South 14th St., St. Joseph, Mo., Sup. Co. 4th Mo., OS-MA.
Smoot, Charles C.	Sergeant	2114 Bartlett St., St. Joseph, Mo., Sup. Co. 4th Mo., OS-MA.
Daubenspeck, George W.	Sergeant	Petroleum, West Va., Co. F. 3rd Kans., OS-MA.
Davis, Claude	Sergeant	Oskaloosa, Kans., Co. B. 3rd Kans., OS-MA.
Anderson, Jesse L.	Sergeant	414 West Second St., Maryville, Mo., Co. A. 4th Mo., OS-MA.
Terror, Joseph D.	Sergeant	Caruthersville, Mo., Co. B 4th Mo., OS-MA.
Pullem, Emerald A.	Corporal	Lathrop, Mo., 4th Mo. Sup. Co., OS-MA.
Letcher, Fred	Corporal	St. Joseph, Mo., 4th Mo. Sup. Co., OS.
Sparks, George	Sergeant	St. Joseph, Mo., 4th Mo. Sup. Co., OS-MA.
Torbert, Mark	Corporal	St. Joseph, Mo., 4th Mo. Co. M, OS.
Burkhardt, William	Hs.	Palmyra, Mo., 4th Mo. Co. E, OS-MA.
Murray, Andrew W.	Corporal	Kensington, Kans., 3rd Kans. Co. M, OS-MA.
Gerlach, Phillip	Corporal	Crown Point, Ind., 4th Mo. Sup. Co., OS-MA.
Johnson, Harold F.	Corporal	Forest City, Ia., Camp Dodge, Ia., OS-MA.
Myers, Lee J.	Corporal	Coffeyville, Kans., Co. A 3rd Kans., OS-MA.
Elmore, Lester R.	Hs.	Coffeyville, Kans., Co. A 3rd Kans., OS-MA.
Hayes, Perry J.	Hs.	Tina, Mo., Co. E 4th Mo., OS-MA.
Shannon, Garland E.	Hs.	Bogard, Mo., Co. E, 4th Mo., OS-MA.
Hooper, Othal L.	Hs.	Huntington, Mo., Co. E 4th Mo., OS-MA.
Reed, George E.	Saddler	Friedensburg, Pa., Sup. Co., 3rd Kans., OS-MA.
Greenland, Donald C.	Saddler	Bellwood, Pa., 3rd Kans. Sup. Co., OS-MA.
Amos, Jake	Mechanic	St. Joseph, Mo., 4th Mo. Co. M, OS-MA.
Amos, Claude L.	Mechanic	St. Joseph, Mo., 4th Mo. Co. M, OS-MA.
Brown, Curtis	Pvt. 1cl.	Coffey, Mo., Co. M 3rd Kans., OS.
Carter, Frank F.	Mechanic	St. Joseph, Mo., 4th Mo. Sup. Co., OS-MA.
Judkins, Carl	Mechanic	Tarkio, Mo., Co. A 4th Mo., OS-MA.
Connett, Carrol H.	Mechanic	St. Joseph, Mo., Hdq. Co. 4th Mo., OS.
Barnes, Eddie A.	Cook	St. Joseph, Mo., Sup. Co., 4th Mo., OS-MA.
Boyd, Henry E.	Cook	Fortescue, Mo., Co. L 4th Mo., OS-MA.
Bryson, George	Cook	Coffeyville, Kans., Co. A 3rd Kans., OS.
Patterson, Edward C.	Cook	Unknown, OS.

NAME AND RANK		HOME ADDRESS AND REMARKS
Smith, Fred	Cook	Niotaze, Kans., Co. D 3rd Kans., OS-MA.
Billington, Allen	Cook	Kewanee, Mo., Co. B 4th Mo., OS-MA.
Lash, Harlow W.	Cook	Enterprise, Kans., Co. E 3rd Kans., OS-MA.
Graff, Walter A.	Cook	Woolridge, Mo., OS-MA. Camp Funston, Kans.
Allbrecht, Edmund C.	Wagoner	Norborne, Mo., 4th Mo. Co. H, OS-MA.
Anderson, Fred	Wagoner	Laclede, Mo., Co. I 4th Mo. OS-MA.
Anderson, Edward V.	Wagoner	Laclede, Mo., Co. I 4th Mo. OS-MA.
Arnold, Hobart	Wagoner	Unknown Co. 3rd Kans., OS-MA.
Bassham, James C.	Wagoner	Moko, Ark.
Beisel, Gotfred F.	Wagoner	Marion, Kans., 3rd Kans. Co. M, OS.
Blake, Halolm L.	Wagoner	812 Brooks St. Avenue, Topeka, Kans., 3rd Kans. Sup. Co., OS-MA.
Brake, Carey G.	Wagoner	1002½ East 8th St., Topeka, Kans., OS-MA. 3rd Kans. Sup. Co.
Brewster, Willard O.	Wagoner	Sedan, Kans., Co. D 3rd Kans., OS-MA.
Brenning, George T.	Wagoner	Unknown, OS. 3rd Kans. Co. M.
Burnam, William M.	Wagoner	Oskaloosa, Kans., Co. B 3rd Kans., OS-MA.
Carter, Daniel	Wagoner	Bentley, Ia., Co. 4th Mo., OS-MA.
Cartright, Claude	Wagoner	Tarkio, Mo., Co. A 4th Mo., OS-MA.
Casselman, Gideon,	Wagoner	Oskaloosa, Kans., Co. B 3rd Kans., OS.
Chaney, David	Wagoner	Tarkio, Mo., Co. A 4th Mo., OS-MA.
Chaney, Roscoe	Wagoner	Tarkio, Mo., Co. A 4th Mo., OS.
Converse, Lloyd F.	Wagoner	Peabody, Kans., Co. M 3rd Kans., OS-MA.
Cooper, Albert E.	Wagoner	Bazaar, Kans., Co. M 3rd Kans., OS-MA.
Corum, Roy J.	Wagoner	Seneca, Kans., Sup. Co. 4th Mo., OS-MA.
Crawford, Oliver L.	Wagoner	Tina, Mo., Co. H 4th Mo., OS-MA.
Creason, Hardie L.	Wagoner	Caruthersville, Mo., Co. B 4th Mo., OS-MA.
Denning, Leonard C.	Wagoner	Oskaloosa, Kans., Co. B 3rd Kans., OS-MA.
Denton, Samuel R.	Wagoner	Kirksville, Mo., Co. C 4th Mo., OS-MA.
Douglas, John J.	Wagoner	Oskaloosa, Kans., Co. B 3rd Kans., OS-MA.
Douglas, Joseph B.	Wagoner	Oskaloosa, Kans., Co. B 3rd Kans., OS-MA.
Dorcas, Everett H.	Wagoner	Vermillion, Kans., Co. B 3rd Kans., OS-MA.
Dyson, Melvin	Wagoner	Oskaloosa, Kans., Co. B 3rd Kans., OS.
Douglas, Levern	Wagoner	416 Spruce St., Herington, Kans., Co. I 3rd Kans., OS-MA.
Duncan, Elmer E.	Wagoner	Williamstown, Kans., Co. B 3rd Kans., OS-MA.
Egbert, Rollin E.	Wagoner	RFD 7, Newton, Kans., Sup. Co. 2nd Kans., OS-MA.
Fennell, Jesse A.	Wagoner	St. Joseph, Mo., Sup Co. 4th Mo., OS-MA.
Fleming, Thomas H.	Wagoner	RFD 1, Lake Wilson, Minn., Camp Dodge, OS-MA.
Fischer, Fred F.	Wagoner	Gackle, N. D., Camp Dodge, OS-MA.
Foley, Harry	Wagoner	Lebanon, Mo., Co. A 4th Mo., OS-MA.
Forth, Arlie M.	Wagoner	Topeka, Kans., Sup. Co. 3rd Kans., OS-MA.
Gardner, Raymond R.	Wagoner	Kansas City, Kans., Co. E 3rd Kans. OS-MA.
Grout, Wilmer O.	Wagoner	Beloit, Kans., Sup. Co. 3rd Kans., OS-MA.
Green, William	Wagoner	Tarkio, Mo., Co. A 4th Mo., OS-MA.
Henson, Everett H.	Wagoner	Tarkio, Mo., Co. A 4th Mo., OS.
Hicks, Luther	Wagoner	Tarkio, Mo., Co. A, 4th Mo., OS.
Horton, James L.	Wagoner	Kirksville, Mo., Co. C, 4th Mo., OS-MA.
Hurst, Millard	Wagoner	Tarkio, Mo., Co. A 4th Mo., OS-MA.

Name	Rank	Address / Unit
Heines, Herman	Wagoner	RFD 3, Kenosha, Wis., Camp Custer.
Jenkins, Sidney	Wagoner	Esbon, Kans., Camp Funston, OS-MA.
Johns, Claude I.	Wagoner	919 West Walnut St., Herington, Kans., Co. I 3rd Kans., OS-MA.
Jorgenson, Albert W.	Wagoner	St. Joseph, Mo., Co. M 4th Mo., OS-MA.
Judkins, Cecil	Wagoner	Lonstrap, Denmark. Camp Dodge, Ia., OS-MA.
Kelsay, Jesse L.	Wagoner	Tarkio, Mo., Co. A 4th Mo., OS-MA.
Kinder, William F.	Wagoner	St. Joseph, Mo.
Kelley, George J.	Wagoner	New Hampton, Mo., Co. G 4th Mo., OS-MA.
Kindler, Ernest	Wagoner	Chapman, Kans., Co. C 3rd Kans., OS-MA.
King, Joseph F.	Wagoner	RFD 1, Collins, Minn., Camp Dodge, OS-MA.
Knox, Fred	Wagoner	Harrisburg, Mo., Co. F 4th Mo., OS-MA.
Luebke, William M.	Wagoner	528 Stool Ave., Milwaukee, Wis., Camp Custer.
Larson, Leonard	Wagoner	Sawyer, N. D., Camp Dodge, OS-MA.
Long, William N.	Wagoner	Oxford, Kans., Co. L 3rd Kans., OS-MA.
Maxwell, Joseph L.	Wagoner	Quitman, Mo., Sup. Co. 4th Mo., OS-MA.
McArthur, Floyd	Wagoner	Caruthersville, Mo., Co. B 4th Mo., OS.
McClure, Norvie J.	Wagoner	Walton, Kans., Co. M 3rd Kans., OS-MA.
McHugh, John E.	Wagoner	Agenda, Kans., Camp Funston, OS-MA.
McNeal, Joe	Wagoner	Tarkio, Mo., Co. A 4th Mo., OS.
Mountain, Delbert	Wagoner	Kirksville, Mo., Co. C 4th Mo., OS-MA.
Nagle, Charles A.	Wagoner	Unknown, Camp Funston., OS.
Olsen, Andy L.	Wagoner	Jamestown, Kans., Camp Funston, OS-MA.
Oglevie, Lloyd V.	Wagoner	Burr Oak, Kans., Camp Funston, OS-MA.
Pauls, Rudolph	Wagoner	Hillsboro, Kans., Co. M 3rd Kans., OS-MA.
Potter, Ray	Wagoner	Kirksville, Mo., Co. C, 4th Mo., OS-MA.
Potter, Floyd	Wagoner	Cottonwood Falls, Kans., Co. M 3rd Kans., OS-MA.
Potter, Kent B.	Wagoner	Cottonwood Falls, Kans., Co. M 3rd Kans., OS-MA.
Powell, Amos	Wagoner	Tarkio, Mo., Co. A 4th Mo., OS-MA.
Robey, Charles	Wagoner	Maryville, Mo., Co. A 4th Mo., OS-MA.
Reilly, John J.	Wagoner	Detroit, Kans., Co. C 3rd Kans., OS-MA.
Ross, William	Wagoner	Stanberry, Mo., Co. A 4th Mo., OS-MA.
Smith, Isaac R.	Wagoner	Florence, Kans., Co. M 3rd Kans., OS-MA.
Reed, James F.	Wagoner	423 Adams St., Minneapolis, Minn. Camp Dodge, OS-MA.
Smith, Charles L.	Wagoner	423 West 12th St. Junction City, Kans., Co. C 3rd Kans., OS-MA.
Snodgrass, Joseph	Wagoner	Herington, Kans., Co. L 3rd Kans., OS-MA.
Snodgrass, George	Wagoner	Herington, Kans., Co. L 3rd Kans., OS.
Snyder, Carrol D.	Wagoner	Wellington, Kans., Co. L 3rd Kans., OS-MA.
Stebbins, Chauncy	Wagoner	Tarkio, Mo., Co. A 4th Mo., OS-MA.
Stevens, William H.	Wagoner	Black, Mo., Sup. Co. 4th Mo., OS-MA.
Stoltz, George W.	Wagoner	Eldorado, Kans., Co. F 3rd Kans., OS-MA.
Stanton, George S.	Wagoner	Unknown.
Sturm, Clarence E.	Wagoner	Rydal, Kans., Camp Funston, OS-MA.
Traub, William	Wagoner	Tarkio, Mo., Co. A 4th Mo., OS.
Vendel, Claude W.	Wagoner	Oskaloosa, Kans., Co. B 3rd Kans., OS-MA.
Walker, Oliver,	Wagoner	Forbes, Mo., Co. L 4th Mo., OS-MA.
Wampler, Charles	Wagoner	Guthrie, Okla., Co. L 4th Mo., OS-MA.
Welch, Henry C.	Wagoner	Havan, Kans., Co. D 3rd Kans., OS-MA.
Wiley, Carter W.	Wagoner	Rogers, Ark., Co. D 3rd Kans., OS-MA.
Wilson, Lorn T.	Wagoner	Perth, Kans., Co. L 3rd Kans., OS-MA.
Williams, Forrest H.	Wagoner	Chapman, Kans., Co. C 3rd Kans., OS-MA.
Williams, Russel H.	Wagoner	Chapman, Kans., Co. C 3rd Kans., OS-MA.
Wheeler, James R.	Wagoner	Oskaloosa, Kans., Co. B 3rd Kans., OS-MA.
Wright, Mike	Wagoner	Kirksville, Mo., Co. C 4th Mo., OS-MA.
Zeek, Floyd	Wagoner	Unknown, OS.
Allen, Leslie	Pvt. 1cl.	Chapman, Kans., Co. C 3rd Kans., OS-MA.
Brumback, David	Pvt. 1cl.	Tarkio, Mo., Co. A, 4th Mo., OS-MA.
Dalton, Charley	Pvt. 1cl.	717 Albermarle St., St. Joseph, Mo., Co. M 4th Mo., OS-MA.
Frantz, Donald	Pvt. 1cl.	Topeka, Kans., Co. B 3rd Kans., OS-MA.
Gray, Earl R.	Pvt. 1cl.	Coffeyville, Kans., Co. A 3rd Kans., OS.
Gunn, Clarence T.	Pvt. 1cl.	Barnard, Mo., Co. M 4th Mo., OS-MA.
Hayes, Chester A.	Pvt. 1cl.	Edgerton, Mo., Co. M 4th Mo., OS-MA.
Lamb, Edward	Pvt. 1cl.	Tyler, Mo., Co. B 4th Mo., OS-MA.
Limle, Harry	Pvt. 1cl.	St. Joseph, Mo., Co. M 4th Mo., OS-MA.
Rossie, Charles	Pvt. 1cl.	St. Joseph, Mo., Sup. Co. 4th Mo., OS-MA.
Vrana, Joseph	Pvt. 1cl.	Agenda, Kans., Camp Funston, OS-MA.
White, Wilfred	Pvt. 1cl.	Maryville, Mo., Hdq. Co. 4th Mo., OS-MA.
Arlt, William H.	Private	Bird Island, Minn., Camp Dodge, MA.
Bennett, Charles A.	Private	McClusky, N. Dak., Camp Dodge, MA.
Blumhagen, Willie	Private	Kief, N. Dak., Camp Dodge, MA.
Byers, Walter J.	Private	Cameron, Mo., Sup. Co. 4th Mo., OS-MA.
Chesky, Joseph	Private	Crystal Falls, Mich., Camp Custer.
Cooper, Noah	Private	Laclede, Mo., Co. I 4th Mo., OS-MA.
Davis, Edwin L.	Private	St. Joseph, Mo., Co. M 4th Mo., OS.
Dawson, Benjamin H.	Private	Perth, Kans., Co. L 3rd Kans., OS.
Douglas, John J.	Private	Caruthersville, Mo., Co. B 4th Mo., OS.
Davis, Charles G.	Private	Dawson Springs, Ky., Camp Custer.
Doramus, Elmer C.	Private	Perth, Kans., Co. L 3rd Kans., OS-MA.
Duckworth, William A.	Private	Jackson, Mich., Camp Custer.
Dowell, George W.	Private	Avalon, Mo., Co. L 4th Mo., OS-MA.
Engler, Louis K.	Private	Chapman, Kans., Co. C 3rd Kans., OS-MA.
Freyer, Alexander W.	Private	Stevensville, Mich., Camp Custer.
Ford, Glee A.	Private	Madison, Kans., Co. L 2nd Kans., OS.
Furey, John L.	Private	Deer Foot, Minn., Camp Dodge, OS.
Grey, Richard L.	Private	Coffeyville, Kans., Co. A 3rd Kans., OS.
Hanson, Martin C.	Private	Unknown, Camp Dodge, OS.
Hoffman, Joe A.	Private	Gackle, N. Dak., Camp Dodge, OS.
Henderson, William	Private	Sacramento, Ky., Camp Custer.
Jackson, William M.	Private	Tarkio, Mo., Co. A 4th Mo., OS.
Johnson, Robert L.	Private	Cape Girardeau, Mo., Co. B 4th Mo., OS-MA.
Kennedy, Leo J.	Private	St. Joseph, Mo., Sup. Co. 4th Mo., OS-MA.
Kearn, Earl R.	Private	Council Grove, Kans., Co. L 3rd Kans., OS-MA.
Krenis, Victor	Private	Kenosha, Wis., Camp Custer.
Kittleson, Oscar A.	Private	Unknown. OS.
Leigh, Lee	Private	Tarkio, Mo., Co. A 4th Mo., OS.
LeVeque, George	Private	Wichert, Ill., Camp Dodge.
Linn, Earl J.	Private	Marion, Kans., Co. M 3rd Kans., OS-MA.
LaCoursiere, Joseph	Private	Unknown, OS., Camp Dodge.
Matson, Mathis	Private	Unknown, OS., Camp Dodge.
Madden, John L.	Private	Albany, Mo., Co. G 4th Mo., OS-MA.
Morgan, Cecil D.	Private	Trenton, Mo., Co. D 4th Mo., OS.
McGarry, James	Private	Chapman, Kans., Co. C 3rd Kans., OS-MA.
Michels, Anton J.	Private	Stacyville, Ia., Camp Dodge, OS-MA.
Myers, Oscar L.	Private	Leavenworth, Kans., Co. E 3rd Kans., OS-MA.
Nolen, Henry	Private	Hayti, Mo., Co. B 4th Mo., OS-MA.
Nordberg, John	Private	Minneapolis, Minn., Camp Dodge, OS.
Persson, Linus	Private	Braddock, N. Dak., Camp Dodge, OS-MA.
Reisenauer, Wendel	Private	Mandan, N. Dak., Camp Dodge, MA.
Scanlon, Leo T.	Private	Chapman, Kans., Co. C 3rd Kans., OS-MA.
Schrader, Charles F.	Private	Stitzer, Wis., Camp Custer.
Sharkey, Walter	Private	Rock Island, Ill., Camp Custer, MA.
Smith, Albert	Private	Hargeline, Mo., Co. H 4th Mo., MA.
Smith, James L.	Private	Annapolis, Ill., Co. F 3rd Kans., OS-MA.
Sailor, Arthur H.	Private	Marion, Kans., Co. M 3rd Kans., OS-MA.
Templeman, Harvey E.	Private	Kenosha, Wis., Camp Custer.
Vaughan, William,	Private	Coffeyville, Kans., Co. A 3rd Kans., OS-MA.

Wheeler, James R,	Private	Oskaloosa, Kans., Co. B 3rd Kans., OS.	

Wheeler, James R, Private — Oskaloosa, Kans., Co. B 3rd Kans., OS.
Bly, Andrew W. Wagoner — Fenton, Mich., Camp Custer.
Blount, Walter L. Wagoner — Peabody, Kans., Co. M 3rd Kans., OS.
Deitz, Ralph Wagoner — Petersburg, Ill., Camp Custer.
Peters, Fred Wagoner — Portonville, Mich., Camp Custer.
Phillips, Harry H. Wagoner — Sturgis, Mich., Camp Custer.
Ransier, Frank A. Wagoner — Hamtramck, Mich., Camp Custer.
Beatie, Harold R. Pvt. 1cl. — Anson, Kans., Co. L 3rd Kans., OS.
Hamel, Melvin A. Pvt. 1cl. — Wichita, Kans., Co. L 3rd Kans., OS-MA.
Swiger, Fred O. Pvt. 1cl. — Cherryvale, Kans., Co. D 3rd Kans. OS-MA.
Grady, George E. Private — Gentry, Kans., Co. A 3rd Kans., OS-MA.
Hollingsworth, Ralph Private — Wellington, Kans., Co. L 3rd Kans., OS-MA.

ATTACHED ORDNANCE

Barnes, Henry E. Ord. Sgt. — Chillicothe, Mo., Co. D 4th Mo., OS-MA.
Collier, Woodson E. Ord. Corp. — Trenton, Mo., Co. D 4th Mo., OS-MA.
Burke, William R. Pvt. 1cl. — Trenton, Mo., Co. D 4th Mo., OS-MA.
Haldeman, Oscar Pvt. 1cl. — Trenton, Mo., Co. D 4th Mo., OS-MA.
Collier, John W. Private — Trenton, Mo., Co. D 4th Mo., OS-MA.
McAuliffe, Joseph T. Private — Trenton, Mo., Co. D 4th Mo., OS-MA.
McMullin, Cecil O. Private — Trenton, Mo., Co. D 4th Mo., OS-MA.
Shea, Daniel B. Private — Trenton, Mo., Co. D 4th Mo., OS-MA.

HEADQUARTERS DETACHMENT, 1st BATTALION, 139th INFANTRY

NAME AND RANK	EMERGENCY ADDRESS
Samuel G. Clarke, Major.	
Marcus J. Morgan, 1st Lieut. Bat. Adj.	
Ross Diehl, 1st Lieut. Bat. Munitions officer.	
Chas. Barndollar, 2nd Lieut., Bat. Int. officer.	
William H. Van Sickler, 2nd Lieut. Bat. Liaison Officer.	
Chas. E. Munn, 1st Lieut. Bat. Gas Officer.	
Pickering, Ben. C., Bat. Sergt. Maj.	
Fields, Chas. W. Private	
Shafer, William F. Private	
McDaniels, Hillary, Private, Orderly.	
Welty, Chas. D., Private, Orderly.	
Croy, William C. Bn. Sgt. Major	Mr. John A. Croy, father, 1611 S. Lamine St., Sedalia, Mo.
Davis, Robert C. Corporal	Mr. R. L. Davis, uncle, 7th and Frances Sts., St. Joseph, Mo.
Sharp, Clarence G. Corporal	Mr. Wm. M. Sharp, father, Craig, Mo.
Smith, Vesper M. Corporal	Mr. Otto A. Smith, father, Green, Kans.
Higgs, Earnest Corporal	Mr. L. E. Higgs, father, Anderson, Mo.
Gilliland, Gilbert L. Pvt. 1cl.	Mr. Joel N. Gilliland, father, Idlewild, Tenn.
Benson, Loren R. Private	Mr. D. J. Benson, father, 501 East 4th St., Topeka, Kans.
Bousfield, George H. Private	Mrs. Josephine Bousfield, mother, Lansing, Kans.
Doering, William Private	Mrs. Elisabeth Block, mother, Hillsboro, Kans.
Gott, Loyd Private	Mrs. Joseph Gott, mother, Jamesport, Mo.
Haines, William H. Private	Mrs. N. Haines, mother, Monett, Kans.
Hadel, Henry W. Private	Mrs. Julia Hadel, mother, Hillsboro, Kans.
Hopkins, Myron E. Private	Mr. J. W. Hopkins, father, Bridgeport, Kans.
Lake, Artie C. Private	Mr. George Lake, father, Rock Creek, Kans.
Shumard, Arthur E. Private	Mr. Walter Shumard, father, Grenola, Kans.
Songer, Lee Private	Mrs. J. A. Songer, mother, RFD 4, Box 101 Neodesha, Kans.
Stockton, Floyd O. Private	Mrs. Florence E. Stockton, mother, 1105 N. Washington Ave., Wellington, Kans.
Testerman, Elmer W. Private	Mrs. Bessie M. Franson, mother, Clay Center, Kans.
Welty, Charles Private	Mr. Charles Welty, father, 1828 High St., St. Joseph, Mo.

SANITARY DETACHMENT

Read, Lathrop B., Jr. Sergeant	Mr. L. B. Read, father, 445 Tenn. St., Lawrence, Kans.
McLeod, Alvin C. Pvt. 1cl.	Mr. Dan McLeod, father, Washington, Kans.
Van DeWalker, Earl G. Pvt. 1cl.	Dr. J. W. Van De Walker, father, Washington, Kans.
Wright, Paul C. Pvt. 1cl.	Mr. J. R. Wright, father, Washington, Kans.
Bonar, Verlin E. Private	Mr. D. C. Bonar, father, Washington, Kans.
Bonesteel, Guy M. Private	Mr. Bert Bonesteel, father, Haddam, Kans.

NAME AND RANK	EMERGENCY ADDRESS
Combs, George M. Private	Mr. George Combs, father, RFD 4, Washington, Kans.
Gray, Robert C. Private	Mr. James Gray, father, Washington, Kans.
King, Fred E. Private	Mrs. E. W. King, mother, Washington, Kans.
Philbrook, Merell F. Private	Mr. C. H. Philbrook, father, Washington, Kans.
Rose, Charles Private	Mr. J. B. Rose, father, RFD 1, Louisiana, Mo.
Rutherford, John L. Private	Mr. Thomas Rutherford, Sr., father, Rose, Ia.
Cummings, Charles C. Sergeant	Mrs. Hattie Cummings, mother, 912 S. 14th St., St. Joseph, Mo.
Pullem, Emerald A. Corporal	Mrs. L. W. Mullemux, sister, Tuny, Mo.
Shannon, Garland E. Horseshoer	Mr. G. C. Shannon, father, Route 1, Bogard, Mo.
Judkins, Carl Mechanic	Mrs. Albert Judkins, mother, 316 West Scott St., St. Joseph, Mo.
Barnes, Eddie A. Cook	Mr. J. H. Barnes, father, RR 5, St. Joseph, Mo.
Douglass, John J. Wagoner	Mrs. Anna Douglass, mother, Steel, Mo.
Green, William Wagoner	Mr. E. P. Green, Albany, Mo.
Jackson, William W. Wagoner	Mr. W. R. Jackson, father, Collins, Mo.
Johnson, Harold F. Wagoner	Mrs. Mattie Krucock, mother, Forest City, Ia.
Knox, Fred Wagoner	Mr. John Knox, father, Harrisburg, Mo.
Mountain, Delbert Wagoner	Mr. John Mountain, brother, Kirksville, Mo.
Oglevie, Loyd V. Wagoner	Mr. Louis B. Oglevie, father, Burr Oak, Kans.
Potter, Ray Wagoner	Mrs. Sadie Potter, mother, W. Harrison St., Kirksville, Mo.
Vendel, Claude W. Wagoner	Mr. William A. Vendel, father, Oskaloosa, Kans.
Williams, Russel H. Wagoner	Mrs. H. H. Williams, mother, Chapman, Kans.
Williams, Forrest H. Wagoner	Mr. H. H. Williams, father, Chapman, Kans.
Denton, Samuel R. Wagoner	Mrs. Given Denton, wife, Kirksville, Mo.
Wilson, Lorn T. Pvt. 1cl.	Mrs. Hazel McEchern, sister, Perth, Mo.
Carter, Charley Private	Mrs. Maggie Carter, mother, Hatfield, Mo.
Cooper, Noah Private	Mr. John Murphy, step-father, Laclede, Mo.
Dowell, George W. Private	Mr. E. W. Dowell, father, RFD 1, Avalon, Mo.
Hansen, Martin Private	Mr. John E. Hansen, father, Mentor, Minn.
Huck, Casper Private	Mr. George Huck, father, Youngstown, N. D.
Kearn, Earl R. Private	Mr. Emmit Kearn, father, Council Grove, Kans.
Myers, Oscar L. Private	Mrs. L. Meyers, mother, RR 1, Leavenworth, Kans.
Green, William Private	E. P. Green, uncle, Albany, Mo.

ORDNANCE

Burke, William R. Private	Mr. W. J. Burke, father, 802 Olive St., Trenton, Mo.
Shea, Daniel B. Private	Mrs. George Shea, mother, Plattsburg, Mo.

DETACHED SERVICE TO SUPPLY COMPANY

J. W. Frazier, 2nd Lt.	Mrs. C. E. Yingling, mother, Lexington, Mo.

HEADQUARTERS DETACHMENT, 2nd BATTALION, 139th INFANTRY

NAME AND RANK	EMERGENCY ADDRESS
James E. Rieger, Major	Mrs. Alma Rieger, Kirksville, Mo.
Charles A. Lusk, Captain	Mrs. Hattie Lusk, Butler, Mo.
Arthur A. Axline, 1st Lt.	Mrs. Leah A. Axline, Bethany, Mo.
Arthur F. Amick, 1st Lt.	Mrs. A. F. Amick, Loup City, Neb., Box 505.
John F. Coffman, 1st Lt.	Mrs. Elizabeth G. Coffman, Marion, Kans.
Otto L. H. Hine, 1st Lt.	T. S. Hine, Muskogee, Okla.
McCutchen, Robert J. Reg. Sup. Sgt.	Mrs. Anna McCutchen, 614 Angelique St., St. Joseph, Mo.
Allen, William A. Bn. Sgt. Major	D. C. Allen, Topeka, Kans.
Dreyer, Arthur N. Sergeant	Mrs. Roy Lewis, Home City, Kans.
Myers, Lee J. Sergeant	Charles E. Myers, Coffeyville, Kans., RFD 1.
Dietrich, Joseph H. Corporal	Mr. H. R. Dietrich, Utica, Mo.
Dennison, Charles Corporal	J. A. Dennison, 1726 Fulton Ave., Hannibal, Mo.
Miller, Karl D. Corporal	Mrs. Catherine Miller, 1415 Clay St., Topeka, Kans.
Rettig, Fred W. Corporal	F. F. Rettig, 1006 5th Ave., Oswego, Kans.
Daubenspeck, George	A. F. Daubenspeck, Petroleum, West Va.
Hayes, Perry F. Horseshoer	Samuel G. Hayes, Tina, Mo.
Murry, Andrew A. Mechanic	Mary E. Allen, Kensington, Kans.
Billington, Allen Cook	Mattie Billington, Kewanee, Mo.
Albrecht, Edmond C. Wagoner	Frank Albrecht, Norborne, Mo.
Blake, Halcolm L. Wagoner	Clara R. Blake, 812 Brooks Ave., Topeka, Kans.
Burnam, William M. Wagoner	Tom Harding, McLouth, Kans.
Chaney, David Wagoner	Jacob Chaney, Tarkio, Mo.
Doramus, Elmer C. Wagoner	C. T. Doramus, Perth, Kans.
Denning, Leonard C. Wagoner	Dave Denning, Oskaloosa, Kans.
Fennell, Jesse A. Wagoner	James Fennell, Schaler, Ia.
Fleming, Thomas H. Wagoner	John Fleming, Lake Wilson, Minn. RFD 1.
Hurst, Millard Wagoner	John Hurst, Rogersville, Mo.
Hass, John Wagoner	George Hass, McClusky, N. Dak.
Jorgenson, Albert W. Wagoner	P. M. Jorgenson, Lonstrap, Denmark.
King, Joseph F. Wagoner	Mrs. James King, Collis, Minn. RFD 1.
Long, William N. Wagoner	G. H. Long, Oxford, Kans.
McNeal, Joe Wagoner	W. A. McNeal, Tarkio, Mo.
Pryczynski, John L. Wagoner	Mary Pryczynski, 1029 East Main St., Decatur, Ill.
Ross, William Wagoner	Mrs. Ella Bacon, Stanberry, Mo.
Stebbins, Chaucey Wagoner	Mrs. D. H. McNeal, Tarkio, Mo.
Stoltz, George W. Wagoner	G. W. Stoltz, Eldorado, Kans.
Smith, Isaac R. Wagoner	L. J. Smith, Florence, Kans.
Welch, Henry C. Wagoner	W. Welch, Havana, Kans., Box 117.
Baird, Hoyt Pvt. 1cl.	Mrs. Jennie E. Baird, 108 N. 8th St., Herington, Kans.
Dunmire, Joseph A. Pvt. 1cl.	Geo. Dunmire, Valley Center, Kans.
French, Lawrence L. Pvt. 1cl.	B. F. French, 132 W. 4th St., Trenton, Mo.
Fetrow, Ward W. Pvt. 1cl.	G. D. Fetrow, Haddam, Kans.

NAME AND RANK	EMERGENCY ADDRESS
Grafford, James A. Pvt 1cl.	Henry Harrison Grafford, 808 E. Monroe St., Mexico, Mo.
Gore, Paul W. Pvt. 1cl.	W. T. Gore, Hannibal, Mo., RR 4.
Myers, William C. Pvt. 1cl.	William M. Myers, 1415 Byers Ave., Joplin, Mo.
Black, Jessoe Private	Mrs. Chas. Dunn, Caruthersville, Mo.
Carter, Alfred E. Private	Mrs. Ella Hudson, Stewartsville, Mo.
Chesnut, Raymond L. Private	Henry Chesnut, Linn, Kans.
Doty, James T. Private	James T. Doty, 122 N. Ninth St., Louisiana, Mo.
Gerloch, Philip Private	A. G. Gerloch, Crown Point, Ind.
Garrett, Ralph L. Private	Mrs. Eddie Garrett, 725 W. 4th St., Sedalia, Mo.
Kelly, Newton B. Private	Rev. N. B. Kelly, Washington, Kans.
Laird, Thomas E. Private	Mrs. Elizabeth E. Laird, Halliday, Ark.
McMullin, Cecil O. Private	Alice J. McMullin, 1515 E. 9th St., Trenton, Mo.
McGrillen, James P. Private	Hugh A. McGrillen, Quinville Terrace, Down, Ireland.
McAuliffe, Joseph F. Private	Michael McAuliffe, 415 E. 8th St., Trenton, Mo.
Mansfield, Harry N. Private	Harry Mansfield, Des Moines, Ia., care Chicago-Great Western R. R.
Nolen, Henry Private	Henry Nolen, Hayti, Mo.
Oliver, Laben C. Private	Luther Oliver, New Hampton, Mo.
Quiett, William E. Private	C. E. Quiett, Ozawkie, Kans.
Stoffle, Herbert F. Private	W. L. Stoffle, Morrowville, Kans.
Shuck, John W. H. Private	Mrs. Tennie Shuck, 3903 Washington Ave., St. Louis, Mo.
Turner, James A. Private	C. D. Turner, Placerville, Cal.
Trower, Marvin, Private	A. L. Trower, 500 Douglas St., Louisiana, Mo.
VanDoren, Chester G. Private	Mrs. E. E. VanDoren, 1001 Mulberry St., Abilene, Kans.
Wyatt, John O. Private	G. W. Wyatt, Green City, Mo.

ATTACHED 110TH F. S. BN.

NAME AND RANK	EMERGENCY ADDRESS
Masterson, William F. 1cl. Sgt.	Mrs. W. F. Masterson, 2115 Linwood Blvd., Kansas City, Mo.
Momyer, Harry H. Sergeant	Geo. R. Momyer, Morte Vista, Colo.
Shawhaw, Harold R. Corporal	Mrs. E. B. Shawhaw, 321 10th West, Hutchinson, Kans.
Miller, William B. Corporal	Mrs. W. H. Miller, 316 E. Jackson St., Chillicothe, Mo.
Anderson, William H. Corporal	Mrs. W. H. Anderson, 1325 Dillon St., St. Louis, Mo.
Arnold, Claude A. Pvt. 1cl.	T. E. Arnold, 16 and Jefferson, Charleston, Ill.
Jones, John D. Pvt. 1cl.	J. H. Jones, 1211 South Main, Wichita, Kans.
Ragsdale, Lawrence E. Pvt. 1cl.	E. E. Ragsdale, 1228 Cook St., Denver, Colo.
Peck, Ralph F. Pvt. 1cl.	A. R. Stahly, 713 7th East Hutchinson, Kans.
Spath, Julius T. Pvt. 1cl.	Mrs. M. Spath, 5314 Winona Ave., Chicago, Ill.
Delmas, Edward F. Private	Mrs. Chmelik, 5039 Atgen Ave., Cicero, Ill.
Schwenker, William J. Private	Mrs. H. Schwenker, 209 S. Bassett, Madison, Wis.

ROSTER OF 110th FIELD SIGNAL BATTALION, ATTACHED TO HEADQUARTERS COMPANY

Name and Rank	Emergency Address
Kernal, Delbert L. Sgt. 1cl.	S. A. Kernal, father, 302 S. 11th St., Monmouth, Ill.
Hutchinson, Roland R. Sergeant	Mrs. J. G. Shacklett, mother, 410 Ellis Ave., Wichita, Kans.
Davis, Curtis E. Sergeant	William B. Davis, father, Shellburn, Ind.
Moore, Carl E. Sergeant	Mrs. Ada L. Moore, mother, 511 South St., Iola, Kans.
Channell, Floyd V. Sergeant	J. W. Channell, father, Weatherby, Mo.
Thompson, William C. Corporal	Mrs. H. A. Stege, mother, 3518 Illinois Ave., St. Louis, Mo.
Magie, Albert E. Corporal	Mr. C. N. Magie, father, Healy; Kans.
Halley, James W. Corporal	H. W. Halley, father, 123 E. Clarke St., Hutchinson, Kans.
Richards, Paul J. Acting Corporal	Mrs. P. J. Richards, wife, 7403 Wise Ave., St. Louis, Mo.
Ash, Carl Pvt. 1cl.	Mrs. Nettie Ash, mother, Wellington, Kans., 606 N. B St.
Dreher, Walter F. Pvt. 1cl.	Mrs. Caroline M. Dreher, mother, 3641 Cass Ave., St. Louis, Mo.
Hoppe, Eugene A. Pvt. 1cl.	Mr. Fred A. Hoppe, father, Syracuse, Kans.
Holt, Newman H. Pvt. 1cl.	Mr. R. H. Holt, father, Clay, Ky.
Hauser, Frank Pvt. 1cl.	John H. Hauser, father, 1318 N. Monroe St., N. Topeka, Kans.

Name and Rank	Emergency Address
Kitson, William T. Pvt. 1cl.	Mrs. Nancy Kitson, grandmother, 923 A So. Sarah St., St. Louis, Mo.
Mahoney, Erwin J. Pvt. 1cl.	Mr. John A. Mahoney, father, 1420 Sherwin Ave., Chicago, Ill.
Moore, Harry C. Pvt. 1cl.	Mr. Robert B. Moore, father, 219 N. Market St., Wichita, Kans.
Nutter, Earl I. Pvt. 1cl.	I. L. Nutter, father, Middletown, Mo.
Shaughnessy, George J. Pvt. 1cl.	Mrs. E. Shaughnessy, mother, 22 Leburnum Cresent, Rochester, N. Y.
Turner, Claude D. Pvt. 1cl.	Mrs. Myrtle Teel, sister, RFD 4, Dexter, Mo.
McDonald, Patrick F. Pvt. 1cl.	Mrs. E. H. McDonald, mother, 602 W. Howard St., Pontiac, Ill.
Boucek, William Private	Lena Boucek, mother, Ada, Kans.
Lang, Ferdinand B. Private	Mrs. F. B. Lang, wife, Kimmswick, Mo., RFD 1.
Oliver, John L. Private	Mrs. Anna Oliver, mother, 5320 Theodosia Ave., St. Louis, Mo.
Yager, Leslie Private	Mrs. Leslie Yager, wife, 9 St. and 2nd Ave., Nebraska City, Neb.
Zimmerman, Henry W. Private	Mrs. William Zimmerman, mother, Enterprise, Kans.

HEADQUARTERS DETACHMENT, 3rd BATTALION, 139th INFANTRY

Name and Rank	Emergency Address
William D. Stepp, Major USNG	Mrs. Mabel Stepp, wife, 820 Custer St., Trenton, Mo.
John F. Kaster, 1st Lt. Adjutant USNG	Dr. J. P. Kaster, father, 616 Madison St., Topeka, Kans.
Edwin V. Burkholder, USNG 1st Lt.	Sam Burkholder, father, Marion, Kans.
Halley A. Smith 1st Lt. MRC	Charles H. Smith, father, Antioch, Ill.
Roy H. Heil, 1st Lt. DCNG	Mrs. Susan Heil, mother, 1273 Garfield Ave., Topeka, Kans.
Lewis, Lon A. Bn. Sgt. Major	Mrs. R. B. Lewis, mother, Rosendale, Mo.
Humphreys, James Corporal	Mrs. Edna Humphreys, wife, Winchester, Kans.
Holley, Francis J. Corporal	Miss Ruth Holley, sister, St. Joseph, Mo.
Hamilton, Lewis B. Corporal	Wood H. Hamilton, father, Gallatin, Mo.
Hainer, Maurice Corporal	Oscar Hainer, father, Wiley, Colo.
Duncan, Robert L. Pvt. 1cl.	Edward L. Duncan, father, Dearborn, Mo.
Freeburne, Clarence L. Pvt. 1cl.	Mrs. Edna Freeburne, wife, Peabody, Kans.
Meyer, Walter C. Pvt. 1cl.	H. L. Meyer, father, Cicero, Kans.
O'Brien, William M. Pvt. 1cl.	Miss Florence O'Brien, sister, 216 Blondran Ave., Keokuk, Ia.
Reed, William J. Pvt. 1cl.	Mr. Sherman W. Reed, father, 405 West 9th St., Newton, Kans.
Rhoads, Marvin E. Pvt. 1cl.	J. M. Rhoads, father, Tucumcari, N. Mex.
Thogmartin, Quincy E. Pvt. 1cl.	Chas. Thogmartin, father, Princeton, Mo.
Adkins, Ira Private	Nathan Adkins, father, Carrollton, Mo.
Dobyns, Louie Private	Joe Dobyns, brother, Percy, Ill.
Hanes, Harry Private	Mrs. William Kohlmpi, mother, Kirksville, Mo.
Koennicke, Paul A. Private	Mrs. Johanna Koennicke, mother, Perham, Minn.
Siegenthal, Albert Private	S. D. Clawson, friend, Peabody, Kans.
Turner, George D. Private	Samuel G. Turner, father, Ludlow, Mo.
Williams, Charles D. Private	John D. Williams, father, 220 N. N. St., Herington, Kans.

FROM SUPPLY COMPANY, 139TH INFANTRY

Name and Rank	Emergency Address
Donnell, Calvin Reg. Sup. Sgt.	Mrs. Myra Andrews, sister, O'Keene, Okla.
Smoot, Charles S. Sergeant	Mrs. S. F. Smoot, mother, 3209 Raleigh St., Denver, Colo.
Egbert, Rollin E. Corporal	Mrs. J. A. White, wife, RFD 7, Newton, Kans.
Amos, Claude L. Mechanic	George W. Amos, father, RFD 4, St. Joseph, Mo.
Elmore, Lester R. Horseshoer	James Elmore, father, RFD 2, Coffeyville, Kans.
Blount, Walter L. Wagoner	Mrs. J. M. Morelock, mother, Peabody, Kans.
Brake, Carey G. Wagoner	Mrs. Sarah Brake, mother, 1002½ East 8th St., Topeka, Kans.
Converse, Lloyd F. Wagoner	M. S. Converse, father, Peabody, Kans.
Cooper, Albert E. Wagoner	Mrs. Annie Cooper, mother, Bazaar, Kans.
Douglas, Laverne Wagoner	Mrs. Louis Douglas, mother, 416 E. Spruce St., Herington, Kans.
Johns, Claude I. Wagoner	Elizabeth Traub, friend, 1601 Mass St., St. Joseph, Mo.
Maxwell, Joseph L. Wagoner	Frank Maxwell, father, Burlington Jct., Mo.
McClure, Norvie J. Wagoner	Jennie McClure, mother, Walton, Kans.
Pauls, Rudolph Wagoner	John Pauls, father, Hillsboro, Kans.
Potter, Floyd Wagoner	J. M. Potter, father, Cottonwood Falls, Kans.
Potter, Kent B. Wagoner	J. M. Potter, father, Cottonwood Falls, Kans.
Powell, Amos Wagoner	Cora Cox, sister, Gentry, Mo.
Smith, Charles L. Wagoner	Mr. J. B. Smith, father, 432 West 12th St., Junction City, Kans.
Snodgrass, George Wagoner	Mrs. Thomas Buckles, mother, Nodaway, Mo.
Snodgrass, Joseph M. Wagoner	Adeline Buckles, mother, Nodaway, Mo.
Snyder, Carrol D. Wagoner	Mrs. C. E. Dickson, friend, Wellington, Kans.
Wampler, Charles Wagoner	W. M. Wampler, father, Guthrie, Okla.
Graff, Walter A. Wagoner	Mrs. Caroline Graff, mother, Wooldridge, Mo.

Name and Rank		Emergency Address
Persson, Linus	Private	Iver Edholm, brother, Braddock, N. Dak.
Reisenauer, Wendel	Private	John M. Reisenauer, father, 2nd St. and 7th Ave., Mandan, N. Dak.
Walker, Oliver	Wagoner	Mrs. Hattie Gillwater, sister, Forbes, Mo.

ATTACHED ORDNANCE MEN

Haldeman, Oscar	Pvt. 1cl.	F. C. Haldeman, brother, Hideman, Calif.
Collier, John W.	Pvt. 1cl.	Luther Collier, father, 603 E. 8th St., Trenton, Mo.

SANITARY DETACHMENT

Macleod, Percy A.	Sergeant	A. D. Macleod, father, Washington, Kans.
Erps, Harry R.	Pvt. 1cl.	Mrs. Elizabeth Erps, mother, Morrowville, Kans.
Fuhrken, Arnold C.	Pvt. 1cl.	William Fuhrken, father, Washington, Kans.
Jackson, Forrest,	Pvt. 1cl.	J. W. Jackson, father, 524 North Third St., Louisiana, Mo.
Lull, Elmer	Pvt. 1cl.	V. S. Lull, father, Haddam, Kans.
Newkirk, Urie	Pvt. 1cl.	H. J. Newkirk, father, 1220 Shanklin Ave., Trenton, Mo.
Mazanec, William	Private	Joe Mazanec, father, Louisiana, Mo.
Owens, Eugene C.	Private	Mrs. L. B. Owens, mother, RFD 6, Leavenworth, Kans.

Tilton, Jettie F.	Private	Mrs. Nannie Tilton, mother, 1021 Iowa St., Louisiana, Mo.
Whetstine, Sylvester	Private	E. J. Whetstine, father, Washington, Kans.
Wood, Oliver S.	Private	J. W. Wood, father, Weskin, Kans.

FIELD SIGNAL MEN ATTACHED

Johnston, Richard	Sergeant 1cl.	Mrs. A. J. Hadley, mother, 3722 Wayne, Kansas City, Mo.
Priest, Howard O.	Sergeant	Mrs. Fred L. Priest, mother, 1009 Union St., Emporia, Kans.
Schomberg, Otto Joseph	Corporal	
Waldron, Hugh Wilbur	Corporal	Mrs. J. M. Waldron, mother, 1134 S. Seneca, Wichita, Kans.
Heasty, Kearns W.	Pvt. 1cl.	Mrs. R. M. Heasty, mother, 818 N. Popular, Wellington, Kans.
Howell, Lloyd S.	Pvt. 1cl.	Mrs. H. B. Howell, mother, 108 Washington St., Chillicothe, Mo.
Martin, Hillery R.	Pvt. 1cl.	Mrs. Mary E. Teague, mother, Sterling, Kans.
Zeiber, Warren	Pvt. 1cl.	W. M. Zeiber, father, Pawnee Rock, Kans.
Wahl, Roy W.	Pvt. 1cl.	Mrs. A. H. Wahl, mother, Washburn, N. D.
Lovett, Ernest R.	Private	Mrs. S. H. Lovett, mother, Miles City, Mont.
Mann, Walter T.	Private	Mrs. Anna Mann, wife, 217 E. Maryland St., Evansville, Ind.
Weddle, Cecil M.	Private	Mrs. H. T. Weddle, mother, Reserve, Kans.

ROSTER OF MEN OF 110th SIGNAL BATTALION

Name and Rank		Emergency Address
Anderson, Erie E.	Sgt. 1cl.	Mr. A. E. Anderson, father, 408 N. Chestnut, Iola, Kans.
Strange, Russel E.	Sergeant	Mrs. Jessie L. Strange, mother, Rogersville, Mo.
Adams, Charles H.	Corporal	Mrs. Howard B. Adams, mother, Iola, Kans.
Buchanan, Glyn	Corporal	Mrs. Lizzie A. Buchanan, mother, Dexter, Mo.
Lindquist, Hjalmer H.	Corporal	Mrs. Claus J. Lindquist, mother, Wichita, Kans.
Davis, Isaac E.	Private	Mrs. Chas. W. Davis, mother, Homestead, Penn.

Name and Rank		Emergency Address
Dizmang, Roy L.	Private	Mrs. Drusie E. Dizmang, mother, Doniphan, Mo.
Endsley, Robert W.	Private	Mrs. William L. Oliver, mother, Kansas City, Mo.
Johnston, Valentine	Private	Mr. John McDonald, father, Salt Lake City, Utah.
Montgomery, Everett L.	Private	Mrs. Mattie Montgomery, mother, Seattle, Wash.
Snyder, Dean F.	Private	W. F. Snyder, father, 1109 Mansfield, Winfield, Kans.
Zenk, John A.	Private	Mrs. Anna Zenk, mother, Gary, Ind.

ROSTER OF CASUALS

Name and Rank		Emergency Address
Gibson, Hugh J.	Sergeant	Anne Jane Gibson, mother, Mound City, Mo.
Havens, William P.	Sergeant	W. S. Havens, father, 314 S. Gregory St., Carthage, Mo.
Stovall, Woodson,	Private	Mrs. W. E. Stovall, wife, 1407 Main St., St. Joseph, Mo.
England, Raymond D.	Private	Mrs. Ida England, 2058 N. Thompson, Kansas City, Kans.
Smith, William R.	Private	Mr. B. J. Smith, father, Chattahoochee, Ga.
Taylor, Willard R.	Private	Mrs. C. L. Carson, mother, 328 N. Francis, Carthage, Mo.
Gilliland, David E.	Private	E. H. Gilliland, father, Coffeyville, Kans.
Ronde, Paul,	Private	Rasmus Ronde, Sharon, N. Dak.
Peterson, Carl E.	Private	Charles O. Munson, uncle, Jct. City, Kans.
Darnell, William B.	Private	Mr. J. L. Darnell, father, Albertville, Ala.
Staley, Henry H.	Private	Mrs. Sophia Arnbrester, mother, Kiowa, Tex.
Sterling, Joseph A.	Private	Mrs. J. A. Elliott, mother, Dillon, Kans.
Smith, Joseph E.	Private	Mrs. Frank McCall, mother, Mansfield, Ill.
Edens, Harry H.	Private	Mr. W. T. Edens, father, Council Grove, Kans.
Reese, Hamilton G.	Private	Herberand Reese, father, Edinburg, N. Dak.
Sevier, Ernest	Private	Mrs. Ernest Sevier, wife, Coffeyville, Kans.

Name and Rank		Emergency Address
Packstein, Conrad A.	Private	Henry Packstein, father, 1028 Concert St., Keokuk, Ia.
Swift, Claud J.	Private	Mrs. S. H. Swift, mother, 909 E. Lincoln St., Wellington, Kans.
Veeder, Howard C.	Private	Mrs. C. H. Veeder, mother, Sauk Centre, Minn.
Banghart, Marl R.	Private	Mrs. Alice Banghart, mother, Oxford, Kans.
Doyle, Joseph	Private	Mrs. J. O. Doyle, mother, Lamoure, N. Dak.
Lowe, Charles	Corporal	Mrs. Charles Lowe, wife, 1420 Clay St., Chillicothe, Mo.
Kneer, Clare S.	Pvt. 1cl.	Mrs. C. S. Kneer, wife, Abilene, Kans.
Wikus, Julius L.	Corporal	G. A. Schmersey, cousin, Marion, Kans.
Carter, James J.	Pvt. 1cl.	Mrs. L. B. Carter, mother, Iatan, Mo.
Rogers, Clyde J.	Private	W. C. Rogers, father, Nortonville, Kans.
Lowe, Leroy,	Pvt. 1cl.	A. H. Lowe, father, Sampsel, Mo., RFD 7.
Ruby, Glen O.	Private	Mrs. Arilla Ruby, mother, Oskaloosa, Ia.
Henson, John C.	Private	Fred Henson, brother, Balaton, Minn.
Pugh, Guy	Private	Mrs. Joe Mayer, mother, 421 W. 13th St., Trenton, Mo.
Row, Earl	Private	Mrs. W. Row, mother, Walhalla, N. Dak.
Rich, Clarence	Private	J. A. Beecher, guardian, Wayne, Kans.
Smith, Alden	Private	

FIELD AND STAFF

These hard-looking citizens were known as the "Field and Staff." They were fairly good looking men in less strenuous times.

CASUALS FIRST BATTALION

Sergeant		Edward Miller	E	Charles L. Mapes	E	Willis Ira Johnson	F
Frank J. Kilfoyle	M	Russell Aye	I	Hans E. Lien	Hq.	Carl G. Zeaske	M
Privates:		Leo Takes	F	James Conley	E	J. W. Peterson	Hq.
Frank Petry	H	Owen Nowland	H	Clarence Bowen	E	Knud Knudson	M.G.
Ole Sewell	K	A. Fuller	E	Roy H. Epley	E	T. H. Thompson	I
Bryan Salisbury,	M	C. P. Olmstead	F	Bastiaan J. Wolters	G	Arley Dwight	E
Olie Robinson	F	F. O. Ramey	Hq.	Ralph H. Viola	H	David R. James	H
Clifford Phillips	E	Norman S. Lowell	Hq.	Howard D. Stechoffer	I	Ralph E. Jones	H
Henry Minor	E	M. A. Tantow	F	Doyle Hooper	H	James Allen	I
Paul E. Mentzer	E	A. Pierson	Hq.	John Myres	M.G.	Henry W. Black	I
Lee Kerr	E	Wesley Coleman	Hq.	L. E. Dial	G	Isom W. Ward	I
Elwood Leach	E	J. M. Raisch	M.G.	John B. Howery	E	Harry B. Cookston	F
Corporals:		J. Lien	M.G.	John A. Stringham	H	Tracy Logan	E
Edward Blockberger	E	C. E. Londin	E	A. S. Stone	H	Harry A. Montague	F
Jess Scott	E	H. H. Palmer	F				

FIRST ASSIGNMENT OF OFFICERS

Pursuant to the provisions of G. O. 10 of the 35th Div. dated Oct. 1st, 1917, the following assignment of officers was made.

Col. John D. McNeely
Lt. Col. Alex A. Sharp

Other officers are assigned as follows:

1st Battalion
Major:
 C. C. MacDonald (Commanding)
 Baxter D. McLain (Attached)
1st Lieutenant:
 Donald M. MacDonald (Adj.)

2nd Battalion
Major:
 Albert H. Krause (Commanding)
 James E. Rieger (Att.)
1st Lieutenant:
 Hugh B. Dudley (Adj.)

3rd Battalion
Major:
 William D. Stepp (Comm.)
 Thomas R. Campbell (Att.)
1st Lieutenant:
 James H. McCord (Adj.)

Headquarters Co.
Captain:
 John J. Haskell (Com.)
 Walter M. Mann (Reg. Adj.)
1st Lieutenant:
 Paul C. Bodkin
 Guss B. Ridge
2nd Lieutenant:
 George J. Woodward
 Arthur F. Amick
 Earl G. Pitts

Supply Company
Captains:
 Charles J. Hall (Supply Officer)
 James F. Going (Att.)
1st Lieutenant:
 John B. Sharp

Machine Gun Company
Captains:
 W. F. Logan (Com.)
 Peyton (Att.)
1st Lieutenants:
 Richard B. Wilson
 Walter A. Wood
2nd Lieutenants:
 Louis C. Northrup
 George J. Hunt
 Joseph L. Darr

A Company
Captains:
 Thomas E. Herridge (Com.)
 Edgar H. Dale (Att.)
1st Lieutenants:
 Blanton V. Bentley
 M. H. Hall
2nd Lieutenants:
 Homer Yale
 Charles Barndolar

B Company
Captains:
 William B. Hitchcock (Com.)
 Guy N. Walling (Att.)
1st Lieutenants:
 William A. Smith
 Victor Malloure
2nd Lieutenants:
 Clinton Kanaga
 Harry Malloure

C Company
Captains:
 Jasper N. Gates (Com.)
 William H. Perrigo (Att.)
1st Lieutenants:
 Samuel A. Daugherty
 Raymond W. Cater
2nd Lieutenants:
 Charles O. Hall
 John D. Heiny

D Company
Captains:
 William C. Williamson (Com.)
 George W. Wark (Att.)
1st Lieutenants:
 Angus J. Nicholson
 Gus. S. Gehlbach
2nd Lieutenants:
 Jesse H. Wilson
 Homer B. Loman

E Company
Captains:
 Karl C. Bostwick (Com.)
 Robert W. Lindenstruth (Att.)
1st Lieutenants:
 Paul C. Radford
 William McDonald
2nd Lieutenants:
 Humphrey Biddle
 James W. Paynter

F Company
Captains:
 Irving A. Otten (Com.)
 Asbury Roberts (Att.)
1st Lieutenants:
 Charles W. Clark
 William E. Galligan
2nd Lieutenant:
 George H. Klinkerfuss

G Company
Captains:
 Randall Wilson (Com.)
 Arthur W. Snyder (Att.)
1st Lieutenants:
 Edward Hanby
 Arthur A. Axline
2nd Lieutenants:
 Carlyle Wilson

H Company

Captains:
Joseph H. McQueen (Com.)
Charles H. Brown (Att.)

1st Lieutenants:
John W. McManigal
Brown Dyer

2nd Lieutenants:
Ralph F. Lucier
Ralph H. Cox

I Company

Captains:
A. M. Ellett (Com.)
James B. Garrett (Att.)

1st Lieutenants:
Matthew Guilfoyle
Robert W. Roberts

2nd Lieutenants:
Ralph W. Martin
Ross Diehl

K Company

Captains:
John E. Wells (Com.)
Howard M. Randall (Att.)

1st Lieutenants:
George C. Brewster
Coburn Hull

2nd Lieutenants:
John F. Kaster
W. L. Crockett

L Company

Captains:
Ray W. Carter (Com.)
Thomas L. Crow (Att.)

1st Lieutenants:
Asa R. Black
Charles E. Munn

2nd Lieutenants:
William H. Haupt
Moss Fomet

M Company

Captains:
Charles E. Holt (Com.)
George L. Allison (Att.)

1st Lieutenants:
Edvin V. Burkholder
George T. Worthen

2nd Lieutenants:
Walter C. Dickey
William R. Carpenter

Medical Officers

Major Henry D. Smith (Com.)
Major G. O. Cuppaidge (Att.)

Captains:
George W. Belshe
Charles P. Lewellen

1st Lieutenants:
George M. Boteler
Herbert M. Webb
John F. Coffman
A. Eugene Harrison

Dental Surgeons

1st Lieutenants:
Robert H. Heil
Forrest Kutz
James A. Taylor
Walter Cronkite

Chaplains

1st Lieutenant:
Myron Collins

ROSTER OF OFFICERS, 139TH INFANTRY, FEBRUARY 28TH, 1919

FIELD AND STAFF

Colonel Carl L. Ristine, Commanding Regiment

Lieutenant Colonel:
Major Robert C. Heyward, Com. 3rd Battalion
Major William C. Williamson, Com. 2nd Battalion

Major:

Captains:
Angus J. Nicholson, Personnel Adjutant
Hugh B. Dudley, Adjutant, on leave
Matthew Guilfoyle, Operations Officer
John D. Heiny, Intelligence Officer, on leave

1st Lieutenants:
Lewis E. Hansen, Adjutant 1st Battalion
William J. Oakes, Adjutant 2nd Battalion
Coburn Hull, Adjutant 3rd Battalion
Charles W. Barndollar, Int. Officer—1st Battalion

2nd Lieutenants:
Andrew G. Osborn, Int. Officer 2nd Bn—DS
2nd Army Hq.
Thomas R. Donoghue, Int. Officer, 3rd Bn.

1st Lieutenants:
Myron S. Collins, Chaplain, on leave
William V. Meredith, Chaplain, 2nd Bn.
Daniel Lane, Chaplain, 3rd Bn. DS-School.
Jesse W. Wilson, Asst. Operations Officer

Regiment at Large

2nd Lieutenant:
Earl M. Robertson, Regimental Gas Officer.

Captain:
James B. Garrett (Attached)

Headquarters Company

Captain:
Ralph F. Lucier, Commanding Co.

1st Lieutenants:
R. E. Littleton
Edward S. Carmack, Acting Regt. Adjutant.

2nd Lieutenants:
Albert D. Pitts
H. L. Brown

Supply Company

Captain:
Charles J. Hall, Regt. Supply Officer

1st Lieutenants:
Harry E. Malloure
Edwin V. Burkholder, DS-French University
Olin Ruth

2nd Lieutenant:
John L. Creech, DS-French University.

Machine Gun Company
Captain:
Albert E. Cooper, Com. company
2nd Lieutenants:
Roy C. Ireland
Edward Ennis
Forrest T. Sark
Attached.
2nd Lieutenant:
Wilford D. Mills (Assigned to regiment)

A Company
Captain:
Ross Diehl, On leave
1st Lieutenant:
Edward Johnson Commanding company
2nd Lieutenants:
George S. Downing
Harry Ross

B Company
Captain William A. Smith, Commanding company
1st Lieutenants:
Paul A. Cannady, Sick in Base Hospital 91
Charles F. Fowler
2nd Lieutenants:
William C. Winter
Gordon K. Goltz, Town Major-Vignot

C Company
Captain Raymond W. Cater, Commanding 1st Bn.
1st Lieutenants:
George L. Prindle
Frank L. Armistead, Commanding Company
George H. Stephens, On leave
2nd Lieutenants:
Joseph M. Forsthove
Attached
Richard P. McDonald, Sick in Base Hospital No. 91.

D Company
Captain Gus S. Gehlbach, Commanding company
1st Lieutenant:
Thurston J. Morris, SD-Division Football Team
2nd Lieutenants:
Lawrence L. O'Kelley, On leave
Ralph C. Davis
James D. Gillespie

E Company
Captain George H. Klinkerfuss, on leave
1st Lieutenants:
Herbert C. Smith, Commanding company
James D. Martin
2nd Lieutenants:
Alvin G. Steier
Clarence B. Connell

F Company
Captain Homer B. Loman, Commanding company
1st Lieutenants:
John A. Hoffman
Byrl J. Hilt
2nd Lieutenants:
Norwood K. Lillybridge
Glen W. Davis

G Company
Captain Jesse D. Clarke, Sick in hospital
1st Lieutenants:
George T. Worthen, Commanding company
Edward Rode
Homer Yale, Sick in Field Hospital
Ralph D. Henderson
2nd Lieutenant:
Noah W. Wagnon, Town Major-Euville

H Company
Captain Rodney J. Ludlow, Commanding company
1st Lieutenants:
William S. Gray
Edward S. Axline
2nd Lieutenants:
Donald A. Eskridge
Charles F. Lynch

I Company
Captain Ralph W. Martin, Commanding company
1st Lieutenants:
Eugene A. Hirsch, Prison Officer
William D. Turnbull
2nd Lieutenant:
Robert L. Lovern

K Company
Captain Marcus J. Morgan, Commanding company
1st Lieutenants:
William H. Ellenburg
Oliver F. Crockett, on leave
Charles M. Flynn
Frederick E. Swanson, Regt. Inst. of Schools
Truman O. Pooler
Burr A. Davidson
Homer J. Henney, DS-French University
2nd Lieutenants:
James M. Brown, Sick in Base Hospital No. 91
Stanislaus Lafond, Regt. Billeting Officer.

L Company
Captain Charles Haftle, Commanding company
1st Lieutenants:
George Walters
Spencer Otis, Jr.
2nd Lieutenants:
Lonnie N. Young
George A. Gleason

M Company
Captain John E. Ray, Commanding company
1st Lieutenants:
William R. Carpenter, on leave
Walter E. Ruch
Elvin L. McCormick
Howard N. Frizzell, DS-Hq. 35th Div.
2nd Lieutenants:
Thomas H. MacMahon
Isaac Morrison

Sanitary Detachment
Major Henry D. Smith, Commanding Detachment
Captain Earle F. Ristine, Regt. Sanitary Officer.
1st Lieutenants:
Richard P. Lewis
Halley A. Smith
Paul C. Rohde
John F. Coffman, SD-Division Football Team.
Otto L. H. Hine (D.C.)
Loos E. Wiley (D.C.)
Daniel L. Taylor (D.C.) Sick in Field Hospital.
Warren S. Whittle (D.C.)

WINNING A COMPETITION

Headquarters 35th Division
American Expeditionary Forces
21 February, 1919

G-3 MEMORANDUM: Inter-Regimental Competitions.

1. The inter-regimental competitions as prescribed by G-3 Memorandum of 30th January have been completed, and a summary is given below:

(a) Basis of marking:

1) Condition of billets	15
2) Condition of kitchens	15
3) General appearance of officers and men.............	10
4) Condition of transportation and stable management....	15
5) Rendering of courtesies by officers and men..........	10
6) March discipline	5
7) Battalion close order drill competition................	10
8) Company close order drill competition................	10
9) Most effective method of handling athletic hour......	5
10) The best established educational system..............	5

(b) Results of competition, showing standing of various regiments:

No.	137th Infty.	138th Infty.	139th Infty.	140th Infty.	110th Eng..
1	10.95	9.50	12.75	11.50	12.00
2	11.00	9.00	12.00	12.00	11.00
3	8.10	6.37	8.10	7.56	5.75
4	11.00	13.00	13.66	7.00	13.00
5	8.80	7.18	8.67	7.96	6.37
6	4.00	4.00	4.00	4.00	4.00
7	8.50	8.00	9.00	7.00	— —*
8	9.00	8.50	8.50	6.00	— —*
9	3.50	4.00	4.00	3.00	5.00
10	2.50	1.50	2.50	3.00	5.00
Total	77.35	71.05	83.18	69.02	62.12

*Engineers had left divisional area before competition was held.

By command of Brigadier General Dugan:
H. S. HAWKINS
Colonel, General Staff
Chief of Staff

N. HARROWER
Capt., Infty.,
Acting G-3.
To all organisations
Second Army, G-5
IX Corps, G-3
C. G. Officers' Combat Depot, GONDRECOURT.

STEADY OF HEART, BUT SHAKY IN ENGLISH

ADDRESS OF THE FRENCH COMMANDER TO THE MEN OF THE 139TH

Fortress of Vaux
Address to the American Soldiers

The commander of this fortress is happy to wish his most hearty welcome to the American officers, sergeants, corporals and privates, who come and take garrison in this historical fortress and to express to them his feelings of high sympathy and best companionship.

He enjoys himself with the coming of these new companions in arms, glittering of tenacity in purpose and valor, full of clear energy and spirit.

The glorious President, Woodrow Wilson, irresistible champion of justice, pursuing high an ideal, put in the scales with his powerful hand the highest force of liberty in the world to assure the victory of the allied over the savage Huns.

The United States with their wonderful mind of organization, their colossal abilities, their huge supplies, succeeded the wonder of gathering armies like by enchantment, crossing the Atlantic with innumerous battalions and throwing them in the battle field of liberty. It is on that everlasting stream we placed our final triumph, our hope of finishing the utter defeat of the savage enemy whom we are struggling against for more than four years.

The fruitful and generous blood of the American soldiers already spread in the front of Chateau Thierry, Saint Mihiel, Verdun and Argonne, the splendid success of the Yanks obtained and that history had already been engraved on bronze tablets, are a certain warranty of which we can hope from them in future days.

The same generous passions, the same love of peace built on right, the same respect of the will of nations fill us up to the same degree. Our fraternity in arms is strengthened by the community of ideal and mutual esteem.

Hurrah for American people!

Fortress of Vaux 25-10-18.
The Commander.

WHEN A FELLER NEEDS A FRIEND

REGIMENTAL ORDER IN THE VOSGES.

HEADQUARTERS 139TH INFANTRY, A. E. F.,
July 3, 1918.

MEMORANDUM:

1. Effective July 4, no bugle calls will be sounded henceforth at this station. All formations will be by the watch, the town clock being the official time or if the clock is not running, the Regimental Adjutant's watch. All units and individuals will be in place and all formations completed exactly at the prescribed time. The following schedule will govern:

	DAILY (Except Sat. & Sun.)	SATURDAY	SUNDAY
Reveille (Assembly)	5:45 A.M.	5:45 A.M.	5:45 A.M.
Stables	6:00	6:00	6:00
Mess	6:30	6:30	6:30
Sick	7:00	7:00	7:00
Fatigue	7:00	7:00	—
Inspection of Quarters	7:15	7:15	—
Drill	7:30	7:30	(General inspection by Bn. commanders) 8 to 10
Recall	11:30	11:30	Church 10:30
Stables	11:45	11:45	11:45
Mess	12 noon	12 noon	12 noon
Fatigue	1:00 P.M.	—	—
Drill	1:30	—	—
Recall	5:00	—	—
Guard Mount Adjutant's Call	5:45	5:45 P.M.	5:45 P.M.
Mess	6:00	6:00	6:00
Stables	6:40	6:40	6:40
Retreat	7:30	7:30	7:30
Inspection of rifles (By platoons)	7:35	7:35	—
N. C. O. School	8:00	—	—
Call to Quarters	9:00	9:00	9:00
Taps	9:15	9:15	9:15

FORMATIONS—Reveille and Retreat.

Reference Point: *Road intersection at Pont des Champions.* 2nd Bn. will form in line with right of line at fork of road near Pont des Champions and line extending north along the Chemin Vicinol. 3rd Bn., will form in like manner on road extending over the bridge with the left of line at intersection of roads. Formations will be by platoon units, the platoon sergeant reporting to the platoon leader who in turn will report to the company commander. The Officer of the Day will take post at the crossroads and receive the report of the company commanders.

Twenty minutes before the time prescribed for the reveille and retreat formations the Band will take post at the Pont des Champions and play lively marches in 130 cadence while the units march to their positions, at attention. Two minutes before the prescribed time for the formation the band will cease playing, and at retreat will play the Star Spangled Banner. Following retreat the band will play a concert during the inspection. Independent companies will form under direction of their immediate commander in their respective areas.

DRILL.

Battalion and independent company commanders will prepare their own weekly schedule of instruction, in conformity to the Division schedule, and submit in advance to these headquarters three copies of their instruction schedule. Battalion and separate units will form under the direction of their respective commanders; and will have not less than forty minutes close order drill daily (twenty minutes squad and twenty minutes platoon drill). Manual of arms will be frequently practiced while enroute to and from drill. During all drills and other instruction battalion commanders will keep up liaison with Regimental Headquarters, sending in hourly reports by runners or cyclists to the Adjutant's office, showing the present location and the exercises engaged in. These reports will be checked up.

UNIFORM AND APPEARANCE.

For reveille and retreat formations: O. D. Wool, with blouse, overseas cap, wrap puttees, field shoes. All officers and men will shave daily and preserve at all times a clean, neat appearance. Battalion and independent company commanders may prescribe the uniform for drill and field exercises.

GAS MASKS.

Will be worn by all officers and men from 9:30 to 10:30 A.M., no matter what duty engaged in.

By order of Lieut. Colonel Ristine:

WALTER M. MANN,
Captain 139th Infantry,
Adjutant.

WELL WON PRAISE

Following are some of the Divisional Orders in which men of the 139th Infantry are mentioned.

Headquarters 35th Division
American Expeditionary Forces,
5th August, 1918.

GENERAL ORDERS
NO. 59.

I. The Division Commander takes great pride in honoring the memory of Second Lieutenant Thomas Hopkins, 139th Infantry. Lieutenant Hopkins during a raid on July 20, 1918, and although not a member of the raiding party, voluntarily left his combat group, and, passing through the enemy barrage of artillery and machine gun fire, went to the rescue of a private soldier, who, wounded and crippled, had become entangled in the wire. Successful in reaching the wounded man, he himself was fatally wounded while assisting him to cover.

This brave and unselfish act, which ended a most promising career, is only an incident in this great world's struggle, but it serves to show that in the desperate hour of need the officer and enlisted man fight shoulder to shoulder in the brotherhood of arms.

II. The Division Commander desires to commend the soldierly conduct of the officers and enlisted men of the following units participating in a raid on Landersbach July 20, 1918:

American Units
First Battalion, 137th Infantry
Company D, 129th Machine Gun Battalion
Sanitary Detachment, 1st Bn., 137th Infantry
Company G, 139th Infantry.

French Units
1st, 2nd, 3rd and 8th Batteries 35th R. A. C.
7th, 8th, 9th and 13th Batteries 2nd R. A. M.
10th and 11th Batteries 125th A. T.
1st Battery, 8th R. A. P., 2nd, 3rd, and 24th Batteries, VIII C/III R. A. M.

III. The Division Commander takes great pleasure in citing in General Orders the following named officers and enlisted men for gallant conduct in action against the enemy in a raid at Landersbach on July 20th, 1918.—

Captain Roy W. Perkins, 137th Infantry,
1st Lieut. Emil Rolf, 137th Infantry,
1st Lieut. Paul W. Masters, 137th Infantry,
1st Lieut. Louis R. Scott, 137th Infantry,
1st Lieut. Walter H. Kirkpatrick, Medical Corps, N. G.,
2nd Lieut. Arthur L. Theiss, 137th Infantry,
Sergeant Jackson E. Walker, Company G, 139th Infantry,
Corporal Carl W. Turner, Company G, 139th Infantry,
Private Earl D. Sullivan, Company B, 137th Infantry,
Private Earl P. Busser, Company D, 137th Infantry.

By command of Major General Traub:
E. B. HASKELL,
Lieut. Colonel, General Staff,
Chief of Staff.

OFFICIAL:
WM. ELLIS
Major, N. G., U. S.,
Acting Division Adjutant.

Headquarters 35th Division
American Expeditionary Forces
14th October, 1919.

GENERAL ORDERS
NO. 82

1. It is with great pride and pleasure that I make record, and publish in General Orders, my appreciation of the courage and devotion to duty of the officers and men of the following units under my command during the six days' battle against the picked troops of the enemy, from September 26th to October 1st, 1918:

Headquarters 35th Division,
Headquarters and Headquarters Detachment, 69th Infantry Brigade,
The 137th Infantry Regiment,
The 138th Infantry Regiment,
Headquarters and Headquarters Detachment, 70th Infantry Brigade,
The 139th Infantry Regiment,
The 140th Infantry Regiment,
Headquarters and Headquarters Detachment, 60th Field Artillery Brigade,
The 138th Field Artillery Regiment,
The 129th Field Artillery Regiment,
The 130th Field Artillery Regiment,
The 128th Machine Gun Battalion,
The 129th Machine Gun Battalion,
The 130th Machine Gun Battalion,
The 110th Regiment of Engineers,
The 110th Field Signal Battalion,
The 110th Supply Train,
The 110th Ammunition Train,
The 110th Sanitary Train,
The 110th Trench Mortar Battery,
Headquarters Troop 35th Division,
2nd Brigade Tank Corps,
Provisional Squadron, 2nd Cavalry, Troops, B, D, F and H.

2. The task of making of record the individual acts of courage and devotion to duty in the face of a most deadly artillery and machine gun fire is an impossible one, for many of them will never be known. No greater praise nor commendation to the officers and men of the units mentioned above can be bestowed than to say that they have performed the tasks set for them, in a spirit and manner worthy of the best ideals and traditions of the American Army. You have met and defeated picked divisions of the enemy. You never failed to respond cheerfully to whatever difficult and dangerous tasks may have been let for you to perform. You have accomplished these tasks with a fearlessness, courage and disregard of danger and hardship which fully justifies the pride which those at home have in you. VAUQUOIS, BOIS de ROSSIGNOL, OUVRAGE d' ADEN, CHEPPY, CHARPENTRY, RAULNY,

BOIS de MONTREBEAU, EXERMONT, are names that you may take just pride in passing on to your native States as having been the scenes of your feats of arms.

3. The spirits of our dead comrades are with us to urge us on to greater deeds in Our Country's Noble Cause. To their families and friends we extend our heartfelt sympathy. To our wounded we hope for a speedy and safe return to our ranks that they may add their great spunk and enthusiasm to those of their more fortunate brothers in arms.

4. I direct that this General Order be read to all units of this command at the first formation at which they are assembled after receipt thereof.

PETER E. TRAUB,
Major General, U. S. Army,
Commanding.

Headquarters 35th Division
American Expeditionary Forces
17th October 1918.

GENERAL ORDERS
    NO. 83

*   *   *   *   *   *   EXTRACT   *   *   *   *   *   *

1. The Division Commander takes great pleasure in citing in General Orders the following named Officers and Enlisted Men, for gallantry in action during the six days' battle from September 26th to October 1st, 1918:

*   *   *   *   *   *   *   *   *   *   *   *   *

First Lieutenant Otto L. H. Hine, Dental Corps, and his enlisted assistant, Private 1st Class W. C. Myers, Medical Department. Displayed wonderful determination and courage in rescuing the wounded under heavy shell fire, rendered great assistance in dressing and evacuating the wounded, securing litters and litter bearers over difficult terrain, where it was impossible for ambulances to operate.

*   *   *   *   *   *   *   *   *   *   *   *   *

By Command of Major General Traub:
H. S. HAWKINS
Colonel, General Staff,
Chief of Staff.

OFFICIAL:
    WM. ELLIS
Lt. Col., Inf., U. S. Army
    Division Adjutant

Headquarters 35th Division
American Expeditionary Forces
17th October 1918.

GENERAL ORDERS
    NO. 83

*   *   *   *   *   *   EXTRACT   *   *   *   *   *   *

2. The Division Commander takes great pleasure in citing in General Orders the following named Officers and Enlisted men for gallantry in action during the six days' battle from September 26th to October 1st, 1918:

*   *   *   *   *   *   *   *   *   *   *   *   *

Major James E. Rieger, Commanding the Second Battalion, 139th Infantry. Ascertaining that the attacking battalion of the ——— Infantry was temporarily checked in the advance, immediately collected about eighty men and pushed forward two or three hundred meters in advance of said battalion, thereby driving a wedge in the defensive fortifications of the enemy. (September 26th.) Personally led the two leading companies of his battalion in an attack on Charpentry, which attack resulted in the capture of that town and the taking of many prisoners, machine guns and material of different kinds. (September 27th.) Personally led a detachment of mixed elements in an attack on Exermont, assisted in the capture of that town and pushed beyond said town several hundred meters, until told to retire. (September 29th.) Took charge of re-organization of the right half of our defensive line, after the withdrawal, and prevented the withdrawal beyond the defensive line as chosen. (September 29th.)

Captain Joe W. McQueen, 139th Infantry. Led his company on the front line in the attack on the enemy artillery and machine gun positions between Charpentry and Baulny, resulting in the capture of prisoners, artillery and machine guns; this after the advance of other troops had been checked by the enemy fire. (September 27th.) Led his company in the attack on Exermont, reaching that village and was there wounded while directing his company. This advance was made against artillery and machine gun fire and after other troops had fallen back. (September 29th.)

Captain Randall Wilson, 139th Infantry. Commanded a small detachment in an advanced position north of Chaudron Farm, and covered the evacuation of many wounded from said Farm, remaining on duty twenty-six hours, repelling attacks made by the enemy and retired only when evacuation of the wounded was completed. (September 29th-30th.)

First Lieutenant John W. McManigal, 139th Infantry. Led his platoon on the front line in the attack on the enemy artillery and machine gun positions between Charpentry and Baulny, resulting in the capture of prisoners, artillery and machine guns; this after the advance of other troops had been checked by the enemy fire. (September 27th.) Led his platoon in the attack on Exermont, reaching that village, and was there wounded while directing his platoon. This advance was made against artillery and machine gun fire and after other troops had fallen back. (September 29th.)

Sergeant Stephen Lake, Company E, 139th Infantry. After all officers of his company had been either killed or wounded he assumed command of his company, advanced and captured several German machine guns. (September 28th.) Commanded his company in the attack on Exermont and while leading his company he was wounded severely. (September 29th.)

By command of Major General Traub:
H. S. HAWKINS
Colonel, General Staff,
Chief of Staff.

REGIMENTAL INTELLIGENCE SECTION

The gallantry of this band in battle won the highest praise. Reading from left to right, they are Capt. John D. Heiny, Corwin F. Foster, Lawrence Holloway, Franz Veercamp, William Vermerhen, Ferdinand W. Meyer, Jr., Lawrence Elder, Garland Ramsey and Raymond O. Bernauer. Vermerhen, Meyer and Bernauer were Sergeants. The others were First Class Privates.

Headquarters 35th Division,
American Expeditionary Forces,
17th October, 1918.

SPECIAL ORDERS
  NO. 83
*   *   *   *   *   *   EXTRACT   *   *   *   *   *   *

The Division Commander takes great pleasure in citing in General Orders the following named Officers and Enlisted Men, for gallantry in action during the six days' battle from September 26th to October 1st, 1918:

Captain S. M. Brown, Jr., 139th Infantry. While Regimental Adjutant on September 26th and 27th, fearlessly exposed himself to intense artillery and machine gun fire in order to assist his commanding officer by assuring the proper execution of orders. He was killed while assisting in forming his regiment for the attack on Charpentry. At the time of his death he was wearing the insignia of First Lieutenant as he had not been advised of his promotion to Captaincy which occurred on September 18, 1918.

Sergeant Alonzo L. Reed, Company I, 139th Infantry. On September 26th displayed excellent leadership in leading his platoon in a heroic charge against machine gun nests under machine gun and artillery fire near Charpentry and was among the first to enter that town, at which place his platoon captured a number of prisoners.

Major William D. Stepp, 139th Infantry. On September 26th fearlessly and gallantly led his battalion in the face of severe and intense machine gun and artillery fire advancing against enemy strong points and machine guns which had held up another battalion for eight hours. In the attack southeast of Varennes he was killed while leading his troops.

By command of Major General Traub:
H. S. HAWKINS
Colonel, General Staff,
Chief of Staff.

OFFICIAL:
  WM. ELLIS
Lt. Col., Inf., U. S. Army,
  Division Adjutant.

GENERAL ORDERS
NO. 88

Headquarters 35th Division,
American Expeditionary Forces,
27th October 1918.

The Division Commander takes pleasure in citing in General Orders the following named officer whose courage and devotion to duty in the face of the enemy is typical of the fighting of this Division.—

Major Clay C. Macdonald, 139th Infantry, until September 28th, Postal Agent, 35th Division; learning of the death in action of his son, a First Lieutenant of this Division, he came forward to the front lines and volunteered for service. He was assigned to command a Battalion and conducted himself with courage and good judgment, and, although 61 years of age, endured great physical hardships with a fortitude and determination that would have done credit to many a younger man.

By command of Major General Traub:
H. S. HAWKINS
Colonel, General Staff,
Chief of Staff.

OFFICIAL:
WM. ELLIS
Lt. Col., Inf., U. S. Army
Division Adjutant.

Headquarters 35th Division,
American Expeditionary Forces,
13th November, 1918.

GENERAL ORDERS
NO. 98

* * * * * * EXTRACT * * * * * *

2. Special credit for courage and resourcefulness, under fire, and for the effective handling of their detachments, is due the following Regimental Surgeons.

Captain Oscar Hansen, Regimental Surgeon, 137th Infantry,
Major Emil Burgher, Regimental Surgeon, 138th Infantry,
Major Henry D. Smith, Regimental Surgeon, 139th Infantry.

By command of Major General Traub:
H. S. HAWKINS
Colonel, General Staff,
Chief of Staff.

OFFICIAL:
WM. ELLIS
Lt. Col., Inf., U. S. Army
Division Adjutant.

Headquarters 35th Division,
American Expeditionary Forces,
17th October, 1918

GENERAL ORDERS
NO. 83

* * * * * EXTRACT * * * * *

8. The Division Commander takes great pleasure in citing in General Orders the courage and devotion to duty, in the face of the enemy, of the following named Officers and Enlisted Men of this Division:

Corporal Forest L. Spidle, Company I, 139th Infantry. At about 5:00 P.M. on September 26th, 1918, Corporal Spidle, with three men was sent out to reconnoiter and outflank a machine gun nest. While endeavoring to perform his duty he was twice severely wounded but persisted in going forward to accomplish his task, which, on account of his wounds, he was unable to do.

* * * * * * * * * * *

11. The Commanding General, 35th Division, takes pleasure in citing in Division Orders the following named Officer of the Medical Corps, 35th Division, for his courage and devotion to duty in the face of the enemy, during the action of September 26th -October 1st, 1918.

Captain Charles A. Lusk, M. C. while with the 139th Infantry, on the night of September 29th, 30th, supervised the collection and evacuation of the wounded from Chaudron Farm, working continuously for hours, under heavy enemy fire, and by his courage inspired those about him to the full performance of their duty.

By command of Major General Traub:
H. S. HAWKINS
Colonel, General Staff,
Chief of Staff.

OFFICIAL:
WM. ELLIS
Lt. Col., Inf., U. S. Army
Division Adjutant.

DISTINGUISHED SERVICE CROSSES

The following were awarded Distinguished Service Crosses and the citations given are the official record:

COSGROVE, JOHN D., Second Lieutenant

Deceased. 139th Infantry. For extraordinary heroism in action near Charpentry, France, September 26-27, 1918. As battalion intelligence officer, he repeatedly went in front of his own and adjoining battalions to secure information which he conveyed to regimental headquarters over fields swept by artillery and machine-gun fire. When the advance of his battalion was checked by destructive hostile fire, this officer, disregarding personal danger, conducted a personal reconnaissance, locating many machine guns and strongholds. He was killed while voluntarily leading and placing troops in advantageous positions to reduce these machine-gun nests. Next of kin, Mrs. Sarah Agnes Nare, 1002A Glasgow Avenue, St. Louis, Mo.

DUNCAN, GEO. E., Private (First Class)

Company K, 139th Infantry. Upon seeing his brother killed by a bursting shell as he was leading his platoon forward, Pvt. Duncan displayed the utmost bravery and initiative in rushing forward, taking command of the platoon, which had become depleted by casualties, and was in danger of becoming disorganized, and leading it forward in the advance. Home address, E. L. Duncan, father, Dearborn, Mo.

FOUST, BENJAMIN E., Mechanic.

Company F, 139th Infantry. For extraordinary heroism in action near Exermont, France, September 29, 1918. After having one eye shot out, Mechanic Foust refused to avail himself of the opportunity to be evacuated to the rear, but rendered first aid to himself and continued to dress the wounds of his comrades, until a heavy concentration of gas so affected his wounded eye that he was forced to go to the rear. His work was the means of saving the lives of many of his comrades. Home address, Miss Grace Foust, Columbia, Mo.

GENTRY, CARL C., Private (First Class)

Company D, 139th Infantry. For extraordinary heroism in action near Baulny, France, September 30, 1918. Upon his own initiative, Private Gentry organized a platoon composed of disorganized men from various units, and led it through terrific machine-gun fire, stopping an advance of the enemy. In performing this courageous feat he was severely wounded. Home address, John Gentry, father, Twenty-first and Lulu Streets, Trenton, Mo.

GRISWOLD, LEVI W., Corporal.

Deceased. Company C, 139th Infantry. For extraordinary heroism in action in the Montrebeau Woods, France, September 29, 1918. During a hostile counterattack Corporal Griswold, with absolute disregard for personal safety, crept out from a shell hole under terrific machine-gun fire and gas bombardment in an attempt to assist a wounded comrade to adjust his gas mask. He was killed in the performance of this self-sacrificing mission. Next of kin, Mrs. Alice McAninch, mother, Yarrow, Mo.

HEINY, JOHN D., Captain.

139th Infantry. For extraordinary heroism in action near Charpentry, France, September 27, 1918, in order to secure important information as to the position of hostile batteries he passed through the enemy's artillery fire and was twice severely wounded. In spite of his wounds he remained on duty throughout the entire engagement and gave assistance in the reorganization of advanced positions.

HINE, OTTO L. H., Captain.

Dental Corps, 139th Infantry. For extraordinary heroism in action at Chaudron Farm, France, September 29-30, 1918. Upon his own initiative, Captain Hine (then first lieutenant) went to a dressing station in advance of the line, after the infantry had withdraw, and worked under heavy bombardment of gas and high explosive shells, dressing the patients and directing their evacuation. That night he returned to our lines through heavy artillery and machine-gun fire to arrange for ambulances and litters. Later he made another trip to the rear for the purpose of securing an artillery barrage to protect his dressing station. Through his exceptional courage and energy, all the wounded men were safely evacuated. Next of kin, T. S. Hine, father, 217 Court Street, Muskogee, Okla.

HOPKINS, THOMAS, Second Lieutenant.

Deceased. 139th Infantry. Near Wesserling, July 20, 1918, he left his own post of comparative safety and voluntarily went through a heavy artillery barrage to rescue a private who was wounded and entangled in barbed wire. While engaged in this self-sacrificing effort he was killed. Next of kin, Mrs. Edna Hopkins, wife, 1124 Bittling Avenue, Wichita, Kansas.

KELSEY, HARRY R., First Sergeant.

Deceased. Company E, 139th Infantry. For extraordinary heroism in action near Charpentry, France, September 27, 1918. Sergeant Kelsey volunteered to carry an important message from his company commander to battalion headquarters and, knowing the extreme importance of the message, proceeded by the most direct route through the heavy, machine-gun fire and artillery barrage, with entire disregard for his personal safety. He was killed while performing this heroic service. Next of kin, Mrs. Mattie Kelsey, mother, Easton, Kansas.

KEMMERER, BURTRUS, Corporal.

Company H, 139th Infantry. For extraordinary heroism in action near Baulny, France, September 26, 1918. Seeing his battalion adjutant lying several hundred yards in front of our lines, and in great danger from heavy machine-gun and rifle fire, Corporal (then private) Kemmerer, with a total disregard for personal danger, went to the assistance of this officer and succeeded in carrying him to safety. This gallant soldier was himself wounded while performing this heroic act. Home address, John Kemmerer, 410 East Benton Street, Carrollton, Mo.

KILFOYLE, FRANK J., Sergeant.

Company M, 139th Infantry. Under heavy machine-gun and artillery fire, Sergeant Kilfoyle led an automatic rifle squad into Varennes and captured an enemy machine-gun nest, which had been inflicting heavy casualties on our forces, killing or wounding all the members of the crew, including a German major. Two days later he again displayed skilful leadership in organizing his platoon against an enemy counterattack, which was successfully repulsed. Home address, Mrs. Mary B. Kilfoyle, mother, 1015 Henry Street, St. Joseph, Mo.

MOTLEY, FRANK L., Corporal.

Company M, 139th Infantry. For extraordinary heroism in action near Apremont, France, September 29, 1918. When the enemy was counterattacking, having succeeded in planting machine-guns behind a smoke screen, he advanced with utter disregard of personal danger and jumped into an enemy machine-gun nest where there were about 15 Germans. Single-handed, he killed the gunner and loader, and engaged the remainder of the Germans until he received help from his platoon. Home address, William B. Mitchell, uncle, in care of Meuller-Keller Candy Company, St. Joseph, Mo.

NORTON, EVERETTE C., Private (First Class)

Machine Gun Company, 139th Infantry. For extraordinary heroism in action near Cheppy, France, September 27, 1918. After being wounded by a machine-gun bullet, Private Norton refused to be evacuated to the rear, but continued in his duties for two days thereafter, and only stopped when weakened by the loss of blood. Home address, Joseph Clarence Norton, Moran, Kansas.

OLDFIELD, WILLIE A., First Sergeant.

Company H, 139th Infantry. For extraordinary heroism in action near Baulny, France, September 26-27, 1918. Sergeant Oldfield was in charge of his platoon when it was subjected to heavy enemy machine-gun fire, causing numerous casualties. By his word and example he held his men in line as a unit until nightfall, when they intrenched. Next day when the tanks appeared he led the charge upon the machine-guns which were holding up the advance. Inspired by his gallantry, his men went forward and cleared out the guns and assisted in the capture of Charpentry, with many prisoners. Home address, Mrs. Anna Oldfield, mother, Canton, Kansas.

PALMER, ALVA W., Corporal.

Company K, 139th Infantry. For extraordinary heroism in action south of Exermont, France, September 28, 1918. When his battalion commander asked for a volunteer to carry a message to the battalion commander on the right, Corporal Palmer (then private) volunteered and carried the message through an area exposed to intense machine-gun and artillery fire. By this utter disregard for his own personal safety, and his example of bravery, he inspired all those near him. Home address, Cleve Finney, brother-in-law, Weston, Mo.

RIEGER, JAMES E., Lieutenant Colonel.

138th Infantry. For extraordinary heroism in action near Charpentry, France, September 27, 1918. He commanded the battalion which had, with conspicuous gallantry, captured Vauquois Hill and the Bois de Rossignol, and which was later held up for some hours in front of Charpentry by severe artillery and machine-gun fire. He placed himself in front of all his men, and, thus starting them forward, led them to the attack with such speed and dash that a large number of the enemy were cut off and captured. Home address, Mrs. James E. Rieger, Kirksville, Mo.

SEGRAVES, VICTOR L., Sergeant.

1st Battalion, Scout Platoon, 139th Infantry. For extraordinary heroism in action near Baulny, France, September 28, 1918. Sergeant Segraves voluntarily formed and led a patrol against an enemy machine-gun nest, which was causing many casualties in his battalion, and captured one of the guns. With utter disregard for his personal safety he advanced alone on another gun of the nest but was severely wounded by the intense fire, in the performance of this heroic act. Home address, Mrs. Patrick Segraves, mother, Perry, Kansas.

SHAHAN, WINFIELD F., Corporal.

Company M, 139th Infantry. For extraordinary heroism in action in the Meuse-Argonne offensive, September 26-28, 1918, and near Exermont, France, September 29, 1918. Corporal Shahan, regimental liaison noncommissioned officer, with great courage constantly exposed himself to heavy enemy machine-gun and shell fire for three days in maintaining liaison between his regimental headquarters and the companies in the front line. On September 29, he attacked, single-handed, an enemy machine-gun nest, killing several of the enemy and taking one prisoner. While making his way back to his lines, he was fired upon by another German machine-gun, which wounded him in the right arm, and was at the same time attacked by his prisoner. In spite of his wound, he killed the German with his pistol, and reached his lines in safety. Home address, Mrs. Flora Shahan, mother, Marion, Kansas.

WILSON, CARLISLE R., First Lieutenant.

Deceased. 139th Infantry. For extraordinary heroism in action near Montblainville, France, September 27, 1918. In order to establish and maintain liaison with the adjacent division, Lieutenant Wilson, although wounded, led his men along the valley of the Aire River and across a bridge through the heaviest kind of artillery and machine-gun fire. He died soon after this exploit from the wounds received. Next of kin, Judge J. C. Wilson, father, Bethany, Mo.

WORTHEN, GEORGE T., First Lieutenant.

139th Infantry. For exrtraordinary heroism in action near Varennes, France, September 26, 1918. Arming himself with a rifle, Lieutenant Worthen personally led an attack on a hostile machine-gun nest which was holding up the advance, capturing the position and killing or capturing the entire enemy unit, including two officers. Home address, Mrs. Dora E. Worthen, wife, 2739 South Eighteenth Street, St. Joseph, Mo.

WRIGHT, EARL, Corporal.

Company I, 139th Infantry. For extraordinary heroism in action near Charpentry, France, September 27-28, 1918. After being wounded in the knee, Corporal Wright refused to be evacuated, but remained at his post for nearly 24 hours until his wounds became so serious that he was ordered to the dressing station. His example of bravery and fortitude was an inspiration to his comrades. Home address, J. F. Wright, father, Bucklin, Mo.

WHAT COL. DAVIS SAID

Headquarters 35th Division,
American Expeditionary Forces,
1st February, 1919.

MEMORANDUM: To Commanding Officer, 139th Infantry Regiment.

1. In a report from the IX Corps on the problem conducted January 31st, the following comments were made:

"The problem was well handled and worked satisfactorily. The following points were observed: selection of defensive position excellent; use of auxiliary weapons, excellent; disposition of troops, very good; troop leadership very good; orders of regimental and battalion commanders, very good; liaison fair; tactical decisions, very good."

DWIGHT F. DAVIS,
Lieutenant-Colonel, Infty.,
A. C. of S., G-3.

LIEUTENANT COFFMAN'S STORY

Headquarters 130th M. G. Bn.,
Office of Battalion Surgeon,
American E. F., Jan. 5, 1919.

From: John F. Coffman, Jr., Bn. Surgeon, 2nd Bn. 139th Inf.
To: Division Surgeon.
Subject: History of Sanitary Detachment, 2nd Bn. 139th Inf. during Argonne Meuse Battle, Sept. 25th to Oct. 2nd, 1918.

September 25th, 1918. Battalion was located in woods about 12 kilometers South-east of Vauquois. At 10:00 A.M. our Battalion Commander notified us that in a few hours we were to take part in an offensive against one of the German's strongest positions and that we should make necessary preparation and hold ourselves in readiness.

Immediately we had 12 men to report to us from each Company, making a total of 48 men, to act as litter bearers. There being no arm bands for these men, we quickly improvised one for each man out of an old blue blanket, stating specifically to them what their duties were to be and what was expected cf them, at the same time going over various ways of administering first aid.

We then took the personnel of each Company separately and talked to them for one hour, going over the methods of checking hemorrhage and administering first aid. This was done to freshen their memories, as they had been given lectures along these lines numerous times. In talking to them we would draw an imaginary picture of every conceivable wound and then have them apply first aid, first on themselves and then on others, all the time assuring them of the necessity of keeping a good cool head. This all paid a large dividend, as was proven by the number of men that were wounded and reported to Aid Station with their wounds dressed in fine shape, either by themselves or by a companion laying close thereby, requiring only the necessity of evacuation. We then took our enlisted personnel for one hour, having them adjust various splints and administer first aid to various imaginary wounds, equipping all but two of them with two shell dressing cases (improvised by using empty gas mask covers) containing 50 dressings. The other two were carrying 100 doses of Anti-Tetanic Serum, all that was available at the time. We then assigned two of our men to each of the Companies, instructing them of their duties and positions.

At 4:00 P.M. we received an order to move at 6:00 P.M. and take up our position which was just back of the front line trenches, one kilometer South of Vauquois in an old orchard. Right here we wish to state that there was not a single man in this Battalion but what knew this Battle was coming off in a very few hours and we are pleased to state that not a single one of them presented himself at the Infirmary with any form of sickness.

At 6:00 P.M. sharp we swung down the road in column of squads, marching in this formation for six kilometers, then in column of twos for four kilometers and into our position at 2:00 A.M. Sept. 25th, there waiting to perform the duties that we had so faithfully trained for during 14 long months. While laying there it started to rain and mist and a heavy fog started forming. At 4:00 A.M. we were informed by our Major that there was a dug-out about 100 meters to our right in the trench which we could use as a First Aid Station, so there we established our first Station. At this station we evacuated only one casualty, a man from the 129th M.G.Bn., wounded in the neck by a piece of Bosche shell. At 3:00 A.M. our barrage started and at 5:30 A.M. the Battalion went over the top. Here we wish to state that we figured it a poor policy to have only one Aid Station to the Battalion, as a direct hit by artillery would put us all out of commission, thereby leaving our Battalion in a bad way, so we there and then resolved to have at least two and some times three stations.

At 6:15 A.M. we went over the top, strung out behind our Battalion with no man closer to another than 20 meters, which was just as far as one could see in the fog. This formation was also necessary, as being spread out we could locate casualties. We advanced in this formation for 2 kilometers, only finding one casualty, that being 1st Lt. Malcomb McDonald who had been instantly killed by a burst of machine gun bullets. By this time, 7:30 A.M., we had taken Vaquois Hill and prisoners were being brought to the rear. We advanced about one-half a kilometer further and were held up for a time as we were then right behind our Battalion; here we established two Aid Stations, marked on map as 2A and 2B. 2A was established on the South side of a steep hill which was thought to be and also proved to be defalated. While we were informed about 11:00 A.M. that there were a great many wounded about 300 meters to our right in the woods; on looking around we noticed passing us about 30 German prisoners under guard. We explained the circumstances to the guards, stating that we needed litter bearers, and we had no trouble in getting these prisoners, after further assuring the guards that they could stay with us and in due time have the prisoners returned to them.

Our Chaplain, one of the most fearless young men we saw during the entire battle, volunteered to act as foreman over the Bosche litter squads, so he gave them "about face" and into the woods they went and in a very short time he had them littering in wounded on improvised litters such as limbs of trees with their coats on them, old bunks and blankets. We in turn dressed them and laid them along in rows on the ground on the side of the hill, as no better place was available. By 4:00 P.M. we had them all out, dressed and fairly comfortable, a total of 59 casualties. We then picked out eight of the most severely wounded and had them put on litters by the Bosche, called the two guards and turned the prisoners back to them with orders to litter these eight men to the rear as quick as possible. At 4:30 P.M. we turned the balance over to the advance litter bearers of the 140th Ambulance Co. Nearly all these casualties were from the 137th Infantry.

This work was performed under an almost continual artillery and machine gun fire. 2B was established in a trench which had been widened out and made fairly comfortable by Bosche prisoners under the supervision of our Dentist, Lt. Hine, and his assistant. He also used German prisoners as litter bearers and from here evacuated 19 casualties. One hour prior to establishing this Aid Station Lt. Hine was on the North side of Vaquois Hill and, after following the board walks past large, well constructed concrete caves and dug-outs, he noticed a crowd of men through the fog about 30 meters ahead of him. Not being able to distinguish who they were, he turned to his assistant, Private Wm. C. Myers, who was following him, and asked him if he thought they were Bosche. As the assistant affirmed his suspicions, Lt. Hine held up his revolver which he had in his hand, and while trying to make up his mind as to exactly what course to pursue, the Germans saw him and all held up their hands and started toward him. There were some steps leading up to a trench that led back over the knoll between Lt. Hine and the Germans, so he waved to them to go up those steps and counted 32 of them. Falling in behind them he took them across the valley and up into the trenches from where he had started that morning, turning them over to guards who were returning with other prisoners.

At 4:30 P.M. we went forward about one kilometer and established Aid Station Number 3 on the South slope of a deep ravine. From here we evacuated 21 casualties. Here we had the honor of a short visit by Major General Traub, who shook hands with all of us, inquiring as to what organization we belonged, stating that he was pleased to see the Doctors so close to the front. At 6:00 P.M. we again started forward, going about 2 kilometers without finding any casualties until we caught up with our Battalion, which was then digging in for the night on top of a hill. At this time it was dark. Here we established Aid Station Number 4. We lay here all night sleeping in shell holes. No casualties during the night. At daylight our Battalion advanced about one kilometer and were held up. We then moved up to an old cellar and there established Aid Station Number 5 at 7:00 A.M. Sept. 27th. Here we stayed until 5:00 P.M. evacuating 34 casualties. At 9:00 A.M. a runner came to us with a statement of several wounded men back South of us on the hill, so the Chaplain and I went back and dressed six men that had been severely wounded by one shell, procured litter bearers and evacuated them. We then started toward the road to get some water in our canteens as we had been told of a spring. We had not gone very far until the Bosche started dropping some shells quite close to us, so we dived into a shell hole. It had about four inches of water in it. The Chaplain hit the bottom and I on top of him. Here we lay for 30 minutes while 75 shells dropped around us, none further than 200 meters and several as close as 15 feet, which when they exploded would nearly burst our ear drums, caused by the concussion. While laying there I saw a little mouse run around the edge of the shell hole and dart into his hole; believe me, that is the only time in my life that I wished to be a mouse. After this had been going on for about 20 minutes I said to the Chaplain: "Do you suppose they are trying to kill a Doctor and Chaplain?" To this he was about to agree when I stuck my head over the top and saw 10 tanks coming down the road; these beyond question were what was being shot at, but the Bosche were over-shooting and the Chaplain and I in our shell hole were the goat. After this had quieted we gave our canteens to one of our men that was going past and he took them back to the dressing station with him. We then started back ourselves. While walking along I noticed two litter bearers coming along with a man on the litter, also noticed blood spurting in the air from the wounded man's shoulder. I ran to them quickly, had them lower the litter to the ground and very quickly tore off the dressing and clamped the arteries with two haemostats, applied dressing over all and sent him on back. This man proved to be Lt. Col. Dickey. He was at this time in very bad shape. We then walked forward to our dressing station again, it then being 11:00 A.M. We just got comfortably situated when they started dropping shells around us again, a few of them being gas shells. One very large one dropped about 50 feet from us, the gas quickly volatilized and was blown directly over us by the wind. I happened to be looking in that direction and saw it coming and yelled "gas" and into our masks we went, wearing them for about 15 minutes and it was all over. Lt. H. P. Lewis, who was with me, was at this time in a shell hole about 20 feet from me and did not see what was coming or did not hear me at first and thereby got a breath of it before he could get in his mask and get away. This gave him a severe headache, eyes watered and some vomiting. He then went to the rear, the last I saw of him.

At 5:00 P.M. our Battalion was ordered over the top again under our machine gun barrage. I was on high ground and could easily see them go over. Never shall I forget the sight as the men went forward against the Bosche artillery and machine gun bullets: the men tipped their heads forward and reminded me by their actions of cattle facing a hail storm. Every few yards a man would fall wounded. Just as the last Plattoon of our H Company was forming to go over a large shell hit among them. This I saw and we quickly gathered our equipment together and ran down to them and pulled six of them into shell holes and were dressing them when two Bosche air planes swung down from the sky and started toward us up the valley firing their machine guns. They wounded nine of our boys in the back, as I dressed them shortly afterwards.

From here we established an Aid Station in a cement culvert four feet high, 3 feet wide and 30 feet long, marked No. 6 on Map. By this time it was dark, but we managed by the aid of candles to evacuate from here 42 casualties: would have the wounded littered into the ends of the culvert, dress them and line them along the ditches along each side of the road on the ground, as we needed the litters. We got an ambulance in a very short time, which worked with us all night. About 10:00 P.M. one of my men informed me that there was a dug-out just to the left of us about 200 meters, which was nice and dry. As it was raining we moved our Station, No. 7 on Map, there, continuing our work, keeping the wounded men in a dry place. Here we stayed working all night until 1:00 P.M. Sept. 28th, evacuating 65 casualties.

At 1:00 P.M. we again went forward about 2 kilometers to a place shown as St. Quenteen, just South from Baulny about 300 meters. Here we established Aid Station No. 8 in an old mine. We did not feel very comfortable here for the first hour as on examining the place we found about one ton of dynamite in one of the rooms. As we had a man in our detachment who had had experience handling it, he and one other volunteered to put it in a car and take it away, which they did. We then felt much safer. Here we worked all night evacuating 125 casualties, many of them wounded severely and when littered in were wet to the skin, as it rained the entire night. From here we had splendid ambulance service, having one every twenty minutes. This was remarkable as at this time we were only about one kilometer behind our front lines. Fully 75 per cent of our casualties up to the time of establishing this Aid Station had been caused by machine gun bullets. From here until we were relieved they were 75 per cent caused by fragments of shells. Did not have a casualty during the entire battle caused by shrapnel.

At 6:00 A.M. Sept. 29th we again went forward. At the bottom of the hill at Baulny we met Major General Traub for the second time, he again inquiring as to who we were and again expressed himself as being pleased to see the Doctors so close to the front. On going a few yards further we saw Capt. Nesbitt, Co. A 130th M.G. Bn., and he informed us that his Company had just been badly shelled further up along this road, so up the road we went dressing 11 casualties and had them littered back to Baulny. While going further up the road we had to keep down in a ditch on West side of road which had about one foot of water in it. We kept one behind the other, about 50 meters between men, as all along here the Bosche would snipe at one man with their Austrian 88, named by the men "Whiz Bangs." We finally came to a large stone bridge over a little creek that was running like a mill race; this affording some protection, we waited one-half an hour standing in water up to our knees. On looking around we noticed up the road and to the right about 200 meters was an old stone house standing against a steep bank. In this house we established Aid Station No. 9A at 10:00 A.M. From here we only took care of three casualties, keeping them with us as it had now become impossible to get out of here on account of artillery and machine gun fire. While here we watched the 28th Division take Exermont, which was one kilometer to our left. At 3:30 P.M. the shelling had let up considerably, so we sent two of our men forward with instructions to locate an appropriate place for our next Aid Station. These men being gone about fifteen minutes came running back with the information that our Infantry was falling back, so we went out and looking to our right saw that their information was true. Looking to the North we could see the reason for it, as there was what looked to us to be a million Bosche coming over a hill about two kilometers away. Without further hesitation we took our three casualties on litters and returned to the Aid Station at St. Quenteen, which had now been acting as our Regimental Aid Station.

At 9:00 A.M. Lt. Hine established Aid Station 9B at Baulny, from here evacuating 16 casualties, and then returned to St. Quenteen. At 10:30 A.M. Herbert Stoffle, one of our personnel, who had been detailed with G Company and was serving with them on the front line, and who was afterwards captured by the Germans, came in and said that he knew where there was a dressing station with lots of wounded, but they were being taken care of; but as there were quite a few of these men, thinking that he could be of assistance, Lt. Hine with his assistant accompanied him to Chaudron Farm, where he established Aid Station No. 10, evacuating altogether 80 casualties. There, after going into a room which was about half full of wounded men and asking if there were any who had not been dressed and receiving the reply that none of them had been dressed since coming from the field, he began to work. The first two or three he dressed and tagged, then to speed up with the dressing, he quit tagging, but soon the litter bearers brought them in so fast and as he was the only medical officer there at that time, he could only devote his time to placing them. That room, which was about 75 feet long and 20 feet wide, was filled and another room of the same dimensions and yet another and then the sheds and the barn received their portion. During this time heavy shelling was going on and the report that the line was falling back necessitated the withdrawal of several officers and men. By this means Lt. Hine sent back word of his plight with the urgent request for help and for means of evacuation. Two gas attacks were also put over, which necessitated the adjusting of gas masks for the wounded that had them or could be supplied.

About 6 o'clock of this same day Captain Randall Wilson, who was holding the line out in front and who did hold the Germans from entering the dressing station with 75 men after doggedly fighting their way twice from the very walls of the place, came and asked how they were getting along. After he found out the condition he gave Lt. Hine 50 men to help with the work of evacuating the wounded. With these 50 men 37 men were evacuated on litters, improvised litters and riding guns. Then after an actual count by Lt. Hine and Lt. John D. Heiny, Regimental Intelligence Officer, who had also been helping hold the line and who had helped with the evacuation, there remained 95 litter patients, the walking cases having been sent back upon entering the Station. This was at 10:00 P.M. September 29th, 1918. At this time Capt. Wilson came in and asked if all had been evacuated. Upon being informed as to the true state of affairs Captain Wilson said: "Hell, Doc, you have got to get these men out of here by daylight. There are only 25 men between you and the Bosche. The main line has fallen back to the top of the hill about a half mile behind you." At twelve o'clock, midnight, after deciding that there was no help coming and that something had to be done, Lt. Hine got on a mule, which was in the barn of the farm, bare backed and with a rope halter, started back to get help or protection, and if possible both. On his way back he met a Lieutenant with a detail of 50 men coming to help, but as they had no litters he took them back to the dressing station at Charpentry. There the Doctor in charge gave him 5 litters, but that was not sufficient, so Lt. Hine went to the Major in command for help. The Major, Major Gist, said that there were no litters and that ambulances could not go past Charpentry under existing general orders. "Give me the order for the ambulances and I will go to the General and get the order removed," said Lt. Hine. "We have got to have action and I know the General will let them by." The Major wrote the order for the ambulances and the Lieutenant then started to see the General. In the square in front of the dressing station he met a boy asking for Major Gist. Upon finding that perhaps the order was from the General and pertained to the evacuation of wounded, Lt. Hine took him to the Major. There he found that two ambulances with 7 litters were to be used for this purpose. Loading the litters, 12 in all, on the ambulances and starting the detachment of 50 men forward, they all started for the farm. The ambulances could not make it up the hill, due to the steepness and the mud, so the 50 men took the litters and the ambulances were stationed at the bottom of the hill to carry the wounded from there. Knowing that all the wounded could not be gotten out of the way by daylight and that infantry protection could not be obtained, Lt. Hine got on his mule and went to the Headquarters of the 129th Field Artillery, hoping that protection could be secured from there. The Captain in charge could not get information enough in detail so he was sent to the advance observation post, which was at Balny. There he ran into a dug-out full of officers, principally Colonels, and after telling them the situation, with emphasis laid on the fact that only 25 men separated the dressing station from the Germans, he was promised a barrage across the road in front of the farm with quite heavy shell fire until all of the patients were evacuated. But his barrage was to begin at 4:30; it was then 5 minutes of four and Captain Wilson and his 25 men were across the road, so Lt. Hine again mounted his mule and made it down the hill to Charpentry and up over the hill to the farm in 15 minutes flat and got Captain Wilson and his 25 men back before the barrage started. Not knowing what else to do, Captain Wilson went back to report that he had withdrawn. All followed the men back, but about 100 meters out they met four men with a litter, so Lt. Hine, his assistant and the four men with the litter went back and got 3 more wounded men. Thinking that with all the protection gone, no means available for evacuation and daylight nearly there about 45 or 50 wounded men would be found there by the Bosche when they came over looking around next morning. When the last of the three men there were being put into the ambulance Captain Wilson had reported and had been told he was not intended to withdraw entirely, so he came up and said that they had to go back in. Captain Wilson at that time had only 12 men left, but as they went through the line where the Infantry was dug in he took 12 more men. When they took up their position again it was already daylight. Captain Wilson promised to hold off the Dutch to the last man and Lt. Hine first went to Major

163

Smith, his Battalion Medical Commander, and he helped him secure Lt. Deal and about a hundred men to help. They then went back again to Major Gist and, as he had two ambulances full of litters coming, they waited and while waiting Major Gist had a cook fry up a mess pan full of pan-cakes with butter and molasses for each, which they will never forget. The litters came and Lt. Deal and Lt. Hine took the men and litters up over the hill through one of the worst shellings a hill ever got. A report that about a third of the litter bearers were being employed to carry a fellow litter bearer back later came to the dressing station.

It was about 1:00 P.M. September 30th that Captain Wilson came back to find out how near the work of evacuation had been completed. There were only two Americans, who were wounded so badly that it was thought they could not live and who were unconscious, and 5 Germans left. Captain Wilson said: "Well, I have just seven men left. They are all my men and they will stay on the job to the last one." They waited until 3 o'clock and no more litter bearers came, so Lt. Hine again went for litter bearers. He went to the Lt. Colonel of the Regiment who replied: "Give him anything he wants," so he took 50 men and started back to the Farm, but as he started up the hill that had been the "Waterloo" to the ambulances the night before he met 4 men carrying a German and he recognized the German as one that was in the Dressing Station. He stopped them and asked what was left and they replied that he was the last one. It was 5:00 P.M. Sept. 30th. Lt. Hine reported to his Medical Major that the job was completed. He was then sent over to Charpentry for ambulances to evacuate dressed men that had accumulated in the Regimental Dressing Station. No ambulances were to be had so he took a truck, but getting only about half way back and getting stuck he went back to wait for an ambulance. At 10:30 no ambulance had showed up so he went to the Major and the Major said that they had been evacuated.

Work all over, Lt. Hine reposed on a litter, but one hour of slumber was enough, as he froze out. Major Rieger, the Battalion Commander, seeing him up and around invited him to share his bed, which was a 14 inch board nailed against the wall and one blanket. This they both occupied until 3:30 P.M. Oct. 1st when an orderly brought word to the Major that they were being relieved.

Then came a three days march from the lines, and being nearly overcome from dysentery, bronchitis, diarrhoea and a slight attack of gas, Lt. Hine was evacuated to a hospital.

Now, going back to the remainder of the Detachment: At 5:00 P.M., Sept. 29th, we left St. Quenteen, as there was plenty of help there, going back South one kilometer and there establishing Aid Station No. 11 at the same place where we had Aid Station No. 7. On arriving we found about 40 men laying asleep and on questioning them we found they represented nearly every unit in the Division and that they had become lost from their organizations. We put them in charge of a Sergeant and instructed him to take them up to the front and attach themselves to some fighting unit, as they were needed badly. Only about one-half of them had guns, but there were plenty of them laying around that had been left by men whom we had evacuated the day before, also plenty of ammunition. So we soon had them all equipped and off they went without hesitating. The spirit of the men at all times was something wonderful; on numerous occasions we would find small groups of men lost from their organizations and on explaining to them that they should attach themselves to the first unit they found, they would cheerfully go forward and do so. All they wanted was just some one to suggest what to do and they were always found ready and willing. At no time did we see a man going to the rear unless it was to perform a specific duty that required going there. We did not evacuate a single medical case during the entire battle. We were not bothered by a single malingerer. One peculiar incident while here was that a young man was brought in on a litter with a machine gun wound in left arm and left leg and while dressing his wounds I noticed that his skin felt quite hot and I said to him: "Young man, do you feel as though you had some fever, or do you feel bad any other way?" He replied: "Doctor, my throat has seemed a little sore for a couple of days." On examination I found a typical diphtheritic membrane over each tonsil and onto the uvula. I said to him: "Why didn't you report to a Doctor?" He replied: "I was not very sick; besides I wanted to stay here in the drive with the rest of the boys, and I was afraid if I saw a Doctor he would send me back to a hospital." This young man sent me word from a hospital in Southern France a few days ago stating that he was real well. From this Station we evacuated this time 16 casualties.

At 8:00 A.M. Sept. 30th we again went forward about one and one-half kilometers and established Aid Station No. 12 in a dug-out between Charpentry and Balny, evacuating from here 14 casualties. We stayed here until 4:30 P.M. Oct. 1st when our Battalion was relieved. We marched South about 7 kilometers, arriving there about 11:00 A.M., where we pitched tents and stayed for the night. We here established Station No. 13, evacuating 3 casualties, caused by mustard gas burns received during the battle.

Strength of Battalion when we took up our position on September 26th 2:00 A.M. was 22 Officers and 962 Enlisted Men.

Strength of Battalion on October 1st at 1:00 P.M. was 5 Officers and 382 Enlisted Men.

Number of Aid Stations established..............................13
Number of Men evacuated from all Aid Stations.................720
Number of Bosche casualties evacuated...........................12
Number of prisoners taken.......................................32
Number of men becoming casualties from Detachment...............3
Number of men taken prisoner by Germans....1, Pvt. Herbert Stoffle.

MEMBERS OF THE DETACHMENT:

OFFICERS:

1st. Lieut. John F. Coffman, Jr.
1st. Lieut. R. P. Lewis—Sept. 26th and 27th.
1st. Lieut. Otto H. Hine, Dentist.
1st. Lieut. Wm. V. Meredith, Chaplain.
1st Lieut. Paul C. Rhodie—Sept. 29th, 30th, Oct. 1st.

ENLISTED MEN

Sgt. Arthur N. Dreyer.
Sgt. Harry R. O'Brien.
Pvt. 1st Cl. Paul W. Gore.
Pvt. 1st Cl. Russell Dudley.
Pvt. 1st Cl. William C. Myers.
Pvt. 1st Cl. Ward W. Fetrow.
Pvt. James Wheeler.
Pvt. Harry Vance.

Pvt. Raymond L. Chestnut.
Pvt. John W. H. Shuck.
Pvt. Newton B. Kelley.
Pvt. James Doty.
Pvt. Harry Mansfield.
Pvt. Marion Trower.
Pvt. Herbert Stoffle.
Pvt. Jesse Black.

JOHN F. COFFMAN, JR.,
1st. Lieut. M.C., U.S.A.,
Battalion Surgeon.

A RECORD OF MOVEMENTS

All movements except early Kansas.

Initial Return Aug. 20/17.   4th Mo. Inf

Various companies of the regiment mobolized at their home rendevouz on August 5/17 in response to the President's Proclamation of July 3/17.
Left Home Stations August 13/17.
Completed Muster-in to Federal Service August 20/17.

Monthly Return August, 1917, nothing. 4th Mo. Inf.
September, 1917. 4th Mo. Inf.

In accordance with Special Orders 213 Hqrs. Central Department September 20/17 this regiment changed station from Camp Clark, Missouri to Camp Doniphan, Oklahoma, departing from the former station September 24, 1917 and arriving at this station September 25/17.

October, 1917.   139th Infantry.

Pursuant to G. O. No. 213 Hqrs. 35th Division September 20/1917 the Third Kansas Infantry and Fourth Missouri Infantry were consolidated on October 1/17 forming the 139th Infantry.

November, 1917, nothing.
December, 1917, nothing.
January, 1918, nothing.
February, 1918, nothing.
March, 1918, nothing.

Field Return, September 25/17. 4th Mo. Inf.

In accordance with S. O. 213 Headquarters Central Department, Sept. 20/17, this regiment changed station from Camp Clark, Mo., to Camp Doniphan, Okla. First section, Major C. C. Macdonald, 1st Bn., Supply Co., 2 officers, 11 enlisted men M. D. Left Camp Clark 11:50 A.M., Sept. 24/17. Ar. Camp Doniphan 2:00 P.M., Sept. 25/17. Second section, Major James E. Rieger, 2nd Bn., Hqrs. Co., 1 Medical officer, 1 D. S., 11 enlisted men M. D. left Camp Clark 12:25 P.M., Sept. 24/17, ar. Camp Doniphan 3:30 P.M., Sept. 25. Third section, Major William D. Stepp, 3rd Bn., M. G. Co., 1 Medical officer, 1 D.S., and 11 enlisted men of M. D. left Camp Clark 1:30 P.M. Sept. 24, ar. Camp Doniphan 4:00 P.M. Sept. 25/17.

The Regimental Commander and Staff travelled with first section.

Monthly Return April, 1918. 139th Infantry.

Pursuant to confidential S. O. Hq. 35th Div. No. 97, 7 Apr., 1918, this regiment left Camp Doniphan in eight section as follows: Apr. 8, 1st section composed of Hq. Co., Sup. Co.; 2nd section, M. G. Co.; 3rd Sec., Co's A & B, Apr. 22, 9th; Sec. 4, Co's C & D; Sec. 5, Co's E. & F; Sec. 6, Co's G & H, Apr. 10; Sec. 7, Co's I & K; Sec. 8, Co's L & M. A detachment of the Medical Detachment accompanied each Section. Sections arrived at Camp Mills, New York, as follows: Apr. 12/18, 1st, 2nd and 3rd Sections. Apr. 13/18, 4th, 5th & 6th Sections. Apr. 14/18, 7th & 8th Sections.

Pursuant to Confidential Memorandum Hq. 35th Div. Apr. 18/18, this regiment embarked for overseas service in two sections as follows: 1st Sec., Field & Staff Officers, Hq. Sup. and M.G. Co's A, B, C, D, E, F, G, H and I and Med. Det. sailed Apr. 24/18 on Transport No. 552. Second Section composed of Co's K, L, and M and Detachment of Medical Detachment sailed on Transport No. 501.

March, 1918. 139th Infantry. Nothing.

Monthly Return May, 1918. 139th Infantry.

This regiment minus Co's K, L and M docked at Huskisoon Dock, Liverpool, England, 11:30 A.M., May 7/18. Debarkation commenced 2:30 P.M., completed 4:45 P.M. Marched to Waton on the Hill R. S. Station. Entrained in five sections, Great Central R. R. First Sec. left 6:55 P.M. Last Sec. left 4:30 P.M., May 8/1918. First Section detrained Romsey, England, 5:15 A.M., May 8, 1918. Arrived American Rest Camp, Camp Woodley, 6:15 A.M. Departed from A. R. C. 7:50 A.M., May 15/18, arrived Romsey Station 8:30 A.M. Left Romsey Station via L. & S. W. R. R. 9:50 A.M. Arrived at Docks, Southampton, England, 10:35 A.M. Boarded Transport "H. W. Miller" 5:00 P.M. (First Section.) Arrived at Havre, France, 3:15 A.M., May 16/18. Debarked 6:00 A.M. Marched to Rest Camp No. 2, Havre, France. Departed Rest Camp No. 2 6:25 P.M., May 17/18 on foot. Arrived Rest Camp No. 1 9:15. Departed Camp No. 1 4:30 P.M., May 20/18. Arrived R. R., Point No. 4, 5:55 P.M. Entrained and departed Point No. 4 8:00 P.M. Arrived Eu, France, 8:10 A.M., May 21/18. Detrained and marched to Staging Camp 8:50 A.M. Departed Staging Camp 10:25 A.M. on March to le Mesnil Reaume. Arrived le Mesnil Reaume 3:00 P. M., May 21/18. Co's K, L and M billeted at Melleville, France, again carried as present with regiment.

Monthly Return June, 1918. 139th Infantry.

Left le Mesnil Reaume June 6/18. Marched to Morgny, arriving June 8/18. Entrained on June 9/18, arriving at Harol June 11/18. Marched to Archettes June 12/18. Left Archettes by motor train June 23/18, arriving in Moosch same day. 2nd Bn. in front line trenches June 19th to 28th. Pvt.Warren L. Day electrocuted 5:10 A.M. June 24/18 in enemy wire, front line, Wesserling Area. Pvt. John C. Lovall, Co. H, killed by shrapnel 11:15 P.M., June 26/18 in front line, Wesserling Area. Sgt. Walter R. McCurdy, Co. F, seriously wounded in Camp Hennequin West by shrapnel 5:20 P.M., June 26/18. Corp. Frank O. Pierce, M. G. Co., slightly wounded in front line, Wesserling Area, June 27/18. Marched from Moosch to Cornimont June 28/18. From Cornimont to LaBresse June 29/18. 3rd Bn. Detached from Regiment June 23rd to July 2nd/18. Stationed at Jarmenil and Pouxioux.

Monthly Return July, 1918. 139th Infantry.

Third Battalion left Jarmenil and Pouxioux for LaBresse July 1/18. 2nd Battalion left LaBresse from Kruth July 12/18. 2nd Battalion left Kruth for sub-sector E July 15/18. Regiment minus 1st Battalion and 2nd Battalion left LaBresse for sub-sector E July 19/18. 1st Battalion left Cornimont for Kruth July 22/18. 1st Battalion left Kruth for Felleringen July 27/18. 1st Battalion left Fellering for sub-sector E July 30/18.

Monthly Return August, 1918. 139th Infantry.

2nd Bn. left Felleringen, Alsace, for sub-sector E August 16th, relieving the 3rd Bn., same moving to Kruth. 3rd Bn. left Kruth, Alsace, for Mentron, France, August 29th.

Monthly Return September 1918. 139th Infantry.

1st Bn., 2nd Bn., and Regt'l Hdqrs. changed station from Robinson Sector, Alsace, to Kruth, Sept. 1, 1918. 1st Bn. and Regt'l Hdqrs. from Kruth to Cornimont, Sept. 2/18. 2nd Bn. changed station from Kruth to Cornimont Sept. 3/18. Regt'l Hdqrs. and Hq. Co. and 1st Bn. from Cornimont to Einvaux by rail, from Einvaux to woods near Tonnoy by marching, on Sept. 4/18. 3rd Bn. marched from Ventron to Cornimont ,from Cornimont to Einvaux by rail, from Einvaux to Flavigny on foot, Sept. 4/18. 2nd Bn. from Cornimont to Einvaux by rail Sept. 4/18. Regt'l Hdqrs. and Hq. Co. from woods near Tonnoy to Neuves Maisons on foot Sept. 5/18. 2nd Bn. from Einvaux to Flavigny on foot Sept. 5/18. 2nd Bn. from Flavigny to Neuves Maisons on foot Sept. 6/18. Regiment from Neuves Maisons to Foret de Haye on foot Sept. 11/18. Regiment from Foret de Haye to Poste de Velaine on foot Sept. 18/18. From Poste de Velaine, 2:30 P.M., Sept. 18/18 to Charmontois, 4:30 A.M., Sept. 19/18. Regt'l Hdqrs. and Hdqrs. Co. from Charmontois to Eclaires, 8:00 A.M., Sept. 19/18. Regiment minus Regt'l Hdqrs. and Hdqrs. Co. from Charmontois to bivouac near Le Chemin Sept. 19/18. Regimental Hdqrs. and Hdqrs. from Eclaires and rest of Regiment from bivouac near Le Chemin to bivouac in Foret de Argonne Sept. 20/18. Changed place of bivouac next morning to Beauchamps Farm. 1st Bn. from bivouac at Beauchamps Farm to cross-roads near Clermont Sept. 25/18. 2nd Bn. (attached to 69th Inf. Brigade) from bivouac at Beauchamps Farm to Camp Baussot, 2:30 A.M., Sept. 26/18. 3rd Bn. from bivouac at Beauchamps Farm to Aubreville, 4:30 A.M., Sept. 26/18. In battle from 5:00 A.M., Sept. 26/18, to and including Sept. 30/18.

Monthly Return October, 1918. 139th Infantry.

1st Bn. from battle to field west of Cheppy Oct. 1, 1918. 2nd Bn. from battle to Hill 253 October 1, 1918. 3rd Bn. from Cheppy to Auzeville October 2, 1918. 1st Bn. from Cheppy to Auzeville October 2, 1918. 2nd Bn. from Hill 253 to Auzeville October 2, 1918. Regiment from Auzeville, 7:30 A.M., Oct. 3/18, to Camp Grand du Fosse, 3:45 P.M., Oct. 3/18. Regiment from Camp Grand du Fosse to Louppy le Petit afternoon of Oct. 5/18. Regiment from Louppy le Petit to woods near Benoite Vaux afternoon of October 12/18. 1st Bn. from Benoite Vaux to Camp Les Senegalias. 2nd Bn. from Benoite Vaux to Camp Chiffoure, 3rd Bn. from woods near Benoite Vaux to Camp Henvaux, Regt'l Hdqrs. from woods near Benoite Vaux to P. C. Massa Oct. 13/18. 3rd Bn. from Camp Henvaux to P. C. Murat Oct. 23/18. Regt'l Hdqrs. from P. C. Massa to 34 Rue de Etain, F.B.G. Pave, Verdun, Oct. 24/18. 3rd Bn. from P. C. Murat to trenches north of Verdun (C.R.Fort) 2:30 A.M., Oct. 25/18. 2nd Bn. from Camp Chiffoure to F.B.G. Pave, Verdun, 8:00 P.M., Oct. 24/18. 1st Bn. from Camp les Senegalias to F.B.G. Pave, Verdun, 10:30 P.M., Oct. 25/18. Regt'l Hdqrs. from 35 Rue de Etain, F.B.G. Pave, Verdun, to P. C. Normandie, 9:00 P.M., Oct. 25/18. 1st Bn. from F.B.G. Pave, Verdun, to P. C. Simone, 11:35 P.M., Oct. 26/18. 2nd Bn. from F.B.G. Pave, Verdun, to C. R. Fort, relieving 3rd Bn., 11:15 P.M., Oct. 28/18. 3rd Bn. from C. R. Fort to F.B.G., Pave, Verdun, 2:00 A.M., Oct. 29/18. 3rd Bn. from F.B.G., Pave, Verdun, to Pouderie, 7:00 P.M., Oct. 29/18.

Monthly Return November, 1918. 139th Infantry.

2nd Bn. from P. C. Murat to C. R. Fort (Verdun) to Senoncourt Nov. 6/18. 1st Bn. from P. C. Simone (Verdun) to Senoncourt Nov. 7/18. 3rd Bn. from Pouderie (Verdun) to Senoncourt Nov. 6/18. 1st Bn. from Senoncourt to Bannoncourt Nov. 9/18. 2nd Bn. from Senoncourt to Bannoncourt Nov. 9/18. 3rd Bn. from Recourt to Eppecourt Nov. 7/18, to Recourt Nov. 9/18, to Bannoncourt Nov. 10/18. 1st Bn. from Bannoncourt to Camp Marcalieu Nov. 10/18. Regt'l Hdqrs. from P. C. Normandie to Lemmes (via F.B.G. Pave) Nov. 7/18, to Bannoncourt Nov. 9/18. From Bannoncourt to Rupt Nov. 13/18. 2nd Bn. from Bannoncourt to Kouer le Grand and Kouer le Petit Nov. 13/18. 3rd Bn. from Bannoncourt to La Belle Vallee Nov. 13/18.

Monthly Return December, 1918. 139th Infantry.

Regimental Hq. from Rupt to Vignot Dec. 8/18. 1st Bn. from Camp Marcalieu to Camp Negra Dec. 3/18, to Vignot Dec. 8/18. 2nd Bn. from Kouer la Grande and Kouer la Petite to Euville Dec. 8/18. 3rd Bn. from LaBelle Vallee to Vignot Dec. 8/18. Machine Gun Co. from Camp Marcalieu to Rupt Dec. 3/18, to Euville Dec. 8/18. Mentioned in G.O. 232 HAEF, 1918, for service with First Army in the Meuse-Argonne Operation. Mentioned in G.O. 238 HAEF, 1918, for service with the First Army in the taking of the Saint Mihiel Salient (reserve). 2nd Battalion and Machine Gun Co. stationed at Euville, Meuse.

Monthly Return January, 1919. 139th Infantry.

M. G. Co. changed station from Euville to Granvoisin (Meuse) 19th Jan./19 for the purpose of attending provisional Machine Gun School. Returned to Euville 25th Jan./1919. 2nd Bn. stationed at Euville during month. Remainder of regiment stationed at Vignot.

Monthly Return February, 1919. 139th Infantry.

2nd Bn. and M. G. Co. stationed at Euville (Meuse), France, during month. Remainder of Regiment stationed at Vignot (Meuse), France, during month.

Monthly Return March, 1919. 139th Infantry.

Regimental Headquarters moved from Vignot (Meuse), France, to Borg-de-Torce (Sarthe), France, March 9th to 12th, 1919. Hq. Co. and Supply Co. moved from Vignot (Meuse), France, to Torce (Sarthe), France, March 9th to 12th, 1919. M. G. Co. moved from Euville (Meuse), France, to Torce (Sarthe), France, March 9th to 12th, 1919. 1st Bn. Hq. and Co's A and B moved from Vignot (Meuse), France, to Beaufay (Sarthe), France, March 9th to 12th, 1919. Co. C moved from Vignot (Meuse), France, to Sille-le-Phillippe (Sarthe), France, Mch. 9 to 12/19. Co. D moved from Vignot to Chantiloupe (Sarthe) Mch. 9 to 12/19. 2nd Bn. moved from Euville to Lombron (Sarthe) Mch. 10th to 13th/19. 3rd Bn. Hq. and Co's I and K moved from Vignot to LaChapelle (Sarthe) Mch. 10th to 13th/19. Co's L and M moved from Vignot to St. Celerin (Sarthe) Mch. 10 to 13/19. 1st and 2nd Battalions moved to Tent Section Belgium Camp March 19th, 1919. Reg. Hq., Hq. Co., Supply Co., M. G. Co. and 3rd Bn. moved to

Tent Section Belgium Camp Mch. 20/19. 1st and 2nd Bn. moved to Permanent Barracks Section Belgium Camp American Embarkation Center March 24th, 1919. Reg. Hq., Hq. Co., Supply Co. and M. G. Co. and 3rd Bn. moved to Permanent Barracks Section Belgium Camp, American Embarkation Center, March 25th, 1919.

Monthly Return April, 1919. 139th Infantry.

Regiment entrained at Permanent Barracks, Belgian Camp. A. E. C., Apr. 1/19, arriving at St. Nazaire, May 2nd, 1919, less Companies E, F, I, K, L, M. Went into Camp at Camp Guthrie. Companies E, F, I, K, L, M entrained at Permanent Barracks Section, Belgian Camp, A. E. C., April 2nd, 1919, arriving at St. Nazaire May 3rd, 1919. Went into camp at Isolation Camp. Hq. Co., M. G. Co., San. Det., Co. B, G and H embarked at St. Nazaire, France, on U. S. S. Matsonia April 13th, 1919, arriving at Newport News, Va., April 24th, 1919. Marched 2½ miles to Camp Stuart, Va. Companies E, F, I, K, L, M embarked at St. Nazaire, France, on U. S. S. Matsonia April 13th, 1919, arriving at Newport News, Va., April 24th, 1919. Marched 2½ miles to Camp Stuart, Va. Companies A, C, D, and Supply embarked at St. Nazaire, France, on U. S. Nansemond April 15th, 1919, arriving at Newport News, Va., April 28th, 1919. Marched 2½ miles to Camp Stuart, Va.

Movements during the month of May.

Regiment entrained in four sections at Camp Stuart, Va., May 1st, 1919. Paraded in St. Joseph, Missouri, Sunday, May 4th, 1919. Paraded in Topeka, Kansas, Monday, May 5th, 1919. Arrived at Camp Funston, Kansas, 4:00 P.M., May 5th, 1919. Regiment less Hq. Co. discharged May 8th, 1919, per Instructions Adjutant General April 14th, 1919. Hq. Co. discharged May 9th, 1919, same authority.

SOME ODD SIZES

CPSIA information can be obtained at www.ICGtesting.com
Printed in the USA
BVOW020700220513

321364BV00001B/31/A